ME NO DUMB DUMB, ME LEARN GOOD

Things Everyone Should Know
Even Though It Is Not Taught In School

TODD EMERSON

MILTON & HUGO L.L.C.

1001 3rd Avenue West,
Suite 430 Bradenton, FL 34205, USA

Website: *www. miltonandhugo.com*
Hotline: *1- 888-778-0033*
Email: *info@miltonandhugo.com*

Ordering Information:
Quantity sales. Special discounts are granted to corporations, associations, and other organizations. For more information on these discounts, please reach out to the publisher using the contact information provided above.

Library of Congress Control Number: 2025927002
ISBN-13:   979-8-89285-749-9   [Paperback Edition]
                    979-8-89285-750-5   [Digital Edition]

Rev. date: 12/09/2025

This Old Man's Opinions And Observations. I started life as a racist then a racist Republican.

Then A Racist Republican Married Military Man, Me No Dumb Dumb Me Learn Good

Things Everyone Should Know Even Though It Is Not Taught In School.

This Old Man's Opinions And Observations. I started life as a racist then a racist Republican.

Then A Racist Republican Married Military Man.

Morphed and accepted I was a gay man and I came out.

Became a very vocal out LGBTQ and civil rights activist in Mississippi.

Became A Business man and Grandfather. In 2005 -2010 was an active addict.

Now a married business man, grandparent and great grandparent that is determined to end racism and discrimination.

Became Politically Aware In 2015 When Trump Turned Our Government Into A Shit Show And Now He Wants To Become A Dictator.

I suggest you read this book and learn what Trump and people in power do not want you to know.

Remember trump said he loves the poorly educated. U.S. your common since. Trump loves the stupid because he can manipulate the ignorant.

Well I Received My Senior Citizen Welcome Package Today So That I Can Understand How To Act And What To Expect When My Birthday Arrives
And Oh, the big 6-0! The age when the warranty on your neurons apparently expires and you start getting ads for the latest in "hip" replacements.

I mean, seriously, who knew that the brain cells had a union and could go on strike the moment you blew out those 60 candles?

And trust me, those candles will put up a fight akin to a tiny bonfire on my cake—because at 60, it's less a birthday cake and more a pyrotechnic display.

Welcome to the Silver League, where I'm again the rookie and my once trusty memory has decided it's time for early retirement.

It's like my brain decided to play a lifelong game of hide and seek, except it's really good at hiding and terrible at seeking.

It's the kind of game where I'll walk into a room and forget why I'm there, but hey, it's great exercise, right?

Cardio and brain puzzles combined.

And let's talk about the "Stupid Gene Subscription Service," which, by the way, comes with a lifetime membership once I hit the big six-oh.

It's like my smart genes will pack their bags and leave a "Gone Fishin'" sign on my cerebral cortex.

But not to worry, the under-40s are the customer service reps here to guide me through the terms and conditions of this new subscription that I never signed up for.

I've now entered the era where my back goes out more than I do, and "sleeping wrong" will become a legitimate injury.

But on the bright side, I can now legitimately pull the "back in my day" card and regale y'all with tales of when phones had cords and "tweeting" was something only birds did.

Here I am, a fresh-faced senior-in-training, ready to navigate the labyrinth of modern life where the Minotaur is replaced by smart homes that are smarter than all of us combined. I tell my phone "call Mike" and it starts a microwave. Fascinating times, indeed.

Aging is like a crash course in humility, with a syllabus designed by my own body and the universe's sense of humor.

Every day's a pop quiz where I learn new things, like how the term "lit" no longer applies to the status of a lamp.

But remember, with age comes the superpower of not caring as much, which is the universe's way of saying, "Congrats! Here's your diploma in the art of living."

So, here's to my, the noble neophyte of the 60s guild, tiptoeing through the minefield of modernity with the elegance of a cat on a hot tin roof.

My quest is noble, My spirit is willing, and my body... well, it's getting there.

As I embark on this comedic odyssey of forgetting why I entered the room, remember, I'm not losing my mind; I'm just running out of RAM.

And that's okay, because of us youngsters?

We're basically walking, talking, tech support with the added bonus of being able to Google anything, anytime.

Thank you for your patronage to the society of the 'young at heart but not quite in the joints.' We salute you, brave adventurer.

I will carry on being a wonderful work-in-progress, and may my journey through the jungle of "jeez, when did that get there?" be as hilarious as it is heartwarming.

Remember, aging might be mandatory, but growing up is still optional.

So, keep the laughter coming, because in the end, it's not the years in my life, but the life (and the laughs) in my years that count.

Fasten your seatbelt because this ride on the senior citizen roller coaster only gets wilder from here.

I'm thinking of my new 60-year-old self as a smartphone that's just received its latest software update, only to find that with new features come new bugs.

Suddenly, I'm autocorrecting "grandkids" to "grandlizards," and let's not even start on the predictive text that thinks I'm more interested in "napping" than "rapping."

And every time I try to "swipe left" on life's annoyances, I remember that's not how reality works, and instead, i accidentally swipe a knick-knack off the shelf.

But here's the silver lining – I'm not just a senior, I'm a "senior edition."

That means I come with vintage charm and a classic vibe that the young 'uns, with their avocado toasts and TikTok dances, can only aspire to.

I've got stories that don't start with "So I saw this meme..." and experiences that don't require a Wi-Fi connection.

Now, about my newfound penchant for historical accuracy when the under-40s start reminiscing about the 2000s like it's ancient history.

"Back in my day,"I begin, and eyes may roll, but they also sparkle with intrigue because nothing beats a firsthand account of a world without hashtags and when "trolls" were just dolls with funky hair.

As for my position on always being wrong?

Well, let's call it "alternative wisdom."

After all, I come from a time when Pluto was a planet, and that kind of cosmic perspective is invaluable.

Besides, in this brave new world where everyone's opinion can be broadcasted, being wrong is just being a part of the conversation – and that's before i even get to politics.

And don't worry about the times I find myself standing in the middle of the kitchen wondering if I was going for the fridge, the pantry, or that I just enjoyed the view.

These are the moments where I'm not forgetful, I'm just deeply philosophical, contemplating the great fridge-pantry dichotomy.

So, as I strap on my metaphorical explorer's hat (which looks suspiciously like a comfy beanie) and dive headfirst into the next decade, remember that I'm not alone.

Y'all, the under-40 brigade, are here to be my Google translators, my tech troubleshooters, and occasionally my fashion consultants (because no, dad jeans haven't made a comeback, not yet at least).

Thank you for letting me join the ranks of the "I can't believe I'm 60" club, where the password is always "What was I saying?" and the secret handshake is forgetting I'm supposed to shake hands. I'm not just growing older; I'm also becoming a legend, one "what's-this-thing-called-again?" at a time.

So, keep on laughing, because each chuckle is a reminder that while the body may slow, the spirit keeps sprinting.

And at the heart of it, whether someone is a sprightly 20-something or a s easoned 60-something, we're all just kids with more sophisticated toys, trying to figure out how to play the game of life.

And if I can find humor in the mix-up, I've already won half the battle.

This is the part where the plot thickens, and my epic journey into the 60s starts to resemble a sitcom where I'm the beloved main character.

You see, at 60, I'm not just a year older, I'm a year bolder.

I've earned every stripe in the game of life, and now I've leveled up.

I've got the wisdom of a sage, the mystique of a time traveler, and the tech-savviness of someone who's watched at least two YouTube tutorials.

I'm not out of touch; I'm "retro," and let's be honest, retro is in.

My new status comes with a fantastic array of superpowers.

For instance, I've now got the uncanny ability to locate the best early-bird specials in town – because who wants to eat dinner after 6 pm when I can be comfortably digesting while watching the sunset at 5:15?

And let's not forget the new newfound talent for giving zero hoots about the judgment of others.

That's right, I'm now the proud owner of a Teflon coating against societal expectations.

Want to wear socks with sandals? Go ahead.

Feel like declaring that lawn bowling is the next big thing? Do it.

The world is my oyster, and I'm ready to shuck it with gusto.

The under-40 crowd will come to me, seeking my sage advice, not realizing that inside, I'm chuckling because I've started measuring time not by clocks or calendars, but by the length of your "to watch" list on Netflix.

And when they ask for my wisdom on love, careers, or the meaning of life, you can impart kernels of knowledge wrapped up in anecdotes that start with, "Well, in the pre-Instagram era..."

But let's talk about the elephant in the room – or should we say the elephant-sized pile of gadgets and gizmos that have somehow accumulated in my living space?

"What's this dongle for?" I wonder.

"Was this gizmo a gift, or did I buy it in a moment of late-night shopping rebellion?"

It's okay. Each device is a story, a battle won against the forces of "user-unfriendly" and a testament to my enduring spirit.

As for the memory, who needs to remember trivial things like passwords when I've mastered the art of password recovery?

It's not forgetfulness; it's an advanced form of cyber security.

And when it comes to names, everyone can be "buddy" or "pal" in a pinch.

It's endearing and covers all bases.

So I wear my "senior citizen in training" badge with pride.

Each wrinkle is etched with the laughter of a joke well told, and every gray hair is a shimmering thread in the tapestry of my storied life.

The under-40s might have the edge on what's trending, but me, my friend, is timeless.

Thank you for being the extraordinary protagonist in the comedy series of life.

My audience – is the tech-laden, meme-sharing, avocado-eating under-40s – are here for it all.

They're ready to binge-watch my adventures, laugh at my bloopers, and cheer for me victories.

And remember, as the saying goes, age is an issue of mind over matter – if I don't mind, it doesn't matter.

So here's to not minding, to finding the hilarity in the hiccups, and to boldly going where no 60-year-old has gone before.

Because, in the end, the biggest joke would be to take life too seriously when the world is so full of possibilities to smile about.

And so, brave voyager of the sixtieth year, as I sail the seas of this brave new age, remember:

I am the captain of my own ship, a ship that may creak a bit more than it used to, but one that's weathered many a storm and is still afloat.

It's not just about staying afloat, though; it's about enjoying the cruise, even if I occasionally forget where I docked my boat.

Now, my treasure map might look a little different.

The X that marks the spot is less about finding buried treasure and more about remembering where I parked at the mega-mall.

But the real treasure? It's the stories I've got stashed in the hold, ready to be shared with any soul brave enough to inquire, "What was it like before the internet?"

As the tides of technology bring in new gadgets, I might find myself marveling at a world where refrigerators can talk to me, and watches tell me much more than the time—they practically forecast when I need my next cup of tea.

And while I'm figuring out how to silence my chatty appliances, the younger generation looks on with a mix of admiration and amusement—because I'm proof that you can teach an old dog new emojis.

My so-called "stupid gene" is nothing more than a mischievous imp, playing hide-and-seek with my keys, my glasses, and occasionally, my train of thought.

But fear not, for every time the imp strikes, I have a deck of get-out-of-jail-free cards, lovingly known as "senior moments," which are universally accepted and often come with a side of sympathetic nods.

And let's not overlook my role as the keeper of the "back in my day" archives, where stories of rotary phones and dial-up internet become mythic tales for the Snapchat generation.

I provide a link to a time when "streaming" was something you did in a canoe, and "clouds" were strictly meteorological.

In this new chapter, I'm not just getting older; I'm leveling up in wisdom.

Sure, the under-40s may have their digital savvy, but I have a PhD in Life. My dissertation? Every single one of those laugh lines etched around my eyes, each one a testament to a joke well-told or a smile generously given.

And let's be honest, while the younger folks are busy capturing moments on their smartphones, I'm living them—fully, richly, with the gusto of someone who knows that the best filter in life is a good sense of humor.

So, while I may occasionally misplace my spectacles (which, by the way, are indeed on my head), I never lose sight of what's important: family, friends, and a good belly laugh. And when all else fails, I've got the under-40s, my loyal crew, ready to navigate the GPS when I take a wrong turn, to stream my favorite show when the remote control becomes elusive, and to share a meme that'll make me chuckle.

So let's raise a glass (with extra large print on it, so i know it's mine) to the adventures ahead, to the laughs we've yet to share, and to the wonderful, whimsical world of being 60. Because if laughter is the best medicine, then I, my friend, is my best doctor on call.

Where Love, Develop And Acceptance Should Fall In Your Life

Let me know where you agree or disagree.

The tiered system is a way to conceptualize relationships and prioritize them based on their perceived importance and impact on someone's life.

It's not necessarily a hierarchy of love, but rather a structure for managing different types of relationships and their demands on your time and emotional energy.

These tiers encapsulate a broader range of relationships.

Tier One: Immediate Family

Spouses (Husbands/Wives):

Your life partner, with whom you've chosen to share your life's journey. This relationship typically holds a high degree of intimacy, mutual support, and shared goals. If you ever drop them out of tier one you need to be honest with you spouse and let them go.

Children:

Your offspring, whether biological, adopted, or stepchildren that you're raising as your own. This tier represents your legacy and the continuity of care, nurturing, and guidance. This tier is non negotiable.

Tier Two: Close Family Extensions

Grandchildren:

They represent the next generation and the continuation of your family line. Your relationship with them is often characterized by unconditional love and the joy of seeing your lineage flourish.

Parents:

Your primary caregivers from birth, who have shaped your early life. As adults, the dynamic should evolve to one of mutual respect and care, with the understanding that the authoritative role is over. If they demand to be in tier one or you demand they be in tier one you both have an unhealthy relationship and you should both avoid having anyone in tier one.

Stepchildren:

If not included in Tier One, these are children you've not taken a significant role in raising usually due age when the partnership with their biological parent began. Your connection with them is often carefully cultivated and may not be as strong as with biological children.

Tier Three: Chosen Family and Lifelong Friends

Best Friends:

These are individuals you've chosen to be part of your life due to shared experiences, trust, and mutual support. These relationships can sometimes rival the closeness of family ties.

Tier Four: Extended Family and Daily Life Associates

Siblings:

Your brothers and sisters with whom you share a familial bond and a common upbringing. The closeness of this relationship can vary greatly from person to person.

In-Laws:

Your spouse's family, with whom you share significant life events and holidays. These relationships can enrich your family life and provide additional support.

Coworkers:

People with whom you spend a significant amount of time due to professional circumstances. These relationships can be important for your career and daily social interactions.

Tier Five: Community and Social Circle

Neighbors:

Individuals living in close proximity who can become important for local support, community involvement, and everyday socialization.

Acquaintances:

People you know on a casual basis, with whom you share common interests or activities, but not necessarily a deep personal connection.

Tier Six: Peripheral Contacts

Professional Services Providers:

Such as your doctor, lawyer, or accountant, who play a specific role in your life.

Online Friends:

People you may not have met in person but with whom you've formed connections through social media, gaming, or forums.

Tier Seven: Influence and Inspiration

Mentors:

Individuals you look up to, who provide guidance and inspiration in various aspects of your life.

Public Figures:

Celebrities, authors, or thought leaders who influence you through their work or public personas.

Let's delve into how this system can be applied and managed in everyday life, as well as the intricacies and potential adjustments that might be necessary.

Managing Relationship Tiers

1. Establishing Boundaries: It's crucial to set clear boundaries for each tier to maintain harmony and balance. This includes understanding the level of commitment, time, and emotional energy you are willing to invest in each relationship.

2. Communication: Effective communication is key to any relationship. Be open and honest about your expectations and your capacity to engage with each tier. This helps prevent misunderstandings and resentment.

3. Time Management: Prioritize your time according to the tiers. For instance, immediate family often takes precedence over extended family or acquaintances. Yet, also recognize the importance of investing in friendships and social networks.

4. Flexibility: Life events such as marriages, births, and deaths can shift the dynamics of relationships, requiring you to reevaluate and possibly adjust your tier system. Be adaptable to these changes.

5. Mutual Support and Reciprocity: Relationships are a two-way street. Ensure that the support you provide is reciprocated in some form. This

doesn't mean keeping score but recognizing that healthy relationships involve give and take.

Intricacies and Adjustments

Inter-tier Movement: Relationships can shift between tiers. A coworker may become a close friend, or a close friend might drift away and become more of an acquaintance. Be aware of these shifts and adjust your emotional investment accordingly.

Cultural and Individual Differences: Different cultures and individuals place varying levels of importance on certain relationships. Be mindful of these differences and respect them in your own tier system.

Crisis and Support: During times of crisis, the tier system might temporarily change. For example, a friend or a distant relative going through a difficult time might temporarily take precedence over others.

Personal Growth: As you grow and change, your relationships will too. Periodic reflection on your relationships and their tiers can help you stay aligned with your values and goals.

Navigating Life Changes and Relationship Dynamics

As life progresses, relationships will inevitably shift due to a myriad of factors such as geographic moves, life stages, and personal development. Acknowledging and embracing these changes is key to maintaining a healthy tiered system.

1. Life Transitions: Major life transitions, such as going to college, starting a new job, or retirement, can significantly impact your relationships. For example, college friends may move from Tier Four to Tier Three as you form closer bonds through shared experiences.

2. Re-evaluating Priorities: Regularly take stock of your relationships to see if they still align with your priorities. An old friend may have grown

apart from you in interests and values, suggesting a need to adjust their place in your tiered system.

3. Investing in Quality: It's not just about the quantity of time spent but the quality of interactions. Even relationships in lower tiers can be deeply meaningful if the time spent together is engaging and fulfilling.

4. Dealing with Conflict: Conflict is a natural part of relationships. How you manage conflicts, especially in higher tiers, can determine the strength and longevity of those relationships. It's important to address issues head-on, with empathy and a willingness to find resolutions.

Cultivating Intimacy and Depth

While the tiered system helps with organization, it's also important to cultivate depth and intimacy in your relationships, especially those in the higher tiers.

1. Shared Experiences: Create meaningful memories with individuals in your top tiers to strengthen bonds. This can include family vacations, traditions, or regular one-on-one outings.

2. Personal Growth Together: Encourage and support mutual growth within your relationships. This could involve pursuing shared goals or supporting each other's personal ambitions.

3. Vulnerability: Be willing to be vulnerable with those in your closest tiers. This opens the door to deeper connections and trust.

Maintaining Balance and Self-Care

In managing a tiered system of relationships, never forget the importance of self-care.

Balancing the needs of others with your own is essential to avoid burnout and resentment.

1. Self-Reflection: Regular self-reflection can help you understand your needs and how your relationships impact your well-being.

2. Saying No: It's okay to say no or to set limits on your time and energy. This is especially important for relationships in lower tiers that may demand more than you can give.

3. Self-Care Practices: Engage in activities that replenish your energy, such as hobbies, exercise, or meditation, so that you can be fully present in your relationships.

Adapting the System for Individual Needs

Finally, it's essential to remember that this tiered system is not one-size-fits-all.

Adapt it to fit your unique circumstances and be willing to make changes as needed.

1. Personal Values: Let your core values guide how you categorize and prioritize relationships. For some, extended family might be on the same level as immediate family, while for others, chosen friends might take precedence.

2. Unique Relationships: Some relationships defy categorization. For example, a mentor might also be a close friend, blurring the lines between tiers.

3. Life's Unpredictability: Life can be unpredictable, and sometimes relationships change in ways we never expected. Be open to these changes and adjust your system as life unfolds.

Harmonizing Inter-tier Relationships

The interplay between different tiers can be complex, with each relationship potentially affecting the others. Here are ways to harmonize these inter-tier relationships:

1. Inclusive Events: Organize events that bring together people from different tiers, such as family gatherings, community events, or group outings. This can help foster understanding and build a sense of community among your social circles.

2. Cross-tier Introductions: Introduce people from different tiers to each other when appropriate. This can help broaden social networks and create new connections that may enrich everyone involved.

3. Managing Jealousies and Competition: Sometimes, individuals from different tiers may feel jealous or competitive for your attention. Address these feelings openly and reassure them of their importance in your life.

Adapting to Relationship Endings and Evolutions

Not all relationships last forever, and some may evolve in unexpected ways:

1. Closure and Letting Go: When a relationship ends, seek closure if possible. Acknowledge the role the person played in your life and the impact of their departure.

2. Transitioning Tiers: As relationships evolve, some may transition to different tiers. A sibling you were once close to might move to a lower tier due to life circumstances, or an acquaintance might become a trusted confidant.

Revisiting and Revising the Tiered System

As with any system, periodic reviews ensure it remains relevant and effective:

1. Annual Reviews: Consider conducting an annual review of your relationships, possibly at the end of the year, to reflect on any changes and make adjustments to your tiers.

2. Life Checkpoints: Use major life events, such as the beginning of a new decade of your life, a marriage, or the birth of a child, as opportunities to reassess your relationship tiers.

Educating Others About Your System

While this tiered system is personal, sharing your approach with those closest to you can help them understand your boundaries and expectations:

1. Discussing Boundaries: Have conversations with those in your higher tiers about your system and why you find it helpful. This can prevent misunderstandings and set clear expectations.

2. Being an Example: By managing your relationships well, you can serve as a model for others, demonstrating the benefits of a balanced and intentional approach to personal connections.

Integrating New Relationships

New relationships can emerge at any time, and integrating them into your system requires thought:

1. Observation Period: Allow new relationships an observation period before deciding which tier they belong to. Over time, their placement will become more apparent.

2. Flexibility for Growth: Be open to the potential growth of new relationships. Someone may enter your life in a lower tier but become significant over time.

Using the Tiered System as a Guide, Not a Limitation

Remember that the tiered system is a guide to help manage relationships, not a rigid framework that restricts the natural flow of life:

1. Emotional Nuance: Understand that the depth of your feelings for someone may not always align with their tier placement.

2. Prioritizing Well-being: Always prioritize your emotional and psychological well-being when managing relationships. If a relationship in a higher tier is toxic, it's okay to distance yourself.

3. Openness to Change: Be open to the idea that the system itself may change as you grow and learn more about yourself and others.

In conclusion, the tiered system for managing relationships is a living framework that can help you navigate the complexities of human connections. It's important to use it thoughtfully, with compassion and flexibility, allowing it to evolve as you do. By doing so, you can maintain a rich and fulfilling social life that supports not only your personal happiness but also contributes positively to the lives of those around you.

Cultivating Each Tier with Intentionality

While managing the tiers, it's essential to engage with each intentionally:

1. Tier One:

Prioritize quality time, create meaningful family traditions, and ensure open lines of communication to foster strong bonds within the family unit.

2. Tier Two:

Show appreciation for the roles these individuals play in your life, and be there for significant milestones and support during challenging times.

3. Tier Three:

Stay connected through regular check-ins and mutual activities that reinforce the bond, while respecting the independence and individual growth of these friends.

4. Tier Four:

Maintain a healthy balance of involvement, offering support when needed but respecting the autonomy of these extended relationships.

Handling Transitions and Mergers Between Tiers

Occasionally, individuals from different tiers may form relationships among themselves, which requires a nuanced approach:

1. Celebrating Connections:
Encourage and celebrate positive relationships that develop between people in different tiers, as this can create a more interconnected and supportive network.

2. Navigating Complexities:
Be prepared to navigate complexities that may arise from these inter-tier relationships, such as when in-laws form bonds with friends, potentially altering the group dynamics.

Encouraging Independence Within Tiers

While it's important to nurture relationships, it's equally crucial to encourage independence:

1. Empowering Family Members:
Encourage family members in Tier One to pursue their own relationships and interests, fostering a healthy independence even within the closest relationships.

2. Supporting Autonomy:
For friends and extended family, support their autonomy by celebrating their achievements and supporting their decisions, even when they lead to less frequent contact.

Rebalancing During Life's Shifts

As life changes, the tier system may require rebalancing:

1. Assessing Life Stages:
Different life stages may necessitate different levels of engagement with various tiers—for instance, when children leave home, or when retirement allows for more social activities.

2. Responding to Needs:
Be responsive to the shifting needs of those within your tiers, such as when an aging parent may require more attention or when a friend is going through a crisis.

Maintaining Your Own Center

In the midst of managing these tiers, don't lose sight of your own center—your personal well-being:

1. Personal Time:
Ensure you carve out time for yourself to engage in activities that replenish your energy and bring you joy.

2. Reflective Practices:
Engage in reflective practices like journaling or meditation that can help you stay in tune with your own needs and feelings as you navigate your relationships.

Embracing Life's Full Spectrum

Life's full spectrum of relationships brings richness and complexity:

1. Valuing Diversity: Embrace the diversity of relationships in your life, understanding that each brings unique perspectives and experiences that can enrich your understanding of the world.

2. Learning from Relationships:

Use each relationship as a learning opportunity, whether it's learning patience from a challenging family member or gaining wisdom from a mentor.

Continual Learning and Growth

Finally, view the tiered system as part of a continual process of learning and growth:

1. Evolving Understanding:
Recognize that your understanding of relationships and their importance will evolve over time, and with it, so will your tiered system.

2. Seeking Feedback:
Be open to feedback from those in your tiers about how you manage and prioritize your relationships, and be willing to make adjustments based on that feedback.

3. Sharing Insights:
Share the insights you gain about relationship management with others, as they may benefit from your experiences and the intentional approach you've cultivated.

In this expanded tier system, it's important to note that the boundaries between tiers can be fluid, as relationships evolve over time.

Also, the value you place on each relationship is subjective and can depend on personal values, cultural influences, and life experiences.

While maintaining harmony in higher tiers is often seen as a priority for personal happiness, it is equally important to manage relationships in lower tiers effectively, as they too contribute to a well-rounded and fulfilling life.

This tiered approach can help you think strategically about where to invest your emotional energy and time, ensuring that those relationships that are most critical to your well-being are nurtured and protected.

However, it's also important to remain flexible and recognize that the significance of a relationship can change over time, and thus, its tier placement may also need to be adjusted.

This tiered approach to relationships is a tool for personal organization and prioritization. It is not meant to dehumanize or commodify relationships but to help you navigate the complex web of social interactions in a way that maintains your well-being and respects the emotional needs of others. Remember, the tiers are not static, and love is not finite. The amount of love you have for someone is not necessarily diminished by their placement in a lower tier—it's more about the practical aspects of how you manage your relationships.

Ultimately, each person's tier system is deeply personal and should be tailored to their unique circumstances, values, and life experiences. It serves as a framework for understanding the different roles people play in your life and for making intentional decisions about how to nurture each relationship in a way that contributes to a fulfilling and balanced life.

In summary, the tiered system of relationships is a dynamic and flexible tool designed to help you navigate the complexities of interpersonal connections. It should serve as a guideline, not a strict rulebook, allowing for personalization based on individual needs and circumstances. By regularly evaluating and adjusting your approach to relationships, you can maintain a healthy social ecosystem that supports your overall happiness and well-being.

By continuing to nurture each relationship with care, acknowledging the fluid nature of human connections, and staying true to your own needs, the tiered system can serve as a valuable compass in the journey of life, helping you to maintain a balanced and harmonious social existence.

Consistently being late sends negative messages to others about your time management skills and respect for their time.

It creates the perception that you value your time more than that of others and that you may not prioritize the commitments you make.

Being punctual is a sign of respect for others and can help establish trust and credibility in professional and personal relationships. It shows that you are reliable, organized, and considerate of other people's schedules.

By making an effort to be more punctual, you can demonstrate respect for others and enhance your reputation as a dependable and considerate individual.

My dad has always said there is never an excuse for being late.

Other People and their time are just as important as your time is to you. If you have any doubt you may be late leave early enough to change a tire and be on time.

My dad's perspective is one that places a high value on punctuality and respect for others' time.

His view is rooted in personal responsibility and consideration for others, and it reflects a strong work and social ethic and sense of integrity.

Here are a few reasons why his philosophy is beneficial and widely respected:

Respect for Others:

By prioritizing punctuality, my dad was showing that he values other people's time as much as his own.

This consideration is fundamental to building trust and maintaining good relationships, both personally and professionally.

Reliability:

Being consistently on time is a sign of reliability. It indicates that you are someone who can be counted on to fulfill obligations and commitments.

Professionalism:

In the workplace, punctuality is often equated with professionalism. Being on time for meetings, appointments, and work shifts is essential for smooth operations and shows dedication to one's role.

Preparedness:

Planning to arrive early enough to account for unexpected delays, like changing a tire, demonstrates foresight and preparedness.

It shows that you have thought ahead about potential obstacles and have taken steps to mitigate them.

Reputation:

Your punctuality can positively affect how others perceive you.

It can enhance your reputation as someone who is organized, thoughtful, and respectful.

Stress Reduction:

Being late can cause stress for both the person who is late and those who are affected by the tardiness.

Planning to be on time, or even early, can reduce this stress and lead to a more peaceful and productive environment.

Fairness:

When everyone makes an effort to be on time, it creates an environment of fairness where no one's time is considered more or less important than anyone else's.

Positive Example:

By valuing punctuality, my dad set a positive example for others, potentially influencing them to also consider the importance of being on time.

In many cultures, punctuality is a virtue and is expected in social and professional settings.

Of course, unexpected situations can arise, but the general principle is to plan ahead to mitigate these potential issues as much as possible.

When delays are truly unavoidable, it's considered courteous to notify those waiting as soon as possible.

By instilling the value of punctuality, my dad was teaching a lesson in personal accountability and respect for others—a lesson that often serves people well in all aspects of their lives.

After Affirmative Action Was Overturned to have Designed an employee employer app that will erase any conscious or unconscious bias when hiring or accepting employment.

This is the second one I have started on.

Part one

EQUINOX

The concept of an app that aims to stop bias in the hiring process and match employers and employees based on skillsets and preferences it is innovative and socially conscious.

This app would leverage technology to promote fair employment practices and could potentially disrupt traditional hiring processes that can be influenced by conscious or unconscious biases.

Here's a breakdown of some considerations and steps that I want to be taken to bring this concept to life:

1. Market Research and Legal Compliance:

Conduct thorough market research to understand the demand for such an app and to identify any potential competitors.

Ensure that the app complies with all employment laws and regulations, such as the Equal Employment Opportunity Commission (EEOC) guidelines, the Americans with Disabilities Act (ADA), and global privacy regulations like GDPR if applicable.

2.Technology Development:

Develop a sophisticated algorithm that can accurately assess and score the various skills and traits without bias.

Use anonymized profiles to ensure that personal information isn't used in the decision-making process.

Implement secure databases to protect sensitive user information.

3. User Experience Design:

Create an intuitive user interface for both employees and employers.

Ensure the registration process is straightforward and the criteria for matching are clear and comprehensive.

Make sure the feedback and counter-offer systems are user-friendly and effective.

4. Verification and Trust Building:

Develop a system to verify the credentials and past employment history of job seekers to ensure the reliability of the information provided.

Consider incorporating a rating system or reviews for employers based on past employee experiences to build trust among users.

5. Pilot Testing:

Before a full rollout, conduct a pilot test with a limited user base to gather feedback and make necessary adjustments.

Use this phase to refine the matching algorithm and user interface.

6. Launch and Marketing:

Launch the app with a strong marketing campaign that highlights its benefits and unique selling points.

Target both job seekers and employers who value diversity and merit-based hiring.

7. Monitoring and Improving:

Continuously monitor the app's performance and user satisfaction to make iterative improvements.

Be open to user feedback and ready to adapt the app's features to better serve its user base.

8. Sustainability and Monetization:

Consider the sustainability of the revenue model, as charging employers a week's salary per hire might need to be adjusted based on market feedback.

Explore additional revenue streams, such as premium features or services for users.

9. Legality of the Hiring Process:

Ensure that the app's process complies with legal hiring practices, especially when formalizing employment agreements.

Consult with legal experts to draft the terms and conditions for both employers and employees.

10. Post-Hiring Engagement:

Develop a mechanism for post-hiring engagement to ensure that both parties are satisfied with the match.

Offer resources or assistance in the event of any disputes or issues that arise after hiring.

11. Feedback Loops and Machine Learning:

Implement machine learning algorithms that use feedback from both employers and employees to refine and improve the matching process over time.

Analyze satisfaction surveys and job longevity to identify patterns that predict successful matches, and use these insights to refine the app's algorithms.

12. Community Building and Support:

Create an online community platform within the app where users can share experiences, tips, and advice.

Provide resources for professional development, such as webinars, articles, and online courses, to help users enhance their employability.

13. Inclusivity Training for Employers:

Offer optional training modules for employers on inclusivity, unconscious bias, and creating a diverse workplace.

By educating employers, the app not only acts as a matching platform but also as a tool for social change and improvement in workplace culture.

14. Flexible Work Options:

Incorporate filters and options for different types of work arrangements, such as remote work, flexible hours, and freelance opportunities.

As the workforce becomes more dynamic, accommodating different work preferences will be essential.

15. Security and Privacy:

Ensure the highest standards of data security to protect user information from breaches.

Be transparent about how data is used and provide users with control over their personal information.

16. Integration with Other Platforms:

Consider integrations with professional networking sites, online resume databases, and job boards to streamline the process of importing user information and credentials.

These integrations can also extend the app's reach and make it easier for users to maintain their professional profiles.

17. Global Expansion and Localization:

Plan for the possibility of expanding the service to different countries and regions.

Localize the app's content and functionality to meet the legal requirements and cultural expectations of each market.

18. Performance Metrics and Reporting:

Provide employers with analytics and reporting tools to help them understand the effectiveness of their hiring practices and the demographics of the candidates they are attracting.

Offer insights into market trends and the app's impact on diversity and inclusivity in the workplace.

19. Legal and Ethical Advisory Services:

Offer access to legal and ethical advisory services for both employers and employees to consult on matters related to employment law, discrimination, and workplace disputes.

This feature could add value by helping users navigate complex employment situations with expert guidance.

20. Continuous Legal Review:

Regularly review the app's features and processes with legal experts to ensure ongoing compliance with employment laws, which can change over time.

Stay updated on legal precedents and cases related to hiring discrimination and bias to proactively adjust the app's framework.

21. Success Stories and Case Studies:

Showcase success stories and case studies of matches made through the app that led to positive employment outcomes.

These narratives can serve as powerful testimonials to attract new users and validate the app's effectiveness.

22. Accessibility:

Ensure the app is accessible to users with disabilities by following web content accessibility guidelines (WCAG) and making the interface user-friendly for everyone.

Accessibility features can include screen reader compatibility, voice commands, and customizable text sizes.

23. Robust Onboarding Process for Users:

Develop an informative onboarding process for new users that guides them through the features and benefits of the app

Use interactive tutorials or walkthroughs that help users understand how to complete their profiles, take assessments, and interpret their scores.

24. Bias-Awareness Features:

Implement features that help to detect and minimize bias within the app, such as flagging potentially biased language in job descriptions or providing tips for writing inclusive job posts.

Use anonymization techniques to hide certain information during the initial matching phase to prevent unconscious biases from influencing decisions.

25. Partnerships with Educational Institutions:

Partner with universities, trade schools, and other educational institutions to connect students and recent graduates with employment opportunities.

Offer specialized services or features for entry-level job seekers who may not have extensive work experience but possess relevant skills and potential.

26. Customizable Matching Criteria:

Allow both employers and employees to prioritize certain criteria over others when creating their profiles, providing a more personalized and relevant matching process.

For example, an employer may prioritize problem-solving skills and a positive attitude over specific educational qualifications.

27. Multilingual Support:

Offer the app in multiple languages to cater to a diverse user base and ensure that language barriers do not impede access to employment opportunities.

This is especially important in regions with a high level of linguistic diversity or where multiple languages are commonly spoken.

28. Responsive Customer Support:

Establish a responsive customer support team that can assist users with technical issues, questions about the app, and any concerns related to employment matches.

Consider offering support through multiple channels, such as live chat, email, and phone, to accommodate user preferences.

29. Strategic Marketing Campaigns:

Launch targeted marketing campaigns that speak to various demographics and highlight the app's commitment to reducing bias and promoting diversity.

Utilize success stories and endorsements from respected figures in the industry to enhance credibility and attract a wider audience.

30. Post-Hire Follow-Up:

Implement a process for following up with both employers and employees after the hiring decision to gather feedback on the app's effectiveness and the satisfaction of both parties.

Use this data to continuously refine the matching process and address any areas for improvement.

31. Regular Feature Updates:

Regularly release updates to the app that introduce new features, improvements, and bug fixes based on user feedback and technological advancements.

Keep users informed about upcoming changes and encourage their input to foster a sense of community and co-ownership of the platform.

32. Ethical Use of Data:

Adhere to ethical standards in the collection, analysis, and use of user data, ensuring that it is used to further the app's mission of fair hiring practices and not for exploitative purposes.

Be transparent with users about data usage and give them control over their personal information.

33. Sustainability and Environmental Considerations:

Highlight the environmental benefits of the app, such as reducing the need for travel during the initial stages of the hiring process, which can lower the carbon footprint associated with job searching.

Promote remote work options and environmentally sustainable companies, aligning with the values of eco-conscious job seekers.

34. Adaptive Testing and Assessments:

Use adaptive testing techniques where the difficulty of assessment questions adjusts based on the user's previous answers to provide a more accurate measure of skills and abilities.

Ensure that assessments are designed to be fair and valid across various demographic groups.

35. User Control and Flexibility:

Allow users to have control over their visibility and availability in the job market, enabling them to pause or deactivate their profiles as needed.

Offer flexibility in job preferences, such as part-time, freelance, or contract work, to appeal to a broader spectrum of job seekers.

36. Cross-Industry Opportunities:

Encourage cross-industry matching where feasible, allowing candidates with transferable skills to explore opportunities in different sectors. This can open doors for employees and provide employers with fresh perspectives.

37. Dynamic Skill-Mapping:

Implement dynamic skill-mapping to continuously update the skills profiles of candidates based on their latest experiences and learning, keeping their profiles relevant and competitive.

38. Integration with Continuous Education Providers:

Collaborate with online course providers, certification programs, and continuous education platforms to offer candidates the opportunity to improve their skills and qualifications directly through the app.

39. Advanced Analytics for Career Development:

Provide users with advanced analytics about their career trajectory, skill gaps, and recommended paths for development to help them make informed decisions about their professional growth.

40. AI-Powered Interview Coaching:

Offer AI-powered interview coaching within the app, using natural language processing and machine learning to provide personalized feedback and training to job seekers.

41. Social Impact Initiatives:

Develop social impact initiatives, such as partnerships with non-profits and social enterprises, to support job seekers from underrepresented or disadvantaged backgrounds.

42. Evolving Industry Standards Monitoring:

Keep track of evolving industry standards and requirements to ensure that the skills assessments remain current and relevant, providing realistic job readiness insights.

43. Gamification Elements:

Incorporate gamification elements to engage users in completing their profiles, taking assessments, and engaging with the platform, making the job search process more interactive and less daunting.

44. Emergency Hiring Feature:

Design an emergency hiring feature for employers who need to fill positions urgently, with a streamlined process that matches them with immediately available candidates.

45. Seasonal and Project-Based Work Features:

Integrate specific features for seasonal and project-based work, accommodating the unique needs of industries with variable employment cycles.

46. Scalable Infrastructure:

Ensure that the app has a scalable infrastructure to handle a growing number of users and data without compromising performance or security.

47. Work-Life Balance Metrics:

Integrate work-life balance metrics into the matching criteria to align with the modern workforce's emphasis on a healthy work-life balance.

48. Ongoing User Education:

Provide ongoing education and updates to users about the hiring process, new features, and best practices for using the app to ensure they maximize its potential.

49. Virtual Reality (VR) and Augmented Reality (AR) Integration:

Explore the potential integration of VR and AR for virtual job fairs, immersive job previews, or realistic job simulations as part of the assessment process.

50. Global Networking and Mentorship:

Facilitate global networking and mentorship opportunities within the app, connecting users with experienced professionals and industry leaders worldwide for guidance and support.

51. Cultural Fit Assessment:

Incorporate a cultural fit assessment to match employees with employers who share similar values and work culture preferences, which can significantly impact job satisfaction and retention rates.

52. Freelancer and Gig Economy Support:

Provide specialized features for freelancers and gig economy workers, including project-based matching, reputation management, and secure payment facilitation within the app.

53. Real-Time Labor Market Insights:

Offer real-time labor market insights to both job seekers and employers, enabling them to understand current demand for specific skills, salary benchmarks, and industry trends.

54. Employee Retention Tools:

Integrate tools for employers to track and improve employee retention, offering insights into turnover rates, employee engagement, and areas for organizational improvement.

55. Mobile Optimization:

Ensure the app is fully optimized for mobile devices, providing a seamless experience for users who prefer to search for jobs and manage their profiles on the go.

56. Collaborative Hiring Processes:

Enable collaborative hiring processes within the app by allowing teams to provide collective feedback on candidates, fostering a more comprehensive evaluation process.

57. Transparent Feedback Mechanism:

Create a transparent feedback mechanism where both employers and job seekers can receive constructive feedback post-interview, aiding in professional development and better future matching.

58. Work Authorization and Visa Support:

Offer guidance and support for international job seekers regarding work authorization, visas, and relocation considerations, expanding the talent pool for employers.

59. Personal Branding Tools:

Provide job seekers with tools and resources to build their personal brand, such as resume builders, portfolio showcases, and personal website templates.

60. Advanced Search and Filter Options:

Develop advanced search and filter options to allow users to narrow down opportunities based on very specific criteria, such as company size, social impact, tech stack for tech jobs, and more.

61. Confidential Job Search Options:

Offer options for job seekers to conduct a confidential job search, ensuring their current employer does not discover their potential interest in other opportunities.

62. AI-Driven Role Evolution Predictions:

Use AI to predict how certain roles may evolve and what skills will be required in the future, helping users to prepare and adapt their career paths accordingly.

63. Integration with HR Systems:

Provide seamless integration with popular HR systems to allow for easy transition of candidate data once hired, simplifying the onboarding process for employers.

64. Sponsorship and Advertising Opportunities:

Create sponsorship and targeted advertising opportunities within the app for educational institutions, professional services, and other relevant businesses to reach a large audience of job seekers and employers.

65. User Experience Personalization:

Utilize data to personalize the user experience, such as recommending jobs and content based on user activity, preferences, and past interactions with the app.

66. Dispute Resolution Services:

Offer mediation and dispute resolution services for conflicts that may arise between employers and employees, aiming to resolve issues fairly and efficiently.

67. Eco-Friendly Company Badges:

Introduce eco-friendly badges or certifications for companies that meet certain environmental sustainability criteria, appealing to job seekers who prioritize environmental responsibility.

68. Skills Verification and Endorsements:

Allow users to have their skills verified or endorsed by peers, mentors, or previous employers, adding credibility to their professional profiles.

69. Career Transition Support:

Provide specialized support for individuals looking to make a career transition, including tailored assessments, resources, and job matching that takes into account transferable skills and interests.

70. Impact Measurement and Reporting:

Measure and report the app›s impact on diversity, equity, and inclusion in the workforce, sharing success metrics and stories to demonstrate the app›s contribution to social change.

71. Extended Reality (XR) Onboarding Experiences:

Integrate extended reality technologies to offer immersive onboarding experiences, allowing new hires to familiarize themselves with the workplace, colleagues, and company culture virtually before their first day.

72. Smart Notification System:

Develop a smart notification system that alerts users to potential opportunities and deadlines, ensuring they don't miss out on applications or follow-ups.

73. Peer-to-Peer Learning Networks:

Facilitate peer-to-peer learning networks within the app where users can share knowledge, skills, and experiences, fostering a collaborative learning environment.

74. Predictive Career Pathing:

Use predictive analytics to help users understand potential career paths and the likelihood of success in different roles based on their skills, experiences, and industry trends.

75. Flexible Compensation Modeling:

For employers, include tools to model flexible compensation packages that can be customized to the preferences of the candidate, such as options for stock, bonuses, and other benefits.

76. Micro-credential Integration:**

Allow users to add micro-credentials to their profiles, reflecting specialized knowledge and skills acquired through short, focused educational courses.

77. Customizable Company Culture Profiles:

Enable employers to create customizable profiles that showcase their company culture through videos, testimonials, and interactive media, giving job seekers a deeper insight into their potential work environment.

78. Talent Pooling:
Offer talent pooling features where employers can keep track of and nurture relationships with potential candidates for future opportunities.

79. Apprenticeship and Internship Matching:

Include a dedicated section for apprenticeships and internships, connecting students and young professionals with opportunities for hands-on learning and experience.

80. Diverse Language Support in Assessments:

Provide assessments in multiple languages to ensure that non-native speakers are not at a disadvantage and can accurately demonstrate their skills and competencies.

81. Integration with Public Employment Services:

Collaborate with public employment services and governmental job programs to widen the app's reach and support wider employment initiatives.

82. AI-Powered Salary Negotiation Assistant:

Introduce an AI-powered salary negotiation assistant that can provide job seekers with guidance on how to negotiate salaries based on industry standards, experience, and location.

83. Wellness and Mental Health Resources:

Embed wellness and mental health resources within the app, recognizing the importance of these aspects in overall job satisfaction and performance.

84. Remote Work Efficacy Tools:

As remote work becomes more prevalent, provide tools and resources to help both employers and employees maximize the efficacy of remote work arrangements.

85. Blockchain for Credential Verification:

Utilize blockchain technology to provide a secure and immutable record of users' credentials, work history, and achievements, simplifying the verification process for employers.

86. Dynamic Reference Checking:

Automate and streamline the reference checking process, allowing candidates to submit references easily and employers to receive feedback quickly.

87. Job Match Guarantees:

Explore the possibility of offering a job match guarantee, where the app provides additional support or refunds the hiring fee if a match does not meet the agreed-upon criteria within a certain period.

88. Corporate Social Responsibility (CSR) Metrics:

Allow companies to display their CSR initiatives and achievements, enabling job seekers to align with employers that share their values on social and environmental issues.

89. User-Generated Content and Success Stories:

Encourage users to share their success stories and content, such as career advice or industry insights, creating a rich ecosystem of user-generated content.

90. Event and Webinar Hosting:

Provide a platform for hosting virtual events and webinars, allowing employers to showcase their organizations and job seekers to learn more about industry trends and career advice.

91. Advanced Role Customization:

Offer advanced customization for job role descriptions, including the ability to define new or emerging roles, to ensure employers can accurately represent the positions they're offering.

92. Integration with Freelance Marketplaces:

Link with freelance marketplaces to provide users with access to short-term projects and freelance work, expanding the app's utility to a broader range of work preferences.

93. Accessibility Compliance:

Regularly audit and update the app to ensure it meets or exceeds accessibility standards, making sure that it is usable by job seekers and employers with disabilities.

94. Multi-factor Authentication:

Implement multi-factor authentication to enhance security and protect user accounts from unauthorized access.

95. Job Search Autopilot:

Develop a 'job search autopilot' feature that automatically applies to jobs on behalf of the user based on their preferences and qualifications, streamlining the job search process.

96. Green Jobs Specialization:

Highlight and specialize in 'green jobs' that contribute to the environment and sustainability, catering to a growing market of environmentally conscious job seekers and companies.

97. On-Demand Career Counseling:

Integrate on-demand career counseling services within the app, offering users the opportunity to receive personalized advice and guidance from career experts.

98. Portfolio Showcasing Platform:

Create a platform within the app for users, especially those in creative fields, to showcase their portfolios, allowing them to present their work effectively to potential employers.

99. Youth Employment Focus:

Develop features and resources tailored specifically towards youth employment, including entry-level positions, tips for first-time job seekers, and links to scholarship and training opportunities.

100. Senior Professional and Executive Track:

Offer a dedicated track for senior professionals and executives, with higher-level matching, networking opportunities, and features appropriate for advanced career stages.

101. Localized Economic Development Support:

Work with local governments and economic development agencies to support employment growth in specific areas, contributing to the economic well-being of communities.

102. User Privacy Controls:

Provide robust user privacy controls, allowing users to decide how much information they want to share and with whom, ensuring they feel secure in their job search.

103. Comprehensive Onboarding for Companies:

Offer a comprehensive onboarding process for companies to help them understand how to best use the app, present their brand, and attract top talent.

104. International Work and Exchange Programs:

Facilitate international work and exchange programs through the app, providing users with opportunities to gain experience abroad.

105. Sector-Specific Advisory Panels:

Establish sector-specific advisory panels comprising industry experts who can provide insights and guidance on trends and best practices within their sectors.

106. Advanced Filtering for Remote-Only Jobs:

With the rise of remote work, include advanced filtering options for users specifically looking for remote-only employment, ensuring they can easily find relevant opportunities.

107. Social Media Integration:

Allow users to integrate their professional social media profiles, enabling a richer presentation of their professional brand and easier sharing of their profiles.

108. Data-Driven Job Market Reports:

Regularly publish in-depth job market reports based on aggregated app data, providing valuable insights into job market trends, skills demand, and salary benchmarks.

109. Interactive Company Roadshows:

Enable companies to hold interactive virtual roadshows on the app, allowing them to engage with potential candidates in a dynamic and informative format.

110. Recruiter and Headhunter Portal:

Create a specialized portal for recruiters and headhunters to access curated talent pools, making it easier to find candidates for specialized roles.

111. Volunteering and Non-Profit Opportunities:

Include a section dedicated to volunteering and non-profit opportunities, connecting users with ways to give back to the community and gain experience in the process.

112. Continuous Feedback Loop:

Establish a continuous feedback loop where the app learns and evolves based on user interactions, feedback, and success rates, ensuring constant improvement.

113. Holistic Wellness Tracking:

Offer holistic wellness tracking for employees, linking job satisfaction and performance with factors such as stress levels, work-life balance, and overall well-being.

114. Mature Workers Program:

Develop a program within the app to help mature workers navigate the job market, with resources and matching for those who may be facing age bias.

115. AI-Enhanced Job Descriptions:

Use AI to help employers craft job descriptions that are clear, inclusive, and appealing, maximizing their chances of attracting suitable candidates.

116. Lifelong Learning Partnerships:

Partner with lifelong learning platforms to encourage continuous education and upskilling, offering discounts or exclusive content to app users.

117. Job Security Scoring:

Provide a job security score for listed positions based on factors such as industry stability, company financial health, and historical turnover rates, helping users make informed decisions.

118. Flexible Benefits Matching:

Allow employees to indicate their preferred benefits, such as healthcare, retirement plans, or wellness programs, and match them with employers offering compatible benefits packages.

119. Environmental Impact Tracking:

Track and report the environmental impact of job placements, such as reduced commuting due to remote work, contributing to an organization's sustainability goals.

120. Expandable and Customizable Profiles:

Give users the ability to expand and customize their profiles to include certifications, publications, patents, or other unique professional accomplishments.

121. Experiential Learning Opportunities:

Partner with organizations to offer experiential learning opportunities, like live projects or simulations, that job seekers can participate in to demonstrate their skills in a real-world context.

122. Cross-Cultural Competence Training:

Provide resources and training modules on cross-cultural competence for both employers and employees, which is essential for global companies and diverse work environments.

123. AI Career Advisor:

Develop an AI career advisor feature that uses machine learning to provide personalized career advice, suggest potential career moves, and recommend upskilling opportunities based on market trends.

124. Job Compatibility Index:

Introduce a job compatibility index that rates how well a job seeker's skills, experiences, and preferences align with the job's requirements and the company's culture.

125. Return-to-Work Programs:

Offer support for individuals returning to the workforce after an extended absence, with tailored job matching and resources to ease the transition.

126. Frictionless Application Processes:

Streamline the application process with one-click applications, resume parsing, and autofill capabilities to minimize the time and effort required to apply for jobs.

127. Company Transparency Ratings:

Implement a company transparency rating system where employees can rate employers on their transparency regarding company performance, expectations, and culture.

128. Alumni Networks and Rehire Programs:

Create alumni networks within the app for companies to maintain relationships with former employees and potentially rehire them for new opportunities.

129. Skill Decay Alerts:

Notify users when their skills may be at risk of becoming outdated and provide suggestions for refresher courses or new skills to learn.

130. Workplace Accessibility Ratings:

Allow users to rate and review companies on workplace accessibility, providing valuable insights for job seekers with disabilities.

131. Predictive Turnover Analytics:

Offer predictive turnover analytics to employers, helping them identify patterns and risk factors for employee turnover and address them proactively.

132. Childcare and Eldercare Resources:

Provide a resource hub for job seekers that includes information on childcare and eldercare options, recognizing the importance of these services in work-life balance.

133. Interview Scheduling Automation:

Automate the interview scheduling process with calendar integration and real-time availability matching to facilitate seamless coordination between job seekers and employers.

134. Employee Value Proposition (EVP) Builder:

Equip employers with an EVP builder to help them articulate and communicate their unique value proposition to potential candidates.

135. Geolocation-Based Job Searches:

Incorporate geolocation features to allow job seekers to find jobs in their vicinity or in specific areas they are interested in moving to.

136. Contingent Workforce Management:

Offer features for managing a contingent workforce, including contract workers, freelancers, and part-time staff, accommodating the growing trend towards flexible work arrangements.

137. Startup Ecosystem Support:

Create a startup ecosystem within the app that connects startups with talent passionate about working in a dynamic, entrepreneurial environment.

138. Ergonomics and Workplace Well-being:

Include information and tips on ergonomics and workplace well-being for both remote and in-office environments, helping employees maintain a healthy workspace.

139. Career Path Visualization:

Provide a tool for visualizing career paths that allows users to see potential future job roles and the skill and experience requirements for each step.

140. Social Impact Job Matching:

Emphasize social impact in job matching, allowing job seekers to find positions in companies that prioritize social responsibility and align with their values.

141. Regulatory Compliance Resources:

Offer resources and checklists for companies to ensure they are compliant with all relevant employment regulations and laws, reducing the risk of legal issues.

142. Mid-Career Change Support:

Cater to individuals looking to make a mid-career change, with resources and job matching services that recognize the value of transferable skills and diverse experiences.

143. Relocation Assistance Features:

For jobs that require relocation, provide features that assist with the process, such as cost-of-living calculators, housing resources, and community insight.

144. Job Shadowing Opportunities:

Facilitate job shadowing experiences where individuals can spend time observing professionals in their desired field to gain insight into a typical workday, industry practices, and job responsibilities.

145. Industry Networking Events:

Organize industry-specific networking events, conferences, or seminars where job seekers can connect with professionals, recruiters, and potential employers to expand their professional network and explore career opportunities.

146. Wellness Programs and Benefits:

Implement wellness programs and benefits that focus on physical, mental, and emotional well-being, such as mindfulness sessions, fitness classes, employee assistance programs, and flexible work arrangements to support overall employee wellness.

147. Entrepreneurship Support Services:

Provide resources, mentorship, and training for individuals interested in entrepreneurship, including business planning assistance, access to funding opportunities, and networking events with successful entrepreneurs.

148. Skill-Based Volunteer Opportunities:

Connect job seekers with skill-based volunteer opportunities where they can apply their expertise, gain hands-on experience, and contribute to meaningful projects while expanding their professional network and enhancing their resume.

149. Professional Development Stipends:

Offer professional development stipends or allowances for employees to pursue further education, attend conferences, workshops, or training programs to enhance their skills, knowledge, and advance their careers.

150. Job Search Support Groups:

Establish job search support groups or online communities where job seekers can share resources, advice, job leads, and emotional support during their job search journey.

151. Technology Skills Training:

Provide training programs and workshops to help individuals develop in-demand technology skills, such as coding, data analysis, digital marketing, or cybersecurity, to increase their employability in tech-driven industries.

152. Lifelong Learning Accounts:

Introduce lifelong learning accounts or benefits that allow employees to access funds or resources for continuing education, skill development, and personal growth throughout their careers.

153. Cultural Sensitivity Training:

Offer cultural sensitivity training to educate employees on different cultures, perspectives, and communication styles to promote a more inclusive and respectful work environment that celebrates diversity.

154. Job Rotation Programs:

Implement job rotation programs that allow employees to gain experience in different roles or departments within the organization, helping them develop new skills, expand their knowledge, and explore various career paths.

155. Flexible Work Arrangements:

Provide flexible work arrangements such as telecommuting, flexible hours, compressed workweeks, or job sharing options to accommodate diverse work styles, improve work-life balance, and increase employee satisfaction and productivity.

156. Career Development Workshops:

Conduct career development workshops on topics like resume writing, interview skills, networking strategies, personal branding, and career planning to empower individuals with the tools and knowledge needed to advance in their careers.

157. Employee Recognition Programs:

Establish employee recognition programs that acknowledge and reward employees for their contributions, achievements, and dedication, fostering a positive work culture, boosting morale, and increasing employee engagement.

158. Digital Skills Bootcamps:

Offer intensive digital skills bootcamps or training programs to help individuals quickly develop proficiency in high-demand digital skills like coding, data analytics, UX/UI design, or digital marketing to enhance their job prospects in the digital economy.

159. Workplace Mental Health Resources:

Provide access to mental health resources, counseling services, mental health awareness training, and initiatives to create a supportive and stigma-free environment for employees to prioritize their mental well-being.

160. Job Sharing Platforms:

Create job sharing platforms or networks where individuals can find job sharing opportunities with another professional, allowing them to split a full-time role based on their preferences and commitments.

161. Green Skills Training:

Offer training programs on green skills and sustainability practices to equip individuals with the knowledge and expertise needed to pursue careers in environmentally conscious industries and contribute to a more sustainable future.

162. Conflict Resolution Workshops:

Conduct conflict resolution workshops to provide employees with strategies and skills to effectively manage conflicts, foster positive workplace relationships, and maintain a harmonious work environment.

163. Gig Economy Skill Development:

Provide training and resources to help individuals thrive in the gig economy, including skills such as self-employment, marketing, customer relationship management, and financial management for gig workers and freelancers.

164. Emotional Intelligence Training:

Offer emotional intelligence training to help individuals develop self-awareness, self-regulation, empathy, and social skills, which are essential for effective communication, collaboration, and leadership in the workplace.

165. Job Crafting Workshops:

Host job crafting workshops where employees can learn how to redesign their roles, tasks, and responsibilities to better align with their strengths, interests, and values, increasing job satisfaction and engagement.

166. Parental Leave Support Programs:

Provide parental leave support programs that offer resources, guidance, and flexible return-to-work options for employees transitioning back to work after parental leave, promoting work-life balance and supporting working parents.

167. Microlearning Modules:

Develop microlearning modules or bite-sized learning resources on specific topics or skills that employees can access on-demand to support continuous learning and skill development in a convenient and time-efficient manner.

168. Job Referral Incentives:

Implement job referral programs with incentives for employees who refer qualified candidates, encouraging employee referrals and helping companies attract top talent through their employees' networks.

169. Cybersecurity Awareness Training:

Provide cybersecurity awareness training to educate employees on best practices for data security, privacy protection, recognizing phishing attempts, and safeguarding company information from cyber threats.

170. Resilience Building Workshops:

Offer resilience building workshops and training sessions to help employees develop coping strategies, stress management techniques, and resilience skills to navigate challenges, setbacks, and uncertainties effectively.

171. Reverse Mentoring Programs:

Establish reverse mentoring programs where younger or less experienced employees mentor senior or more experienced professionals, facilitating knowledge exchange, fostering diversity of thought, and promoting mutual learning and growth.

172. Job Redesign Initiatives:

Explore job redesign initiatives to optimize job roles, tasks, and workflows for increased efficiency, employee engagement, and job satisfaction, taking into account changing business needs and employee preferences.

173. Workplace Innovation Challenges:

Organize workplace innovation challenges or hackathons where employees can collaborate, brainstorm, and propose creative solutions to business problems, fostering a culture of innovation, creativity, and continuous improvement.

174. Language Skills Development Programs:

Offer language skills development programs or language courses to help employees enhance their communication abilities, cultural understanding, and global business prospects by learning a new language or improving existing language skills.

175. Wellness Challenges and Programs:

Implement wellness challenges and programs that promote healthy behaviors, physical activity, mindfulness practices, and overall well-being among employees, creating a supportive and health-conscious work environment.

176. Cross-Functional Team Projects:

Encourage cross-functional team projects and collaborations where employees from different departments or areas of expertise work together on initiatives, fostering diversity of thought, knowledge sharing, and innovation.

177. Job Satisfaction Surveys and Feedback Mechanisms:

Conduct regular job satisfaction surveys and establish feedback mechanisms to gather employee input, identify areas for improvement, and take proactive measures to enhance job satisfaction, engagement, and retention.

178. Professional Certification Support:

Provide support for employees seeking professional certifications or credentials relevant to their roles, offering financial assistance, study materials, exam preparation resources, and dedicated study time to help employees advance their careers.

179. Digital Literacy Training:

Offer digital literacy training programs to enhance employees' proficiency with digital tools, software applications, online communication platforms, and information technology, empowering them to leverage technology effectively in their work.

180. Job Flexibility Options:

Introduce job flexibility options such as job sharing, part-time work, flexible schedules, or remote work arrangements to accommodate employees' personal needs, preferences, and lifestyle choices while maintaining productivity and work quality.

181. Innovation Incubator Programs:

Establish innovation incubator programs that provide resources, mentorship, and funding for employees to develop and prototype innovative ideas, products, or solutions within the organization, fostering a culture of creativity and entrepreneurship.

182. Conflict Resolution Mediation Services:

Offer conflict resolution mediation services facilitated by trained professionals to help employees resolve interpersonal conflicts, misunderstandings, or disputes in a constructive and collaborative manner, promoting healthy work relationships.

183. Job Market Skills Assessments:

Conduct job market skills assessments or competency evaluations to help employees identify their strengths, areas for development, and skill gaps, guiding them in setting career goals and pursuing relevant training or upskilling opportunities.

184. Employee Resource Groups (ERGs):

Support and promote employee resource groups (ERGs) or affinity groups that bring together employees with common interests, backgrounds, or identities to foster inclusivity, diversity, and a sense of belonging within the organization.

185. Job Embeddedness Programs:

Implement job embeddedness programs that focus on increasing employees' connections, fit, and satisfaction within the organization, reducing turnover intentions, and enhancing employee commitment and loyalty.

186. Generational Diversity Training:

Provide generational diversity training to educate employees on the characteristics, preferences, and communication styles of different generations in the workforce, promoting understanding, collaboration, and effective teamwork across age groups.

187. Personal Development Budgets:

Allocate personal development budgets or allowances for employees to invest in their personal and professional growth, including courses, workshops, coaching, or resources that support their individual learning and development goals.

188. Remote Team Building Activities:

Organize remote team building activities, virtual games, and collaborative projects to foster team cohesion, strengthen relationships, and boost morale among remote or dispersed teams.

189. Innovation Training and Workshops:

Provide innovation training and workshops to equip employees with creative problem-solving skills, design thinking methodologies, and innovation techniques to drive continuous improvement and innovation within the organization.

190. Job Crafting Tools and Resources:

Offer job crafting tools, resources, and self-assessment exercises that empower employees to customize and redesign aspects of their job roles, tasks, and responsibilities to align with their strengths, interests, and values.

191. Employee Well-being Check-ins:

Conduct regular employee well-being check-ins, one-on-one meetings, or pulse surveys to assess and address employees' emotional well-being, job satisfaction, stress levels, and overall happiness at work.

192. Professional Networking Platforms:

Provide access to professional networking platforms, online communities, or industry-specific forums where employees can connect, share knowledge, seek mentorship, and explore career opportunities within and outside the organization.

193. Agile Work Methodologies Training:

Offer training on agile work methodologies, such as Scrum or Kanban, to help employees adapt to dynamic work environments, improve collaboration, prioritize tasks effectively, and deliver results efficiently in iterative work cycles.

194. Employee Recognition and Appreciation Programs:

Implement employee recognition and appreciation programs that celebrate individual and team achievements, milestones, and contributions through rewards, public recognition, and personalized appreciation gestures.

195. Professional Growth Opportunities:

Create pathways for professional growth and career advancement within the organization through opportunities for promotions, lateral moves, cross-training, leadership development programs, and succession planning initiatives.

196. Continuous Feedback Culture:

Foster a culture of continuous feedback and open communication by encouraging regular feedback exchanges between managers and employees, promoting constructive feedback, recognition of achievements, and opportunities for growth and improvement.

197. Skill Swapping Initiatives:

Facilitate skill swapping initiatives where employees can exchange skills, knowledge, or expertise with their peers through informal learning sessions, workshops, or collaborative projects to enhance cross-functional capabilities and promote a culture of learning.

198. Health and Wellness Benefits:

Offer comprehensive health and wellness benefits, including medical insurance, mental health support, gym memberships, wellness programs, ergonomic workstations, and other initiatives to support employees' physical and mental well-being.

199. Workplace Diversity Training:

Provide workplace diversity training to raise awareness, foster inclusivity, prevent bias, and promote respect for individuals from diverse backgrounds, cultures, genders, and identities within the workplace.

200. Cross-Training Programs:

Implement cross-training programs that enable employees to learn new skills, gain knowledge about different roles or departments, and increase their versatility within the organization, enhancing teamwork and flexibility.

201. Employee Resource and Information Centers:

Establish employee resource and information centers that centralize important resources, policies, benefits information, professional development opportunities, and support services to empower employees to access relevant information easily.

202. Job Sharing Networks:

Create job sharing networks or platforms where employees can explore job sharing arrangements, find compatible job sharing partners, and negotiate flexible work schedules that allow them to share responsibilities and maintain work-life balance.

203. Innovative Rewards and Recognition Programs:

Design innovative rewards and recognition programs that go beyond traditional incentives to include personalized rewards, experiential perks, skill development opportunities, or social recognition initiatives that motivate and engage employees.

203. Virtual Leadership Development Programs:

Offer virtual leadership development programs tailored for remote or distributed teams to enhance leadership skills, communication effectiveness, team management strategies, and virtual collaboration capabilities among leaders and managers.

204. Professional Ethics Training:

Provide professional ethics training to employees at all levels within the organization to promote ethical behavior, integrity, and compliance with company values and standards. This training can help employees make sound decisions, navigate ethical dilemmas, and contribute to a positive organizational culture built on trust and accountability. Professional ethics training can cover topics such as conflicts of interest, confidentiality, respect in the workplace, diversity and inclusion, and ethical decision-making processes. By investing in professional ethics training, organizations can foster a culture of integrity and demonstrate a commitment to ethical conduct in all aspects of their operations.

205. Learning Circles and Study Groups:

Facilitate learning circles and study groups where employees can engage in peer-to-peer learning, knowledge sharing, and collaborative learning experiences on specific topics, skills, or areas of interest to deepen their expertise.

206. Community Engagement Initiatives:

Engage employees in community service, volunteering opportunities, or corporate social responsibility initiatives that align with the organization's values, promote social impact, and encourage employees to give back to their communities.

207. Agility and Resilience Training:

Provide training on agility and resilience to help employees adapt to change, navigate uncertainties, bounce back from setbacks, and thrive in dynamic work environments by developing a growth mindset and flexible approach to challenges.

208. Wellness Programs and Initiatives:

Implement wellness programs and initiatives to support employees' physical, mental, and emotional well-being. These programs can include activities such as fitness challenges, mindfulness sessions, health screenings, mental health resources, and stress management workshops. By promoting a culture of wellness, organizations can help employees maintain a healthy work-life balance, reduce stress, increase productivity, and enhance overall job satisfaction.

209. Diversity and Inclusion Training:

Offer diversity and inclusion training to educate employees on the importance of diversity, equity, and inclusion in the workplace. This training can help employees develop cultural competency, understand unconscious bias, and foster a more inclusive and equitable work environment. By promoting diversity and inclusion, organizations can leverage the unique perspectives and talents of their diverse workforce, improve collaboration, and drive innovation and performance.

210. Continuous Feedback and Coaching Programs:

Establish continuous feedback and coaching programs to provide ongoing support and development opportunities for employees. Regular feedback sessions and coaching conversations can help employees set goals, identify areas for improvement, and receive guidance on how to enhance their performance. By fostering a culture of continuous feedback and coaching, organizations can empower employees to grow, learn, and succeed in their roles, ultimately contributing to their professional development and career advancement.

211. Flexible Work Arrangements:

Introduce flexible work arrangements such as telecommuting, flextime, compressed workweeks, or job sharing to accommodate employees' diverse needs and preferences. Flexible work options can help employees achieve better work-life balance, reduce commuting stress, and increase job satisfaction and productivity. By offering flexibility in how and where work is done, organizations can attract and retain top talent, boost employee morale, and create a more inclusive and adaptable workplace culture.

212. Knowledge Sharing Platforms:

Implement knowledge sharing platforms or systems that facilitate the sharing of information, best practices, and expertise among employees across different teams and departments. These platforms can include intranet portals, collaboration tools, or online forums where employees can exchange ideas, seek advice, and collaborate on projects. By promoting knowledge sharing and collaboration, organizations can harness their collective intelligence, foster innovation, and improve efficiency and decision-making processes.

213. Conflict Resolution and Mediation Services:

Provide conflict resolution and mediation services to help employees address and resolve conflicts in a constructive and collaborative manner. Trained mediators or conflict resolution specialists can facilitate conversations between parties, help them clarify issues, and work together to find mutually acceptable solutions. By offering conflict resolution and mediation services, organizations can promote a culture of open communication, trust, and respect, and prevent conflicts from escalating and negatively impacting team dynamics and productivity.

214. Employee Assistance Programs (EAP):

Implement Employee Assistance Programs (EAP) to provide employees with confidential counseling, support services, and resources to address personal or work-related challenges. EAPs typically offer services such as mental health counseling, financial counseling, legal assistance, and referrals to community resources. By offering EAPs, organizations demonstrate a commitment to the well-being of their employees and help them navigate difficult situations, manage stress, and improve their overall quality of life.

215. Cross-Functional Project Teams:

Form cross-functional project teams composed of employees from different departments or areas of expertise to collaborate on specific projects or initiatives. Cross-functional teams can bring diverse perspectives, skills, and knowledge to problem-solving and decision-making processes, promote creativity and innovation, and improve communication and collaboration across the organization. By leveraging the strengths of cross-functional teams, organizations can drive successful project outcomes, foster a culture of teamwork and mutual learning, and enhance organizational agility and performance.

216. Succession Planning and Talent Development:

Establish succession planning and talent development programs to identify high-potential employees, provide them with opportunities for growth and advancement, and ensure a pipeline of skilled and capable leaders for key roles within the organization. Succession planning involves assessing current talent, identifying future leadership needs, and developing strategies to fill critical roles with internal candidates. By investing in talent development and succession planning, organizations can nurture their employees' potential, retain top performers, and build a sustainable leadership pipeline for long-term organizational success.

217. Mentorship and Coaching Programs:

Create mentorship and coaching programs that pair employees with experienced mentors or coaches who can provide guidance, support, and career development advice. Mentors can share their knowledge and expertise, offer insights into the organization's culture and practices, and help mentees set and achieve their professional goals. Coaching programs can focus on specific skills development, leadership competencies, or personal growth areas tailored to individual needs. By fostering mentorship and coaching relationships, organizations can promote skill development, career advancement, and employee engagement.

218. Learning and Development Opportunities:

Provide ongoing learning and development opportunities for employees to enhance their skills, knowledge, and capabilities. This can include offering training programs, workshops, seminars, online courses, and tuition reimbursement for further education. By investing in employee learning and development, organizations can empower their workforce to stay current with industry trends, adapt to new technologies and practices, and contribute effectively to the organization›s success. Continuous learning also helps employees feel valued, engaged, and motivated in their roles.

219. Employee Surveys and Feedback Mechanisms:

Conduct regular employee surveys and establish feedback mechanisms to gather insights, opinions, and suggestions from employees regarding their work experiences, job satisfaction, and organizational culture. Employee feedback can provide valuable information for identifying areas of improvement, addressing concerns, and enhancing employee engagement and morale. By listening to employee feedback and acting on it, organizations can demonstrate a commitment to employee voice, foster a culture of transparency and trust, and make data-driven decisions to create a positive and inclusive work environment.

220. Community Engagement and Corporate Social Responsibility (CSR) Programs:

Engage employees in community service projects, volunteering opportunities, or corporate social responsibility (CSR) initiatives that align with the organization's values and contribute to social impact. Community engagement programs can foster teamwork, build camaraderie, and instill a sense of purpose and pride among employees. By participating in CSR activities, employees can make a positive difference in their communities, enhance their sense of social responsibility, and strengthen their connection to the organization's broader mission and values.

221. Agile Work Practices:

Implement agile work practices and methodologies to increase organizational agility, responsiveness, and collaboration. Agile principles emphasize iterative development, continuous improvement, and cross-functional teamwork to deliver value to customers efficiently and adapt to changing circumstances. By embracing agile practices, organizations can enhance innovation, speed up project delivery, and empower employees to work more collaboratively and flexibly.

222. Employee Well-being Initiatives:

Launch employee well-being initiatives that focus on promoting physical, mental, and emotional health in the workplace. These initiatives can include wellness challenges, mindfulness programs, health screenings, mental health resources, ergonomic assessments, and initiatives to reduce workplace stress. By prioritizing employee well-being, organizations can create a supportive and healthy work environment, improve employee morale and productivity, and reduce absenteeism and turnover.

223. Technology Adoption and Training Programs:

Provide technology adoption and training programs to help employees leverage new tools, software, and technologies effectively in their roles. Training programs can include workshops, online courses, and hands-on sessions to enhance employees' digital skills, increase their productivity, and adapt to technological advancements. By investing in technology training, organizations can empower employees to work more efficiently, stay competitive in the digital age, and drive innovation and growth.

224. Sustainability Initiatives:

Integrate sustainability initiatives into the organization's operations and culture to promote environmental responsibility and social impact. Sustainability initiatives can include reducing carbon footprint, conserving resources, supporting eco-friendly practices, and engaging employees in green initiatives. By incorporating sustainability into business practices, organizations can demonstrate corporate citizenship, attract environmentally conscious employees and customers, and contribute to a more sustainable future.

225. Continuous Improvement Culture:

Foster a culture of continuous improvement where employees are encouraged to identify inefficiencies, suggest process enhancements, and implement innovative solutions to drive organizational excellence. Continuous improvement involves ongoing evaluation, feedback, and learning to optimize operations, enhance quality, and deliver value to customers. By promoting a culture of continuous improvement, organizations can adapt to change more effectively, increase operational efficiency, and foster a mindset of innovation and excellence among employees.

226. Knowledge Management Systems:

Implement knowledge management systems and tools to capture, organize, and share knowledge and information within the organization. Knowledge management systems can include databases, wikis, intranets, or collaboration platforms that enable employees to access relevant information, best practices, and expertise easily. By leveraging knowledge management systems, organizations can enhance knowledge sharing, improve decision-making, and foster a culture of learning and collaboration.

227. Remote Work Policies and Guidelines:

Establish clear remote work policies and guidelines to support employees who work remotely or in a hybrid work environment. Remote work policies should outline expectations, communication protocols, performance metrics, and guidelines for maintaining work-life balance while working outside the traditional office setting. By providing structure and guidance for remote work, organizations can ensure productivity, collaboration, and cohesion among remote teams.

228. Crisis Management and Business Continuity Planning:

Develop comprehensive crisis management and business continuity plans to prepare for and respond to emergencies, disasters, or unforeseen events that may disrupt business operations. These plans should outline protocols, roles, and communication strategies to ensure the safety of employees, protect critical assets, and maintain essential services during a crisis. By proactively planning for emergencies, organizations can minimize disruptions, mitigate risks, and safeguard their business continuity.

229. Innovation Labs and Incubators:

Establish innovation labs or incubators as dedicated spaces or programs to foster creativity, experimentation, and innovation within the organization. Innovation labs provide a structured environment for employees to explore new ideas, collaborate on projects, and develop innovative solutions to business challenges. By creating a culture of innovation and providing resources for experimentation, organizations can drive creativity, spark innovation, and stay ahead of the competition in a rapidly evolving marketplace.

230. Employee Empowerment and Autonomy:

Empower employees by granting them autonomy, decision-making authority, and ownership over their work and projects. Employee empowerment involves trusting employees to make decisions, take initiative, and contribute their unique skills and perspectives to achieve organizational goals. By fostering a culture of empowerment, organizations can increase employee engagement, motivation, and job satisfaction, leading to higher performance, creativity, and innovation.

231. Workplace Diversity and Inclusion Initiatives:

Implement workplace diversity and inclusion initiatives to create a more diverse, equitable, and inclusive work environment. These initiatives can include diversity training, recruitment strategies to attract a diverse talent pool, affinity groups or employee resource groups, and policies to prevent discrimination and promote diversity at all levels of the organization. By fostering diversity and inclusion, organizations can leverage the benefits of a diverse workforce, enhance creativity and innovation, and create a culture where all employees feel valued and respected.

232. Employee Recognition and Appreciation Programs:

Establish employee recognition and appreciation programs to acknowledge and reward employees for their contributions, achievements, and dedication to the organization. These programs can include recognition ceremonies, awards, peer-to-peer recognition platforms, or personalized notes of appreciation. By recognizing and appreciating employees' efforts, organizations can boost morale, motivation, and employee engagement, leading to increased job satisfaction and retention.

233. Conflict Resolution Training:

Provide conflict resolution training to equip employees with the skills and techniques needed to effectively manage and resolve conflicts in the workplace. Conflict resolution training can help employees improve their communication, negotiation, and problem-solving skills, enabling them to navigate disagreements and disputes constructively. By offering conflict resolution training, organizations can promote a positive work environment, enhance team dynamics, and prevent conflicts from escalating and affecting productivity.

234. Agile Leadership Development Programs:

Offer agile leadership development programs designed to cultivate leadership skills that are adaptive, collaborative, and responsive to change. Agile leadership programs focus on developing leaders who can inspire and empower teams, foster innovation, and navigate complexity and uncertainty effectively. By investing in agile leadership development, organizations can build a resilient leadership pipeline capable of driving organizational agility, growth, and success in dynamic business environments.

235. Data Analytics and Decision-Making Training:

Provide training in data analytics and decision-making to help employees leverage data-driven insights to make informed decisions and drive business outcomes. Training in data analytics equips employees with the skills to collect, analyze, and interpret data to identify trends, opportunities, and risks. By enhancing employees' data literacy and decision-making capabilities, organizations can improve their strategic planning, operational efficiency, and competitive advantage in the data-driven digital age.

236. Health and Safety Programs:

Implement health and safety programs to ensure the well-being and security of employees in the workplace. These programs encompass practices such as conducting risk assessments, providing safety training, promoting ergonomic workspaces, and establishing emergency response protocols. By prioritizing health and safety, organizations can create a safe and secure work environment, reduce accidents and injuries, and demonstrate a commitment to employee welfare.

237. Continuous Performance Feedback Systems:

Establish continuous performance feedback systems that provide ongoing feedback and coaching to employees throughout the year. These systems can include regular check-ins, goal setting, performance reviews, and development discussions to support employees in achieving their objectives and improving their performance. By offering continuous performance feedback, organizations can enhance employee development, motivation, and engagement, leading to increased productivity and performance.

238. Emotional Intelligence Training:

Provide training in emotional intelligence (EI) to help employees develop self-awareness, empathy, and relationship management skills. Emotional intelligence training can enhance employees' ability to understand and manage their emotions effectively, navigate interpersonal relationships, and communicate empathetically. By cultivating emotional intelligence in the workforce, organizations can improve teamwork, leadership effectiveness, and conflict resolution capabilities.

239. Remote Team Building Activities:

Facilitate remote team building activities and initiatives to foster collaboration, camaraderie, and engagement among remote or distributed teams. Remote team building activities can include virtual team challenges, online games, video conferencing social events, or virtual coffee breaks. By promoting remote team building, organizations can strengthen relationships, boost morale, and create a sense of connection and belonging among team members working in different locations.

240. Job Rotation Programs:

Implement job rotation programs that allow employees to rotate through different roles, departments, or projects within the organization. Job rotation programs offer employees the opportunity to develop new skills, gain diverse experiences, and broaden their understanding of the business. By providing job rotation opportunities, organizations can increase employee engagement, retention, and career growth, while also fostering a more versatile and adaptable workforce.

241. Remote Work Skill Development:

Provide training programs and resources to help individuals develop essential skills for remote work, such as time management, communication in virtual environments, and collaboration tools proficiency.

These initiatives aim to support employees' professional growth, well-being, and engagement while fostering a positive and inclusive work culture within the organization.

By focusing on a comprehensive range of features and services that cater to diverse needs, the hiring app can become a holistic platform that not only connects job seekers with employers but also supports them throughout their professional journey. From career inception to retirement, the app can serve as a companion, advisor, and catalyst for career success and satisfaction.

By continuously expanding the functionality and services of the hiring app, it can not only match talent with opportunity but also play a pivotal role in shaping a more adaptive, inclusive, and forward-looking global job market. Whether it's through leveraging the latest technologies or providing comprehensive support and resources, the app can become an indispensable tool for career advancement and business success.

By continuously innovating and adding valuable features, the hiring app can stay ahead of the curve and remain a powerful tool for facilitating employment opportunities. The goal is to not only match the right candidate with the right job but also to empower individuals in their career journeys and help businesses thrive through inclusive and diverse hiring practices.

By addressing these areas and maintaining a focus on user experience, ethics, and continuous improvement, the hiring app can serve as a leading tool in the movement towards equitable and inclusive employment practices. The success of such an app is not just in its technological prowess but also in its ability to inspire change and represent a new standard for how we approach the hiring process in the digital age.

By addressing these additional considerations and continuously evolving based on user feedback and societal changes, the hiring app can maintain relevance and effectiveness in a competitive job market. The ultimate goal is to create a platform that not only facilitates fair and merit-based hiring but also contributes to a more inclusive and equitable workforce.

In summary, this app could fill an important niche in the job market by promoting equality and focusing on skills and fit rather than demographics. It would require substantial investment in technology, legal guidance, and user experience design to be successful. With the right execution, such an app could make a significant impact on the hiring landscape around the globe.

If you own or run a company and the company is worth hundreds of millions or billions, and your staff needs assistance to live, you and your company owners are Shitty People.

If you're rich and your employee's pay doesn't reflect an income that raises them far above the standard of living, you don't deserve to be in business.

Providing for employees

As a company owner or leader, you are responsible for ensuring that your employees are fairly compensated for their work and have access to a decent standard of living.

This includes providing competitive wages, benefits, and a safe working environment.

Wealth of the company

When a company is worth hundreds of millions or billions of dollars, that indicate it is highly successful and generating significant profits.

In this case, the company should allocate resources to ensure its employees are well cared for.

Corporate social responsibility

Many believe that companies must give back to society and support their employees, not just focus on maximizing profits for their owners.

This can take the form of paying fair wages, providing benefits, investing in employee well-being programs, and supporting the communities in which they operate.

Perception of leadership

Suppose a company's leaders are seen as neglecting the needs of their employees while the company is highly successful. In that case, it can lead to negative perceptions of the company and its leadership. This can impact employee morale, public perception, and even shareholder trust.

In summary, while there are differing opinions on the responsibilities of company owners and leaders, many would argue that if a company is worth a significant amount and its employees are struggling to make ends meet, there is a moral obligation to ensure that employees are adequately supported. Failing to do so can lead to negative consequences for the company and its reputation.

Okay White Straight People Quit Whining About How There Is A Two Tiered Judicial System Just Because Trump Was Indicted And Has To Stand Trial For His Crimes.

However, You Are Right There Is A Two-Tiered Judicial System You Set It Up So That You Can Remain In Power And You Could Keep Your Feeling Of Superiority.

I Wish Trump Could Actually Get The Tier Meant For The Citizens of Color, Immigrants of Color and The LGBTQ+ Communities.

Charged with actual trumped up and bogus claims.

Held Without Bond.

Given Higher than regular fines.

A longer prison sentences.

A longer than normal parole or probation.

Go Ahead And Use The Bottom Tier Of That Two Tiered System.

Could be even worse he could have been murdered just because of racial bias or gender and orientation bias.

Here is how to go about erasing the two-Tiered system by achieving equality, eliminating privilege, increasing representation, and promoting social justice, here is a cohesive summary along with actionable steps that anyone can take to contribute to positive change:

1. Equality and Privilege:

Acknowledging and addressing systemic inequalities, biases, and privileges is essential for creating a more just and inclusive society where all individuals have equal opportunities and rights.

2. Representation and Advocacy:

Increasing representation of marginalized communities in leadership roles, such as in politics, is crucial for amplifying diverse voices, challenging bias, and advocating for inclusive policies that benefit all members of society.

3. Empowerment and Action:

Empowering individuals to engage in advocacy, education, and dialogue can drive meaningful progress towards social justice, equity, and diversity by fostering empathy, understanding, and collective action.

Actionable Steps:

1. Educate Yourself:

Take the time to educate yourself on issues related to privilege, bias, inequality, and social justice. Read books, attend workshops, and engage with diverse perspectives to deepen your understanding.

2. Support Diverse Candidates:

Encourage and support people of color and individuals from the LGBTQ+ community who are running for office or seeking leadership positions. Volunteer for their campaigns, donate.

3. Amplify Marginalized Voices:

Use your platform, whether it's on social media or in your community, to amplify the voices of marginalized individuals and communities. Share their stories, experiences, and perspectives to raise awareness and promote understanding.

4. Advocate for Inclusive Policies:

Advocate for policies that promote diversity, equity, and inclusion in your workplace, community, and society at large. Support initiatives that address systemic inequalities and work towards creating a more just and equitable world for all.

5. Engage in Difficult Conversations:

Have open and honest conversations with friends, family, and colleagues about privilege, bias, and social justice issues. Listen actively, show empathy, and be willing to challenge your own beliefs and assumptions.

6. Support Organizations:

Support organizations that are dedicated to promoting social justice, equality, and diversity. Volunteer your time, donate resources, or participate in events and campaigns that aim to create positive change in your community.

7. Take Action:

Take concrete actions in your daily life to challenge privilege, combat inequality, and promote social justice. Stand up against discrimination, speak out against injustice, and be an ally to those who are marginalized or oppressed.

8. Participate in Diversity and Inclusion Training:

Seek out opportunities to participate in diversity and inclusion training programs to deepen your understanding of privilege, bias, and systemic inequalities. These programs can provide valuable insights and tools for promoting a more inclusive and equitable environment in various settings.

9. Support Minority-Owned Businesses:

Make a conscious effort to support minority-owned businesses in your community. By doing so, you can help create economic opportunities for marginalized groups and contribute to building a more diverse and vibrant local economy.

10. Vote and Advocate for Policy Change:

Exercise your right to vote and advocate for policy changes that advance social justice, equality, and diversity. Stay informed about key issues, support candidates who prioritize these values, and engage in grassroots efforts to push for meaningful legislative reforms.

11. Challenge Stereotypes and Microaggressions:

Be vigilant about challenging stereotypes and addressing microaggressions in your interactions with others. Speak up when you witness discriminatory behavior or harmful assumptions, and strive to create a more inclusive and welcoming environment for everyone.

12. Support Intersectional Approaches:

Recognize the intersectionality of identities and experiences within marginalized communities. Support initiatives and organizations that take an intersectional approach to social justice, addressing the interconnected nature of privilege and oppression across various dimensions of identity.

13. Practice Self-Reflection and Growth:

Engage in ongoing self-reflection and growth to identify and unlearn your own biases and privileges. Be open to feedback, seek out opportunities for personal development, and commit to continuous learning and improvement in your journey towards becoming a more effective ally and advocate for social justice.

14. Support Mental Health and Well-Being:

Recognize the impact of systemic inequalities and social injustices on mental health and well-being. Advocate for accessible mental health services and resources for marginalized communities, and prioritize self-care practices that promote resilience and healing for yourself and those around you.

15. Engage in Allyship and Solidarity:

Actively engage in allyship and solidarity with marginalized communities by amplifying their voices, supporting their causes, and standing up against discrimination and injustice. Listen to and center the experiences and perspectives of those who are most affected by systemic inequalities.

16. Promote Equity in Education:

Advocate for equitable access to quality education for all individuals, regardless of their background or identity. Support initiatives that address disparities in educational opportunities and resources, and work towards creating inclusive learning environments that empower students from diverse backgrounds to thrive.

17. Foster Inclusive Spaces:

Create and nurture inclusive spaces in your workplace, community, and social circles where individuals of all backgrounds feel welcome, valued, and respected. Challenge exclusionary practices and policies, and actively work towards building a culture of belonging and diversity.

18. Collaborate with Community Organizations:

Collaborate with local community organizations and grassroots movements that are dedicated to advancing social justice, equity, and diversity. Volunteer your time, skills, and resources to support their initiatives and contribute to positive change at the grassroots level.

19. Advocate for Police and Criminal Justice Reform:

Advocate for police and criminal justice reform to address systemic racism, bias, and inequalities within the criminal justice system. Support efforts to promote accountability, transparency, and community-based approaches to public safety that prioritize equity and justice for all.

20. Celebrate Diversity and Cultural Heritage:

Celebrate the diversity of cultures, identities, and experiences within your community and beyond. Participate in cultural events, festivals, and activities that showcase the richness and vibrancy of different traditions and heritages, and embrace opportunities for cross-cultural learning and solidarity.

21. Support LGBTQ+ Rights:

Advocate for the rights and equality of LGBTQ+ individuals by supporting policies and initiatives that protect their rights, promote inclusion, and combat discrimination based on sexual orientation and gender identity. Stand in solidarity with LGBTQ+ communities and work towards creating a more accepting and affirming society for all.

22. Combat Environmental Injustices:

Recognize the disproportionate impact of environmental injustices on marginalized communities and advocate for environmental policies that prioritize equity, sustainability, and environmental justice. Support initiatives that address environmental racism, pollution disparities, and climate change impacts on vulnerable populations.

23. Promote Economic Equity:

Advocate for economic equity by supporting initiatives that address income inequality, wealth disparities, and barriers to economic mobility for marginalized communities. Champion fair wages, workplace diversity, and economic empowerment programs that create opportunities for all individuals to thrive economically.

24. Challenge Systemic Oppression:

Challenge systemic oppression in all its forms, including racism, sexism, ableism, and other forms of discrimination. Educate others about the ways in which systemic oppression operates and work towards dismantling oppressive structures and creating a more just and equitable society for all.

25. Engage in Legislative Advocacy:

Get involved in legislative advocacy efforts at the local, state, and national levels to influence policy decisions that promote social justice, equity, and human rights. Contact your elected representatives, participate in advocacy campaigns, and use your voice to push for legislative changes that advance equality and fairness.

26. Prioritize Racial Justice:

Center racial justice in your advocacy work and daily actions by actively working to combat racism, promote anti-racism initiatives, and support policies that address racial disparities and discrimination. Listen to and uplift the voices of communities of color, and commit to being an ally in the fight for racial equity.

27. Practice Empathy and Compassion:

Cultivate empathy and compassion in your interactions with others, especially those who may have different lived experiences or perspectives. Listen actively, seek to understand diverse viewpoints, and approach conversations with kindness and a willingness to learn from others.

28. Support Mental Health Awareness and Accessibility:

Advocate for increased awareness and accessibility to mental health resources, especially for marginalized communities who may face additional barriers to seeking help. Promote destigmatization of mental health issues and support initiatives that prioritize mental well-being for all individuals.

29. Combat Digital Inequities:

Address digital inequities and disparities in access to technology and internet connectivity that can exacerbate existing social inequalities. Support efforts to bridge the digital divide and ensure that all individuals have equal access to digital tools and resources for education, communication, and opportunity.

30. Promote Gender Equity and Women's Rights:

Advocate for gender equity and women's rights by supporting initiatives that address gender-based discrimination, promote gender equality in all aspects of society, and empower women and girls to realize their full potential. Stand up against gender-based violence and inequality in all its forms.

31. Engage in Intergenerational Dialogue:

Foster intergenerational dialogue and collaboration to bridge divides, share knowledge, and work towards a more inclusive and equitable future. Listen to the perspectives and experiences of different generations, learn from each other, and collaborate on initiatives that promote intergenerational solidarity and understanding.

32. Support Refugee and Immigrant Rights:

Stand in solidarity with refugees, immigrants, and displaced populations by advocating for policies that protect their rights, ensure their safety and well-being, and promote pathways to integration and empowerment. Support organizations that provide assistance and support to refugees and immigrants in need.

33. Promote Restorative Justice Practices:

Advocate for restorative justice practices that prioritize healing, accountability, and community-based solutions over punitive measures. Support initiatives that address the root causes of harm, promote reconciliation, and prioritize the well-being of both victims and offenders in the pursuit of justice.

34. Embrace Lifelong Learning and Growth:

Commit to lifelong learning and personal growth by seeking out opportunities for education, self-reflection, and skill development that deepen your understanding of social justice issues and empower you to be an effective advocate for positive change. Stay open to new perspectives and experiences that challenge and expand your worldview.

35. Support Disability Rights and Inclusion:

Advocate for disability rights and promote inclusion for individuals with disabilities by supporting policies and initiatives that ensure equal access, accommodations, and opportunities for all. Raise awareness about the needs and contributions of individuals with disabilities and work towards creating a more accessible and inclusive society.

36. Promote Cultural Diversity and Exchange:

Celebrate cultural diversity and promote cross-cultural exchange by engaging with different cultures, traditions, and perspectives. Attend cultural events, participate in diversity initiatives, and learn from the richness and diversity of global cultures to foster mutual respect and understanding.

37. Combat Hate Speech and Discrimination:

Take a stand against hate speech, discrimination, and intolerance in all forms. Speak out against bigotry, xenophobia, and prejudice, and work towards creating a culture of respect, acceptance, and inclusivity where all individuals are treated with dignity and equality.

38. Support Indigenous Rights and Sovereignty:

Stand in solidarity with Indigenous communities and advocate for the protection of Indigenous rights, sovereignty, and self-determination. Support initiatives that address historical injustices, promote Indigenous rights and cultures, and advance efforts towards reconciliation and justice.

39. Engage in Community Building and Mutual Aid:

Participate in community building initiatives and mutual aid efforts that promote solidarity, cooperation, and support among members of your community. Work together to address local challenges, build resilience, and create a sense of belonging and interconnectedness.

40. Practice Active Citizenship and Civic Engagement:

Engage in active citizenship and civic participation by voting, staying informed about current events, and participating in community activities and initiatives. Exercise your rights and responsibilities as a citizen to contribute to a more just, equitable, and democratic society for all.

41. Embrace Intersectional Approaches:

Embrace intersectional approaches to social justice and equity by recognizing the interconnected nature of identities and experiences. Advocate for policies and initiatives that address overlapping forms of oppression and privilege to promote more comprehensive and inclusive solutions.

42. Promote Global Solidarity and Cooperation:

Support global solidarity and cooperation by advocating for international human rights, peace, and development initiatives. Stand in solidarity with marginalized communities worldwide, support global efforts towards social justice, and work towards building a more equitable and peaceful world for all.

43. Promote LGBTQ+ Inclusivity in Education:

Advocate for LGBTQ+ inclusivity in educational curricula and school environments to create safe and supportive spaces for LGBTQ+ students. Support policies that promote LGBTQ+ awareness, acceptance, and inclusion in schools and educational institutions.

44. Combat Food Insecurity and Support Food Justice:

Get involved in initiatives that address food insecurity, promote food justice, and ensure access to nutritious and affordable food for all individuals and communities. Support food banks, community gardens, and programs that address food inequities and promote food sovereignty.

45. Advocate for Affordable Housing and Homelessness Support:

Advocate for affordable housing initiatives and support programs that address homelessness and housing insecurity. Work towards policies that ensure access to safe and affordable housing for all individuals, particularly those facing housing challenges and homelessness.

46. Support Workers' Rights and Fair Labor Practices:

Advocate for workers' rights, fair labor practices, and equitable working conditions for all individuals. Support initiatives that promote fair wages, workplace safety, and protections for workers, including marginalized and vulnerable populations.

47. Promote Environmental Sustainability and Climate Justice:

Support environmental sustainability initiatives and advocate for climate justice to address environmental challenges and promote a healthy and sustainable planet for future generations. Get involved in climate action efforts and support policies that prioritize environmental conservation and sustainability.

48. Combat Gender-Based Violence and Support Survivors:

Stand against gender-based violence and support survivors by advocating for policies that prevent violence, provide support services, and promote gender equality. Support organizations and initiatives that work towards ending gender-based violence and supporting survivors in their healing journey.

49. Engage in Community Organizing and Grassroots Movements:

Get involved in community organizing and grassroots movements that advocate for social justice, equity, and positive change at the local level. Collaborate with community members, activists, and organizations to address pressing issues and work towards collective solutions.

50. Promote Youth Empowerment and Engagement:

Support youth empowerment and engagement by creating opportunities for young people to participate in advocacy, leadership, and decision-making processes. Foster youth voices, perspectives, and initiatives that drive positive change and contribute to a more inclusive and equitable society.
By incorporating these actionable steps into your advocacy efforts and daily actions, you can contribute to building a more just, inclusive, and equitable society where all individuals have the opportunity to thrive and reach their full potential.

Together, let's continue to work towards a future where social justice, equality, and human rights are upheld and respected for everyone, creating a more just and harmonious world for all.

What happened to the day when drag shows and female impersonations meant something.

There was a day that men in drag were men in drag. When it took work took long ok like a woman. Not a man with so many enhancements that you didn't once w if you were looking at a man or woman.

There was a day where you actually appreciated watching the show because you were amazed at to how he did it. Today they have so many enhancements that it is boring.

I do realize that as time goes on so does standards. It is just so upsetting to see a part of our history die.

It is like today everyone forgot the stonewall riots of 1969 and feel privileged today without remembering how they got here.

It would be nice for our community to figure out that girls with enhancements are girls and boys that spend the time to give you the illusion of women are true shows.

I find it very sad that people, those in my community and the world around me will no longer ever get to know what female impersonation actually was and should be.

I am saddened that we have spent the last 50 years for equal rights just to lose it in the the need for performers to get get tits and asses to look the sale as everyone else.

Here is an example what the power of drag as an illusion can accomplish

The historic LGBTQ+ pride parade and festival in Biloxi, Mississippi, in 1994 is indeed a significant piece of LGBTQ+ history, especially considering the sociopolitical climate of the area at the time. Let me reiterate and emphasize the story with the recognition it deserves.

The Historic Pride Event in Biloxi, Mississippi, 1994:

The year 1994 in Biloxi, Mississippi, marked a watershed moment for the LGBTQ+ community.

Activists like myself, along with a brave group of illusionists and drag queens, set out to organize the first LGBTQ+ pride parade and festival in a state known for its conservative views and stringent laws against LGBTQ+ expressions.

Obtaining Permits

Our group successfully secured the necessary permits to hold the event at a park on Biloxi Bay a feat in itself given the local government's stance on LGBTQ+ events.

But the real challenge emerged when officials learned of the drag show and country and western band that were to be part of the festivities.

The Mayor's Ultimatum

Faced with the threat of having the permits revoked, the mayor issued an ultimatum that the drag performers could only proceed if they were covered "from head to toe," an attempt to suppress the visibility of the LGBTQ+ community and its expressions.

A Bold Response

Undeterred, the community rallied around the event. Tommie, the MC and host, responded to the mayor's restrictive rule with a bold and ingenious act of protest.

In front of an audience that included more law enforcement officers than attendees, Tommie used the power of performance art to make a stand.

Tommie's Performance

He crafted an outfit that adhered to the letter of the mayor's demand but defied its spirit.

Clothed in a skin-toned ensemble that covered him from neck to toe, including pasties and a tuck that was nothing short of a work of art, Tommie performed with a level of skill and fearlessness that would become legendary.

His acrobatic performance won over not just the LGBTQ+ community and allies in attendance but also the very police officers who were there to potentially enforce the mayor's mandate.

The Impact

Tommie's act of courage set a precedent for the rest of the evening. It was a statement that resonated far beyond the festival, a declaration that the LGBTQ+ community would not be shamed or forced into invisibility.

The remaining performers were able to take the stage without the fear of persecution, thanks to the boundary-pushing bravery of their peer.

This event in Biloxi was far more than a drag show; it was an act of political resistance and a pivotal moment in the fight for LGBTQ+ rights in one of the most conservative states in the USA.

The success of this event, despite the intense opposition and the real risk of arrest faced by the performers, is a testament to the resilience and solidarity of the LGBTQ+ community.

The Significance of Mississippi's Story

The story of Biloxi's pride event exemplifies the struggle for LGBTQ+ rights in environments that are hostile to progress.

Mississippi's ranking as 50th in civil rights underscores the bravery required to host such an event and the profound impact it had on those who were part of it.

It also symbolizes the ongoing fight for equality and the importance of remembering and honoring these milestones in LGBTQ+ history.

By sharing these narratives, we ensure that the sacrifices and victories of those who came before us are not forgotten.

They serve as a reminder that while progress has been made, the work continues, and it is through understanding our past that we can forge a more inclusive future.

Every LGBTQ+ members role and the role of every person that attended performed and organized the 1994 Biloxi pride event are pivotal chapters in the story of LGBTQ+ resilience and empowerment.

When Drag Was An Illusion Performed By A Boy Or Girl As The Opposite Sex And Convincing Everyone That For That Number They Were That Star.

Today for me drag has lost all or at least most of its appeal. Almost everyone performing at the shows I've been too all have body enhancements such as breast and but augmentation. You no longer need an imagination. You a girl pretending to be a boy being a girl and I find it to be an insult not only to the craft but I feel like it does a disservice to the trans and non binary community.

Trans want you to see them as the person they know they are and it's not a perceived choice for entertainment.

Okay, I may be too old to understand what's happening today. I can be totally off base. However this is how I see things. If I'm wrong please enlighten me so I understand. Just remember I come from a world that being caught in a gay act could be life in prison and marriage was unheard of. It's our sacrifice that got us where we are today.

I need someone to explain to me what happened to the drag Performances.

Back when I was young and fresh out of the closet. Like before anyone believed we would get sodomy laws struck down. Some states still have them in the books, whether you believe them or not. Such laws still exist in Florida, Georgia, Kansas, Kentucky, Louisiana, Massachusetts, Michigan, Mississippi, North Carolina, Oklahoma, South Carolina and Texas.

Anyway, I digress. Drag in the past meant a boy who taught himself how to do his makeup, make himself a gown, and practice his number in the mirror until he built up the confidence to perform in public in front of his friends and sometimes family.

Then, there occasionally was the girl who learned the mannerisms if the boy they wanted to portray practiced bought the right outfit performed and for that number convinced you they were a boy.

However, when the shows were over, the illusion ended. Most were surprised to find out who was who.

In 1994, I and a few activists, along with a group of illusionists and drag queens, organized and put on our first LFBTQ+ gay pride parade and festival in Biloxi, Mississippi, at the park on Biloxi Bay.

We had no problem getting permits. That was until they found out we had a gay country and western band, and we finally planned to be a drag show.

Immediately, they tried to pull our permits. Finally, mayor Bigot said he would allow it if they were covered from head to toe.

Do you think that deterred our drag show? No, Tommie, my Mcee and host, before he opened the show, we had more police than attendees because we were still taboo in Mississippi; you digress,

Tommie announced over the PA, "I just want to tell all of you men in blue. I am a boy in an outfit, and I'm covered from neck to toe, so before you rush the stage to arrest me, remember I have done everything the mayor said I have to do."

Immediately, every guest at the festival and every vendor abandoned their stands and surrounded the stage to block the police from storming him, doing his number as her.

He spent the 24 hours before the festival and right after the mayor gave his rule, making himself utterly nude to his skin tone from his neck to where it even covered his toes. Three pasties, a tuck you would never believe, and a couple of socks where his chest was.

He did a number with backflips, forwardflips, splits, and everything you could think of. When it was over, I believe the police and sheriff departments were louder than we were when clapping and yelling for more.

After Tommie took that risk and did that, he was scared shitless he would go to jail after he did that. However, our group already had attorneys at the department and jail prepared.

However, that didn't happen; what did happen was the rest of the illusionist did not have to go extreme and were allowed to do their regular performances without fear of persecution.

That's drag. What we have today are trans pretending to be boys being girls. I fear that this is contributing to the trans community being persecuted today.

Why? Every time I end up in an argument with a bigot about bathrooms or trying to explain gender as a concept, not a biological form, I set it in stone. I get okay if they are girls and should be able to the Women's restroom. Why are they advertising themselves as drags in gay bars? They use a more vulgar term.

I find it hard to answer their questions.

Drag has lost its definition. I haven't seen a boy or girl pulling off the pollution in a performance in years.

I would probably enjoy the shows today more if there were more truth in the bar's advertising.

There are no drag shows anymore. At least if they were advertised correctly, I believe it would help the trans community go a lot further in acceptance in society.

However, if you can't accept you're trans, how do you expect people who don't understand trans to accept you?

————————

It's usually useless to try to educate someone with deeply ingrained biases and bigotry but here it goes this is my attempt.

Educating anyone requires a combination of patience, factual information, and often an appeal to empathy.

When discussing transgender and non-binary identities with someone who is resistant or uninformed, it's crucial that I present clear facts and explain the nuance behind these concepts.

Here's a detailed argument that I use if you like it you are more than welcome to use some or all of it:

"Let's begin by distinguishing between 'sex' and 'gender,' as these terms are often conflated.

Sex is assigned at birth based on physical characteristics, including genitalia, chromosomes, and reproductive anatomy. Typically, this assignment is either 'male' or 'female.' However, biological sex itself is more complex than this binary suggests:

Intersex Variation

Some individuals are born with intersex trait, variations in chromosomes, hormones, or genitalia that do not fit typical definitions of male or female.

This is not rare; intersex conditions are as common as having natural red hair (about 1 in 2,000 births).

The existence of intersex individuals shows that sex is not strictly binary but exists on a spectrum.

Chromosomal Diversity

While XX and XY are the most well-known sex chromosome configurations, there are others, such as XXY (Klinefelter syndrome) or XO (Turner syndrome), and these also affect physical development in ways that challenge the simple binary.

Gender, on the other hand, is a social and psychological concept.

It encompasses the roles, behaviors, activities, and attributes that a given society considers appropriate for men and women.

Cultural Variation

Different cultures have recognized more than two genders throughout history.

For example, some Indigenous cultures in North America have long recognized the existence of Two-Spirit people, who embody traits of both male and female genders, or have unique gender roles not tied to binary sex.

Gender Identity

This is a person's internal, deeply-held sense of their own gender, whether that be male, female, a blend of both, or neither.

Transgender people have a gender identity that does not match the sex they were assigned at birth. Non-binary individuals do not exclusively identify as male or female.

The recognition of transgender and non-binary identities is supported by medical and psychological consensus.

Major health organizations, including the American Medical Association and the American Psychological Association, affirm that being transgender or non-binary is a legitimate expression of human diversity, not a mental disorder.

Moreover, research shows that affirming a transgender individual's gender identity by using their chosen name and pronouns, as well as respecting their right to socially and medically transition if they choose, has a significantly positive effect on their mental health and well-being.

When we talk about inclusivity and respect for transgender and non-binary individuals, we are also talking about basic human rights.

Denying someone's identity or discriminating against them because of their gender identity is a violation of their human rights, as stated by international human rights law.

Understanding that both sex and gender are more complex than a binary classification allows us to recognize and respect the diversity of the human species and experience.

It is not about denying biological facts but about understanding that our social interpretations of these facts can and should include the full range of human diversity."

Using this approach, you're providing concrete information, citing authoritative sources, and framing the issue within a broader context of human rights and respect for individual dignity.

It's important to note that while facts and empathy can be persuasive, deeply held beliefs often take time and repeated exposure to new perspectives to evolve.

It's essential to address common misconceptions and provide further context to support the validity of transgender and non-binary identities:

Mental Health and Recognition

Acceptance and Mental Health

Studies have consistently shown that transgender individuals face higher rates of mental health issues, not because of their gender identity itself, but largely due to discrimination, stigma, and lack of acceptance.

When transgender people are supported and accepted for who they are, their mental health outcomes improve significantly.

This is a strong argument against the idea that transgender identities are inherently pathological.

Legal and Medical Support

Legal Recognition

Many countries around the world recognize the importance of affirming gender identity.

Laws are increasingly supporting the right to change one's legal documents to match their gender identity, reflecting an understanding that gender identity is a core aspect of a person's identity and social existence.

Medical Transition

For some transgender individuals, medical transition (which may include hormone therapy or surgeries) is an important part of aligning their physical appearance with their gender identity.

Access to transition-related healthcare is associated with positive mental health outcomes and reduced dysphoria.

Social Impact and Inclusivity

Social Integration

Inclusive policies and practices that recognize transgender and non-binary individuals' identities contribute to healthier, happier, and more cohesive communities.

When people are free to express their true selves, without fear of discrimination, society as a whole benefits from the diversity of experiences and perspectives.

Biological Notions of Sex and Gender

Neurological Underpinnings

Research into the neurobiology of gender identity suggests that there may be innate differences in the brains of transgender individuals that align more closely with their gender identity than their assigned sex at birth.

This further supports the notion that gender identity is a deeply rooted aspect of human experience.

Evolutionary Diversity

From an evolutionary perspective, diversity is beneficial to species survival. Just as there's a wide variety in sexual orientation, gender diversity can be seen as part of the spectrum of human variation that has existed across cultures and history.

Appeal to Empathy and Shared Humanity

Personal Stories

Sharing the personal stories of transgender and non-binary individuals can be a powerful tool for fostering empathy.

When people hear about the real-life experiences of others, it can help humanize abstract concepts and break down prejudices.

Common Ground

It's important to find common ground and emphasize that everyone has a stake in supporting human rights.

Just as one would not choose to be discriminated against for an intrinsic trait, transgender and non-binary individuals deserve the same respect and opportunity to live without fear of discrimination.

Remember, the goal isn't necessarily to "win" an argument but to plant seeds of understanding that may grow over time.

You may not change someone's mind in one conversation, but by consistently providing factual information, showing empathy, and appealing to universal values of dignity and respect, you can contribute to a gradual shift in perspective.

"Let's debunk the myth of immigrant crime sprees and acknowledge the truth:

Immigrants are one of the safest groups in the U.S., with a minuscule crime rate of just 0.001%.

It's important to recognize that immigrants often face more crime from prejudiced individuals than they themselves commit.

When immigrants join our communities, they bring diversity, hard work, and a shared desire for a better future.

By welcoming them, we not only make our neighborhoods stronger but also safer.

Let's stand against prejudice, promote empathy, and build unity. Together, we can create a more inclusive and secure society. #UnityOverDivision"

By highlighting the double standard that immigrants face in terms of crime, this message aims to raise awareness about the challenges immigrants encounter and the importance of fostering a welcoming and supportive environment for all individuals. Thank you for advocating for a more just and compassionate society.

Now For A Comparison Between Immigrants Whether Undocumented Or Not Living In Your Community And A Bigot Living In Your Neighborhood.

WHEN BIGOTRY IS ACCEPTED AND TOLERATED IN YOUR COMMUNITY

Bigotry refers to intolerance, prejudice, or discrimination against individuals or groups based on factors such as race, ethnicity, religion, nationality, gender, sexual orientation, or other characteristics. When bigotry exists in a neighborhood, it can have various negative implications:

Social Division:

Bigotry can create divisions within a community, leading to tensions and conflicts between different groups. It can foster an "us vs. them" mentality that hinders social cohesion and unity.

Fear and Anxiety:

Residents who are targeted by bigotry may experience fear, anxiety, and a sense of insecurity in their own neighborhood. This can have a detrimental impact on their well-being and quality of life.

Isolation and Exclusion:

Bigotry can lead to the isolation and exclusion of marginalized groups, making them feel unwelcome or unsafe in their own community. This can result in social alienation and a lack of sense of belonging.

Limited Opportunities:

Discrimination based on bigotry can limit the opportunities available to individuals from marginalized groups, such as access to housing, employment, education, and social services. This perpetuates inequality and hinders overall community development.

Undermined Trust and Relationships:

Bigotry erodes trust and undermines relationships between neighbors, making it difficult to build a sense of community and cooperation. It can breed resentment and hostility, hindering collective efforts to address shared challenges.

Negative Reputation:

Neighborhoods known for bigotry and intolerance may develop a negative reputation, affecting property values, economic development, and overall community well-being. This can deter potential residents, businesses, and investments.

Addressing bigotry in a neighborhood requires a collective effort to promote understanding, respect, and inclusivity. By challenging prejudices, fostering empathy, and celebrating diversity, communities can create a welcoming and supportive environment where all residents feel valued and respected. It is essential to nurture a culture of acceptance and openness to ensure a thriving and harmonious neighborhood for everyone.

WHEN BIGOTRY IS NOT ONLY UNWELCOME IN A COMMUNITY BUT IS TREATED AS AN OUTCAST REVERSING BIGOTRY AND ACCEPTANCES ROLL:

When rejected Bigots can also experience negative effects as a result of their beliefs and behaviors.

Here are some potential consequences that bigots may face:

Isolation and Alienation:

Bigots may find themselves isolated or alienated from others, as their prejudiced views can lead to strained relationships with friends, family, colleagues, and community members. Their attitudes may result in social exclusion and disapproval from those who reject bigotry.

Limited Perspectives:

By holding onto prejudiced beliefs, bigots limit their own perspectives and understanding of the world. This narrow-mindedness can hinder personal growth, empathy, and the ability to appreciate the diversity and richness of different cultures and backgrounds in their communities.

Conflict and Tension:

Bigots may experience conflict and tension in their interactions with others, especially with individuals or groups who are the targets of their prejudice. This can lead to confrontations, misunderstandings, and a perpetuation of negative attitudes and behaviors.

Legal and Social Consequences:

In some cases, expressing or acting upon bigoted beliefs can lead to legal ramifications, such as being subject to anti-discrimination laws or facing social consequences like public backlash, loss of reputation, or exclusion from certain spaces or opportunities.

Emotional Toll:

Holding prejudiced views can also take an emotional toll on bigots. Their beliefs may be rooted in fear, insecurity, or misinformation, leading to feelings of anger, resentment, or defensiveness. Over time, these negative emotions can impact their mental well-being and overall quality of life with an increase in suicide.

Missed Opportunities for Growth:

By clinging to bigotry, individuals miss out on opportunities for personal growth, learning, and meaningful connections with a diverse range of people. Embracing inclusivity and openness can lead to enriched experiences and a more fulfilling life.

It's important to recognize that addressing bigotry requires a willingness to challenge one's own beliefs, cultivate empathy, and strive for understanding and respect toward others. Encouraging dialogue, education, and self-reflection can help individuals overcome prejudice and contribute to a more inclusive and harmonious society.

We can only reflect to a longing for a past era and a respect for the origins and traditions of drag culture, which is a vital part of LGBTQ+ history and has played a significant role in the fight for equality and acceptance.

Drag has a rich and varied history that can has evolved significantly over time.

Traditionally, drag shows were a form of entertainment that involved men dressing as women, with an emphasis on the art of illusion and performance. It required skill, creativity, and dedication to craft a feminine appearance and persona, often without the aid of surgical enhancements or modern cosmetic procedures.

The art of drag has always been about more than just the external transformation; it is a form of self-expression and rebellion against societal norms.

It has roots in theater and performance art, with a long-standing tradition of challenging gender roles and stereotypes.

Drag queens have been key figures in the LGBTQ+ community, contributing to the visibility and fight for rights.

As we have mentioned, the Stonewall riots of 1969 were a pivotal moment in the struggle for LGBTQ+ rights, with drag queens and transgender individuals playing a significant role in the uprising against police brutality and discrimination.

The bravery shown during those riots laid the groundwork for the modern aLGBTQ+ rights movement.

Over time, the availability of cosmetic enhancements and the rise of shows like "RuPaul's Drag Race" have brought drag culture into the mainstream, introducing new aesthetics and performance styles.

This has led to a diversification of what drag can mean, including those who use surgical enhancements to achieve their look.

While some lament the shift away from traditional drag, it's essential to recognize that cultures evolve, and this evolution can encompass both preservation of historical practices and the embrace of new forms of expression.

The current generation of drag performers exists in a world that is more accepting of diverse gender expressions and identities, and this has naturally influenced the art form.

To address my concerns about the loss of historical perspective, education and dialogue within the community are key.

Celebrating the pioneers of drag and ensuring the stories of past struggles and triumphs are remembered can coexist with embracing the diversity of current expressions.

Ultimately, the spirit of drag is about pushing boundaries, questioning norms, and celebrating individuality.

As society's understanding of gender continues to evolve, so too will the expressions of drag.

It's important to remember that drag, at its core, is about the freedom to be one's true self, in whatever form that may take, and that this can look different for everyone.

For those who share my perspective, creating spaces and events that honor traditional drag practices can help keep the history alive.

Documentaries, story-telling, and community events can educate new generations about the roots of drag and the importance of the LGBTQ+ movement's history.

This way, the rich tapestry of the past is not lost but rather woven into the ongoing narrative of the community's evolution.

The desire to return to the roots of traditional drag performance, where the artistry lay in the skill of transformation without surgical or significant bodily enhancements, is a call to celebrate and preserve a specific aspect of drag history.

This style of performance emphasizes the craftsmanship of makeup, costume, and character to create a feminine illusion, and it showcases the performer's ability to metamorphose using these tools alone.

Traditional drag has always been more than just dressing up; it's a performance art that plays with the concepts of gender and identity.

Performers like Julian Eltinge and Divine became icons in the early and mid-20th century, known for their ability to convincingly portray women on stage, and they did so without the modern-day cosmetic procedures that are more accessible today.

To advocate for a return to these traditional roots, consider the following approaches.

Education and Storytelling:

Share the true history of drag through documentaries, books, and oral histories.

Highlight the lives and performances of legendary drag queens who practiced their art prior to the widespread use of cosmetic enhancements.

This can instill a sense of tradition and respect for the craft.

Workshops and Masterclasses:

Organize events where experienced drag queens teach the art of makeup, costuming, and performance.

This can help new performers learn the techniques that create the illusion of femininity without relying on physical alterations.

Themed Nights and Competitions:

Encourage local drag venues to host nights dedicated to classic drag performances.

Competitions could be organized with specific rules that focus on traditional transformation methods, celebrating performers who excel in creating the female illusion through skill and creativity alone.

Cultural Recognition and Awards:

Establish awards or recognition within the drag community for those who excel at traditional female impersonation.

This can provide an incentive for performers to pursue and perfect this style of drag.

Social Media and Online Content:

Use the power of social media to showcase and promote artists who are dedicated to traditional drag.

Create online content, such as tutorials and performance videos, to reach a wider audience and inspire a new generation of performers.

Collaborations with LGBTQ+ Organizations:

Partner with LGBTQ+ groups and history organizations to ensure that the story of drag and its impact on the community's rights and visibility is not forgotten.

This can help educate both the public and new performers about the significance of traditional drag within the broader context of LGBTQ+ history.

Supportive Spaces.

Foster the creation and maintenance of venues that specifically cater to traditional drag performances.

These spaces can serve as cultural hubs for those who appreciate and wish to engage with the art form in its classic sense.

It's important to note that advocating for traditional drag does not have to negate the value or validity of contemporary expressions of drag.

The beauty of the drag community lies in its diversity and inclusivity. There's room for many styles and interpretations, from the most traditional to the avant-garde.

By promoting and preserving traditional drag, you add to the rich tapestry of drag culture without dismissing the evolution that has allowed the art form to reach new heights and audiences.

Certainly! Here's a reflective way that addresses the sentiment of returning to the traditional art of drag performance.

The Timeless Art of Illusion: Revisiting the Roots of Traditional Drag Performance.

In a world that praises the new, the innovative, and the boundary-pushing, there's a quiet yearning among some for the return to an art form that captivates through the power of transformation:

Traditional drag performance. It's an art that harkens back to a time when female impersonation was about craftsmanship, artistry, and the sheer will to create an illusion so convincing that it left audiences spellbound.

Drag, in its essence, is an intricate dance with identity, gender, and presentation.

It has always been a bold statement, a resolute act of defiance against societal norms that seek to box in the fluidity of self-expression. Yet, as the years have passed, and as the LGBTQ+ community has bravely carved out spaces of acceptance and celebration, the art of drag has morphed and evolved, branching out in a myriad of directions, each with its own merit and beauty.

However, within this kaleidoscopic expansion, some voices echo a sentiment for tradition—the kind of drag that doesn't lean on the advancements of cosmetic surgery or body modifications but instead on the transformative magic of makeup, wigs, and costuming.

This traditional drag doesn't just create an image; it weaves a story. It's a tale told with every stroke of the brush, every sequin sewn into fabric, and every character quirk meticulously rehearsed.

The performers of yesteryears were not only artists but also illusionists, crafting their personas with the tools of the stage, leaving no stone unturned in their journey to embody the essence of womanhood.

What made these traditional performances so enthralling was the visible journey from one's everyday self to the heightened persona on stage.

The absence of permanent physical enhancements meant that each show was a resurrection of the character, a testament to the performer's dedication and skill.

The transformation was ephemeral, lasting only for the duration of the performance, and therein lay the magic.

Today, the call to revisit and celebrate this form of traditional drag is not a dismissal of contemporary evolution but rather an homage to the roots that have nourished the diverse landscape of drag culture we see today.

It's a recognition that amidst the clamor for what's next, there's profound beauty in remembering and preserving what came before.

It's about acknowledging the sweat, the toil, and the ingenuity that laid the foundations of the art.

For the up-and-coming generation of drag enthusiasts, understanding and appreciating this heritage is crucial.

It's a connection to the past that informs the present and shapes the future.

It's an acknowledgment that before the glitz, the glam, and the mainstream appeal, there were performers who dared to dream and dared to bring those dreams to life through sheer force of will and talent.

These pioneers stood on the stages of dimly lit bars and clubs, not just as entertainers but as revolutionaries.

Their performances were acts of courage, each one chipping away at the monolithic structures of gender expectations.

They were, and continue to be, an integral part of the struggle for equality and acceptance.

As we look to the future of drag, let us not forget the legacy of the past.

Let us continue to create spaces where traditional drag is not just a memory but a living, breathing art form.

Let us celebrate the new while still honoring the old, for it's in this delicate balance that the true spirit of drag—resilient, defiant, and ever-transforming—continues to shine.

This article seeks to capture the essence of traditional drag and invites the new generation to respect and participate in the timeless tradition of female impersonation without permanent physical enhancements.

It's a tribute to the past as much as a beacon for the future, nurturing a space where the art of illusion thrives in its most authentic form.

Continuing from where we paused, let's delve deeper into the bridge between past and present, as well as into the future of traditional drag artistry.

The resilience of traditional drag lies in its adaptability and its timeless appeal.

While new forms of expression are celebrated, there's a unique enchantment in the meticulous process of becoming, which traditional drag encapsulates.

The personas created are not static; they are reborn with each performance, renewed by the performer's evolving interpretation and the audience's perception.

This dynamic process of creation is an open invitation to the up-and-coming generation to engage with the art form at a level that transcends the physical.

It challenges performers to become masters of illusion, to use their bodies as canvases, and to transform not through permanent change but through the ephemeral alchemy of artistry. It is a homage to the ingenuity of the human spirit and the power of creativity.

Moreover, traditional drag serves as a historical lens through which we can view the progress of LGBTQ+ rights and culture.

These performances are a living archive, a repository of the bravery, humor, and pathos of those who came before.

They remind us that drag is not just entertainment but a poignant narrative of struggle, triumph, and the quest for visibility.

As we move forward, it is imperative that we honor the pioneers by continuing their legacy.

By creating platforms for traditional drag artists, by championing their work, and by ensuring that the stories of the past remain integral to the fabric of the present.

The call to uphold the traditions of drag is not a call to stifle innovation but to remember the essence of what made drag revolutionary in the first place.

It is about understanding that the heart of drag beats with the pulse of transformation and that each generation has the power to redefine what that means while paying homage to its origins.

It is a testament to the art form's resilience that traditional drag can coexist with modern interpretations.

The community is vast and varied, and there is room for all expressions under the umbrella of drag. We can revel in the diversity of our expressions while still holding a special place for the traditions that brought us here.

To the up-and-coming drag artists, embrace the rich tapestry of drag culture. Learn the histories, master the techniques of old, and infuse them with your unique flair. To the audiences, approach traditional drag with the reverence it deserves, for in its reflection, you are witnessing not just a performance but a piece of living history.

Traditional drag is more than nostalgia.

It is a testament to the transformative power of performance art.

As we celebrate the evolution of drag in all its forms, let us also preserve the traditional arts that have paved the way.

Let the spirit of creativity and the joy of illusion continue to inspire us all, as we pay tribute to the past, revel in the present, and look forward to the future of this vibrant and enduring art form.

This is only to aim to inspire a balance between honoring the traditions of drag performance and embracing the future as it unfolds, encouraging a holistic appreciation of the art form's history and its potential for continuous evolution.

In this spirit of reverence and forward-thinking, let us consider how the torch of traditional drag is carried and shared in today's rapidly changing world.

The wisdom of the past is not lost; rather, it is the eternal flame that lights the path for the new guard to follow and, eventually, to lead.

The practice of traditional drag is not merely an act of looking back but a conscious choice to engage with the art form in its most elemental sense.

It is a discipline that demands a deep understanding of the history, techniques, and cultural significance of drag.

Through this understanding, new performers can draw connections between their art and the broader narrative of LGBTQ+ history and identity.

What does this mean for the future of drag?

It suggests a symbiosis between the traditional and the contemporary, where each informs and enriches the other. The new generation of drag artists have at their disposal an array of media and platforms to showcase their talents.

They have the power to broadcast the subtleties of traditional drag to a global audience, to educate, to inspire, and to provoke thought.

Traditional drag, with its emphasis on the transformative journey, also serves as a powerful metaphor for personal growth and self-discovery.

It reminds us that identity is multifaceted and fluid, and that the exploration of self can be a beautiful, complex, and artistic process.

By embracing the roots of drag, performers connect with a fundamental human experience.

The ability to redefine oneself, to step into another's shoes, and to see the world from a different perspective.

This is the call to action for the up-and-coming: to become stewards of an art form steeped in legacy.

By doing so, they become part of a lineage of performers who have used their craft to challenge perceptions, to entertain, and to create spaces for those who have been marginalized.

The responsibility is great, but so too is the opportunity to contribute to the rich tapestry of drag culture.

As we look to the horizon, we see a world where traditional drag is not only remembered but revered and revitalized.

We envision festivals and showcases dedicated to the art of illusion, where the old school and the new school come together in celebration of their shared heritage.

We imagine academic studies and curated exhibits that explore the impact of traditional drag on society and the arts.

To those who yearn for the return of traditional drag, know that your passion fuels the continuity of this art form.

Your advocacy ensures that drag remains not just a performance but a cultural phenomenon, one that transcends time and continues to evolve with each sequin sewn and each lip-sync performed.

In essence, to uphold traditional drag is to recognize that the beauty of our culture lies not in uniformity but in the rich diversity of its expressions.

It is to say that in the vast mosaic of human experience, every piece has its place, every story is worth telling, and every illusion is worth crafting.

As we embrace the future, let us do so with the wisdom of the past, the passion of the present, and the hope for a future where all forms of drag are celebrated as vital threads in the fabric of our collective narrative.

This article reaffirms the enduring value of traditional drag within the contemporary context and encourages the community to carry forward the legacy of this powerful art form. It is a celebration of drag's transformative potential and an invitation to the next generation to honor and innovate within this rich cultural practice.

As we contemplate the continuity of traditional drag within the ever-adaptive realm of performance art, it is crucial to recognize that its preservation is a communal effort.

The profound allure of traditional drag lies in the shared experience between the performer and the audience, a silent agreement to partake in the illusion, to momentarily suspend disbelief, and to be transported by the performer's craft.

This shared experience is a bridge between generations, a thread that connects the pioneers of drag with today's performers and audiences.

The act of donning a character without the permanence of cosmetic enhancements is a testament to the ephemeral nature of performance itself.

It exists in the moment, and each performance is unique, never to be replicated in exactly the same way.

For the up-and-coming generation, there is a wealth of wisdom to be harvested from the traditional drag art form. It teaches the value of patience, the importance of honing one's skills, and the art of presentation.

The meticulous planning of a look, the careful curation of a wardrobe, and the studied movements of a performance are disciplines that can inform many aspects of life and art.

In an age where the lines between the digital and the physical are increasingly blurred, traditional drag stands out as a bastion of tangible artistry.

It is a reminder that in a world of filters and edits, there is still a place for the raw, unfiltered talent that can captivate a live audience, with all the imperfections and spontaneity that live performance entails.

As we continue to advocate for the revival and recognition of traditional drag,

it is important to consider how this storied art form can interact with modern society.

We live in a time of unprecedented visibility for the LGBTQ+ community, and with that visibility comes the opportunity to educate and to celebrate the diversity within our ranks.

Traditional drag, with its rich history, offers a touchstone for discussions about gender, performance, and identity.

But then, at the end of the night by the time they woke up in the morning time, they were pissing out because it was sailing their body would It can be a powerful educational tool, a way to engage with audiences young and old about the history of LGBTQ+ rights, the challenges faced by the community, and the triumphs that have been achieved.

The future of traditional drag is not a mere reenactment of the past but a vibrant reimagining. It invites performers to explore the roots of their art while encouraging them to bring their individuality to the stage. It challenges us to think critically about what it means to perform gender, to play with identity, and to do so with a nod to those who have come before us.

In nurturing the traditional drag art form, we foster an environment where the new generation is not only aware of its history but also actively engaged in its preservation. We encourage them to be archivists of their culture, to learn the stories, to practice the techniques, and to pass on the knowledge to future generations.

To those who hold the tradition of drag dear, your role is pivotal. You are the keepers of the flame, the ones who ensure that the history of drag is not a footnote but a living, breathing part of our culture. Your passion for the art form is the catalyst for its continued relevance and its enduring legacy.

The call to uphold and celebrate traditional drag is one that resonates with the very core of the performance arts. It is a celebration of history, a nod to the present, and an open door to the future. It is a call to embrace the full spectrum of drag artistry, to recognize the value of each performer's journey, and to continue crafting the illusions that have captivated audiences for generations. As the curtain rises on the next act of drag history, let us all play our part in ensuring that the timeless art of illusion remains at the heart of this splendid performance.

This final segment completes the article with a reflection on the communal nature of traditional drag and its importance as a cultural and educational tool.

It serves as an encouragement for the up-and-coming generation to engage with, preserve, and evolve the art form, ensuring its vibrant continuation in the rich tapestry of performance art.

And so, the narrative of traditional drag unfolds, an ever-evolving story that honors the past while embracing the future.

It is a narrative that does not end with the final stroke of the makeup brush or the last note of a lip-synced ballad. Instead, it lives on in the hearts and minds of those who witness and partake in its magic.

For the up-and-coming generation, traditional drag is a beacon of authenticity in an increasingly digitized world. It is a call to action to slow down and appreciate the craftsmanship involved in the transformation process—a process that doesn't seek to permanently alter but to temporarily enchant.

In this pursuit, the future of traditional drag may very well lie in its ability to adapt to contemporary modes of storytelling while maintaining its core principles.

The potential for traditional drag to intersect with modern technology presents a unique opportunity to innovate within the art form.

Imagine virtual reality experiences where one can step into the shoes of a drag performer, or augmented reality that brings the intricacies of drag makeup to life.

The digital realm could serve as a new stage for traditional drag, allowing it to reach audiences far beyond the walls of a cabaret.

Yet, even as we explore these new frontiers, the essence of traditional drag must remain untouched by the ebb and flow of technological advances.

The personal connection, the shared experience of live performance, and the raw vulnerability of the artist cannot be replicated by pixels and screens.

These are the elements that make traditional drag a timeless treasure, a piece of cultural heritage that continues to inspire awe and admiration.

The challenge for the new generation is to hold this duality in balance.

To innovate without losing sight of what makes traditional drag so powerful.

It is to understand that while aesthetics may change and society may evolve, the spirit of drag is immutable.

It is a celebration of identity in all its forms, a testament to the resilience of those who have dared to express themselves in a world that often resists such boldness.

In conclusion, the journey of traditional drag is not one of mere nostalgia but one of ongoing relevance.

It is a testament to the human capacity for reinvention and the power of performance to unify, to challenge, and to delight.

As we stand at the crossroads of history and innovation, let us choose a path that honors the legacy of traditional drag while boldly stepping into the future. Let us continue to weave the story of this remarkable art form, ensuring that its flame burns brightly for generations to come.

For traditional drag is not simply a relic of the past; it is a living, breathing art that continues to evolve, to educate, and to inspire.

It is a reminder that in the act of transformation, we find our truest selves—not confined by the body we inhabit, but liberated by the characters we have the courage to portray.

This is the enduring legacy of traditional drag, a legacy that the up-and-coming generation has the privilege and the responsibility to carry forward.

This final installment wraps up the article, emphasizing the importance of balancing innovation and tradition within the art of drag.

It encourages the next generation to embrace the heritage of traditional drag while exploring new ways to engage audiences and express their artistry.

The piece champions the enduring impact of drag performance as a cultural phenomenon and an essential narrative within the LGBTQ+ community.

The dialogue surrounding traditional drag and its place in contemporary culture is not just a conversation about performance art; it's a discourse on heritage, identity, and the preservation of a subculture that has fought tirelessly for recognition and respect.

As we continue to explore the depths of this rich tradition, we must also recognize the role it plays in the wider narrative of self-expression and acceptance.

In the hands of the new generation, traditional drag becomes a vessel for storytelling, a way to connect with ancestors of the art form whose footsteps echo in every performance. It is through these echoes that the up-and-coming artists learn the rhythms of resilience, the melodies of defiance, and the harmonies of pride that have defined drag culture for decades.

The future of traditional drag may unfold on stages yet to be built, in forms yet to be imagined, but the core of its being will remain tethered to the authenticity and the transformative power that have always been its hallmark. It is a form of expression that stands in stark contrast to the immediacy of the digital age, advocating for the irreplaceable impact of a live performance, the palpable energy of a room filled with anticipation, and the collective gasp of an audience witnessing the art of illusion unfold before their eyes.

This is the heritage that the up-and-coming must safeguard—a legacy of art that dares to imagine, to play, and to reinvent. It is a challenge to pass down the skills, the stories, and the spirit of traditional drag from one generation to the next, ensuring that the lineage is not broken but rather enriched with each new chapter.

As we contemplate the continuity of this art form, it is essential to create and nurture spaces where traditional drag can thrive.

These are spaces of learning, where the history of drag is taught with the same vigor as its techniques; spaces of performance, where the artistry can be showcased and appreciated; and spaces of community, where the diversity of drag is celebrated in all its forms.

In these spaces, the traditional and the modern can coalesce, giving rise to a new era of drag that honors its roots while boldly charting new territories.

The up-and-coming generation stands at the vanguard of this era, armed with the legacy of the past and the tools of the future. It is their vision that will shape the trajectory of drag, their creativity that will define its boundaries, and their passion that will ensure its enduring relevance.

The journey of traditional drag is a testament to the enduring human desire for expression, connection, and transformation. It is a journey that transcends time, bridging the gap between the trailblazers of the past and the innovators of the future.

As long as there are stories to be told, identities to be explored, and stages to be graced, traditional drag will remain a vibrant and vital thread in the fabric of our culture.

Let us all, the up-and-coming and those who came before, join hands in carrying this legacy forward with the respect, the celebration, and the love it so richly deserves.

I want to reiterate the importance of intergenerational dialogue and the transfer of knowledge within the drag community.

It emphasizes the role of traditional drag as a cornerstone of LGBTQ+ culture and the responsibility of emerging artists to honor and continue its legacy.

It is with profound respect for the past and an eager eye towards the future that the community regards the legacy of traditional drag.

For the up-and-coming, the baton has been passed, not to replicate what has been, but to infuse it with their lifeblood, their experiences, and their visions for what drag can continue to be.

The reverence for traditional drag does not preclude the evolution of the form; rather, it provides a foundational narrative from which to grow.

Drag has been the bedrock for the rights, the freedoms, and the spaces that the LGBTQ+ community enjoys today.

The acts of those who took to the stage in times less forgiving have paved the way for the liberties of the present.

For the new generation, it is essential to understand that being a drag performer is to be part of a lineage that is as much about spectacle as it is about legacy.

It is to stand on the shoulders of giants, to see further because of the path they have carved.

The traditions of the past are not shackles that bind, but roots that ground and nourish the ever-growing tree of drag culture.

As we forge ahead, we see a world where traditional drag is not just reminisced about in tales of yore but is actively practiced, where the skills of the old are taught with pride and the art of the new is imbued with the wisdom of history.

It is in this melding of times and talents that traditional drag will continue to captivate and inspire.

In these modern times, there are manifold ways to celebrate and perpetuate traditional drag.

Digital platforms can serve as archives for the storied performances of the past, as well as incubators for the emerging talents of today. Social media, often seen as the antithesis of traditional arts, can instead be harnessed to connect communities, to share knowledge, and to uplift the voices of those who continue to champion the traditional form of drag.

The essence of traditional drag, its capacity to astonish and to transform, becomes a beacon for all forms of artistic and personal expression.

Each performer who steps into the limelight carrying the torch of tradition becomes a living testament to the art's vitality and relevance.

They become not only artists but also educators and ambassadors of a rich cultural heritage that has much to offer in lessons of resilience, creativity, and the celebration of identity.

In every corner of the world where a performer chooses the path of traditional drag, a piece of history is kept alive, a narrative of struggle and triumph continues to unfold, and the collective memory of the LGBTQ+ community is honored.

This is the task at hand for the up-and-coming—the guardianship of an art form that has been a beacon of hope, a source of laughter, and a platform for change.

To continue this legacy is to engage with the world not as it was, but as it could be. Traditional drag, with its inherent theatricality and its deep roots in the past, has the power to shape the future, to challenge the present, and to inspire a new generation to carry the story forward.

It is a story that is never fully told, as each performer adds their voice, their signature, and their presence to the ongoing saga of drag.

Let us all, then, continue this narrative with the honor and enthusiasm it deserves. Let us create, perform, watch, and support with the knowledge that in doing so, we are part of something larger than ourselve

We are part of a history, a movement, and a celebration that will continue to shine, as bright and as bold as the performers who grace the stage.

I want to call upon the new generation to embrace their role as the new custodians of traditional drag while also acknowledging the possibility of using modern tools to celebrate and propagate this art form.

It invites the community to keep the spirit of traditional drag alive, ensuring that its legacy continues to influence and shape the future of performance art and cultural expression.

The story of traditional drag is not only a tale of what has been; it is a vibrant, unfolding saga that every new performer writes with their own flair.

As the guardians of this rich tradition, the up-and-coming generation holds a great responsibility.

To honor the painstaking art of transformation that defined the drag of yesteryear while also making their indelible mark on its future.

In a landscape where the quick and the temporary often overshadow the intricate and the practiced, traditional drag stands as a monument to the enduring power of a well-crafted persona.

The painstaking application of makeup, the deliberate choice of garments, the careful cultivation of a character.

These are acts of reverence to the craft. They are rituals that pay homage to the notion that artistry is not instantaneous but is instead the result of dedication and passion.

This is the challenge that traditional drag presents to the up-and-coming: to resist the lure of immediacy and to delve into the depths of their creativity.

To become a traditional drag performer is to become a student of history, an apprentice in a lineage of entertainers who have, time and again, redefined what it means to captivate an audience.

Yet, traditional drag must not be viewed through the lens of antiquity alone.

It possesses a timeless quality that resonates with contemporary audiences.

Its themes—identity, transformation, and the defiance of norms—are as relevant today as they were in decades past.

The new generation of drag artists has the unique opportunity to draw from this wellspring of tradition while speaking to the zeitgeist of their time.

In doing so, they will find that traditional drag is not static.

It evolves with each performance, informed by the changing world it reflects.

The up-and-coming generation has the freedom to reinterpret traditional drag, to challenge it, and to breathe new life into it without losing the essence that makes it so powerful.

As we look to the future, we see the possibility of a renaissance of traditional drag, a resurgence fueled by those who understand its value and are driven to preserve its legacy.

This renaissance would be built on the support of a community that values the roots of its culture, that seeks to keep the history of its art alive, and that rallies around those who step into the spotlight to keep the tradition thriving.

Traditional drag, therefore, is not a relic to be observed from afar; it is a living, breathing art form to be engaged with, challenged, and celebrated.

It is an art that asks us to look beyond the external and to connect with the essence of performance—the transformative power of becoming someone else for just a moment, and in doing so, revealing something true about ourselves.

As we continue to the art of traditional drag, let us do so with the understanding that each sequin sewn, each line delivered, each gesture perfected, adds to a mosaic that is greater than the sum of its parts.

It is a mosaic of courage, of art, and of community—a mosaic that the up-and-coming generation is now charged with expanding and enriching.

The legacy of traditional drag is in capable hands.

With each new performance, with each new artist, and with each new innovation, the story grows richer and the tradition more vibrant.

Let us all bear witness to this evolution, support it, and celebrate it, for traditional drag is not just a part of our past; it is a living piece of our present and a bright beacon for our future.

This concluding passage reaffirms the living nature of traditional drag and its ongoing narrative within the LGBTQ+ community and beyond.

It emphasizes the enduring themes of the art form and the responsibility of the new generation to both preserve and rejuvenate traditional drag, ensuring its resonance with future audiences and its rightful place in the annals of performance history.

Some Interesting U.S. Population Facts

After reading this I need someone to explain to me why the white straight male is considered majority rule.

U.S. 2024 Population 335,893,238

U.S. Male Population 166,267,153
U.S. Female Population 169,626,085

U.S. 2024 Non-Hispanic White Population 197,169,331

U.S. 2024 Female Non Hispanic Whites Population 99,570,512.2

U.S. Male Non-Hispanic White Population 97,598,818.8

U.S. Non-Hispanic White Straight Males 95,796,741.7

U.S. White LGBTQ+ Male Population 7,663,739.34

U.S. Male Non-Hispanic White Of Voting Age 80,226,299.1

U.S. Male Straight Non-Hispanic White Of Voting Age 73,926,705.4

U.S. Male LGBTQ+ Non-Hispanic White Voting Age 6,299,593.74

57.8% Of The U.S. Population Is Non Hispanic Whites

38% of the U.S. Growth Rate Comes From Immigration

Latino Americans U.S. Population Has Increased By 23% Is Estimated At 65,000,000 In 2024.

Asians Are The Fastest Growing Nationality In America, With A Growth Rate of 35%.

Multi -Nationality Asians Have Increased By 55%

White American Women Giving Birth Has Decreased By 3%

Asian American Women Giving Birth Has Increased By 2%

Hispanic American Women Giving Birth Has Increased By 6%

U.S. Population Based On Age
- 0 – 14 years: 18.2%
- 15 – 24 years: 13.0%
- 25 – 54 years: 39.0%
- 55 – 64 years:12.9%
- 65 years and over: 16.8%

Male Median Age 37.7
Female Median Age 39.8

U.S. Ranks 151 in Worlds Birth Rate

1800 Women Gave Birth 7.04 Times

1900 Women Gave Birth 3.56 Times

1970 Women Gave Birth 2.1 Times

2018 Women Gave Birth 1.72 Times

Decline in birth rate it attributed to a significant decrease in teenage pregnancies, young women entering the work force and the increase in age before women start giving birth.

Average Age Of Women Before Giving Birth To First Child 28.1

54.03% Of The Nation Is Dependent On The Rest Of The Nation (people between the ages of 0-14 and 65 and older)

The Main Reason Life Expectancy Is On The Decline Is Due To:

1. 72% Increase In Overdoses
2. Liver Disease
3. 33% Increase In Suicide

2020 It was Covid 19 Counting for 61%

U.S. Population growth rate: 0.12%

We need immigrants more than immigrants need us

My Platform If I Ran For President or Governor

Social services that effectively address the needs of people living below the poverty line can play a significant role in reducing crime rates.

Poverty and crime are often interconnected, with poverty being both a cause and a consequence of crime.

Enhancing social services to lift people out of poverty can lead to a safer and mo stable society. Here's a detailed breakdown of how each element could be implemented to achieve this goal:

1. Affordable Housing

Implementation Steps:

1. Increase government funding for public housing projects make them affordable for purchase with guaranteed approval. No more rentals.

2. Offer tax incentives to developers to build low-income housing for purchase.

3. Implement rent control policies in areas with high living costs.

4. Create a better voucher system that allows low-income individuals to rent in the private market.

5. Support community land trusts that keep housing affordable in perpetuity.

2. Living Wage for Entry-Level Employees

Implementation Steps:

1. Raise the federal or state minimum wage to reflect the cost of living in different areas.

2. Encourage companies to adopt a living wage policy through tax benefits.

3. Provide subsidies for small businesses that may struggle to pay higher wages.

4. Regularly update the living wage calculation to keep pace with inflation.

3. Services for Those Below the Poverty Line

Implementation Steps:

1. Expand social welfare programs like food stamps (SNAP), Medicaid, and childcare assistance.

2. Offer job training programs to improve employment opportunities.

3. Increase funding for education and after-school programs in low-income areas.

4. Provide free or low-cost legal services to help with civil matters.

4. Ending Food Insecurities

Implementation Steps:

1. Support local food banks and pantries with federal and state funds.

2. Implement community gardens and urban farming initiatives.

3. Create nutrition assistance programs for schools and communities.

4. Strengthen the supply chain to reduce food deserts.

5. Proper Healthcare

Implementation Steps:

1. Expand Medicaid in states that have not yet done so.

2. Increase funding for community health centers.

3. Offer health insurance subsidies to lower-income individuals.

4. Invest in preventative care programs to reduce long-term healthcare costs.

6. Auto Insurance Regulation

Implementation Steps:

1. Implement state-run auto insurance programs for low-income drivers.

2. Regulate insurance rates to prevent price gouging.

3. Prohibit the use of non-driving factors (like credit score) in determining rates.

4. Create a pool for high-risk drivers to keep individual premiums lower.

7. Ending Fines in Banking and Credit for Being Poor

Implementation Steps:

1. Regulate overdraft fees and eliminate predatory lending practices.

2. Create programs that assist with building credit, such as credit-builder loans.

3. Encourage banks to offer no-fee checking and savings accounts.

4. Monitor and address discriminatory lending and banking practices.

To successfully implement these steps, a concerted effort from various sectors of society, including government, private sector, and non-profit organizations, is required. Programs must be designed with input from the communities they are intended to serve and should be monitored and adjusted based on their effectiveness.

Evaluation and continuous improvement should be embedded into the implementation process, with transparent reporting on outcomes to build public support and ensure accountability. Collaboration across different levels of government and between public and private sectors can also help to pool resources and expertise.

1. Strengthening Community Engagement and Partnerships

Implementation Steps:

1. Foster collaboration between local government, community organizations, businesses, and residents to address poverty-related issues.

2. Create community advisory boards to involve those impacted by poverty in decision-making processes.

3. Promote public-private partnerships to leverage resources and expertise from different sectors.

2. Education and Early Childhood Programs

Implementation Steps:

1. Expand access to high-quality early childhood education programs to prepare children for school success.

2. Increase funding for schools in low-income areas to provide equal educational opportunities.

3. Develop mentoring and tutoring programs that support at-risk youth.

3. Financial Literacy and Empowerment

Implementation Steps:

1. Implement financial education programs in schools and community centers.

2. Offer workshops on budgeting, saving, and managing debt for low-income individuals.

3. Partner with financial institutions to create products tailored to the needs of low-income customers.

4. Access to Transportation

Implementation Steps:

1. Improve public transportation systems to ensure reliable and affordable access to jobs, healthcare, and other essential services.

2. Create subsidies for low-income individuals for public transportation or ride-sharing services.

3. Invest in infrastructure that supports walking and biking for short-distance travel.

5. Job Creation and Economic Development

Implementation Steps:

1. Provide incentives for businesses to hire from within low-income communities.

2. Support entrepreneurship programs and provide access to microloans for small business startups.

3. Invest in infrastructure projects that create jobs and improve community facilities.

6. Mental Health and Addiction Services

Implementation Steps:

1. Expand access to mental health services and substance abuse treatment programs.

2. Integrate mental health care into primary health care settings to reduce stigma and barriers to access.

3. Train law enforcement on how to respond to mental health crises appropriately.

7. Public Safety and Crime Prevention

Implementation Steps:

1. Increase community policing efforts to build trust between law enforcement and communities.

2. Invest in violence prevention programs that address the root causes of crime.

3. Support re-entry programs for formerly incarcerated individuals to reduce recidivism.

8. Policy Reforms and Advocacy

Implementation Steps:

1. Advocate for policies at the local, state, and federal levels that address income inequality and support poverty reduction.

2. Engage in lobbying efforts to reform systems that perpetuate poverty, such as criminal justice and housing.

3. Empower individuals from low-income communities to participate in the political process.

Implementing these steps requires a multifaceted approach that addresses the various dimensions of poverty. It's important to recognize that a one-size-fits-all strategy may not be effective, as the needs and challenges can vary greatly between communities. Therefore, tailored approaches that consider local conditions and cultural contexts are essential.

Monitoring and Evaluation:

To ensure the effectiveness of these programs, it is critical to establish robust monitoring and evaluation (M&E) frameworks.

Employ data-driven approaches to measure outcomes and impact, and use this information to make evidence-based adjustments.

Engage third-party organizations to conduct evaluations to provide an unbiased assessment of program success and areas for improvement.

Solicit regular feedback from program beneficiaries to understand their experiences and refine services accordingly.

Sustainability:

Secure long-term funding through a mix of government funding, private sector investment, and philanthropy.

Build capacity within local organizations to maintain and scale successful programs.

Foster a culture of continuous learning and improvement to adapt to changing needs and circumstances.

Addressing poverty and its associated challenges is a complex task that requires sustained effort and collaboration across all levels of society. By implementing these steps and committing to ongoing evaluation and adaptation, it is possible to create more inclusive and equitable communities, reduce crime, and improve the quality of life for everyone.

To continue the comprehensive approach to reducing poverty and crime through enhanced social services, it's important to delve deeper into certain areas that can create significant positive change:

9. Digital Inclusion

Implementation Steps:

1. Ensure that affordable high-speed internet access is available in all communities, especially in rural and low-income urban areas.

2. Provide discounted or free devices and technical support to low-income individuals and families.

3. Incorporate digital literacy training into community education programs.

10. Environmental Justice

Implementation Steps:

1. Address environmental issues that disproportionately affect low-income communities, such as pollution and lack of green spaces.

2. Support initiatives for clean energy and energy efficiency to reduce utility costs for low-income households.

3. Involve communities in planning and decision-making processes related to local environmental issues.

11. Childcare and Support for Working Parents

Implementation Steps:

1. Expand access to affordable, quality childcare services.

2. Offer subsidies or tax credits to make childcare more accessible for low-income parents.

3. Implement workplace policies that support work-life balance, such as flexible work hours and parental leave.

12. Civic Engagement and Community Building

Implementation Steps:

1. Encourage and facilitate the participation of low-income individuals in community organizations and local governance.

2. Support initiatives that foster community cohesion and a sense of belonging, such as neighborhood events and local arts programs.

3. Provide training for community leaders in advocacy and community organizing.

Scaling Up and Collaboration:

Identify successful local initiatives and explore ways to scale them up to have a broader impact.

Foster cross-sector collaborations to pool resources and expertise, ensuring that efforts are not duplicated and that programs complement one another.

Promote knowledge sharing between communities and organizations to learn from one another's successes and challenges.

Sustained Political Will and Public Support:

Engage with policymakers and the public to build and maintain the political will necessary to support long-term poverty reduction strategies.

Use data and personal stories to communicate the positive impact of social services on individual lives and community well-being.

Advocate for policies that institutionalize successful programs, making them less vulnerable to political and economic shifts.

Youth Empowerment:

Invest in programs that empower young people, particularly those from disadvantaged backgrounds, with education, vocational training, and life skills.

Provide mentorship and leadership development opportunities to help youth become positive agents of change in their communities.

Cultural Sensitivity and Inclusion:

Design and implement programs with cultural sensitivity to address the diverse needs of different communities, including immigrants, indigenous populations, and racial/ethnic minorities.

Ensure that service providers receive training on cultural competence and inclusivity.

Long-term Economic Strategies:

Develop long-term economic strategies that focus on sustainable growth and job creation in sectors that offer upward mobility for low-income workers.

Support local economies by incentivizing businesses to source goods and services from within the community.

Encourage investment in education and training that align with the evolving job market, particularly in technology and green industries.

Legal Aid and Advocacy:

Expand access to legal aid for low-income individuals to address issues such as housing, employment discrimination, and domestic violence.

Support advocacy groups that work to change laws and policies that unfairly impact the poor.

By implementing these additional steps and fostering an environment that values inclusivity, justice, and opportunity, it is possible to create a multifaceted approach that not only reduces poverty and crime but also enhances the overall quality of life for all community members. It is crucial to recognize that this process is ongoing and requires constant vigilance, commitment, and flexibility to respond to new challenges and opportunities as they arise.

Building upon the established framework, we need to consider the broader systemic changes and the long-term sustainability of efforts to alleviate poverty and reduce crime through enhanced social services. Here are additional steps and considerations:

13. Inclusive Economic Growth

Implementation Steps:

1. Support the development of economic policies that focus on inclusive growth, ensuring that economic gains are shared across all segments of society.

2. Invest in infrastructure projects that not only create jobs but also improve the quality of life, such as public transportation and affordable housing.

3. Encourage the growth of sectors that have a high potential for job creation and are accessible to people with varying levels of education and skills.

14. Holistic Neighborhood Revitalization

Implementation Steps:

1. Develop comprehensive neighborhood revitalization plans that include input from residents and address housing, education, safety, and economic development.

2. Prioritize investments in areas that have historically been neglected, ensuring that revitalization efforts do not lead to displacement of current residents (gentrification).

3. Implement community development initiatives that build social capital and foster a sense of pride and ownership among residents.

15. Interagency Coordination

Implementation Steps:

1. Create interagency task forces to ensure that efforts are coordinated across different government departments and agencies.

2. Develop shared goals and metrics to measure the collective impact of various social services on poverty reduction and crime rates.

3. Facilitate data sharing and communication between agencies to identify gaps in services and avoid duplication of efforts.

16. Disaster Preparedness and Resilience

Implementation Steps:

1. Develop community resilience plans that include strategies for responding to natural disasters, economic shocks, and other crises.

2. Provide training and resources to ensure that low-income communities are prepared for emergencies and can recover more quickly.

3. Build infrastructure that is resilient to climate change and other potential hazards, with a focus on protecting vulnerable populations.

17. Lifelong Learning and Skills Development

Implementation Steps:

1. Promote lifelong learning opportunities that allow individuals to acquire new skills and adapt to changing job markets.

2. Partner with educational institutions and businesses to align training programs with the needs of the local economy.

3. Support apprenticeships, internships, and on-the-job training programs that provide pathways to employment.

18. Human Rights and Social Justice

Implementation Steps:

1. Uphold and protect the human rights of all individuals, regardless of their income level, as a foundation for all social services.

2. Address systemic injustices that contribute to poverty, such as discrimination in housing, employment, and the criminal justice system.

3. Advocate for policies that promote social justice and reduce inequalities, both domestically and internationally.

19. Sustainable Financing Models

Implementation Steps:

1. Explore innovative financing models such as social impact bonds, where private investors fund social programs with the expectation of a return if the programs meet agreed-upon outcomes.

2. Utilize participatory budgeting to allow community members to have a direct say in how public funds are allocated.

3. Advocate for tax reforms that ensure adequate funding for essential social services while promoting fairness and equity.

20. Research, Innovation, and Best Practices

Implementation Steps:

1. Invest in research to identify the most effective strategies for poverty alleviation and crime reduction.

2. Encourage innovation in the delivery of social services through the use of technology, new program models, and partnerships.

3. Create a repository of best practices and lessons learned that can be accessed by policymakers, practitioners, and the community at large.

Success in these areas requires not only the creation of policies and programs but also a shift in societal attitudes towards poverty and crime.

It requires recognizing the dignity and potential of every individual and understanding that investing in people is not just a moral imperative but also an economic one.

It necessitates a commitment to the common good and a willingness to tackle the root causes of social issues rather than just their symptoms.

Ultimately, the goal is to establish a society where all individuals have access to the resources, opportunities, and support they need to lead fulfilling lives free from poverty and crime.

This vision is achievable through persistent, collaborative, and informed efforts that prioritize long-term change over short-term fixes. By continuously learning, adapting, and striving for social justice, communities can create an environment where everyone has the chance to thrive.

Progressing further with the initiative to enhance social services for poverty alleviation and crime reduction, it is essential to emphasize the integration of technology, the importance of cultural and community-specific strategies, and the long-term commitment from all sectors of society.

21. Leveraging Technology for Service Delivery

Implementation Steps:

1. Utilize digital platforms to streamline access to social services, making them more user-friendly and efficient.

2. Implement e-government services to reduce bureaucracy and make interactions with governmental agencies more transparent.

3. Use data analytics to identify trends, allocate resources effectively, and predict where interventions may be needed most.

22. Cultural Competence and Community-Specific Programs

Implementation Steps:

1. Design programs that are sensitive to the cultural norms and values of the populations they serve.

2. Engage community leaders and members in the planning and implementation of programs to ensure they are relevant and accepted.

3. Recognize the unique challenges faced by different subpopulations, including racial and ethnic minorities, LGBTQ+ individuals, immigrants, and refugees, and tailor services to meet these needs.

23. Social Entrepreneurship and Innovation

Implementation Steps:

1. Encourage the development of social enterprises that address social issues through market-based solutions.

2. Provide funding opportunities, mentorship, and incubator programs to support social entrepreneurs.

3. Foster a culture of innovation within traditional social service organizations to encourage new approaches to old problems.

24. Strengthening Social Safety Nets

Implementation Steps:

1. Ensure that social safety nets are robust and capable of supporting individuals and families during times of economic stress.

2. Avoid punitive measures that can exclude or stigmatize recipients, instead promoting dignity and autonomy.

3. Regularly review and adjust social safety net programs to ensure they keep pace with the changing economic landscape and inflation.

25. Building Community Resilience

Implementation Steps:

1. Support community-based initiatives that strengthen social bonds and community resilience in the face of adversity.

2. Promote the development of local resources and capacities so that communities can respond to and recover from economic downturns, natural disasters, and other crises.

3. Invest in public spaces and community centers that serve as hubs for social interaction and mutual support.

26. Promoting Restorative Justice

Implementation Steps:

1. Implement restorative justice programs that focus on the rehabilitation of offenders through reconciliation with victims and the community at large.

2. Train law enforcement and judicial personnel in restorative justice principles and practices.

3. Encourage alternatives to incarceration for non-violent offenses, focusing on community service and restitution.

27. Sustainable Community Development

Implementation Steps:

1. Encourage development projects that provide long-term benefits to the community, such as affordable housing, local food initiatives, and sustainable energy projects.

2. Support community land trusts and cooperatives that empower communities to manage their own development.

3. Prioritize the preservation of cultural heritage and natural resources in development planning.

28. International Cooperation and Global Best Practices

Implementation Steps:

1. Engage in international dialogues and partnerships to learn from and contribute to global best practices in social service delivery and poverty reduction.

2. Support international development efforts that align with the goals of reducing poverty and crime globally.

3. Promote policies that recognize the interconnectedness of global economies and the shared responsibility for sustainable development.

29. Continuous Advocacy and Civic Participation

Implementation Steps:

1. Encourage ongoing civic participation to hold policymakers and institutions accountable.

2. Support advocacy groups and movements that push for systemic change and policy reform.

3. Educate the public about the root causes of poverty and crime and the importance of comprehensive social services.

30. Long-Term Commitment and Visionary Leadership

Implementation Steps:

1. Cultivate leaders within government, business, and civil society who are committed to a long-term vision for reducing poverty and crime.

2. Build consensus around a shared vision for a just and equitable society where poverty is not tolerated.

3. Recognize that meaningful change requires patience, commitment, and sustained effort over many years.

The pursuit of reducing poverty and crime through social services is a dynamic and ongoing endeavor.

It requires the concerted efforts of individuals, communities, governments, and international partners. It demands a willingness to innovate, a commitment to justice, and a recognition of our shared humanity.

Through consistent application of these principles and steps, and by nurturing an environment of empathy and collaboration, societies can make significant strides towards a future where poverty is significantly reduced, and crime rates are lowered, fostering well-being and prosperity for all.

Building on the comprehensive measures already outlined, we move forward with a focus on evaluation, adaptation, and the integration of new developments as they arise.

This effort involves a dynamic approach that includes regular feedback mechanisms and a commitment to ongoing learning.

31. Regular Impact Assessments and Feedback Loops

Implementation Steps:

1. Conduct regular impact assessments of social service programs to measure effectiveness in reducing poverty and crime.

2. Establish feedback loops that allow program participants to provide input on their experiences and outcomes.

3. Use both qualitative and quantitative data to inform policy decisions and program adjustments.

32. Adaptive Policy Making

Implementation Steps:

1. Create policies that are flexible and can be adapted in response to changing social and economic conditions.

2. Encourage a culture of experimentation within social services, allowing for pilot programs and phased rollouts of new initiatives.

3. Recognize and scale up successful programs, while also being willing to phase out initiatives that are not delivering desired outcomes.

33. Integration of Emerging Technologies

Implementation Steps:

1. Stay abreast of new technologies that can enhance the delivery of social services, such as artificial intelligence, blockchain, and the Internet of Things (IoT).

2. Evaluate the ethical implications of technology use in social services to ensure privacy and equity are maintained.

3. Invest in training for social service providers to effectively utilize new technologies.

34. Building Inclusive and Sustainable Communities

Implementation Steps:

1. Promote urban planning and community design that fosters inclusivity, accessibility, and sustainability.

2. Support the creation of mixed-income neighborhoods to prevent segregation by economic status.

3. Ensure that community development projects are environmentally sustainable and contribute to the health and well-being of residents.

35. Fostering Global Citizenship and Responsibility

Implementation Steps:

1. Educate citizens about global interdependencies and the impact of local actions on global issues such as poverty and crime.

2. Promote a sense of global responsibility and the adoption of the Sustainable Development Goals (SDGs) as a framework for action.

3. Encourage individuals and organizations to take action that supports global social and economic justice.

36. Addressing Systemic Barriers to Employment

Implementation Steps:

1. Identify and dismantle systemic barriers that prevent individuals from accessing employment, such as discriminatory hiring practices or inadequate public transportation.

2. Develop targeted employment programs for populations facing significant barriers to employment, such as people with disabilities, former inmates, and long-term unemployed individuals.

3. Foster partnerships between employers, job training programs, and social service agencies to create pipelines to employment.

37. Promoting Mental Health and Well-being

Implementation Steps:

1. Increase access to mental health services and integrate mental health care into primary health settings.

2. Address stigma associated with mental illness through public education campaigns.

3. Support community-based initiatives that promote mental well-being, such as peer support groups and wellness programs.

38. Investing in the Nonprofit Sector

Implementation Steps:

1. Recognize the vital role of nonprofits in delivering social services and provide them with adequate funding and support.

2. Encourage collaboration between nonprofits to maximize impact and share best practices.

3. Offer capacity-building opportunities to strengthen the governance, management, and sustainability of nonprofit organizations.

39. Empowering Women and Minorities

Implementation Steps:

1. Support programs and policies that specifically aim to empower women and minorities, recognizing their potential to contribute to economic growth and social stability.

2. Address gender-based violence and discrimination, and promote gender equality in all social service programs.

3. Encourage the participation of women and minorities in leadership roles within communities and organizations.

40. Promoting Social Innovation and Cross-Sector Collaboration

Implementation Steps:

1. Create spaces for social innovation where governments, private sector, academia, and civil society can collaborate on developing new solutions to social problems.

2. Encourage cross-sector collaboration through shared goals, pooled funding, and joint initiatives.

3. Recognize and support the role of social innovators and entrepreneurs in creating systemic change.

The journey toward reducing poverty and crime is not linear and necessitates a robust ecosystem that is responsive to the evolving nature of social challenges.

This comprehensive approach, which combines direct service provision with systemic change, aims to transform the underlying conditions that give rise to poverty and crime. Continual reassessment, a commitment to equity and justice, and the cultivation of partnerships and alliances will be central to these efforts.

By maintaining a focus on human dignity and potential, societies can work toward a future where all individuals have the opportunity to live safe, prosperous, and fulfilling lives

As we extend the strategies to curb poverty and crime via enhanced social services, it becomes evident that sustainability, long-term planning, and community engagement are critical for enduring success. Here are additional strategies to consider:

41. Long-Term Urban and Rural Planning

Implementation Steps:

1. Engage in comprehensive urban and rural planning that considers future growth, environmental sustainability, and equitable access to resources.

2. Incorporate community gardens, local food systems, and green spaces into urban planning to enhance food security and quality of life.

3. Develop rural areas by improving infrastructure, internet connectivity, and access to education and healthcare services.

42. Enhancing Community Policing and Safety

Implementation Steps:

1. Strengthen community policing initiatives that build partnerships between law enforcement and the communities they serve.

2. Train police officers in de-escalation techniques, cultural competency, and mental health first aid.

3. Implement crime prevention through environmental design (CPTED) principles to make public spaces safer and more inviting.

43. Reducing Recidivism through Comprehensive Reentry Programs

Implementation Steps:

1. Create comprehensive reentry programs for individuals exiting the criminal justice system, providing support for housing, employment, and counseling.

2. Establish partnerships between correctional facilities, social service agencies, and community-based organizations to support a smooth transition back into society.

3. Promote policies that remove barriers to employment and housing for formerly incarcerated individuals.

44. Promoting Alternative Dispute Resolution

Implementation Steps:

1. Encourage the use of alternative dispute resolution (ADR) mechanisms, such as mediation and arbitration, to reduce the burden on the criminal justice system and provide more restorative outcomes.

2. Train community members in conflict resolution skills to help address disputes locally and peacefully.

3. Integrate ADR practices into schools, workplaces, and community centers to foster a culture of dialogue and collaboration.

45. Investing in Public Health Initiatives

Implementation Steps:

1. Allocate resources to public health initiatives that address the social determinants of health, such as poverty, education, and housing.

2. Promote preventative healthcare services, including vaccinations, screenings, and health education, to reduce long-term healthcare costs.

3. Support mental health initiatives that are accessible to all members of society, particularly the most vulnerable.

46. Developing Resilient Economic Systems

Implementation Steps:

1. Support the development of local economies that are resilient to global market fluctuations and local disasters.

2. Promote economic diversification to reduce dependence on a single industry or employer.

3. Foster the development of cooperatives and social enterprises that prioritize community benefit over profit.

47. Youth Engagement and Leadership

Implementation Steps:

1. Create opportunities for youth to engage in community service and leadership development.

2. Support mentorship programs that connect young people with positive role models and career guidance.

3. Invest in education and extracurricular programs that provide constructive alternatives to involvement in criminal activity.

48. Enhancing Social Capital and Networks

Implementation Steps:

1. Support the development of local organizations and networks that can provide mutual aid and support to community members.

2. Promote initiatives that encourage volunteering and civic engagement as a means to strengthen social ties and community cohesion.

3. Recognize and celebrate the diverse cultural assets and social capital present within communities.

49. Addressing Climate Change and Sustainability

Implementation Steps:

1. Integrate climate change mitigation and adaptation strategies into poverty reduction efforts.

2. Support sustainable practices in agriculture, industry, and urban development to ensure long-term environmental health.

3. Educate communities about the impacts of climate change and the importance of sustainability for future generations.

50. Fostering International Solidarity and Support

Implementation Steps:

1. Promote international solidarity by supporting initiatives that address global poverty and crime.

2. Engage in diplomatic efforts that focus on peacebuilding, conflict resolution, and international development.

3. Collaborate with international organizations to share knowledge, resources, and expertise in addressing social challenges.

The continuation of these efforts requires a holistic and interconnected approach, where the success of one strategy is often linked to the progress of others. Ensuring that these strategies are well-coordinated, adequately funded, and have the backing of a well-informed and engaged public will be vital to their success. It is also crucial to remain adaptable and responsive to emerging challenges, such as new economic trends, technological developments, or global events, while never losing sight of the ultimate goal: creating a just, equitable, and peaceful society for all.

As we delve further into strategies for reducing poverty and crime through social services, it's important to emphasize the need for a comprehensive, multi-sector approach that promotes resilience, inclusivity, and social cohesion. Here are additional strategies that ensure a holistic continuation of efforts:

51. Promoting Financial Inclusion

Implementation Steps:

1. Support initiatives that increase access to banking and credit for underserved populations, such as microfinance institutions and community banks.

2. Encourage the development of financial products tailored to the needs of low-income individuals, such as low-fee accounts and micro-insurance.

3. Implement financial education programs that teach money management, savings, and investment strategies.

52. Nurturing Local Arts and Culture

Implementation Steps:

1. Invest in local arts and cultural programs that enhance community identity and pride.

2. Support local artists and cultural institutions as catalysts for social change and community development.

3. Utilize the arts as a medium for social commentary and a platform for marginalized voices.

53. Facilitating Access to Legal Representation

Implementation Steps:

1. Provide funding for legal aid clinics that offer free or low-cost services to those unable to afford legal representation.

2. Promote pro bono work among legal professionals to increase access to justice for disadvantaged populations.

3. Educate the community about their legal rights and the resources available to help them navigate the legal system.

54. Promoting Sustainable Agriculture and Food Systems

Implementation Steps:

1. Support sustainable farming practices that increase food security while minimizing environmental impact.

2. Invest in local and regional food systems that connect consumers directly with farmers, such as farmers› markets and community-supported agriculture (CSA) programs.

3. Encourage urban agriculture initiatives to reduce food deserts and provide local, fresh produce.

55. Fostering Social Enterprise and Impact Investing

Implementation Steps:

1. Create a favorable regulatory environment for social enterprises that seek to address social issues through business methods.

2. Encourage impact investing, where investors seek not only financial returns but also social and environmental benefits.

3. Provide support and resources for entrepreneurs focused on creating positive social impact.

56. Developing Cross-Sector Data Sharing Initiatives

Implementation Steps:

1. Facilitate data sharing between government agencies, non-profits, and the private sector to inform better policy-making and service provision.

2. Ensure that data sharing respects privacy concerns and is protected against misuse.

3. Utilize shared data to identify trends, predict needs, and evaluate the effectiveness of interventions.

57. Supporting Caregivers and Dependent Populations

Implementation Steps:

1. Provide resources and support for individuals who act as caregivers for the elderly, children, or persons with disabilities.

2. Develop respite care options to alleviate caregiver burden and prevent burnout.

3. Ensure that dependent populations receive adequate care and support to participate fully in society.

58. Building Ethical Supply Chains

Implementation Steps:

1. Promote corporate responsibility by encouraging businesses to adopt ethical supply chain practices that respect worker rights and the environment.

2. Support certification programs that identify products made with fair labor practices.

3. Educate consumers about the impact of their purchasing decisions and how to support ethical businesses.

59. Promoting Diversity and Inclusion in the Workplace

Implementation Steps:

1. Encourage organizations to adopt diversity and inclusion policies that create opportunities for all individuals, regardless of background.

2. Provide diversity training and resources to businesses to help them create inclusive work environments.

3. Recognize and celebrate businesses that demonstrate a commitment to diversity and inclusion.

60. Advancing Public Health Campaigns

Implementation Steps:

1. Launch public health campaigns that address pressing health issues, such as substance abuse, obesity, and mental health.

2. Utilize media and community outreach to educate the public on health risks and prevention strategies.

3. Partner with healthcare providers, schools, and community organizations to amplify the reach and impact of health campaigns.

These strategies, though diverse in nature, share a common thread: they each contribute to the stability and vitality of communities. It's critical to approach these strategies with a sense of partnership and shared responsibility, acknowledging that the well-being of individuals is deeply interconnected with the health of their communities and society at large.

By continuing to innovate, collaborate, and engage with communities, it's possible to build resilient social systems that not only prevent poverty and reduce crime but also enrich lives and foster a sense of shared prosperity. This long-term vision requires patience, dedication, and a relentless commitment to social justice and equity. It is a journey marked by continued learning and adaptation, but one that holds the promise of a more inclusive and harmonious world.

To ensure these strategies are effective, it's important to follow through with a few key principles:

61. Continuous Monitoring and Evaluation

Implementation Steps:

1. Establish clear metrics and benchmarks to measure the progress and impact of social service programs.

2. Regularly collect data and conduct evaluations to assess the effectiveness of interventions and make necessary adjustments.

3. Share results and best practices with stakeholders to improve program design and delivery across the board.

62. Building Capacity within Communities

Implementation Steps:

1. Invest in training and development programs that empower community members to lead and sustain local initiatives.

2. Create mentorship and peer-to-peer learning opportunities to foster skills and knowledge transfer.

3. Support leadership development among youth and marginalized groups to encourage a new generation of social advocates and change-makers.

63. Leveraging Technology for Social Good

Implementation Steps:

1. Utilize digital tools and platforms to enhance service delivery, outreach, and community engagement.

2. Promote technological literacy and access to ensure that all community members can benefit from digital resources.

3. Support social innovation through technology, such as apps for health management or platforms for civic participation.

64. Strengthening Social Safety Nets

Implementation Steps:

1. Ensure that social protection programs are robust, accessible, and responsive to the changing needs of the population.

2. Integrate social services to provide a more comprehensive support system for individuals and families.

3. Advocate for policies that provide a minimum level of security, such as universal health care or a basic income guarantee.

65. Fostering Global Cooperation and Solidarity

Implementation Steps:

1. Engage in international partnerships to learn from and contribute to global efforts to reduce poverty and crime.

2. Support the United Nations Sustainable Development Goals as a framework for creating better social outcomes worldwide.

3. Encourage the exchange of knowledge, resources, and best practices across borders to address common challenges.

The path to reducing poverty and crime through social services is not a linear one. It requires the collective effort of governments, non-profits, businesses, and citizens. It demands that we look beyond immediate concerns to the systemic issues that underlie social inequalities and work to dismantle them. Crucially, it calls for compassion and a recognition of our shared humanity, as we strive to create a society where everyone has the opportunity to live with dignity and hope.

As we implement these strategies, we should remember that progress may be incremental and that setbacks are inevitable. However, each step forward can have a profound impact on the lives of individuals and the fabric of communities. With sustained effort and a collaborative spirit, we can envision and work towards a future that is brighter and more equitable for all.

Certainly, let's proceed with additional strategies and implementation steps to further our understanding of how to reduce poverty and crime through enhanced social services and community development:

66. Enhancing Disaster Preparedness and Response

Implementation Steps:

1. Develop and implement community-based disaster risk reduction programs.

2. Train community members in emergency response techniques and establish local emergency response teams.

3. Create and maintain an inventory of resources and shelters available in the event of a disaster.

67. Promoting Responsible Media Representation

Implementation Steps:

1. Engage with media outlets to emphasize accurate and sensitive reporting on poverty and crime-related issues.

2. Encourage media literacy programs that help community members critically assess media content.

3. Support initiatives that amplify the voices of those living in poverty, rather than just portraying them as victims.

68. Investing in Renewable Energy and Efficiency

Implementation Steps:

1. Provide incentives for the adoption of renewable energy sources in low-income communities.

2. Support energy efficiency upgrades for housing and community facilities to reduce utility costs and improve living conditions.

3. Educate communities on the benefits of energy independence and sustainability.

69. Addressing Systemic Racism and Discrimination

Implementation Steps:

1. Conduct training and workshops on unconscious bias and cultural competence for public servants, educators, and law enforcement.

2. Review and reform policies that disproportionately affect marginalized communities.

3. Create platforms for dialogue and reconciliation to address historical and ongoing injustices.

70. Promoting Mental Health and Wellness

Implementation Steps:

1. Expand access to mental health services, including counseling and crisis support.

2. Integrate mental health awareness into education curricula to destigmatize mental illness.

3. Establish workplace wellness programs that encourage work-life balance and stress management.

71. Supporting Sustainable Transportation Solutions

Implementation Steps:

1. Develop affordable and efficient public transit options to improve access to jobs, education, and services.

2. Promote cycling and walking through safe infrastructure and community programs.

3. Implement car-sharing or bike-sharing programs to reduce transportation costs for low-income individuals.

72. Cultivating Community Leadership

Implementation Steps:

1. Identify and nurture community leaders who can spearhead local initiatives and represent the interests of their communities.

2. Provide platforms for community leaders to share their experiences and insights with a wider audience.

3. Encourage cross-community collaborations to build solidarity and share strategies for community development.

73. Promoting Intergenerational Programs

Implementation Steps:

1. Develop programs that bring together older adults and youth to foster mutual learning and understanding.

2. Leverage the skills and knowledge of older adults to mentor younger generations.

3. Create spaces where intergenerational dialogues can take place, building stronger community ties.

74. Supporting Community Health Workers

Implementation Steps:

1. Invest in training for community health workers to act as liaisons between healthcare providers and the community.

2. Provide community health workers with the tools and resources needed to perform their roles effectively.

3. Recognize and compensate community health workers for their contributions to improving community health outcomes.

75. Strengthening Tenant Rights and Affordable Housing

Implementation Steps:

1. Advocate for policies that protect tenants from unfair eviction and rent hikes.

2. Invest in the creation and maintenance of affordable housing units.

3. Provide legal assistance for tenants to understand and exercise their rights.

The journey to reduce poverty and crime is multifaceted, requiring persistent and diverse approaches that address the root causes and provide support systems for those affected. It involves creating environments where every individual has access to the tools and opportunities needed to thrive. By combining these strategies with the earlier discussed ones, we can continue to build a framework that promotes social well-being, economic stability, and justice for all.

In a small town nestled along the Mississippi Gulf Coast, where the waters gently embraced the shores and the sun painted the skies with crimson and gold at dusk, there lived a young man named Ethan. Ethan's life was not one of idyllic sunsets, however, but rather one shadowed by ignorance and hate.

Ethan grew up in a household where bigotry and racism were as commonplace as the family dinners his mother prepared. His stepfather, a man with a heart embittered by unwarranted superiority, would often refer to his colleagues with racial slurs, stirring the toxic stew of prejudice at every turn. In this environment, Ethan's understanding of the world was sculpted by the coarse hands of intolerance.

Yet, deep within Ethan, there was an ember of curiosity, a spark that longed to know the truth beyond the dark veil of hate. He could feel the wrongness of it all, but the fear of standing alone against the tide of bigotry kept him silent.

One fateful day, Ethan's life took an unexpected turn. Liz, his manager at the fast-food joint where he worked, invited him to a party. Liz was different; she was a beacon of kindness in Ethan's routine life. The catch was that Liz lived in North Gulfport, a part of town where the lines of segregation, though unspoken, were as clear as day.

The journey to Liz's home was a clandestine operation, with Ethan hiding under blankets in the back of a car, just to avoid the spiteful eyes of those who might wish them harm. It was there, at that party, surrounded by faces of every hue and stories from every walk of life, that Ethan felt a warmth he had never known. The music, the laughter, the shared humanity—it was a melody that played on the strings of his soul.

Two days later, when Ethan's stepfather discovered his visit to North Gulfport, rage and threats of violence followed. It was a wake-up call for Ethan, a signal that the time had come to leave the nest of thorns he had grown up in.

On his seventeenth birthday, Ethan made a life-altering decision. He accelerated his education and enlisted in the military, yearning for an escape, for a chance to redefine who he was beyond the confines of his upbringing. The military, with its diverse tapestry of individuals, became Ethan's crucible. There, amidst discipline and unity, Ethan learned the true meaning of brotherhood and respect.

While Ethan's transformation was a testament to his inner strength, his brother, who followed him into the military, emerged unchanged, his heart still shackled by prejudice. It was a stark reminder that change is a personal journey, one that cannot be imposed but must be embraced.

Years passed, and Ethan found joy in inclusivity and in the vibrant tapestry of cultures that painted the world in colors more brilliant than he had ever imagined. He discovered that ignorance was indeed easy, but the pursuit of understanding and acceptance was a far more rewarding challenge. It was not without effort, but it was an effort that nourished the soul.

The moral of Ethan's story resounds with the truth that hate is a legacy that can be broken. It is the easy path, the path of least resistance, to accept the prejudices handed down to us. But it is through courage, through the willingness to expose ourselves to the unknown, to learn and grow, that we can rise above our inherited biases.

The tale of Ethan's journey teaches us that we should not be mere vessels for the flawed beliefs of our predecessors. Instead, we should seek to be the architects of our own character, building bridges where walls once stood. By embracing diversity and striving to understand those around us, we not only enrich our own lives but also pave the way for a world where love and acceptance are the norm, not the exception.

And so, Ethan's story is a beacon to all who find themselves at the crossroads of change. It serves as a reminder that while the road to shedding the heavy cloak of bigotry is fraught with challenges, it is a road that leads to a light-filled destination, where the heart is unburdened, and the spirit is free.

As the years went by, Ethan became a testament to the transformative power of open-mindedness and the willingness to embrace new experiences. His life, once confined to the narrow perspectives of his childhood, now expanded with every person he met and every culture he encountered. He understood that ignorance was not bliss; it was a chain that bound the spirit and blinded the heart to the beauty of diversity.

Ethan became an avid traveler, using his leave from the military to explore the world. He walked through bustling marketplaces in distant lands, tasted spices that danced on his tongue, and listened to the melodies of languages he did not speak. With every journey, his world grew larger, and the prejudices he had been taught as a child seemed increasingly petty and nonsensical.

He also became a mentor to younger service members, sharing with them the lessons of empathy and understanding he had learned. He told them of his own past, not with shame, but with the hope that his story would inspire them to choose a different path, one of compassion and camaraderie.

One day, Ethan received news that his old manager, Liz, the woman who had first opened his eyes to a world beyond hate, had passed away. He returned to his hometown for the funeral, a place he had not set foot in for many years. As he walked the streets of North Gulfport, memories of his youth came flooding back, but they no longer had the power to haunt him. He had outgrown them, just as he had outgrown the hatred that had once threatened to define his life.

At Liz's service, Ethan spoke of how her simple act of kindness, inviting a confused and prejudiced young man to a party, had sparked the change that reshaped his entire life. He spoke of the importance of reaching out, of being that person who might turn a life around with nothing more than an open heart and an open door.

After the service, many approached Ethan, including some of his old acquaintances who had been trapped in the same cycle of bigotry he had once been a part of. They saw in him something they could not quite understand—a peace and a fulfillment that their prejudice had never afforded them.

Ethan's brother, who had come out of the military with his biases intact, also noticed the change in Ethan. It was a silent, gnawing realization that perhaps he, too, had been wrong. In the quiet moments that followed, Ethan's brother began to reflect on his own choices.

The moral of Ethan's continued journey is that the bridges we build can carry more than just ourselves; they can carry the weight of others who stumble upon them, seeking a way out of their own darkness. Ethan's transformation was not a loud proclamation; it was a quiet revolution that unfolded within him and subtly influenced those around him.

Ethan's story is a reminder that change often comes from unexpected places and that the actions of one person can ripple out to touch the lives of many. It is a call to each of us to be the catalyst for that change, to be the light in someone else's darkness, and to never underestimate the power of a single act of kindness.

As the sun set on Liz's funeral that day, casting long shadows over the town that had once been a cradle of hate for Ethan, it also cast a warm glow on the faces of those ready to follow in his footsteps. It was a new dawn, not just for Ethan, but for all those whose hearts and minds his journey had touched. And therein lies the greatest moral of all: In the end, it is love and understanding that truly conquer all.

Ethan's return to his hometown was not just a farewell to Liz; it became a catalyst for a broader conversation within the community. At the reception following the service, he found himself surrounded by young and old, all eager to hear more about his experiences and the insights he had gained.

Among the attendees was a group of high school students who had been studying civil rights and the impact of racism on society. They listened intently as Ethan spoke of his transformation, of the places he had seen, and the people who had broadened his horizons. His story was not just a narrative; it was a living example of the change they had only read about in textbooks.

Ethan's presence and his openness to discuss his past and his growth sparked something within the community. Conversations began to take place in living rooms, in churches, and even in the local diner. People started to question the long-held beliefs that had silently governed their lives. The seeds of change, sown by Ethan's words and by Liz's legacy, began to sprout.

In the weeks and months that followed, the community started to organize events that celebrated diversity. Ethnic food festivals, cultural exchange programs, and dialogues on race relations became more frequent. The town that once lived in the shadow of segregation was now reaching out, learning, and growing.

Ethan's brother, who had been silently wrestling with his own prejudices, slowly began to see the world through a new lens. Inspired by Ethan's example, he started volunteering at a community center, working with children from all walks of life. It was a small step, but a significant one in his journey towards understanding and acceptance.

The moral of this continued story is one of hope and the enduring impact of positive change. It teaches us that the transformation of a single individual can send ripples through an entire community, challenging and ultimately altering the fabric of long-standing prejudices.

Ethan's story also demonstrates the power of humility and the strength that comes from acknowledging past mistakes. By owning his history and using it as a stepping stone to educate others, Ethan transformed his narrative from one of bigotry to one of enlightenment and unity.

Moreover, Ethan's journey emphasizes the importance of leadership through example. He did not preach to others to change; he simply lived the change he wished to see. His actions, not just his words, showed what could be gained from an open heart and mind.

As time went on, Ethan's influence was felt not just in his hometown but in the broader society as well. His experiences were shared in podcasts, interviews, and even in schools, where his story became part of the curriculum that taught empathy, diversity, and the power of self-reflection.

The moral lesson of Ethan's ongoing story is clear: We are all capable of growth, change, and of breaking the cycles of ignorance and hate. It is a lesson that reminds us that no matter our past, we have the power to choose our future. It is a call to action for all of us to embrace diversity, seek understanding, and, most importantly, to never underestimate the profound effect we can have on the world, simply by being an example of love, acceptance, and change.

Years slipped by, and Ethan's influence on his hometown had settled into the fabric of the community like a quiet revolution. The once seldom-visited cultural festivals had become eagerly anticipated annual events, drawing crowds from neighboring towns and counties. The students who had once listened to Ethan speak of his travels and transformation had grown into community leaders, educators, and advocates for equality themselves.

But the true measure of Ethan's impact was most visible in the lives of the individuals he had touched directly. His brother, for instance, now spent his Saturdays coaching a diverse youth soccer team, where he taught the values of teamwork and respect off the field as much as on it. The community center where he volunteered had become a vibrant hub of activity, a safe place where children learned the beauty of their differences as well as their similarities.

Meanwhile, Ethan's narrative had become a beacon of hope for those struggling with their own prejudices. His story was not a tale of overnight transformation, but one of enduring commitment to personal growth and understanding. It was a journey that showed the winding path toward enlightenment is often fraught with challenges and setbacks, but also filled with moments of profound connection and joy.

Ethan eventually decided to write a memoir, recounting his journey from a place of hate to one of inclusion. His book struck a chord with many, becoming a tool for schools, community groups, and even law enforcement agencies to understand and combat bigotry. It was not just a story; it was a roadmap for change.

The moral of Ethan's ongoing saga is multifaceted. It is a testament to the enduring power of love over hate. It reminds us that our actions, big or small, intentional or inadvertent, have the potential to shape the lives of others. Ethan's life taught that education and exposure to different cultures are keys to overcoming ignorance. But perhaps the most powerful lesson was the power of one's own will to become a force for positive change in the world.

As an old man, Ethan would sit on his porch and watch the children of different races and backgrounds playing together in the street. He saw in them the future he had once dared to dream of—one where labels and prejudices were replaced by understanding and friendship.

In reflections to his readers, he penned a simple yet profound truth: "Change starts within. It is a single step taken in the direction of understanding that leads to a thousand miles walked in the shoes of others."

The legacy of Ethan's story is that the path to a better world is walked one step at a time, one person at a time. It is a story that continues to inspire, reminding each of us that we hold the power to rewrite the narratives of our communities and our lives. It teaches us that while we may not be able to change the entire world, we can change the world around us—one mind, one heart, one act of kindness at a time.

As the sun dipped lower in the sky, casting a golden hue across the porch where Ethan sat, his eyes would often search the horizon, reflecting on the long journey his life had been. In the laughter of the children, he found the greatest hope and the confirmation that the seeds of change he had helped to plant were indeed taking root and flourishing.

Ethan's memoir had not only become a beacon for those seeking to escape the grip of bigotry, but it had also sparked a dialogue among those who had never considered the depth of their own latent prejudices. Reading groups and community discussions popped up, using Ethan's story as a starting point to explore their own biases and the structures that upheld them in society.

The town itself had transformed. Where there had once been a silent acceptance of segregation, now there were concerted efforts to build inclusive spaces. The local library, once a place of quiet study, hosted multicultural book clubs and story hours for children in various languages. The schools, which had once taught a narrow version of history, now celebrated the contributions of all peoples to the nation's fabric.

Ethan's porch became a place of pilgrimage for those who had been moved by his words. They came to share their stories of change, to seek his counsel, or simply to thank him for opening their eyes to a different way of life. He welcomed each visitor with a warm smile, always ready to listen, always ready to encourage.

The moral of Ethan's lifelong journey is one that resonates with timeless truth: Change is a continuous process, not a destination. It is an ongoing commitment to learning, to empathy, and to the hard work of self-examination. It reminds us that the most profound transformations often begin quietly, not in the clamor of grand gestures, but in the willingness to listen, learn, and love.

Ethan's story also encapsulates the idea that leadership is not about power or prestige, but about inspiring others to be better than they were. It's about living one's values out loud and leading by example, not by edict. His influence was not the product of authority, but the result of authenticity and the consistent application of his beliefs in daily life.

In his final years, Ethan started a scholarship fund for students from his hometown who aspired to study abroad. He wanted to give others the chance to see the world as he had, to learn that our common humanity is far greater than the things that divide us. He knew that these experiences could transform others just as they had transformed him.

And so, Ethan's story, which began in a place of darkness and hate, became a narrative of hope and light. It is a reminder to all that it is never too late to change, to reach out, to build bridges where once there were only walls. It underscores the idea that our lives are defined not by the hatred we encounter, but by our response to it—not by the ignorance that surrounds us, but by our quest for truth.

As the twilight of his life approached, Ethan knew that his story would not end with him. It would live on in the hearts and minds of those he had touched, in the community that had transformed, and in the legacy of the scholarship that bore his name. His journey was a testament to the power of one person to make a difference and a call to action for others to do the same.

The moral of Ethan's story is clear: Each of us has the capacity to be a catalyst for positive change. It is through our daily choices, our willingness to confront our own prejudices, and our relentless pursuit of justice and equality that we leave our mark on the world. It is a story that continues, as long as there are those who are inspired to pick up the mantle and continue the work that Ethan and many like him have begun—a never-ending story of hope, change, and the indomitable spirit of love.

This article is accurate; however, I would like to point out that this happens to almost everyone that ends up in the system and has no money to defend themselves.

They Invented This Cruel Plan To Keep People Enslaved.

You might already know about the loophole in the 13th Amendment that allowed slavery. But did you know there's a loophole and THAT loophole is still being used today? And, as always, it's used to brutalize and exploit Black people the most.

Centuries ago, the 13th Amendment abolished slavery – with a few loopholes. The Constitution made it so enslavement could still be legal through incarceration. But there was another hidden loophole, and THAT loophole is still being abused today.

The 13th Amendment allowed slavery for people imprisoned – specifically after due process. So, Southern officials wondered, "How do you convict, incarcerate, and exploit more Black people without a fair trial?"

Their answer was the "plea bargain," where a prosecutor can offer you less time behind bars in exchange for you admitting guilt – whether you did it or not!

Another incentive to pleading "guilty" was financial; following through with a trial was expensive for Black defendants. Plea bargaining ensured that more Black people could be trapped behind bars, so states made substantial financial gains off of Black imprisoned field laborers, too.

Today, over 97% of federal felony convictions and 94% of state convictions are made because of plea bargaining. Only 2% of federal prosecutions end up going to trial!

There's no such thing as honesty or fairness in this criminal legal system, especially not for Black people. The system incentivizes us NOT to tell the truth but to choose between "less" and "more" prison – instead of no prison time at all. History backs us up when we ask, "What kind of freedom is that?"

Why It's Time for Churches and Religious Institutions to Contribute Their Fair Share

As our society strives for fairness and equality, we must address a significant inequity in our tax system: the tax-exempt status of churches and religious institutions. With religious organizations in the United States generating upwards of $1.2 trillion in revenue each year, it's time to re-evaluate their role in our fiscal framework. Here's why these institutions should contribute to our tax base:

1. Economic Power, Fiscal Responsibility:

The sheer scale of the economic activity of religious organizations suggests they have the capacity to support the common good through taxation. Their contributions could help to fund essential services and infrastructure, alleviating the tax burden on individuals and secular businesses.

2. Upholding Fairness:

Tax exemptions for religious institutions create an uneven playing field. Other non-profit organizations and businesses contribute to our tax revenues, and so should religious entities that benefit from the same public goods.

3. Ensuring Transparency:

Taxation would require religious institutions to adhere to the same financial disclosure rules as other entities, fostering an environment of greater transparency and accountability in how they manage and utilize their significant funds.

4. Aligning with Public Benefit:

Taxing religious institutions would encourage them to demonstrate the public benefit of their activities more clearly. This would align their tax-exempt status with a measurable impact on the community, in line with other non-profit organizations.

5. Respecting the Separation of Church and State:

Tax exemptions can be seen as a form of government endorsement of religion. By taxing religious institutions, we reinforce the principle of separation of church and state, ensuring that no religious group is unduly favored by the government.

6. Market Competitiveness:

Religious institutions often engage in activities similar to those of for-profit businesses. Taxing them prevents an unfair advantage and ensures all entities that benefit from the economy contribute to its maintenance.

7. Accountability to the Public:

The vast revenues of religious organizations mean their decisions can significantly impact society. Taxation represents a form of financial accountability, ensuring they contribute to the welfare of the communities that support them.

It's not about hindering religious freedom or practices; it's about economic justice, transparency, and equitable contribution to our society. Taxing religious institutions is a step towards ensuring that every entity, regardless of its mission, contributes its fair share to the flourishing of our communities. As we reflect on the values that define us as a nation, let's consider the role that every organization, including religious ones, should play in supporting the societal fabric that benefits us all.

Consistently being late sends negative messages to others about your time management skills and respect for their time.

It creates the perception that you value your time more than that of others and that you may not prioritize the commitments you make.

Being punctual is a sign of respect for others and can help establish trust and credibility in professional and personal relationships. It shows that you are reliable, organized, and considerate of other people's schedules.

By making an effort to be more punctual, you can demonstrate respect for others and enhance your reputation as a dependable and considerate individual.

My dad has always said there is never an excuse for being late.

Other People and their time are just as important as your time is to you. If you have any doubt you may be late leave early enough to change a tire and be on time.

My dad's perspective is one that places a high value on punctuality and respect for others' time.

His view is rooted in personal responsibility and consideration for others, and it reflects a strong work and social ethic and sense of integrity.

Here are a few reasons why his philosophy is beneficial and widely respected:

Respect for Others:

By prioritizing punctuality, my dad was showing that he values other people's time as much as his own.

This consideration is fundamental to building trust and maintaining good relationships, both personally and professionally.

Reliability:

Being consistently on time is a sign of reliability. It indicates that you are someone who can be counted on to fulfill obligations and commitments.

Professionalism:

In the workplace, punctuality is often equated with professionalism. Being on time for meetings, appointments, and work shifts is essential for smooth operations and shows dedication to one's role.

Preparedness:

Planning to arrive early enough to account for unexpected delays, like changing a tire, demonstrates foresight and preparedness.

It shows that you have thought ahead about potential obstacles and have taken steps to mitigate them.

Reputation:

Your punctuality can positively affect how others perceive you.

It can enhance your reputation as someone who is organized, thoughtful, and respectful.

Stress Reduction:

Being late can cause stress for both the person who is late and those who are affected by the tardiness.

Planning to be on time, or even early, can reduce this stress and lead to a more peaceful and productive environment.

Fairness:

When everyone makes an effort to be on time, it creates an environment of fairness where no one's time is considered more or less important than anyone else's.

Positive Example:

By valuing punctuality, my dad set a positive example for others, potentially influencing them to also consider the importance of being on time.

In many cultures, punctuality is a virtue and is expected in social and professional settings.

Of course, unexpected situations can arise, but the general principle is to plan ahead to mitigate these potential issues as much as possible.

When delays are truly unavoidable, it's considered courteous to notify those waiting as soon as possible.

By instilling the value of punctuality, my dad was teaching a lesson in personal accountability and respect for others—a lesson that often serves people well in all aspects of their lives.

_____

I hear people say that men are gay because they were sexually abused. I say they are wrong men growing up were a used because they are gay.

He was born a very poor white boy, some even use the word trash when describing him. The home he lived in was a small two-bedroom that housed 9 people, his parents, three of his grandparents, and 3 siblings.

He only had one friend while they lived there. He and his friend were inseparable and even got themselves into trouble at the same time. They even started kindergarten together. At the end of the school year his parents moved them a couple of hours away, into a trailer out in the country.

He thought he would never talk or see his best friend again. The funny thing is they are both in their senior years and even though they haven't seen each other in decades they still talk at least once a year.

Anyway even though the boy was poor, white and considered trash he was happy and enjoyed his life. That was until the move.

The move changed it all. First he had no friends and couldn't seem to make any. However, his older sister fell for a older boy down the street.

He pretended to be his friend so he would be invited to stay the night.

One night the older boy talked and manipulated the little boy, who was in the 1st grade, by the selling him it was normal into playing with his private parts. Next it turned into the boy talking the 1st grader into putting it in his mouth.

The little boy thought that was the end of it. That was until that Monday when he went to school. That was when he found out the older boy and told everyone. He was taunted, teased and bullied everywhere he went.

He loved school but didn't want to go back but no one would listen to him. So his remedy was that when his parents left for work he would fane an illness so he could stay home.

all the kids got home before their parents so he thought they would never know.

So he couldn't be more wrong! His mother came home early that day. She stopped at the neighbor up the street to pick up his little brother, they watched him since he was to young for ischool.

Anyway when she showed up she also found the little boy there. She picked him up as well and she acted though everything was okay. Well at lease she acted that way until they walked into the little boys home. The mother beganbeating him and when he tried to explain what happened and that he was being teased she beat him harder for not being a man and for embarrassing her.

Finally the beating and the screaming at him stopped and he thought it was over.

That was far from the truth. Instead when it was time for the bus to drop the neighborhood kids off, they all took one bus 1st-12th grade, there was just one stop for the neighborhood and the little boy's house was the first one you walked past when going home.
So the mother grabbed the boy and dressed him in nothing but a cloth diaper, gave him a bottle, and made him sit in a chair in the front yard so the kids could make fun of him.

Needless to say that from that day on the little boy prayed for death.

Soon after that his parents separated and the mother moved her and the kids away. He was happy because he thought he would finally escape the teasing because of the older boy and the diaper. We was far from wrong because every school he attended the little brother told the diaper story and he still does even though he is almost sixty. The mother was so proud of herself of how she disciplined the little boy she would tell every new friend.

However the mother stopped telling the story when the little boy turned 30. She started to tell the story and he stood up and told her how ever since that incident he had to tried to commit suicide multiple times.

In the saga of the little boy next when he was 10 his mother moved him and his little brother to Mississippi from Texas. She immediately married a very abusive man that was over 30 years older than her. This is when his nightmare truly began between the verbal and physical abuse it would even get worse when he was to meet his teenage years.

Until then let us see what started when he was eleven. The little boys mother had made friends with the woman that always took care of his moms hair.

The woman had a teenage son that attended military boarding school. According to my and his mother when he would come home from school he had no friends.

So the little boy's mother made arrangements for the boy to stay at their house when he was home from school. The first couple of days were great, the little boy was poor but he got to do things there he only dreamed of.

By the end of the first week, that's when the sexual abuse started and it didn't end until he was 14.

There was another incident that took place when he stayed at his friend's house down the street. Their older brother thought he was asleep and began to have his way. The little boy just pretended he was asleep until it was over.

At 16 the stepfather decided that he would move his abuse from verbal and physical abuse into the sexual abuse arena.

That was when the boy had enough finished school, joined the military, and left home. He thought finally it ended.

Nope, it had to happen one more time. While in the services the little boy was raped again. This time it was different it was violent and physically abusive and he feared he would not survive it.

He did and to this day he is still a survivor.

_____

Okay, let me try this again so maybe the MAGA Trumper Cult can understand.

A $5 apple is a $5 apple because people have the money and are willing to pay $5 for the apple.

If no one had the money to buy a $5 apple the $5 apple would be a $1 apple.

You're willing to boycott Bud Light because they gave a special can of beer to a trans person.

So why don't you do something useful and boycott companies that are price gouging. If they can't get their overpriced products off of the shelf the prices will go down.

High Prices Are Due To Corporate Greed.

Unfortunately, Price Gouging Laws Are Only Enforceable Just Before, During And After A Natural Disaster.

_____

Let's talk about why people from all over the world are coming to live in the U.S. can actually be a good thing for all of us.

Think about it this way:

Our country is like a big team. And just like any team, to win, you need all sorts of players. Some are great at scoring goals, others are amazing at defense, and some have the energy that keeps everyone going. Immigrants are like new teammates. They bring skills and talents that can help the whole team succeed.

Now, some people worry that these new teammates might change how the team feels, or that there might not be enough room or resources for everyone. But history has shown us time and again that adding more players to the team doesn't mean there's less to go around. In fact, it usually means we can do more, build more, and achieve more.

As for our team feeling different, that's something that's been happening since the start of the game.

Teams evolve:

Remember, unless you're Native American, your ancestors were new players at some point, too. Embracing new folks doesn't mean losing who we are; it means growing stronger and more diverse.

About the idea of freedom that we're all proud of:

Real freedom means giving everyone a fair shot, no matter what they look like or where they come from. If we shut people out just because they're different, that's not freedom; that's playing the game with one hand tied behind our back.

Look at our friends across the ocean in Europe. Over there, they've got a bunch of countries acting like neighbors, letting folks move around to work and live without lots of red tape. It's not a perfect system, and they've got their own issues, sure. But they're trying to work together to make sure everyone gets a chance to contribute.

At the end of the day, whether we're talking about your neighborhood, school, workplace, or country, being inclusive and welcoming isn't just the nice thing to do it's the smart thing to do.

It helps everyone out. So when we hear folks talking about keeping people out because of where they're from or what they look like, remember that it's like turning away a star player who could help the whole team win.

Let's not let fear call the shots. Instead, let's play the game the way it's supposed to be played: together, as a team, with open arms and a fair chance for all.

Think about your family, your friends, or your community. Everyone has something unique to bring to the table. Your buddy might be the go-to person for fixing cars.

Your aunt might make the best pie in town. Every person adds value in their own way, and it's no different when it comes to people moving here from other countries.

These folks often come ready to work hard, to open businesses, and to share their culture and cuisine ever enjoyed a taco, sushi, or pizza?

That's all thanks to the mix of cultures we have here. They also pay taxes, which help build roads, schools, and hospitals, and sometimes they take jobs that are hard to fill, keeping our economy moving.

Let's not forget that America's always been about giving people a chance to make something of themselves. "The American Dream," right? It's not about where you start; it's about where you're going. Blocking people out because they're from somewhere else goes against that whole idea.

Now, security is important. We lock our doors at night, not because we hate what's outside, but because we want to keep our homes safe. Same thing for our country – it's not about being unwelcoming, but about making sure that the process is done right. That's why we can have strong borders and still open our arms to new folks at the same time. It's not one or the other.

So next time you hear someone saying, "We're full," or "They're not like us," just remember the sports team, your car-fixing buddy, and the best pie you ever had. Remember that most of us wouldn't be here if it weren't for someone taking a chance and coming to America, maybe not even speaking the language at first but having a whole lot of hope and ready to work hard.

We've got a big, beautiful country here, with room to grow and succeed together. Let's not sell ourselves short by being scared of change. Let's be the country that really lives up to that Statue of Liberty promise – give me your tired, your poor, your huddled masses yearning to breathe free.

We can be safe and still be the land of opportunity – for everyone. That's what being free really means. That's what made us great in the first place. Let's keep that spirit alive.

You know, sometimes change can be scary. We get used to how things are, and new faces, new languages, they can seem overwhelming. But think about this – every time a new group has come into this country, they've stirred up the pot a bit, sure, but they've also made it richer. They're like the secret ingredient in the melting pot that makes the flavor pop.

Our country's like a giant patchwork quilt – every piece is different, with its own pattern and color, but when you step back, you see it all comes together into something beautiful. That's what diversity is all about. It's not just a nice word; it's the real strength behind who we are.

Look at our music, our sports, our food – they're all better because of the different influences that come into play. Jazz, blues, rock 'n' roll, hip-hop – they all have roots in different communities and have touched millions of lives. And it's not just about entertainment. Immigrants have been behind some of the biggest innovations and companies in our history, making our lives better and creating jobs.

But I get it, it's not all perfect. There are challenges, like making sure everyone gets along and respects the law. And that's why we have a system in place. It needs work, for sure. We need to fix the way we do things so that it's fair and makes sense – so that it's not too easy or too hard to come here and contribute.

We've got to remember that at the end of the day, whether someone's family came over on the Mayflower, flew in from across the world, or crossed a border, they're here now, and they're part of our community. We can't turn back time, but we can look forward and figure out how to make it work for everyone.

So instead of drawing lines in the sand and saying "us versus them," let's try "us and them." Let's have conversations, even when they're hard. Let's listen to each other's stories and learn from them. Let's remember that a lot of people are just looking for safety, for opportunity, just like our own families did once upon a time.

And for those who are worried about culture changing – culture is always changing, and that's not a bad thing. It's alive, it's dynamic, it's what keeps things interesting. Think about how boring it would be if every day was exactly the same. Our culture is strong, and it's at its best when it's inclusive.

So, let's work together to keep our home safe, to keep it prosperous, and to keep it welcoming. That's the challenge we've got, but it's one we can meet if we remember that we're all in this together. Let's not close the door on what's made us great. Let's build on it, and let's do it in a way that keeps that spirit of opportunity alive for everyone who's got something to contribute.

That's the American way – the way of progress, the way of hope, and the way of a brighter future for all of us, together.

TODD EMERSON

I Believe I Understand Why People Are Bigots And Racist.

It's because it's easy! Ignorance is easy.

Taking the way you think as fact. Just because you thought it that makes it true.

You don't have to learn any nationalities cultures. You don't have to try to understand people with different views.

The only effort you have to put into being a bigot and racist boils down to just reinforcing your belief that you are superior.

Hear me out. I grew up in a racist and bigoted family after my mom divorced my dad and married my stepdad.

My step dad called everyone he worked with and associated with by the N-Word followed by their first name. To him and the people around him took that as normal. Or at least no one spoke up saying it was wrong.

So all of his beliefs, prejudices, bigotry and racism was drummed into our heads as we grew up. I was even as a teenager verbally gay bashing the men and women going in or coming out of the one and only gay bar on the Mississippi Gulf Coast. I was 16 when I was working at a fast food place when my Manger Liz, I will never forget her name, said she was throwing a party at her house after we closed if I wanted to come. I jumped at the chance.

The only hurdle was that she lived in North Gulfport and at that time our city was still segregated, so we had to make sure no white people seen me going into her side of town and she had to make sure she wasn't caught with me. So I laid on the back floorboard covered in blankets.

2 days later my step parent found out and I thought he was going to kill us both.

The man was such a horrible person that the day I turned 17 I told my mother I was going to accelerate my education and graduate that summer and join the military to get away.

I hear people today talking about the military but if it wasn't for the military I would probably be a closeted gay skinhead.

Of course, my brother entered the military as well and he came out even more prejudiced than he went in.

I am much happier being inclusive and I'm even more content the more I get involved in learning more customs.

———————

Imagine a world where every single individual, without exception, embarks on a journey of personal mental health therapy. In this utopian vision, the pervasive shadows of hatred, anger, racism, and prejudice begin to dissipate, making way for a brighter, more empathetic society.

The truth is, each one of us can benefit immensely from the transformative power of therapy. It offers a safe space to unravel the intricacies of our minds, confront our inner demons, and cultivate essential coping mechanisms that pave the way for a harmonious and fulfilling existence.

As we navigate the complexities of life, we often find ourselves ill-equipped to deal with the myriad challenges that come our way. The skills necessary for navigating relationships, managing stress, and fostering emotional well-being are not always innate; they must be nurtured and honed over time. Therapy serves as a vital resource in this regard, providing us with the guidance and tools needed to navigate the labyrinth of our emotions and experiences.

By engaging in therapy, we open ourselves up to a world of self-discovery and growth. We learn to confront our vulnerabilities, confront our biases, and cultivate a deeper understanding of ourselves and others. Through this process, we not only heal our own wounds but also contribute to the healing of our communities and society at large.

So, I implore you to consider the profound impact that personal mental health therapy can have on your life and the world around you. Embrace this opportunity for self-reflection and growth, and take the first step towards a brighter future—one where compassion, understanding, and harmony reign supreme.

In the realm of existential contemplation, individuals are confronted with a fundamental dichotomy:

The choice between mere existence and the profound act of living.

Merely existing entails a self-absorbed state where one's focus remains inward, fixated solely on personal contentment.

However, those who traverse this path often discover that true happiness eludes them, manifesting only as fleeting moments of euphoria.

Contrastingly, to truly live is to transcend the confines of self-centeredness and embrace a broader perspective that incorporates the well-being of others.

Genuine happiness, it seems, is intricately intertwined with the capacity to spread joy among those around us.

This interconnectedness of happiness is vividly illustrated in social settings, where the collective mood of a group can profoundly influence individual experiences.

A night out with four friends serves as a poignant example:

When all revel in happiness and camaraderie, each individual is uplifted and enriched by the shared joy.

Conversely, should even a single member of the group languish in unhappiness, the collective harmony is disrupted, casting a shadow over the entire gathering.

Thus, in the intricate tapestry of human existence, the pursuit of happiness is not a solitary endeavor but a communal voyage.

By embracing the happiness of others, we illuminate our path toward a more prosperous, more meaningful life.

A life not merely of existence but of vibrant, interconnected living.

Voting for pro-choice bills and candidates who support reproductive rights can have several potential benefits for the nation as a whole. Here are some arguments in favor of how supporting pro-choice policies can benefit society:

1. Promoting Women's Health and Well-being:

Access to safe and legal abortion services is essential for protecting women's health and well-being. By supporting pro-choice bills and policies, we can ensure that women have the ability to make informed decisions about their reproductive health, access essential healthcare services, and receive necessary medical care without facing unnecessary barriers.

2. Reducing Maternal Mortality and Health Disparities:

Ensuring access to reproductive healthcare, including abortion services, can help reduce maternal mortality rates and address health disparities that disproportionately affect marginalized communities. Pro-choice policies can promote preventive care, early intervention, and comprehensive healthcare services that benefit women across socioeconomic and demographic backgrounds.

3. Empowering Individuals and Families:

Supporting pro-choice legislation empowers individuals to make decisions about their own bodies, families, and futures. By upholding reproductive rights and autonomy, we foster a culture of self-determination, personal agency, and equality that benefits individuals, families, and society as a whole.

4.Economic Benefits:

Access to reproductive healthcare, including contraception and abortion services, can have positive economic impacts by enabling individuals to plan and space their pregnancies, pursue educational and career opportunities, and achieve financial stability. Pro-choice policies can contribute to workforce participation, economic productivity, and the overall well-being of families.

5. Public Health Outcomes:

Pro-choice measures can have positive public health outcomes by reducing the incidence of unsafe abortions, preventing unintended pregnancies, and promoting reproductive health education and services. By supporting policies that prioritize public health and preventive care, we can improve health outcomes and reduce healthcare costs for individuals and society.

Respecting Diverse Perspectives:

Voting for pro-choice bills and candidates acknowledges the diversity of beliefs, values, and experiences within society. By supporting reproductive rights and choices, we demonstrate a commitment to tolerance, respect, and inclusivity that fosters social cohesion and mutual understanding among individuals with differing viewpoints.

Voting for pro-choice bills and individuals can benefit the nation by promoting women's health, reducing disparities, empowering individuals, spurring economic growth, improving public health, and fostering a culture of respect and inclusivity. Supporting reproductive rights is not only a matter of individual liberty but also a way to advance the well-being and prosperity of society as a whole.

"During July, avoid your doctor, clinic, and hospital if the word University is in their name or if they are used as a teaching facility"

This advice is based on the academic calendar in certain countries where medical universities or teaching hospitals have a major turnover of staff, students, or interns during the month of July. Let's break down the reasons why this advice is given:

Transition Period

July is often the month when medical training programs start or end in many academic institutions.

This turnover can lead to a higher number of inexperienced staff, including new medical residents, interns, and students starting their rotations.

This transition period could potentially impact the quality and continuity of care provided to patients.

Inexperienced Staff

With new medical professionals starting their training or rotations in July, there may be a higher likelihood of errors or miscommunications in patient care.

Inexperienced staff members may not have the same level of expertise or familiarity with hospital protocols as more seasoned professionals.

Reduced Staffing Levels

During the transition period, senior staff members may be busy training new recruits or overseeing the transition process, leading to potential understaffing or increased workload for the existing staff.

This can affect the quality of patient care and may result in longer wait times or rushed consultations.

Focus on Teaching

Teaching hospitals and university-affiliated medical facilities prioritize education and training, which could sometimes take precedence over patient care, especially during the transition period when new students are getting oriented.

This might lead to a less patient-centric approach during this time.

Higher Risk of Mistakes

Studies have shown that there may be a slight increase in medical errors and adverse events during the transition period when new medical professionals are starting their training.

Patients might be at a slightly higher risk of experiencing medical complications or errors during this time.

Unraveling Myths and Facts in U.S. Policy Debates

Introduction

Policy debates in the United States are often clouded by myths and misconceptions that can distract from the real issues at hand. By laying out some of the most common myths alongside the facts, we aim to provide a clearer picture of the state of affairs on pressing topics such as gun control, abortion, the death penalty, and more. This structured approach offers a fact-checked foundation for informed dialogue and policy-making.

Gun Control and Violence

Myth: Guns don't kill people. People kill people.
Fact: Firearms significantly increase the lethality of violent incidents. The U.S. has a much higher gun homicide rate compared to other

high-income countries, indicating that gun availability is a key factor in the prevalence of gun-related deaths.

Active Shooter Drills and School Safety

Myth: Regular active shooter drills are the best method to prepare students for potential school shootings.
Fact: While preparedness is important, active shooter drills can cause psychological harm without clear evidence of their effectiveness. Alternative safety measures that do not induce trauma should be considered, including robust mental health services, secure school environments, and preventive programs.

Myth: The only way to stop a bad guy with a gun is a good guy with a gun.
Fact: More guns do not necessarily lead to increased safety. Countries with higher rates of gun ownership do not inherently have lower crime rates. Instead, a combination of responsible gun ownership, effective gun safety laws, and community intervention strategies are needed to reduce gun violence.

Myth: Arming teachers will keep our kids safer in schools.
Fact: Introducing guns into schools increases the risk of accidental or intentional shootings. Safety experts recommend other measures such as threat assessment programs and gun safety laws to protect students and staff.

Domestic Violence and Gun Ownership

Myth: Federal law prohibits all domestic abusers from having guns.
Fact: Current federal law does not cover all individuals who may be involved in domestic violence, such as dating partners not living with the victim. This gap suggests a need for more comprehensive legislation to protect potential victims of domestic abuse.

Shoot First Laws and Racial Disparities

Myth: Shoot First laws provide everyone an equal right to self-defense.
Fact: Stand Your Ground laws have been shown to be applied in a racially disparate manner. Cases with white shooters and Black victims are more frequently deemed justifiable than when the shooter is Black and the victim is white, which raises serious concerns about equality under the law and racial bias.

Gun Ownership and Background Checks

Myth: Everyone already has to get a background check when buying a gun.
Fact: Federal law does not require background checks for all gun sales, particularly those conducted by private sellers, at gun shows, or online. This loophole allows numerous gun transactions to occur without background checks, potentially putting firearms in the hands of people who are legally prohibited from owning them.

Gun Violence and Its Disproportionate Impact

Myth: Gun violence affects Black and white people in the U.S. equally.
Fact: Gun violence disproportionately affects Black communities. Black Americans are more likely to be victims of gun homicides, gun assaults, and fatal police shootings than their white counterparts, highlighting the need for targeted interventions to address these disparities.

Equality in Self-Defense Legislation

Myth: Shoot First laws ensure a fair and equitable application of self-defense for all.
Fact: Data shows that racial bias can permeate the application of Shoot First laws, leading to disparities in legal outcomes. These laws can be applied disproportionately to the detriment of minority communities, suggesting a need for reevaluation to ensure justice is served fairly regardless of race.

Red Flag Laws and Due Process

Myth: Red Flag laws take guns from people without due process.
Fact: Red Flag laws, or Extreme Risk Protection Orders, are designed with due process in mind, requiring evidence and a court hearing before firearms can be temporarily removed from individuals deemed a risk.

Abortion Policies and Outcomes

Myth: Anti-abortion (Pro-Life) laws save millions of babies' lives.
Fact: Restrictive abortion laws do not necessarily lead to lower abortion rates. Instead, they can result in unsafe, unregulated procedures that put women's lives at risk.

Myth: Criminalizing abortions will stop abortions.
Fact: Making abortion illegal does not eliminate the need for the procedure; it simply makes it more dangerous by driving it underground, particularly affecting disadvantaged women who cannot access safe services.

Myth: Anti-abortion laws protect everyone from the baby to the doctor.
Fact: Restrictive abortion laws can prevent healthcare providers from offering essential care and discourage women from seeking post-abortion care due to fear of legal consequences.

Myth: Pro-life policies are unequivocally supportive of child welfare.
Fact: States with stringent anti-abortion measures often lack comprehensive support systems for children, as evidenced by high rates of child poverty, food insecurity, and poor health outcomes.

Child Well-Being and Pro-Birth Versus Pro-Child Policies

Myth: Pro-Life states are committed to the well-being of every child.
Fact: Examination of child well-being indicators in states with strict anti-abortion laws often reveals higher rates of child poverty, food insecurity, and health problems compared to national averages. This

disconnect suggests that a truly pro-child approach would involve broader social support policies that extend beyond the issue of abortion.

Food Insecurity and Abortion-Restrictive States

Myth: States with strict anti-abortion laws ensure that children have adequate nutrition and care.
Fact: Many states with tight restrictions on abortion have significant levels of food insecurity among households with children. Policies in these states do not always reflect a comprehensive approach to supporting families, which would include addressing the basic needs of children and ensuring their access to sufficient and nutritious food.

The Broader Context of Pro-Life Advocacy

Myth: Pro-Life advocacy consistently supports the welfare of both born and unborn children.
Fact: To truly support children's welfare, policy measures must extend beyond the womb. This includes providing robust healthcare, education, and economic support to families. In many states with strict abortion laws, the lack of social support for children post-birth indicates that pro-life policies could be more comprehensive.

Women's Health and Abortion Legislation

Myth: Restrictive abortion laws unequivocally safeguard women's health.
Fact: By limiting access to safe and legal abortion services, restrictive laws can endanger women's health, forcing them to seek unsafe alternatives. These laws also hinder healthcare providers from offering a full spectrum of reproductive services, which can include necessary and sometimes life-saving care.

Border Security and Crime Rates

Myth: Unsecured borders kill millions of people.
Fact: Analysis of crime statistics has demonstrated that border cities tend to have lower crime rates than the national average, challenging the notion that less secure borders lead to more domestic crime.

The Death Penalty

Myth: The death penalty deters crime.
Fact: There is no conclusive evidence that capital punishment effectively deters crime. Countries that have abolished the death penalty, like Canada, have seen a decrease in murder rates, suggesting that other factors contribute to crime reduction.

Myth: The death penalty is cost-effective for taxpayers.
Fact: The costs associated with the death penalty, including legal proceedings and maintaining death row facilities, are significantly higher than life imprisonment without parole, making it a less economically viable option for the state.

Conclusion

In the quest for effective policy solutions, it's paramount that we ground our discussions in fact rather than fiction. The myths debunked here often stem from deeply held beliefs or misconceptions, but they fail to stand up to scrutiny when compared to the data and evidence available. As we continue to debate and shape the policies that govern our society, let's commit to informed discourse, compassionate consideration of all viewpoints, and policies that reflect the complexities and needs of our diverse population.

———————————

Shoot First Laws and Racial Disparities

Myth: Shoot First laws provide everyone an equal right to self-defense.
Fact: Stand Your Ground laws have been shown to be applied in a racially disparate manner. Cases with white shooters and Black victims are more frequently deemed justifiable than when the shooter is Black and the victim is white, which raises serious concerns about equality under the law and racial bias.

Gun Ownership and Background Checks

Myth: Everyone already has to get a background check when buying a gun.
Fact: Federal law does not require background checks for all gun sales, particularly those conducted by private sellers, at gun shows, or online. This loophole allows numerous gun transactions to occur without background checks, potentially putting firearms in the hands of people who are legally prohibited from owning them.

Gun Violence and Its Disproportionate Impact

Myth: Gun violence affects Black and white people in the U.S. equally.
Fact: Gun violence disproportionately affects Black communities. Black Americans are more likely to be victims of gun homicides, gun assaults, and fatal police shootings than their white counterparts, highlighting the need for targeted interventions to address these disparities.

Child Well-Being and Pro-Birth Versus Pro-Child Policies

Myth: Pro-Life states are committed to the well-being of every child.
Fact: Examination of child well-being indicators in states with strict anti-abortion laws often reveals higher rates of child poverty, food insecurity, and health problems compared to national averages. This disconnect suggests that a truly pro-child approach would involve broader social support policies that extend beyond the issue of abortion.

Food Insecurity and Abortion-Restrictive States

Myth: States with strict anti-abortion laws ensure that children have adequate nutrition and care.

Fact: Many states with tight restrictions on abortion have significant levels of food insecurity among households with children. Policies in these states do not always reflect a comprehensive approach to supporting families, which would include addressing the basic needs of children and ensuring their access to sufficient and nutritious food.

The myths and facts addressed across these policy domains reveal the complexity and nuance required in policymaking. Effective policy must be based on credible evidence, consider the lived experiences of those affected, and strive for equitable outcomes. As citizens and policymakers engage with these issues, it remains crucial to challenge misconceptions and advocate for policies that are informed by reality and promote the well-being of all members of society. Only through a commitment to truth, justice, and comprehensive support can we hope to build a more equitable and just nation.

REPUBLICAN FICTION POINTS VERSUS REAL-LIFE FACTS

FICTION: Federal law prohibits all domestic abusers from having guns.

FACT: Federal law does not prohibit current or recent former dating partners subject to a domestic violence restraining order from purchasing or possessing guns.

FICTION: Anti-Abortion (Pro—Life) Laws Saves Millions Of Baby's Lives.

FACT: The abortion rate is higher in anti-abortion areas. 37 per 1,000 people in states that prohibit abortion altogether or allow it only in instances to save a woman's life, and 34 per 1,000 people in states that broadly allow for abortion, a difference that is not statistically significant.

Fiction: Guns don't kill people. People kill people.

FACT: People with guns kill people, and more efficiently than people without guns. The U.S. gun homicide rate is 26x higher than that of other high-income countries.

FICTION: Criminals will always find a way to get their hands on a gun.

FACT: Laws like <u>background checks</u> stop gun sales to criminals every day. Since 1994, these laws have blocked <u>more than 4 million</u> gun sales to people who could not legally own guns.

FICTION: Unsecured borders kill millions of people.

FACT: A recent analysis of 2019 FBI Crime statistics <u>by Axios</u> <u>confirmed this fact</u> - border cities have among the lowest violent crime and property crime rates per capita in the country. Their analysis of 11 border cities showed that on average these communities had a lower violent crime rate than the national average for 2019 (338.5 compared to 366.7 per 100,000 people). Cities of comparable populations and demographics in the interior of the country were shown to have much higher crime rates in some cases. For some cities such as El Paso, violent crime rates have <u>been on decline since 1993</u>.

FICTION: The only way to stop a bad guy with a gun is a good guy with a gun.

FACT: If more guns everywhere made us safer, America would be the safest country on earth. Instead, we have a gun homicide rate 26x that of other high-income countries.

FICTION: Death Penalty Deters Crime

FACT: Evidence from around the world has shown that the death penalty has no unique deterrent effect on crime.

In 2003 in Canada, 27 years after the country abolished the death penalty the murder rate had fallen by 44 per cent since 1975, when capital punishment was still enforced.

Far from making society safer, the death penalty has been shown to have a brutalizing effect on society.

State-sanctioned killings only serve to encourage the use of force and murder by its constituents.

FICTION: Arming teachers will keep our kids safer in schools.

Fact: <u>Arming teachers</u> ignores research that shows the presence of a gun increases the risks posed to children and teachers. School safety experts and law enforcement oppose arming teachers.

FICTION: We don't own guns, so I don't need to worry about my kids getting hold of one.

FACT: 4.6 million U.S. children live in a household with at least one <u>loaded, unsecured gun</u>. <u>Children and teens</u> access guns in homes other than their own.

FICTION: Death Penalty Saves Tax Payers Money.

FACT: The State Spend At Least 10 Times More On One Death Penalty Prisoner Than On One Person Sentenced To Life.

At One Point Maryland Spent $186 million on 5 executions.

Fiction: Everyone already has to get a background check when buying a gun.

Fact: Federal law only requires licensed dealers to perform <u>background checks</u>. That means that millions of guns are bought and sold by unlicensed sellers each year without one—often <u>online</u> or at gun shows.

FICTION: **Criminalising abortions will stop abortions.**

FACT: Preventing women and girls from accessing an abortion does not mean they stop needing one. That's why attempts to ban or restrict abortions do nothing to reduce the number of abortions, it only forces people to seek out unsafe abortions.

Fiction: Red Flag laws take guns from people without due process.

Fact: <u>Red Flag orders</u> are issued only by judges on the basis of evidence that meets certain standards of proof, and judges can only issue a final order following a hearing of which the person is given notice and during which they have an opportunity to be heard. Red Flag laws also allow an individual to petition to terminate an existing order.

FICTION: Execotions like 6 week ban, in case of rape or incest, life of the mother covers women's health issues.

FACT: Only a small percentage of abortions are due to these reasons, meaning the majority of women and girls living under these laws might be forced to seek unsafe abortions and put their health and lives at risk.

Those who are already marginalized are disproportionately affected by such laws as they have no means to seek safe and legal services in another state or access private care.

They include women and girls on low income, refugees and migrants, adolescents, lesbian, bisexual cisgender women and girls, transgender or gender non-conforming individuals, minority or Indigenous women.

FICTION: Shoot First laws provide everyone an equal right to self-defense.

FACT: Shoot First laws, also known as <u>Stand Your Ground laws</u>, have a disproportionate impact on communities of color.

Across the country, <u>research</u> shows that when white shooters kill Black victims, the resulting homicides are considered justifiable far more frequently than when the shooter is Black and the victim is white.

FICTION: Anti-Abortion laws protect everyone from the baby to the doctor.

FACT: Criminalisation and restrictive laws on abortion prevent health-care providers from doing their job properly and from providing the best care options for their patients, in line with good medical practice and their professional ethical responsibilities.

It also deters women and girls from seeking post-abortion care for complications due to unsafe abortion or other pregnancy related complications.

FICTION: Gun violence affects Black and white people in the US equally.

<u>FACT: Black people in the U.S. are disproportionately impacted</u> by various forms of gun violence. They experience 12 times the gun homicides, 18 times the gun assault injuries, and nearly 3 times the fatal police shootings of white Americans.

FICTION: Active shooter drills make students and school staff more safe in the case of an active shooter.

FACT: There is no evidence to show student participation in <u>active shooter drills</u> saves lives and data shows they do cause trauma and

anxiety. The best way to protect schools from school shootings are proven <u>threat assessment programs</u> and gun safety laws.

FICTION: Pro-Life cares about the well being of every child.

FACT: **Of All Thirteen States Banning Abortion Only Two Try To Be Truly Pro-Child Not Just Pro-Birth.**

Child poverty in the 13 states with abortion bans ranges from 16% in South Dakota to 28% in Mississippi. Only two of the states—Missouri and South Dakota—have child poverty rates at or below the national average of 17%. In 10 of the states with abortion bans, one-fifth or more of children live in poverty.

The share of all births with low birth weight exceeds the national average of 8.2% in 11 of the 13 states that have banned abortion. In fact, at least one in 10 births had low birth weight in Alabama, Georgia, Louisiana, Mississippi, and South Carolina.

States that have banned all abortions rank among the 10 worst states for overall child well-being. None of the states with abortion bans ranks in the top 20. While these 13 states may be pro-birth, the evidence suggests they are not equally pro-child.

States that have banned abortions have the highest share of households with children that sometimes or often did not have enough food to eat in the prior week ranged from a low of 13% in Missouri to a high of 27% in Louisiana. In Alabama, Georgia, Mississippi, and Texas, one-fifth or more of households with children were experiencing food insecurity.

The evidence clearly shows these states have not invested sufficient resources to support their at-risk children—even before banning abortion. Although some women in these states will succeed in obtaining abortions in other states, many may not, leading to an increase in the number of vulnerable children. If policymakers and pro-life advocates in these states continue to focus their resources primarily on anti-abortion efforts, they will fail to meet the needs of thousands of vulnerable children who require additional support to thrive.

———————————

This tension within the Republican Party may indeed be a sign of the systemic issues that arise when the balance between the two parties is lost. The role of the Democrats has often been to serve as the counterweight, ensuring that the needs of all citizens are considered and that policies are implemented with compassion and a sense of shared prosperity.

When one side prioritizes the accumulation of wealth at the top, neglecting the basic needs of the majority, the social fabric begins to tear. This is where Democrats have historically stepped in, advocating for programs and policies that distribute opportunities and support more evenly across society. The intent is not to stifle success, but to create a floor from which all can rise.

The pushback from Republicans, and particularly from the MAGA wing, against such measures can create a volatile political environment. It's in this climate that we've seen a growing number of Republicans distancing themselves from the party line, which may be indicative of a broader need for reflection and recalibration within the party.

The stakes are high, as the decisions made by our leaders have real-world consequences. When policies that support food assistance, healthcare, and fair taxation are undermined, it's the most vulnerable who suffer first and most acutely. This suffering extends beyond immediate needs like food and healthcare to long-term economic stability and opportunity.

The departure of Republicans from office might be seen as an opportunity for the party to reassess its priorities and values. It could be a chance to return to a more traditional conservatism that values fiscal responsibility without sacrificing the well-being of the citizenry.

In the end, the vibrancy of a democracy is measured by how well it responds to the needs of all its citizens, not just a privileged few. It's a delicate balance to strike, but it's essential for the health of the nation and the well-being of its people. As we move forward, it's crucial for voters to remain informed, engaged, and critical of the narratives presented to them, ensuring that the policies enacted in their name truly serve the public good.

If you want to be successful, be successful.

The only person that determines your success is you.

If you like where you are, are happy with what you're doing, are comfortable with your life, and feel fulfilled, then you are successful.

Understanding Sexual Victimization in Men: Breaking the Silence

The Need for Research, Beter Laws For Victim Protections and Understanding of Male Sexual Victimization.

The last comprehensive study regarding male sexual victims was done in the early 1970's

Sexual violence is a pervasive issue that crosses gender boundaries, yet the experiences of men who are victims of such crimes remain shrouded in silence.

With current estimates suggesting that over 27% of men have experienced some form of sexual victimization in their lives, the lack of literature and research on this subject presents a concerning void.

This article aims to shed light on the challenges and gaps in addressing male sexual violence, highlighting the need for further empirical investigation and a shift in societal attitudes.

the majority of sex offenders are likely to be heterosexual. It is important to note that only 0.6% of all types of sexual predators are estimated to be gay.

It is crucial to understand that abuse is fundamentally about power and control, not tied to sexual orientation.

In cases where boys have been molested, the perpetrators are predominantly identified as heterosexual individuals.

Historically, the definition of rape was narrowly construed to mean forceful or unconsented vaginal penetration, effectively excluding male victims from legal recognition and protection.

This narrow view persisted until the turn of the 21st century, with all but three states in the U.S. now having gender-neutral rape laws. Georgia, Mississippi, and Idaho being the three exceptions.

However, societal attitudes and legal systems have been slow to adapt to these changes, leaving male victims in a precarious position.

Up until the mid-1990s, male sexual assault was not only underreported, there was no law that protected the victim, and it was also dangerously conflated with criminality, as victims could themselves be arrested due to sodomy laws lacking a rape exception clause.

This historical injustice has had a lingering effect, deterring male victims from coming forward even today.

The fear of not being believed, coupled with the possibility of facing legal and social repercussions, continues to silence many.

One of the most damaging misconceptions about male sexual victimization is the belief that a physiological response such as an erection or ejaculation implies consent.

This myth undermines the reality that such responses are involuntary and are not indicative of consent or pleasure.

Education and awareness are vital in dispelling these myths and ensuring that male victims receive the justice and support they deserve.

Sexual violence against men can lead to severe physical and psychological consequences.

However, due to the stigma and lack of understanding, male victims may be reluctant to seek help or may not have access to appropriate resources.

Recognizing the involuntary nature of physiological responses during an assault is crucial for providing proper medical treatment and psychological support.

The silent suffering of male victims of sexual violence is a pressing issue that demands attention.

Research into male sexual victimization needs to be updated and expanded to reflect the current societal context.

Legal systems must continue to evolve to offer equal protection and redress for victims, regardless of gender.

Moreover, society as a whole must challenge outdated notions of masculinity and victimhood to foster a supportive environment for all survivors.

Only through increased research, education, and policy changes can we hope to address the needs of male victims of sexual violence and move towards a more just and empathetic society.

Studies in the fields of science and case management have demonstrated that regardless of the victim's gender, the majority of sex offenders are likely to be heterosexual. It is important to note that only 0.6% of all types of sexual predators are estimated to be gay.

It is crucial to understand that abuse is fundamentally about power and control, not tied to sexual orientation.

In cases where boys have been molested, the perpetrators are predominantly identified as heterosexual individuals.

Various forms of violent sexual behavior exist, including sexual assault, harassment, non-penetrative acts of sex, and both attempted and committed rape.

According to the Centers for Disease Control and Prevention, sexual victimization is defined as a sexual act that is carried out or attempted by another person without the victim's freely given consent, or against someone who is unable to provide consent or refuse.

The impact of victimization on individuals is profound, affecting both their physical and mental health.

Victims commonly experience short- and long-term physical injuries, fear, anxiety, despair, post-traumatic stress disorder (PTSD), low self-esteem, social challenges, and thoughts of or committing suicide.

It is imperative to recognize and address the prevalence of sexual victimization in men, breaking the silence surrounding this important issue and providing support and resources for all survivors.

Sexual victimization in men is a complex and often overlooked issue that requires greater awareness and understanding from society as a whole.

By shedding light on this topic and acknowledging the prevalence of male victims, we can work towards creating a more supportive and inclusive environment for all survivors of sexual violence.

One of the key steps in addressing sexual victimization in men is to challenge existing stereotypes and misconceptions surrounding masculinity and victimhood.

Men who have experienced sexual violence may face unique barriers in coming forward due to societal expectations and stigma.

It is essential to create safe spaces where male survivors feel comfortable seeking help and sharing their experiences without judgment.

Support services and resources tailored to the specific needs of male victims do not exist but are crucial in providing effective assistance and promoting healing.

If mental health support, counseling, and access to specialized care were available I would play a significant role in helping male survivors cope with the trauma of sexual victimization and navigate their recovery journey.

Furthermore, education and prevention efforts are vital in combatting sexual violence and creating a culture of consent and respect.

By promoting healthy relationships, communication, and bystander intervention, we can work towards preventing sexual victimization from occurring in the first place.

Ultimately, addressing sexual victimization in men requires a multi-faceted approach that involves raising awareness, providing support, and fostering a culture of empathy and understanding.

By standing together as a community, we can empower male survivors to speak out, seek help, and heal from the trauma of sexual violence.

Through open dialogue, education, and advocacy, we can break the silence surrounding sexual victimization in men and ensure that all survivors receive the support and validation they deserve.

It is essential for individuals, communities, and institutions to actively work towards dismantling harmful beliefs and attitudes that perpetuate the cycle of sexual violence.

By promoting respect, empathy, and equality, we can create a safer and more inclusive society for everyone.

If you or someone you know has been a victim of sexual violence, it is important to seek help and support.

There are organizations, hotlines, and resources available to assist survivors in their healing journey. Remember, you are not alone, and it is never too late to reach out for help.

By standing in solidarity with male survivors of sexual victimization, we can foster a culture of compassion, understanding, and empowerment.

Together, we can work towards creating a world where all individuals are treated with dignity and respect, free from the fear of sexual violence.

In order to create a more supportive environment for male survivors of sexual victimization, it is crucial for society to continue challenging harmful stereotypes and biases that may prevent men from coming forward with their experiences.

By encouraging open conversations, providing education on consent and healthy relationships, and offering non-judgmental support, we can help break down the barriers that male survivors often face.

Additionally, it is important for legal systems and support services to be equipped to effectively respond to the needs of male survivors. This includes training law enforcement officials, healthcare providers, and counselors to recognize and address the specific challenges that male victims may encounter.

As a community, we must also work towards holding perpetrators of sexual violence accountable for their actions, regardless of the gender of the victim. By advocating for justice and supporting survivors through the legal process, we can send a clear message that sexual violence will not be tolerated in any form.

Together, by amplifying male voices, challenging societal norms, and providing comprehensive support, we can create a more inclusive and compassionate society where all survivors of sexual victimization, regardless of gender, can heal and thrive.

Let us continue to stand united in our commitment to ending sexual violence and creating a world where everyone feels safe, respected, and valued.

It is crucial for individuals to educate themselves on the signs of sexual victimization, understand the impact it can have on survivors, and learn how to support those who have experienced such trauma.

By being informed and empathetic, we can contribute to creating a culture of belief, validation, and healing for all survivors.

Furthermore, advocacy and activism play a vital role in raising awareness about sexual victimization in men and pushing for systemic changes that prioritize survivor-centered approaches.

By speaking out against victim-blaming, promoting gender equality, and advocating for policies that support survivors, we can work towards creating a more just and compassionate society for all.

Self-care is essential for those who work with or support survivors of sexual victimization.

It is important to prioritize one's own well-being, seek support when needed, and engage in activities that promote mental and emotional resilience.

By taking care of ourselves, we can continue to show up for others and contribute to the collective effort to end sexual violence.

Addressing sexual victimization in men requires a concerted effort from individuals, communities, and institutions to challenge harmful beliefs, provide support, advocate for justice, and promote healing.

Together, we can create a world where all survivors are believed, supported, and empowered to reclaim their lives from the trauma of sexual violence.

As we strive to address sexual victimization in men, it is essential to recognize that every survivor's experience is unique, and healing is a complex and individual journey.

It is important to listen to survivors with empathy, validate their experiences, and respect their autonomy in deciding how they want to move forward.

Creating safe spaces and support networks specifically tailored to male survivors can be instrumental in fostering healing and empowerment.

Peer support groups, counseling services, and survivor-led initiatives can offer invaluable resources and a sense of solidarity to those navigating the aftermath of sexual victimization.

Education and awareness campaigns targeting diverse audiences can help challenge harmful myths and stereotypes surrounding male victimization.

By promoting messages of consent, respect, and survivor support, we can contribute to a culture that values and uplifts the voices of all survivors.

Research and data collection on sexual victimization in men are crucial for understanding the scope of the issue, identifying trends, and informing effective prevention and intervention strategies.

By investing in research and data-driven initiatives, we can further our understanding of male victimization and enhance our collective response to this important issue.

By continuing to advocate for the rights and well-being of male survivors of sexual violence, we can work towards a future where all individuals are treated with dignity, compassion, and respect, free from the trauma of victimization.

Together, let us stand in solidarity with male survivors, amplify their voices, and create a world where healing and justice are accessible to all.

Empowering male survivors to share their stories and seek support is a crucial step in breaking the stigma surrounding sexual victimization in men.

Encouraging open conversations, providing platforms for survivors to speak out, and amplifying their voices in public discourse can help raise awareness and challenge societal norms that may silence male survivors.

It is important for communities to prioritize prevention efforts by educating individuals on healthy boundaries, consent, and respectful relationships from an early age.

By fostering a culture of respect and empathy, we can create a society that values and upholds the rights and dignity of all individuals, reducing the prevalence of sexual violence against men and women alike.

Addressing sexual victimization in men requires a multifaceted approach that involves advocacy, support, education, and empowerment.

By working together to create a more inclusive and compassionate society, we can ensure that all survivors of sexual violence, regardless of their gender, receive the care, validation, and justice they deserve.

Let us continue to stand united in our commitment to ending sexual violence and promoting healing and resilience for all.

Supporting male survivors of sexual victimization also involves challenging harmful societal attitudes that may perpetuate victim-blaming and disbelief.

By promoting a culture of empathy, understanding, and accountability, we can create a safer and more supportive environment for survivors to come forward and seek help without fear of judgment or retribution.

It is essential for policymakers, law enforcement agencies, and healthcare providers to work collaboratively in developing trauma-informed practices and policies that prioritize the needs of male survivors.

By enhancing access to specialized services, training professionals on best practices in supporting male victims, and improving reporting mechanisms, we can ensure that survivors receive the comprehensive care and justice they deserve.

Fostering collaborations between community organizations, advocacy groups, and survivor-led initiatives can strengthen the network of support available to male survivors.

By building partnerships and sharing resources, we can create a more coordinated and responsive system that addresses the unique challenges faced by male victims of sexual violence.

As we continue to advocate for the rights and well-being of male survivors, it is important to remember that everyone has a role to play in ending sexual violence.

By standing together in solidarity, speaking out against injustice, and promoting a culture of respect and consent, we can create a society where all individuals are empowered to live free from the fear of sexual victimization.

Addressing sexual victimization in men requires a collective effort to raise awareness, provide support, advocate for policy changes, and foster a culture of respect and empathy.

By listening to survivors, amplifying their voices, and working towards systemic improvements, we can create a society that values the rights and well-being of all individuals.

It is crucial for individuals to educate themselves on the complexities of sexual victimization, challenge harmful stereotypes, and support survivors with compassion and understanding.

Together, we can create a world where all survivors, regardless of gender, feel empowered to seek help, heal from trauma, and reclaim their lives.

Standing united in our commitment to ending sexual violence and promoting justice and healing for all survivors, we can work towards a future where every individual is treated with dignity, respect, and compassion.

Let us continue to support and uplift male survivors, break the silence surrounding their experiences, and build a more inclusive and supportive community for all.

Sources:

Sexual violence is notoriously difficult to measure, and there is no single source of data that provides a complete picture of the crime.

My own experiences in dealing with the legal system and mental health system as a sexual assault victim. Sexual abuse stated in 1970 until 1979. A violent rape In 1981 and again while in the service in 1985.

On RAINN's website, they have tried to select the most reliable source of statistics for each topic. The primary data source they use is the __National Crime Victimization Survey (NCVS)__.

Does Racism And Hatred Still Exist Today Because Of Politicians And The Media?

Causing Harm to Millions Due to Ignorance and Lack of Education on How Sensationalized Rhetoric Leads to Violence Against Others

Sensationalized Rhetoric Is The Root Cause Of Today's Hatred And Violence Towards The Disenfranchised.

First and foremost, it is crucial to highlight the importance of treating all victims of any violent crime with dignity and respect rather than exploiting them as tools to further a political agenda.

I'm unsure if it's because people are unaware of how national news works or don't care.

When a specific incident receives widespread coverage on national news, it is an uncommon occurrence.

Cases that are common or happen frequently do not garner national news attention.

So, the short answer is that what you see on national news channels is rare and should not cause you or the people around you any concern or panic. It should only evoke empathy for those involved.

Sensationalizing rare events for political purposes and higher network ratings can have detrimental and violent effects on the lives of countless individuals and nationalities.

This is often motivated and driven by personal biases, prejudices, racism, homophobia, and segregation.

It is vital that everyone, regardless of their beliefs, avoid spreading hysteria and fear without solid evidence and that the statistics and events are not exaggerated.

Only when there is concrete proof that entire groups or nationalities are involved, this will never happen, should calls for actions like mass deportation and the apprehension of those responsible be considered justified.

Instead of hastily jumping to conclusions, unfairly implicating entire groups and nationalities that are based on the actions of a few and causing harm, it is more important that we all concentrate on making a positive impact.

Engaging in research and actively participating in initiatives that promote tolerance and acceptance can help bring about positive changes in society.

This can be achieved through educating oneself and advocating for constructive solutions.

Furthermore, fostering a culture of understanding and empathy is critical to addressing societal issues and preventing violence from sensationalized rhetoric.

By engaging in open dialogue, actively listening to diverse perspectives, and seeking to educate oneself on different viewpoints, individuals can build bridges of communication and mutual respect.

It is essential to challenge one's own biases and assumptions, as well as those prevalent in society, to promote inclusivity and unity within communities.

Rather than perpetuating fear and division through sensationalism, individuals can strive to cultivate an environment where compassion, reason, and evidence-based discourse prevail.

Being mindful of the potential consequences of sensationalized rhetoric and actively working towards a more informed, empathetic society, we can contribute to a safer and more harmonious world for all.

Through collective efforts to promote understanding, tolerance, and respect, we can create a society that values diversity and celebrates the richness of different perspectives.

The willingness and open-mindedness to seek an education regarding what we don't understand plays a role in combating ignorance and misinformation.

By supporting educational initiatives that foster critical thinking skills, media literacy, and cultural awareness about the groups, the nationalities, and the disenfranchised, you have to understand their past to understand and accept their present.

We must empower individuals to discern fact from fiction and resist the lure of sensationalized narratives.

Individuals must engage in constructive conversations, seek common ground, and work towards solutions that benefit society.

By focusing on shared values and goals, we can bridge divides and promote unity in facing challenges.

Ultimately, by rejecting sensationalized rhetoric and embracing a more nuanced, empathetic approach to complex issues, we can build a more compassionate and inclusive world for ourselves and future generations.

Let us strive to be agents of positive change and advocates for a more peaceful and just society.

Causing Harm To Millions Because Of The Ignorance And Not Being Educated As How Sensationalized Rhetoric Causes Violence Towards Others.

First, I want to stress that It is essential to emphasize the treatment of all victims of any crime with dignity and respect rather than exploiting them as tools to advance a political agenda.

If a particular incident is widely reported on national news, it is always an uncommon occurrence.

Cases that are commonplace or occur frequently will not get national news coverage.

Sensationalizing rare events for political campaigns and network ratings causes harm to the lives of countless individuals simply because of your personal biases, bigotry, prejudices, racism, homophobia, and segregation.

It is crucial to refrain from spreading hysteria and fear without concrete evidence that the statistics and occurrences are not embellished. Then, using your hysteria, calling for retribution will be justified.

When you have actual verifiable proof, your calls for mass deportation and the apprehension of the guilty class become relevant.

Until then, Rather than rushing to judgment, unfairly implicating entire groups based on the actions of a few, and causing harm, it is essential to focus on making a positive impact.

Research and participation in positive changes that will increase tolerance and acceptance can be achieved through educating oneself, promoting tolerance and acceptance, understanding immigration issues, advocating for equality among all nationalities, engaging with different generations, embracing diverse genders, and fostering constructive dialogue among opposing political factions.

Let us redirect our energies toward initiatives that foster unity, empathy, and mutual respect instead of perpetuating divisions and prejudice.

Let Me repeat This:

It is crucial to treat all victims of any crime with dignity and respect rather than using them as tools to further a political agenda.

If you have seen or heard about it on the national news, it rarely happens.

Otherwise, it would not be reported on or covered by national news agencies.

When something happens regularly and in large numbers, that means it's commonplace and is not newsworthy.

Just stop the hysteria over rare occurrences you are causing harm to millions of people's lives because you don't like them.

Just keep your ignorance to yourself and stop making a fool of yourself when you broadcast your hatred and prejudices publicly.

So don't jump the gun and start spreading hysteria and fear.

Don't decide to make everyone of any nationality, every immigrant, everybody of any generation, everyone of every gender, or every one of that political party must be found guilty of that one crime, so the government must punish all the people in that classification.

Spend your time doing something you can make a difference at.

A good example would be educating yourself and promoting tolerance, acceptance, and understanding of immigration issues, equality for all nationalities, getting involved with other generations, getting to know and understand all genders, and getting back to the point where all opposing political parties can live peacefully.

———————

The Invisible Americans: 3ʳᵈ Class Citizens Denied Equal Rights And Federal Representation.

Summed up in a simple explanation without the entire history or explanation below:

All of the U.S. Territories' are denied representation and statehood because the majority of the populations are people of color and lean more towards the Democratic Party. All of the Territories would be a majority of people of color and would be people of color led stated. The Disenfranchised people that would lead these states would completely erase any chance that any Republican would retain majority rule.

Nearly five million people residents of Washington D.C., Puerto Rico, and the other U.S. territories are taxpaying U.S. citizens who have fundamentally different voting rights and representation in government than residents of the 50 states.

Currently, the United States occupies sixteen territories, six of which are Washington D.C., Puerto Rico, Guam, the Northern Mariana Islands, American Samoa, and the U.S. Virgin Islands have permanent inhabitants who are U.S. citizens.

Those who live in these six territories are <u>U.S. citizens, pay federal taxes, and can travel freely within the United States</u>.

Despite contributing billions in taxes to the federal government, they do not have meaningful representation like U.S. citizens residing in the 50 states.

The only people who do not live in a US state but still receive electoral college votes are the people of the District of Columbia.

They get three electoral votes, the same minimum number for any represented state.

However, the District of Columbia's electoral votes were given to the territory by the Twenty-Third Amendment to the Constitution in 1961.

The unequal treatment of American territories and their inhabitants echoes historical patterns of marginalization and discrimination seen in other contexts, such as indentured servitude and the plight of African Americans after the Civil War in the United States.

Indentured servitude was a system in colonial America where individuals, often immigrants or poor white workers, would agree to work for a set period in exchange for passage to the New World or other benefits.

While not the same as slavery, indentured servants faced harsh conditions and limited rights during their servitude.

Similarly, the residents of American territories, including indigenous peoples, face limitations in their rights and representation compared to those in the states.

After the Civil War, African Americans faced systemic discrimination and violence despite the abolition of slavery.

They were denied full citizenship rights, faced segregation, and encountered barriers to education, employment, and political participation.

This legacy of oppression and inequality continues to impact African American communities today.

In the context of American territories, residents lack full representation. They cannot vote in Federal Elections, including the presidential elections, and face unequal access to federal programs and resources.

This unequal treatment perpetuates a cycle of marginalization and disenfranchisement that hinders the social and economic development of these regions and their indigenous populations.

For over a century, the U.S. Territories residents have encountered systemic barriers akin to the struggles faced by Native Americans, who, despite obtaining citizenship in 1924 and later becoming residents of Guam and Puerto Rico through the Immigration and Nationality Act of 1952, continue to fight for full equality and representation. The disparities in healthcare, education, and economic opportunities are stark reminders of these communities' long-standing injustices.

The Republican and Democratic parties have historically had divergent stances on these issues, with Republicans often resisting statehood due to economic and political concerns. At the same time, Democrats advocate for greater autonomy and statehood to achieve equity and justice. The path to statehood is not only a political challenge but also a moral imperative, requiring an understanding of the democratic principles that should be at the heart of the Union.

The historical narrative of American territories is fraught with complexities. The United States' relinquishment of the Philippines post-World War II and Roosevelt's calculated omission of certain territories from his declaration of war speech because of color and race, he didn't do it because of his belief. Still, out of concern, white Americans would not back the war if it was seen as the white population being attacked. This may help reflect the intricacies of American geopolitical strategy and the enduring invisibility of nonwhite territories.

Today, acknowledging the resilience and hardships indigenous peoples have faced is essential. By honoring their agency and contributions, we can strive for a future that embraces their voices and addresses the colonial legacies that have shaped their past. Recognizing the intricacies of their plight is the first step toward dismantling systemic inequalities that have long defined the political landscape of these territories.

The future of American territories hinges on our commitment to learning from history, advocating for justice, and pursuing policies that empower indigenous communities. Together, we can work towards a more just and inclusive America, where the dream of statehood or the recognition of independence is realized, affirming the value and experiences of every citizen. This is not just a political decision but a moral obligation that speaks to the core values of democracy and human rights for all under the American flag.

As we move forward, the conversation surrounding America's territories must shift from a footnote in history books to a prominent discourse on civil rights and self-determination. It is high time that the invisible barriers that have kept these Americans in the shadows are dismantled, acknowledging that their fate is intertwined with the nation's ideals of liberty and justice.

The denial of statehood or full political rights to the residents of Puerto Rico, Guam, the U.S. Virgin Islands, and others is not just an oversight; it's a reflection of a deeper, systemic issue that stems from centuries-old legacies of colonialism and racial biases. The predominantly non-white populations of these territories have been disenfranchised, and their aspirations for equality have met with reluctance and political maneuvering.

Empathy and action must replace this historical inertia. Policymakers must heed the call for change, recognizing that these Americans serve in our military, contribute to our economy, and enrich our culture, all the while lacking the full political representation afforded to states. The strategic importance of these territories, underscored by their use in global conflicts and as military outposts, demands that we honor their residents with the same rights as those living on the mainland.

The journey toward statehood—or the alternative, a fair and equitable path to independence—requires legislative change and a transformation in the national consciousness. Americans from all walks of life must understand the significance of these territories, the breadth of their histories, and the richness of their cultures. Only through a collective recognition of their importance to the American narrative can these communities achieve the representation and respect they deserve.

The time for half-measures and incremental change has passed. The call for equality and statehood is to fulfill the promises enshrined in the Constitution and the Declaration of Independence. It requires bold leadership, a willing engagement from the public, and a reimagining of what it means to be American—expanding the promise of democracy to every corner of the nation.

As the United States stands as a global leader, it must also lead by example in rectifying the inequalities within its borders. This means championing the cause of its territories, ensuring that their voices are heard, their votes count, and their rights are upheld. By doing so, we not only strengthen the fabric of our nation but also affirm the universal values of democracy and human dignity.

The path ahead is clear. It is a path of recognition, reform, and reconciliation, where the invisible third-class citizens of America's territories emerge into the light of full citizenship. As the United States continues to evolve, let us ensure that all its citizens, no matter where they reside, share in the rights and responsibilities of this great nation. The promise of America's democracy must be unbroken, its reach unbounded, and its commitment to all its people unwavering. Now is the time to act, to embrace the diversity of our nation, and to welcome these territories into the union as equals, forging a more perfect and inclusive America.

Americas Populated Territories:

American Samoa:

Total Area: 77 square miles (199 sq km), Population: 57,663 (2007 estimate)

Guam:
Total Area: 212 square miles (549 sq km), Population: 175,877 (2008 estimate)

Northern Mariana Islands (Saipan, Farallon de Pajaros, Maug Island, Agrihan, Pagan, Guguan, Sarigan, Anatahan, Farallon de Medinilla, Tinian, Rota):

Total Area: 184 square miles (477 sq km), Population: 86,616 (2008 estimate)

Puerto Rico:

Total Area: 3,151 square miles (8,959 sq km), Population: 3,927,188 (2006 estimate)

U.S. Virgin Islands

Total Area: 136 square miles (349 sq km), Population: 108,605 (2006 estimate)

Wake Island

Total Area: 2.51 square miles (6.5 sq km), Population: 200 (2003 estimate)

Washington D.C.:

Total Area: 68.35 square miles, Population 678,972

IS IT POSSIBLE TO HAVE A CRIME-FREE SOCIETY WITHOUT SACRIFICING FREEDOM?

This question challenges the fabric of our social construct. To paraphrase Benjamin Franklin, those who sacrifice liberty for safety deserve neither.

It's a delicate balance between ensuring safety and preserving freedom that societies strive to maintain.

Our perception of the world as a dangerous place is often shaped by the mass media and politicians, who frequently employ fear as a means of control.

Research indicates that the more individuals consume television, the more likely they believe it is a dangerous world.

This phenomenon is exacerbated during election campaigns, plus when elected politicians are trying to ensure re-election and the industries that profit from selling security

P, from home alarms to insurance, by playing on the fears they have been narrating and the nation now believes.

Crime has been a part of human history since the first recorded murder some 430,000 years ago, believed to have been committed by Homo heidelbergensis or Homo antecessor.

Despite the prevalence of crime, Americans are not uninformed or unintelligent, but the media's and politicians' portrayal often makes rare events seem common and common occurrences appear rare. Rule of thumb: if it's on the news, especially national news, it doesn't happen regularly, so don't buy into the hype when they claim the sky is falling.

The United States has the highest prison population in the world, with 25% of the global prison population, giving Americans a 1 in 100 chance of being incarcerated.

Not all criminals choose their path willingly; many are coerced into crime by circumstances, such as exploitation by gangs or mental health issues that lead to criminal behavior.

There is a complex relationship between crime, policing, and the economy. As crime increases, more police are hired, which can lead to a reduction in crime but also a strain on economic resources.

Conversely, unemployment can lead to decreased city revenues and cutbacks in social services, potentially increasing crime.

This cycle indicates that crime can never be eliminated, as societal changes may redefine what is considered criminal behavior.

Crime affects every aspect of our lives, from the locks on our doors to the passwords on our devices. We take precautions to protect our possessions from criminals, who range from shoplifters to terrorists.

Crime by the poor often stems from necessity, while crime by the rich is motivated by greed. Even within the confines of prison, criminal behavior persists, challenging the notion of rehabilitation.

The complexity of human behavior means that achieving a completely crime-free society is an unrealistic goal.

Crime against someone is often committed by those we know, with most incidents occurring between acquaintances, friends, or family.

The motives behind these crimes can be as trivial as small amounts of money or as severe as loss of life.

Americans tend to overestimate the risks of rare events while underestimating the dangers of more prevalent issues like heart disease or cancer.

Media and political sensationalism influence this skewed risk perception and can lead to misguided priorities.

The private prison industry, which is a multi-billion dollar business, has little incentive to reduce prison populations due to the profits made from incarcerating individuals.

Lobbyists for these companies work to prevent prison reform, ensuring the continued existence of a lucrative system that thrives on high incarceration rates.

Despite the various government structures or the severity of laws and punishments, no society is or will be immune to crime.

Whether it be a democracy, republic, monarchy, or any other form of governance, crime persists.

The root causes of crime are multifaceted, ranging from untreated mental health issues and addiction to unmet basic needs and social inequality.

To make significant strides in reducing crime, society must address numerous underlying issues:

Mental health: Accessible and effective treatment for mental health conditions must be available to everyone.

Addiction: Comprehensive support and rehabilitation services are needed for everyone struggling with addiction.

Basic needs: Ensuring that every individual's basic needs are met is crucial to prevent crimes of necessity.

Inequality: Tackling social and economic disparities can reduce the motivation for crime driven by deprivation.

Substance legalization: By legalizing and regulating drugs, society could redirect funds from enforcement to treatment, and the criminal market would significantly reduce. We are doing prohibition that didn't work with alcohol, and it won't work with drugs.

It's important to acknowledge that crime, in some form, will always exist.

Yet, crime also plays a role in societal dynamics, allowing law-abiding citizens to define themselves in contrast to those who break the law.

If crime were eradicated, the resources currently allocated to the criminal justice system could be redirected to vital social programs, potentially improving overall societal welfare.

Crime and defining what constitutes a criminal act evolve with societal values and consciousness.

The justice system aims to distinguish between victims and offenders, but the distinction is not always clear-cut.

While the system works to punish wrongdoing and support the innocent, it has flaws and failures.

Criminals generate over $80 billion for the private sector, with prisons alone accounting for a significant portion.

This creates a perverse incentive for private prisons and businesses that profit off of fear and those that supply the prisons with goods to want not only to maintain but also to increase prisoner populations, as they can earn substantial daily rates for each inmate.

Envisioning a society completely free of crime may seem desirable, but such a utopia is likely impossible.

Moreover, the absence of crime might result in a less dynamic and exciting world.

Crime, in a sense, contributes to societal self-reflection and progress by highlighting areas needing reform and improvement.

While a crime-free society remains an unattainable ideal, it can significantly reduce crime by addressing its root causes.

Through a comprehensive approach that includes equitable social policies, mental health support, addiction treatment, and a fair justice system, we can create a society that minimizes crime without sacrificing the freedoms we cherish.

One of the most significant challenges in striving for a crime-reduced society is finding the right balance between security measures and preserving individual freedoms.

The expansion of law enforcement and surveillance can lead to potential overreach and violations of privacy, which in turn can erode the very liberties that are fundamental to a democratic society.

Addressing crime also involves investing in education and creating opportunities for a more equitable society.

By improving the quality of education and ensuring that everyone has access to it, individuals are less likely to turn to crime.

Education can provide the skills necessary for gainful employment, reducing economic disparities often correlating with higher crime rates.

Community-oriented policing is another strategy to help reduce crime while promoting positive relations between law enforcement and the community.

Police officers engaged with their communities can build trust and cooperation, which is critical for effective crime prevention and intervention.

The criminal justice system may also benefit from a greater focus on restorative justice and rehabilitation over punitive measures.

Programs that aim to rehabilitate rather than simply punish offenders can lead to lower recidivism rates.

Restorative justice approaches, which involve reconciling the offender with the victim and the community, can provide healing and closure while mitigating the long-term social costs of crime.

Advancements in technology offer new tools for crime prevention and detection.

From predictive policing algorithms to community surveillance systems, technology can be a double-edged sword, potentially improving safety and raising ethical concerns about surveillance and data privacy.

On a global scale, international cooperation is essential for combatting crimes that cross borders, such as human trafficking, drug smuggling, and cybercrime.

Collaborative efforts among nations can lead to more effective strategies and shared resources for tackling these complex issues.

I'm still not understanding why we are not working with the Mexican government to end the cartel hold.

It's well known the top third of Mexico is ruled by the cartel because of force, money, and a corrupt government in charge of that area.

When you read anything about it, they refer to the conflict as Mexico's war.

It would benefit both countries if the U.S. Helped Mexico stabilize its economy and make ours better and lower crime and murder rates in both countries and would reduce immigrants and drugs from coming to America.

Oh! Wait, politicians wouldn't have anything to run on, and the media wouldn't have anything to sensationalize.

Ultimately, the perception of crime and the societal response to it are deeply influenced by the prevailing values and norms.

What is considered a crime today may not be tomorrow, and what wasn't today may be one tomorrow.

A crime here or in one culture may not be seen as a crime the same way elsewhere or in a different era.

As societies evolve or political ideas shift, so do the legal systems and their approaches to crime.

While the dream of a society entirely without crime may be unattainable, the continuous effort to reduce crime and mitigate its impact remains essential.

By addressing social injustice, providing support and opportunities to the marginalized, and fostering a culture of respect and empathy, society can move closer to an ideal where crime is the exception rather than the norm.

The quest for a safer society is ongoing and requires the collective effort of all its members.

Through education, policy reform, technological innovation, and community engagement, strides can be made toward reducing crime.

It is through these multifaceted efforts that society can hope to achieve a balance where the rule of law is upheld, justice is served, and individual freedoms are respected.

While it may not be possible to eradicate crime from society entirely, much can be done to minimize its occurrence and impact.

By addressing the root causes of crime, improving the criminal justice system, and fostering a culture that values social welfare and individual rights, society can make significant progress toward safety and harmony without sacrificing the freedoms essential to our way of life.

Creating robust social support systems is crucial for crime prevention.

Programs that support families, education, and healthcare can help prevent the social and economic conditions that often lead to criminal behavior.

By ensuring that all members of society have access to essential services and support, the temptation or necessity to engage in criminal activities can be reduced.

Economic development plays a crucial role in crime reduction.

By fostering a strong economy with ample job opportunities, individuals are less likely to turn to crime out of economic necessity.

Efforts to create jobs, especially in areas with high unemployment rates, can help uplift communities and reduce the allure of criminal activity as a means of survival.

Substance abuse is often closely linked with criminal behavior. Proactive measures, such as providing comprehensive drug education and accessible treatment to everyone for addiction, can prevent the cycle of substance abuse and crime.

By treating substance abuse as a public health issue rather than solely a criminal one, society can reduce the demand for illegal drugs and the crimes associated with their sale and distribution.

The availability of mental health services is also crucial to crime prevention.

Many individuals in the criminal justice system suffer from mental health issues that go untreated.

By providing adequate mental health care and support, these individuals can receive the help they need, which can prevent the occurrence of crimes related to untreated mental health conditions.

Emerging technologies in crime analysis and prediction can provide law enforcement with tools to more effectively allocate resources and prevent crime.

However, these tools must be used responsibly and ethically, focusing on safeguarding civil liberties and preventing discrimination.

Civic education can empower citizens to participate actively in the prevention of crime.

By fostering a sense of responsible citizenship and community involvement, individuals can work together to create safer neighborhoods.

Programs that encourage community responsibility and engagement have been shown to impact reducing crime rates positively.

As society progresses, legal frameworks must evolve to address new crime types and reflect changing societal norms and values.

Keeping legislation updated with technological advancements and cultural shifts is essential for maintaining a practical and just legal system.

A holistic approach to crime prevention that encompasses social, economic, health, and educational policies is necessary for creating an environment where crime is less likely to occur.

By integrating these various facets, society can work towards a comprehensive strategy for reducing crime.

Every individual has a role to play in creating a safer society. By being vigilant, reporting suspicious activities, participating in community watch programs, and supporting initiatives aimed at crime reduction, citizens can contribute to the overall safety and well-being of their communities.

In summary, while an utterly crime-free society may be an unattainable utopia, significant progress can be made toward reducing crime and its impact on society.

Through policy initiatives, community involvement, technological advancements, and a commitment to social justice, society can create conditions that discourage crime and promote a high quality of life for all its members.

The pursuit of such a society is a shared responsibility, one that calls for continuous effort, innovation, and collaboration.

Embracing Respect Across Generations

Dear Friends and Family,

As I approach a meaningful milestone, turning 60, I've been reflecting on the relationships that I cherish and the shared values that I believe should underpin them. One such value is respect, which I consider to be the cornerstone of not only our personal interactions but also our societal norms, particularly when it comes to age.

It's important to me to communicate something that has been weighing on my heart. It seems there have been instances where the gap in our ages has not been met with the traditional respect that is often extended to one's elders. While age alone does not command respect, the wisdom, experience, and perspective gained over the years do merit consideration and a certain level of deference.

I understand that everyone has their own battles and that sometimes past experiences or stresses can cause one to act out of character. However, I firmly believe that these should not excuse a lack of civility or respect towards anyone, especially those who have many more years of life's trials and triumphs under their belt.

If there are unresolved feelings or issues that might be contributing to this behavior, I urge you to seek resolution, as unaddressed grievances can unintentionally affect our interactions with others. It's never too late to work through past challenges, and doing so can often lead to greater peace and improved relationships.

I am addressing this matter now, well in advance of my birthday, to give us all the opportunity to reflect on how we engage with one another. I hope this can be a starting point for all of us to foster an environment where respect for age, experience, and each other is held in high esteem.

The expectation that younger individuals should respect their elders is not merely about upholding tradition but about recognizing the value of every stage of life. In our family and circle of friends, I believe we can embody this principle, not just for the sake of appearances or societal norms, but because it is the right thing to do.

Should the unfortunate situation arise where I am subjected to yelling or disrespect, know that I will choose to remove myself from the negativity. In my home, I would hope that anyone who cannot abide by this principle of mutual respect would understand when I ask them to leave, so that both of us may reflect on the importance of respect and the image we choose to present to the world.

I share this with you from a place of love and the hope that we can all strive for better, more respectful interactions that honor our shared humanity and the age I have reached. I look forward to continuing our relationships with a renewed commitment to these ideals.

With warm regards and anticipation for positive change

Government "Handouts" Wealth Demographics. The First 16 Are Not For The Poor

1. Mortgage Interest Deduction
Government cost $70 Billion

1. Yacht Tax Deduction
$750,000 per yacht

1. 15 days free rental income

People rent their homes for an annual event for whatever they can charge and it's tax free 15 days and under

1. Breast Augmentation if used for work but no for everyday use

1. Cat Food for farms, Ranches and Businesses if used to attract cats for rodent control. (I would think it would also attract rodents)

1. Loophole allows you to deduct deadbeat loans. It's ment for bad business deals but is worded so if you loan money and you're not repaid you qualify

1. Personnel Pool deduction if you claim it›s medically needed

1. **Private Plane Loophole**

Under President Donald Trump's tax reform, some noncorporate taxpayers may be subject to "excess business loss limitations." The IRS defines excess business loss as "the amount by which the total deductions attributable to all of your trades or businesses exceed your total gross income and gains attributable to those trades or businesses plus $250,000

1. Rental Property Tax Deduction

1. Meals Of The Rich Tax Deductible

1. investment income is taxed at a much lower rate than regular income

1. No estate Tax on wealth under 5.4 million.

1. Gambling loss deduction

1. **The Social Security earnings limit.** Social Security taxes only apply to <u>income up to $118,500</u>

1. **Retirement plans. 66% Of the top 20%. Only 1% goes to the lower 20%**

1. **Cost of Tax prep. Tax Deductable**

1. **Social Security**

1. SNAP

1. WIC

1. School lunch program

1. Over 60 Food Assistance

1. Indigenous Americans Food Assistance

1. Emergency Housing

1. Rental Assistance

1. Medicare

1. Medicaid

1. CHIP

1. ACA

Learn and Know

The Difference Between Knowing and Learning:

I've Learned Everything About Ending Racism.

However, I Still Know Nothing About Ending Racism.

When I Start Applying What I've Learned, I Will Begin to Understand From Experience Why the Disenfranchised Do Not Always Trust a Kind Gesture From a "Moral Majority," and I Will Also Learn Stereotypes Work Both Ways.

The More I Apply My Knowledge, the More I Will Know About Ending Racism.

When You Learn About the World Around You and Apply What You've Learned, You May Become an Expert Because You Know What You Learned.

What I Learned Today

You can spend your life chasing genius.

Attend five of the best universities.
Memorizing and soak up everything you hear and read.

However, you still don't know anything.
You've only learned everything.

You will begin to know what you've learned when you start applying and using what you've spent on understanding what you want to know.

When you cut someone off mid-sentence with "I know" you ruin your credibility. How? Because you don't know you may have a suspicion,

Idea, hell you may even be right but only the speaker knows until they say it.

Marjoric Taylor Greene has called for the Speaker Of The House to vacate.

MTG also claims Ukraine has already lost its war. So, the USA should cut our losses and walk away.

We have already walked away from Vietnam and Afghanistan. What have been the consequences

No wonder the world no longer sees us as a superpower.

I can see why NATO is concerned about Trumps call for Russia to invade NATO countries because if he is elected America won't help

It's important to consider various perspectives on the situation in Ukraine. The conflict is complex, and the outcome of Ukraine's fate is uncertain but not doomed. It's crucial for the USA to support efforts for peace and stability worldwide.

The role of the USA, NATO, and other international partners in addressing conflicts is significant in maintaining democracy and to encourage every country to do the same in order to stop the spread of communism, dictatorships, and ensure the preservation of peace.

The challenges surrounding immigration in the United States are multifaceted and extend beyond just the issue of undocumented immigrants.

Let me start by making a statement:

All of our immigration issues in the United States Of America are 100% due to racism.

Before you try to argue, it doesn't honestly answer these questions. Number are from the Pew Research Center

1. Have you ever heard anything from anyone who has any influence in any party mention anything about the estimated 440,000 undocumented white-European immigrants in the USA?

1. Has there ever been a press conference from any party or any elected officials expressing their outrage about how the 440,000 Undocumented non-European immigrants are taking jobs and using government services?

1. When was the last time the general public protested, demanding all 440,000 undocumented white-European immigrants be deported?

1. When was the last time, if ever, you ever heard any national news coverage regarding anything at all about the 440,000 undocumented white European immigrants?

1. How many of you have even heard that there are 440,000 Undocumented White-European Immigrants?

Number is from the Pew Research Center

I will stop here, but I could go on.

A vital aspect of this challenge is the lack of comprehensive immigration reform to address critical issues such as insufficient funding for immigration processing, a shortage of immigration judges and legal counsel, and systemic barriers that contribute to the complexities of the immigration system.

The Immigration and Nationality Act of 1965, a landmark piece of legislation signed by President Lyndon B. Johnson at the base of the Statue Of Liberty, played a pivotal role in shaping US immigration policy.

By the INA abolishing quotas and opening doors to individuals who could contribute significantly to the country's growth and strength, the Act brought about a significant demographic shift in the United States.

The INA allowed immigrants of color and those from regions other than Western and Northern Europe to enter the country, enriching its diversity and contributing to its cultural fabric.

Information above is from the Immigration and Nationality Act

However, the current political climate, particularly among members of the MAGA movement and their elected officials, reflects a sense of entitlement and bigotry that impedes progress toward a more inclusive and humane immigration policy. Instead of working to improve and build upon the successes of the Immigration and Nationality Act of 1965, some seek to dissolve or replace it with regressive policies that prioritize exclusion and discrimination.

Source my opinion from the last 8 years of burying my nose in politics.

Addressing racism, bigotry, and hatred perpetuated by individuals and groups driven by entitlement is crucial to meeting the evolving needs of the labor force, managing population growth, and safeguarding the rights of immigrants. Immigrants already play a significant role in the US workforce, constituting 20%. Without their contributions, the country would face a severe labor force shortage, impacting various sectors of the economy.

My opinion except the workforce percentage it is from the Department of Labor.

Despite the contributions and benefits that immigrants bring to the country, reports indicate that some large cities are expressing reluctance to welcome more immigrants. This reluctance may stem from various factors, including economic concerns, social tensions, and political considerations. However, it underscores the need for a nuanced and comprehensive approach to immigration policy that balances the interests of all stakeholders while upholding the values of inclusivity, diversity, and respect for human rights.

From Democratic Platform.

Certainly! Cities across the United States are crucial in shaping attitudes toward immigration and addressing labor force shortages. In some large cities, there may be resistance to further immigration due to factors such as strain on resources, infrastructure, or existing social tensions.

However, it is encouraging that more miniature cities and towns nationwide actively seek and encourage immigrants to settle at their location. The small towns and cities in Nebraska, a red state, actively welcome immigrants to address their workforce shortages. One city official said we only have 19 citizens for every 100 jobs we need filled. One immigrant said (translated)," My job is challenging work, but I'm glad I have a job." Small towns and cities are beginning to recognize the value that immigrants bring in filling job vacancies and contributing to local economies.

The willingness of smaller cities to actively recruit and convince immigrants to move to their communities demonstrates a proactive approach to addressing labor force challenges. By embracing diversity and welcoming immigrants, these cities not only fill critical employment gaps but also enrich their communities with new perspectives, skills, and cultures.

Above Source NBC News Now mixed with my opinion

Efforts to promote awareness, responsibility, empathy, and education about immigration issues are equally important in cities of all sizes.

By fostering a more inclusive and welcoming environment, cities can combat racism, bigotry, and discrimination while creating opportunities for all residents to thrive.

City leaders, community organizations, and residents can work together to create policies and initiatives that support immigrants and promote understanding and integration. By showcasing the benefits of diversity and highlighting the positive impacts of immigration, cities can build stronger, more resilient communities that benefit everyone.

In conclusion, cities are vital in shaping attitudes toward immigration and addressing labor force shortages. By embracing diversity, promoting understanding, and creating inclusive environments, cities can harness the potential of immigration to drive economic growth, social cohesion, and community prosperity.

Above Source my opinion

According to international law, individuals who enter a country without proper documentation are classified as "undocumented immigrants," not "illegal aliens" or "illegal immigrants."

The issue with undocumented immigrants is not their lack of documentation but rather the insufficient resources and funding allocated to the Border Patrol to process and bring them before judges in a timely manner. Right now, it takes years not months.

This often leads to individuals crossing into the US without going through border checkpoints.

If Border Patrol were adequately funded and able to process immigrants efficiently, there would be a significant reduction in the number of undocumented immigrants in the country.

Ultimately, it is racism, not immigration, that is the root of the problem.

In today's society, the issue of an individual's responsibilities and awareness is no longer taught.

This is my opinion, so if you're looking for sources, you are out of luck except where you find statistics and the report name is listed with it.

This subject won't be necessary if you understand the following four points. You may want to read it just because, but it is long.

1. Everybody needs to become responsible for themselves and their actions. I don't care how you were raised or what you're taught. Let's start with ourselves. We all inherently know the difference between right and wrong. I don't care if there isn't a law against it. Police yourself and train yourself to do what is right. Stop feeling entitled and blaming others; instead, look at yourself and take responsibility for the part you play.

1. Demand Better News. When the news sensationalizes, switch it off. Push back against the media that peddles fear and division for profit. It's high time that news agencies are held to a higher standard and forced to start reporting truthfully and thoughtfully on issues that matter, not just those that sell ads. They must stop reinforcing harmful stereotypes and start healing societal divides.

1. See Immigrants for Who They Are. Immigrants are the backbone of many economic sectors, yet their stories of hardship and contribution often go untold. Let's shift the narrative on immigration. The media must stop the fear mongering and start telling the real stories of how immigrants are essential to our workforce, contribute positively to society, and face challenges that deserve our compassion and understanding. We must expose the injustices they endure and the contributions they make.

1. News agencies need to make gun violence and mass shootings their biggest priority since it is our biggest preventable killer. When I say this, I don't mean sensationalized like it is now. The media's approach to gun issues needs a complete overhaul. Forget giving airtime to extremists; it's time to focus on the actual cost of gun violence in our communities. No more focusing on the hillbilly red kneck gun-toting bozo that claims not only can he own 600 guns and 300 semis automatic he should be able to get whatever weapons he pleases, and it's no one's business because not only is it his second Amendment right, it is also his god given right. Instead, report what matters. How gun violence takes away individual rights, gives the feeling of power to hate groups, and how lives of entire cities change just to protect the right for one person to own a gun. Report regularly the facts of how gun control will improve everyone's lives, including the responsible gun owner.

Our nation today has a perceived sense of entitlement among its citizens, as reflected in the actions and statements like:

"I do not have to operate in a crowd. The crowd has to operate around me."

When it comes to gun control, responsible gun ownership and promoting safety should be required by law and promoted to the general public.

While some may oppose gun control measures, it is essential to recognize that people feel entitled and will not police themselves, so gun controls must be passed, enacted, and enforced to ensure public safety and prevent the misuse of firearms.

The Second Amendment guarantees the right to bear arms. Still, it doesn't guarantee the right to bear arms without regulations, being registered, licensed, legal weapon types and styles, or having a limit to the number of weapons.

Particularly in the context of a well-regulated militia. In modern times, law enforcement agencies like the police, FBI, CIA, DEA, military, and other government agencies where safety is a concern are a few seen as the militia structure.

We must implement effective gun control laws now that guarantee the safety and rights of the individual and protect the public safety.

Because of entitlement, gun control remains a complex and ongoing challenge for policymakers.

The American citizen's safety and rights should supersede uncontrolled gun ownership of the entitled.

It is crucial in addressing issues related to gun violence and ensuring the well-being of society as a whole that society takes priority.

Gun violence is a leading cause of premature death in the United States. According to the Centers for Disease Control and Prevention (CDC), over 42,000 gun-related deaths in 2023. **36,357 The number of firearm injuries in 2023. 6,192**

The number of children and teenagers shot in 2023. Thirty transgender and gender nonconforming people were killed in 2023. 51 The number of times a person has used an AR-style rifle to defend life or property in the last ten years. 656 The number of mass shootings in 2023 killed 712 people and injured at least 2,692. Mass shootings have increased by more than 150 percent since 2013. Statistics are from the CDC and The Trace.

Entitled Pedestrians

"I don't need to be safe crossing the street. I have the right of way. It's the driver's job to look out for me. It doesn't matter that the car is bigger, takes longer to stop, and is easier to see."

The belief that pedestrians do not need to prioritize their safety while crossing the street reflects a mindset that individual entitlement and convenience precede collective well-being.

I watched the news tonight, and the mother of a child who was hit by a vehicle his mother was knowingly upset that he died. I would be distraught as well.

I am in no way trying to take away the significance of the loss of any life. I do believe all life is equal and precious.

However, I also believe that we are responsible for understanding the risks and consequences of our actions.

This mother blamed his death on the size of the vehicle; yes, I understand the more significant the car, the more likely a fatality will occur. However, it was the responsibility of the pedestrian or the driver that caused the incident, not the vehicle.

I am always amazed how no one considers that the pedestrian's actions may be the cause.

Our entitlement to look at pedestrian responsibility that way. We see it as if they followed the rules or laws of pedestrian safety, then it is the car's fault, and if they don't, we say it is still the car's fault.

While lower than gun-related deaths, the number is still substantial, indicating the importance of addressing pedestrian safety and the shared responsibility of drivers and pedestrians to reduce these fatalities.

Pedestrian safety should always be a critical issue, particularly with the growing number of people and vehicles on the road, which will only increase.

Teaching individuals about personal responsibility and safety in public when walking on roads, in parking lots, and crossing any streets from the time we start walking is essential.

Pedestrian safety and the importance of this safety should be drilled into our minds from the beginning. Absorbing the information around you by the adults in our lives is essential in promoting awareness and care.

The main focus on pedestrian safety now has broader implications. Citizens are calling for the maximum size of vehicles to be significantly reduced, and they are influencing the design and features of vehicles to address risks posed by irresponsible pedestrian behavior.

One safety measure people are asking for is for vehicles to stop automatically when they detect movement in front of it automatically.

Research and development alone on that one requirement would include figuring out how the vehicle will detect what the movement is.

If it will be in its path when it reaches the location.

Know when to begin stopping based on road conditions, speed, and the condition of the vehicle and its brakes.

Then, it will have to decide if the movement is just because the object is stationary and moving in place or if it's moving around in place with the intent to begin crossing.

If this one request and all the other changes they want are made, it will increase (more than double) the vehicle purchase price to recoup the cost related to research, development, and the integration of safety features in vehicles.

The National Highway Traffic Safety Administration (NHTSA) reported pedestrians struck and killed 7,508 people walking in 2022. The GHSA estimates that 3,373 pedestrians died on US roads between January and June 2023 (The latest statistics I have). While lower than gun-related deaths, the number is still substantial, indicating the importance of addressing pedestrian safety and the shared responsibility of drivers and pedestrians to reduce these fatalities.

Vermont is the only state that reported no pedestrian deaths in the statistics. Proof it can be done with a decreased sense of entitlement and increased pedestrian education regarding safety and responsibility. Even though pedestrians aren't driving, they must understand the road rules.

Entitled Party And Its Members:

This last one is about the entitlement of an entire party but mainly focuses on MAGA members and their elected officials.

Immigration is a complex and divisive topic, always clouded by misconceptions and biases.

MAGA members and their elected officials blame crime on immigrants. Don't you think we would be hearing many more stories of murder (either offender or victim) if the immigrants significantly impacted the US murder rate? A murder by any immigrant, undocumented or not, would not make national news if it were a common occurrence.

Estimates vary and likely undercount deaths. The International Organization for Migration (IOM) documented 686 deaths and disappearances of migrants on the US-Mexico border in 2022, making it the deadliest land route for migrants worldwide. Where is the national news covering this?

There are no numbers of crimes committed against immigrants because none of the national database systems allow for modeling trends in bias-motivated crimes against immigrants because they do not currently include any measure of immigration status.

However, the current political climate, particularly among members of the MAGA movement and their elected officials, reflects a sense of entitlement and bigotry that impedes progress toward a more inclusive and humane immigration policy.

Addressing these underlying problems is essential for fostering a more inclusive and tolerant United States

The challenges with immigration in the US extend beyond the presence of undocumented immigrants.

MAGA members and their elected officials refuse to pass a bill that will address the following Issues such as insufficient funding for immigration processing, a shortage of immigration judges and legal counsel, and systemic barriers that contribute to the complexities of the immigration system.

The Immigration and Nationality Act of 1965, a landmark piece of legislation signed by President Lyndon B. Johnson at the feet of the Statue of Liberty, played a pivotal role in shaping US immigration policy.

By abolishing quotas and opening doors to individuals who could contribute significantly to the country's growth and strength, the Act brought about a significant demographic shift in the United States.

It allowed immigrants of color and those other than white immigrants to enter the country, enriching its diversity and contributing to its cultural fabric. The Act significantly altered the demographic mix in the country.

However, because of MAGA members and their elected official's sense of entitlement and bigotry, they want to dissolve and replace the Act instead of improving it.

Ongoing efforts like facing racism, bigotry, and hatred by the self-entitled and group entitlement head are needed to address the evolving needs of the labor force, population growth, and the protection of immigrant rights without the immigrants that already fill 20% of the US workforce. Our country faces a significant labor force shortage.

According to a national news report, Cities across the United States play a crucial role in shaping attitudes toward immigration and addressing labor force shortages.

Many major cities are complaining about the influx of immigrants and are calling for a closing of the borders.

One city in Nebraska said they have only 19 people available people for employment for every 100 jobs that need to be filled. They are begging for immigrants. The ironic part is Nebraska is a red state.

These smaller cities recognize the value that immigrants bring in filling job vacancies and contributing to local economics.

The willingness of smaller cities to actively recruit and convince immigrants to move to their communities demonstrates a proactive approach to addressing labor force challenges.

By embracing diversity and welcoming immigrants, these cities not only fill critical employment gaps but also enrich their communities with new perspectives, skills, and cultures.

We must demand that students are taught about our country's different societal issues, challenge all stereotypes, and work towards a more informed and compassionate understanding of immigration so that we can stop racism and bigotry, where it begins the moment we start to understand and speak.

We need a nationwide promotion on how ending racism, bigotry, and discrimination will benefit everyone, and shutting down immigration will hurt everyone. People need to see how these choices will impact our nation and society.

Promoting awareness, responsibility, and empathy can help foster a more inclusive and harmonious community for all individuals, regardless of their background.

Encouraging a culture of mutual respect, responsibility, and awareness among all and erasing this need for entitlement is crucial for enhancing everyone's safety and well-being.

By emphasizing personal responsibility, we are accountable for our actions and behavior and considerate of others.

The nation and its society can move forward, creating a safer and more harmonious environment for everyone.

_____

This is an open letter to everyone over 18

There Is No Excuse For Your Behavior.

You should know respect by then.

I am going to be 60 this year, and there is only one thing I want from each of you, and if you can't give it to me, I will.

I am so over everyone thinking it is okay with any of you to yell at me. Most of you are, at a minimum, 19 years younger than me. I am not a kid. I am either a parent, grandparent, or spouse to most of you that I see regularly.

Today, March 24, 2024, I reached my limit.

I am over everyone thinking they are smarter than me. That I have memory issues, I have never missed an appointment or a birthday, so I don't remember every story you tell and make a big deal about it; in reverse, you claim my memory is fucked, and I made it up, or I never told you.

I am fully aware of my surroundings, and I remember pretty much everything. Most of the time, I let you tell your story the way you want, and I don't interrupt, but most of you cut off anything I'm saying with "I know."

I plan to spend the rest of my life enjoying it instead of wondering what I can say or do without being yelled at.

I'm saying this now because I don't care who it is. If you yell at me after my birth date and I'm out or at your house, I will say nothing. I will get my stuff and go. If you are at my house, I will politely ask you to leave.

Response to a bigoted woman:

I don't understand any perspective when it comes from a place of BIGORTY and hate for America's ability to integrate immigrants smoothly.

It's clear that you value your self-preservation of people like you rather than support the ability for all residents to communicate with whatever they choose as their primary language of choice within the United States, regardless of whatever previeced hindrance it may cause them.

Your hindrance to their choice doesn't matter because you can choose who to interact with them.

So it's impertinent that you recognize that the United States has a long history of linguistic diversity and has never had an official national language.

I see your bigoted argument, but your feelings and beliefs are mute.

Because again, like it or not, since the inception of the first colony in the U.S., this diversity has been part of what makes us the most unique and prosperous country in the world.

Our success is because we can incorporate different languages and cultures to coexist, which is a strength rather than a weakness.

While it is true that, at this moment, English is the primary language spoken and used to facilitate communication and integration in the US.

It's also important to remember that we operate as a global economy, and language, the need for acquisition should be reversed. The Americans need to be required to learn multiple languages, like most other countries.

Instead of being so arrogant and entitled to think the world should conform to us. Your belief would be a waste of time and resources.

Having ballots in multiple languages, everyone's given name is said and spelled the same, at least in my experience in every country I've lived in and every person I've spoken to.

This practice is about ensuring that all citizens, regardless of their native language, have the opportunity to participate in the democratic process.

It's about inclusivity and making sure that language barriers do not prevent citizens from exercising their rights.

While you might feel that your views are not rooted in racism but rather in practical concerns, it is racism.

Yes, ma'am, you are a racist.

———————————————

Having oversight from federal agencies like ICE staring down state law enforcement with anticipation for arrest of Texas authority all to help ensure that immigration enforcement is conducted in accordance with existing laws and regulations, and that individuals are treated fairly and with respect during the process.

Having ICE (U.S. Immigration and Customs Enforcement) present as observers only to ensure that the rights of immigrants are not violated during the immigration enforcement process with the ability to arrest Texas law enforcement if they violate the right of any detainees that my solution to address concerns about human rights and due process.

Having oversight from federal agencies like ICE can help ensure that immigration enforcement is conducted in accordance with existing laws and regulations, and that individuals are treated fairly and with respect during the process.

However, it's crucial to strike a balance between enforcing immigration laws and protecting the rights of individuals, including due process and fair treatment. Any oversight mechanisms involving ICE or other federal agencies should prioritize upholding human rights standards and ensuring that individuals are treated with dignity and respect.

Ultimately, a collaborative and balanced approach involving both state and federal authorities, as well as oversight mechanisms to protect the rights of individuals, may be necessary to address the complex issues surrounding immigration enforcement in a just and humane manner.

Michelle, I don't understand your perspective when it comes from a place of BIGORTY and hate for America's ability to integrate immigrants smoothly. It's clear that you value the self-preservation of people like you than the ability for all residents to communicate with whatever they choose as their primary language of choice within the United States, regardless of whatever previewed hindrance it may cause them. Your hindrance to their choice doesn't matter because you can choose who to interact with them.

So it's impertinent that you recognize that the United States has a long history of linguistic diversity and has never had an official national language.

I see your bigoted argument, but your feelings and beliefs are mute. Because again, like it or not, since the inception of the first colony in the U.S., this diversity has been part of what makes us the most unique and prosperous country in the world. Our success is because we can incorporate different languages and cultures to coexist, which is a strength rather than a weakness.

While it is true that, at this moment, English is the primary language spoken and used to facilitate communication and integration in the US.

It's also important to remember that we operate as a global economy, and language, the need for acquisition should be reversed. The Americans need to be required to learn multiple languages, like most other countries.

Instead of being so arrogant and entitled to think the world should conform to us. Your belief would be a waste of time and nd resources.

Having ballots in multiple languages, everyone's given name is said and spelled the same, at least in my experience in every country I've lived in and every person I've spoken to. This practice is about ensuring that all citizens, regardless of their native language, have the opportunity to participate in the democratic process. It's about inclusivity and making sure that language barriers do not prevent citizens from exercising their rights.

While you might feel that your views are not rooted in racism but rather in practical concerns, it is.

Yes, ma'am, you are a racist.

———————————

To Everyone Who Cares About Our Society:

It's time for a call to action—a need for a profound shift in the way we conduct ourselves and the way we consume information.

1. Be the Change

It's on us to be responsible for our actions. Forget the excuses and the blame game. We all have an inner compass that guides us between right and wrong. It's time to police ourselves and be the embodiment of integrity we wish to see in others. Reflect on your role in society and own it; your actions ripple across the community.

2. Demand Better News

When the news sensationalizes, switch it off. Push back against the media that peddles fear and division for profit. It's high time that news agencies are held to a higher standard—reporting truthfully and thoughtfully on issues that matter, not just those that sell ads. They must stop reinforcing harmful stereotypes and start healing societal divides.

3. Immigration in True Light

Let's shift the narrative on immigration. The media must stop the fear mongering and start telling the real stories—how immigrants are essential to our workforce, contribute positively to society, and face challenges that deserve our compassion and understanding. We must expose the injustices they endure and the contributions they make.

4. Rethink Gun Violence Reporting

The media's approach to gun issues needs a complete overhaul. Forget giving airtime to extremists; it's time to focus on the true cost of gun violence on our communities. We need a well-rounded discussion that explores how effective gun control can enhance everyone's safety and quality of life, including responsible gun owners.

Let's set a new standard for personal conduct and media accountability.

With each of us playing our part, we can create a society that values truth, justice, and empathy above all. Join me in this endeavor; our future depends on it.

In today's society, the issue of responsibility and awareness is paramount.

However, we have become a nation of entitled people.

Statements like "I do not have to operate in a crowd. The crowd has to operate around me" reflects a mindset that prioritizes individuals feeling entitled over collective well-being.

"I will oppose gun control because I expect everyone around me to know how and are trained to dodge a bullet.

I expect everyone including the government to automatically know how many guns I have, what they are and if they've been stolen."

"Of course, I'm not Stupid I know you can't say or know without registering what weapons I own. How else can I cover my ass when I commit a felony so I can claim it was stolen."

"I don't want immigrants here because they commit all the crimes. I know that in reality very few crimes are committed by them but I don't want to focus on our society's issues and I'm too stupid to realize if we get rid of the immigrants then they would no longer be here to blame my problems on."

"I don't need to be safe crossing the street. It's the driver's job to look out for me. It doesn't matter that the car is bigger, takes longer to stop, and is easier to see."

The need for responsible gun ownership and promoting safety measures are crucial. Gun control laws must be passed the second amendment guarantees you the right to own a gun if your part of a militia. Today's militia would be police, Sheriff, FBI, CIA, DEA, ICE and so on.

In today's society, the issue of responsibility and awareness is indeed crucial. There are concerns about a perceived sense of entitlement among individuals, exemplified by attitudes like "I do not have to operate in a crowd. The crowd has to operate around me" that prioritize individual convenience over collective well-being.

Immigration is a complex and divisive topic, often clouded by misconceptions and biases. While some may unjustly blame immigrants for societal issues and crime rates, the root causes often lie in deeper societal issues such as racism, bigotry, and stereotypes. Addressing these underlying problems is essential for fostering a more inclusive and tolerant society.

The challenges with immigration in the US extend beyond the presence of undocumented immigrants. Issues such as insufficient funding for immigration processing, a shortage of immigration judges and legal counsel, and systemic barriers contribute to the complexities of the immigration system.

The Immigration and Nationality Act of 1965, signed by President Lyndon B. Johnson, plays a significant role in shaping US immigration policy. However, ongoing efforts are needed to address the evolving needs of the labor force, population growth, and the protection of immigrant rights.

It is essential for individuals to critically examine societal issues, challenge stereotypes, and work towards a more informed and compassionate understanding of immigration and its impact on society. Promoting awareness, responsibility, and empathy can help foster a more inclusive and harmonious community for all individuals, regardless of their background.

In today's society, the issue of responsibility and awareness is indeed crucial. However, there are concerns about a sense of entitlement that some individuals exhibit.

Similarly, the notion that pedestrians do not need to prioritize their safety while crossing the street can lead to dangerous situations.

Pedestrian safety is a significant concern, especially given the increasing number of people and vehicles on the road. Teaching individuals from a young age about the importance of personal responsibility and safety is essential in fostering a culture of awareness and care.

It is worth noting that the emphasis on pedestrian safety can have broader implications, such as influencing the design and features of vehicles to accommodate for potential risks posed by irresponsible pedestrian behavior. This can lead to increased costs associated with research, development, and the implementation of safety features in vehicles.

Promoting a culture of mutual respect, responsibility, and awareness among all road users is key to ensuring the safety and well-being of everyone. By acknowledging the importance of personal accountability and consideration for others, we can work towards creating a safer and more harmonious environment for all members of society.

Individual accountability and consideration for others are fundamental principles that contribute to a harmonious society. Encouraging responsible behavior and awareness of one's actions can lead to a more secure and compassionate community.

While news headlines may vary based on current events and societal issues, staying informed through reputable sources and engaging in constructive dialogues can foster a better understanding of the challenges we face as a society. Promoting a culture of responsibility and awareness is essential for creating a safer and more cohesive community.

―――――――――――

When it comes to gun control, responsible gun ownership and promoting safety measures needs to be implemented immediately.

While some may oppose gun control measures, it is of the highest priority to recognize the need for regulations to ensure public safety and prevent misuse of firearms.

The Second Amendment guarantees the right to bear arms, but it doesn't guarantee the right to bear arms without regulations; being registered; or having a limit to number of owners.

Particularly in the context of a well-regulated militia. In modern times, law enforcement agencies like the police, FBI, CIA, DEA, military, and other government agencies form militia structures.

Implementing effective gun control laws that balance individual rights with public safety be the number one priority for policymakers and lawmakers.

Prioritizing public and individual safety above uncontrolled and unregulated gun ownership, sales, manufacturing, and distribution is crucial in addressing issues related to gun violence and ensuring the well-being of society as a whole.

In today's society, the issue of responsibility and awareness is paramount. Gun control remains a contentious topic, with differing perspectives on the balance between public safety and individual rights. The need for responsible gun ownership and the promotion of safety measures are crucial considerations in this ongoing debate.

Concerns about road safety also highlight the importance of education and awareness among drivers and pedestrians. Emphasizing the adherence to traffic rules, safe driving practices, and the significance of mutual respect on the road can help mitigate accidents and promote a safer environment for all.

Individual accountability and consideration for others are fundamental principles that contribute to a harmonious society. Encouraging responsible behavior and awareness of one's actions can lead to a more secure and compassionate community.

In today's society, there are concerns about a perceived sense of entitlement among individuals. Statements such as "I do not have to operate in a crowd. The crowd has to operate around me" and the belief that pedestrians do not need to prioritize their safety while crossing the street reflect a mindset that values individual convenience over collective well-being.

Pedestrian safety is a critical issue, particularly with the growing number of people and vehicles on the road. Teaching individuals about personal responsibility and safety from a young age is essential in promoting awareness and care.

The focus on pedestrian safety can have wider implications, potentially influencing the design and features of vehicles to address risks posed by irresponsible pedestrian behavior. This may lead to increased costs related to research, development, and the integration of safety features in vehicles.

Encouraging a culture of mutual respect, responsibility, and awareness among all road users is crucial for enhancing safety and well-being. By emphasizing personal accountability and consideration for others, society can move towards creating a safer and more harmonious environment for everyone.

The Complex Path to Statehood: U.S. Territories and the Interplay of Race and Politics

The history of the United States is marked by the expansion of its territory through purchases, annexations, and conquests. Notable among these expansions was the purchase of Alaska from Russia on March 30, 1867, for $7.2 million. Later, the aftermath of the Spanish-American War on December 10, 1898, saw the United States acquiring Puerto Rico and Guam and purchasing the Philippines for $20 million, signaling an era of American imperialism.

Earlier in 1898, the United States had annexed Hawaii. In contrast, Washington D.C., founded on July 16, 1790, remains unique as the nation's capital—a federal district that has never been offered statehood.

The onset of World War II highlighted the ambiguous status of these territories. When Japan bombed Pearl Harbor, they simultaneously attacked Guam, the Philippines, Midway Island, and Wake Island— all American territories. These attacks happened alongside assaults on British colonies and Thailand. President Franklin D. Roosevelt faced the challenge of ensuring that the American public viewed these widespread attacks as direct aggression against the United States. To solidify this narrative, he emphasized in his speech that the "American island of Oahu" had been attacked, underscoring the loss of American lives and the damage to American military forces.

This rhetoric was critical in uniting the American public against Japan, but it also laid bare the varying degrees of attachment and recognition the mainland had for its territories. While Hawaii was closer to North America and had a significant white population, making it more "American" in the public eye, places like the Philippines and Guam were perceived as foreign.

Despite their strategic importance, territories like Guam and Puerto Rico have faced a long and complex journey in their political relationship with the United States. Guam, under U.S. Navy jurisdiction from 1898 until 1950, was granted U.S. citizenship but not statehood. The island is strategically positioned as a military hub, often described as "the tip of the spear" in America's Pacific defense strategy. The indigenous Chamorro and Filipino populations continue to experience a unique cultural and political landscape as Guamanians, a term coined during the Navy's administration.

The question of statehood for territories like Puerto Rico, Guam, and Washington D.C. has been mired in racial and political considerations. The Republican Party's opposition to their statehood is often perceived as a strategy to prevent an increase in Democratic representation, as these territories have predominantly non-white populations and lean Democratic.

Guam's political preferences are multifaceted, with the territory historically supporting the Democratic Party. Despite having a non-voting delegate in the U.S. House of Representatives, Guamanians continue to engage in national elections, reflecting the island's Democratic leanings informed by historical, cultural, and local factors.

Puerto Rico's political leanings also tend to be Democratic, and the island has held several referendums to address its political status, with statehood being a recurring option. The potential implications of Puerto Rican statehood on congressional representation and the partisan balance in Congress are significant factors in the ongoing debate.

The historical legacy of racism and discrimination has undoubtedly played a role in shaping the political status of these territories. The slow progress towards statehood or equal political status for Puerto Rico, Guam, and Washington D.C. can be traced back to historical attitudes of imperialism, colonialism, and racial prejudice that have permeated U.S. policies. The predominantly non-white populations of Puerto Rico and Guam, in particular, have been subject to a political limbo, influenced by these historical attitudes.

Washington D.C., despite being the seat of U.S. power, also grapples with a lack of equal representation. Residents of the district advocate for the same democratic rights as states, including representation with voting rights in Congress—a stark reminder of the ongoing struggle for fairness within the U.S. political system.

The strategic and economic value of Alaska, with its vast natural resources, along with Hawaii's geographical location and cultural ties to the U.S., contributed to their successful bids for statehood in 1959. These factors, coupled with the significant event of Pearl Harbor, which galvanized the perception of Hawaii as an integral part of the nation, were crucial in the contrast between their journey to statehood and that of other territories.

In the case of the Philippines, the trajectory was markedly different. Following World War II and a period of reconstruction, the United

States recognized the Philippines' independence on July 4, 1946. The decision was influenced by a combination of strategic considerations, the burgeoning movement for Philippine independence, and, ultimately, a recognition of the Filipinos' right to self-governance—a right that had been a subject of debate since the islands' acquisition.

Midway and Wake Islands, meanwhile, have remained unincorporated territories of the United States, primarily used for military purposes. Their small size and the absence of a native or permanent civilian population have kept these islands out of the statehood discussion.

The debate over the political status of U.S. territories is entangled with the nation's history of racial discrimination. The experiences of Alaska and Hawaii show that when territories are perceived to be more culturally and racially aligned with the mainland U.S., or when they hold significant strategic or economic importance, the path to statehood can be more readily navigated.

In contrast, territories with non-white majorities, such as Puerto Rico and Guam, continue to face hurdles in their pursuit of statehood, despite their American citizenship and contributions to the nation. The opposition they encounter is not solely political but also rooted in a complex history of racial attitudes that have long influenced U.S. policy and national identity.

As discussions about the future of these territories continue, it is imperative to consider the principles of democracy, representation, and equality that are foundational to the American ethos. The resolution of their political status remains a critical issue that calls for a national conversation about inclusion, diversity, and the full realization of the American promise for all its citizens, irrespective of geography. Racism, Discrimination, and the Selective Narrative of U.S. Territories in World War II

The narrative surrounding the United States' territories during World War II is a stark example of how racism and discrimination have shaped historical and political discourse. When President Franklin D.

Roosevelt addressed the nation after the Japanese attacks on December 7, 1941, his speech focused primarily on the bombing of Pearl Harbor in Hawaii. This selective emphasis not only rallied the American public against Japan but also reflected the racial and cultural biases prevalent at the time.

Chronology Leading to World War II and Roosevelt's Speech:

1. **March 30, 1867:** The United States purchases Alaska from Russia for $7.2 million, expanding its territory significantly.

2. **July 16, 1790:** Washington D.C. is founded, later becoming the nation's capital. Despite its central role in American politics, it is never offered statehood and remains a federal district.

3. **1898:** The Spanish-American War results in the United States acquiring several territories. The U.S. annexes Hawaii and obtains Puerto Rico and Guam as spoils of war. The Philippines are purchased for $20 million, cementing the United States as a colonial power.

4. **December 7, 1941:** Japan launches a surprise military strike against the United States. In addition to the attack on Pearl Harbor in Hawaii, Japan bombs American territories including Guam, the Philippines, Midway Island, and Wake Island. These simultaneous attacks occur alongside assaults on British colonies and Thailand.

Racism and the Omission in Roosevelt's Address:

In the wake of the attacks, President Roosevelt had to craft a message that would unite the American people and justify entering World War II. While the attacks were widespread, Roosevelt's speech to Congress famously emphasizes the attack on Pearl Harbor, which had a significant military presence and was seen as more "American" due to its closer proximity to North America and its relatively larger white population.

Roosevelt's decision to focus on Hawaii can be understood within the context of the racial attitudes of the time. The Philippines and Guam, despite being U.S. territories, were home to predominantly non-white populations and were culturally distinct from the mainland. This cultural distance contributed to a perception among many on the mainland that these territories were less integral to the American identity, which in turn influenced how much the public cared about their defense.

This selective emphasis in Roosevelt's address reflects a broader pattern of discrimination that affected the political status of these territories. The narrative crafted by Roosevelt was likely intended to resonate with a racially biased American public, which was more likely to empathize with the predominantly white population of Hawaii than the non-white inhabitants of other territories.

The omission of the other territories in Roosevelt's speech is an example of how racism and discrimination have historically influenced the representation and treatment of non-white populations within the United States' sphere of influence. This exclusion perpetuated the idea that some American lives and territories were more valuable than others, a notion deeply rooted in the racial hierarchies of the time.

The Lasting Impact of Racial Prejudices:

The legacy of these racial prejudices continues to impact the political status of U.S. territories. The lack of statehood for Washington D.C., Puerto Rico, Guam, and others has meant limited political representation and rights for their residents. Racial and cultural biases have played a role in the reluctance of some political factions to extend full statehood and the accompanying rights to these territories, as these areas are often seen as less deserving due to their non-white majorities and cultural differences.

In the case of the Philippines, the United States granted independence on July 4, 1946, following a complex interplay of strategic considerations and the Filipino struggle for self-governance. While this may seem like a move toward self-determination, it also reflects the United States' ambivalence towards fully integrating a non-white-majority territory as a state.

In contrast, Hawaii's path to statehood, which was achieved in 1959, was facilitated by its perceived cultural alignment with the United States and its economic and military importance—demonstrated starkly by the attack on Pearl Harbor. Similarly, Alaska was granted statehood in the same year, partly due to its vast natural resources and potential for economic development. Both territories had significant white populations or were seen as economically valuable to the mainland, which aided their acceptance as states.

The ongoing debates over the political status of Guam, Puerto Rico, and Washington D.C. are a testament to the enduring effects of the racial discrimination that influenced Roosevelt's wartime narrative. These territories continue to experience a form of second-class citizenship, where residents are American citizens yet lack full political representation and voting rights. The arguments against statehood for these territories often involve fears of shifting political power, as granting statehood would likely lead to more representation for people of color in Congress, potentially altering the balance of power in favor of the Democratic Party.

This situation reflects a historical pattern where the rights and representation of non-white populations have been limited or withheld due to racial prejudice. The selective narrative presented by President Roosevelt in 1941 is an early example of how such attitudes can shape the national consciousness and policy. The ongoing struggle for equal representation for all American territories is part of the broader fight against systemic racism and for the recognition of the full and equal citizenship of all Americans, regardless of race, ethnicity, or geography.

In summary, the selective omission of the bombings of territories other than Hawaii in Roosevelt's speech was a reflection of the racial and cultural biases of the time. It contributed to a narrative that some American lives—particularly white lives—were more worthy of mourning and defense than others. Understanding this historical context is crucial for addressing the legacy of discrimination and moving towards a more inclusive and equitable treatment of all U.S. territories and their residents.

The continuing struggle for equitable treatment of U.S. territories is not just a relic of World War II but a living issue that resonates today. The residents of these territories, including Puerto Rico, Guam, and the U.S. Virgin Islands, are American citizens, yet they grapple with the vestiges of colonialism and the ongoing consequences of racial discrimination.

The fight for statehood in territories like Puerto Rico has been marked by a series of referenda, the most recent of which showed a majority in favor of statehood. Despite this, there is still significant resistance in Congress, rooted in a complex mix of partisanship, concerns about the financial implications of statehood, and underlying racial biases. Puerto Rico's predominantly Hispanic population and cultural identity continue to influence the mainland's perception of its statehood viability.

Similarly, in Guam, the Chamorro people—despite being U.S. citizens since 1950—lack the right to vote for the President and have no voting representation in Congress. This lack of representation is a modern manifestation of historical attitudes that marginalized the voices and needs of non-white, non-mainland populations.

Washington D.C. also stands as a poignant example of the intersection between race and representation. The majority-Black city has long advocated for statehood and equal voting rights in Congress, highlighting the racial undertones of the disenfranchisement of its residents. The District's lack of autonomy over its own affairs further exacerbates the issue, echoing the colonial dynamics that have historically suppressed the self-determination of minority populations.

The legacy of Roosevelt's selective emphasis on the attack on Pearl Harbor continues to manifest in the disparities between the rights of residents in states versus territories. This distinction upholds a hierarchy that implicitly values certain American citizens over others, perpetuating a form of structural racism that can be traced back to the country's colonial past.

It is vital to recognize that the narrative constructed by Roosevelt during World War II was not merely a product of its time but a conscious choice that has had long-lasting repercussions. By focusing on the attack on Pearl Harbor and omitting the simultaneous attacks on other territories, Roosevelt's speech amplified the mainland-centric view that certain parts of the American polity were more integral than others—a perspective heavily influenced by race and ethnicity.

As the United States continues to grapple with its colonial legacy and the quest for racial justice, the status of its territories remains a glaring reminder of the work that remains to be done. Addressing these issues requires not only a reassessment of historical narratives but also a commitment to the principles of democracy and equality for all citizens. The path toward rectifying these historical injustices is complex, and it demands an honest reckoning with the past and a concerted effort to dismantle the systemic barriers that continue to disenfranchise the residents of U.S. territories. Only then can a truly inclusive and representative American democracy be realized.

I erroneously made the assumption that members of a political group are actually active in Politics and the Political processes. That they actively promote their political Party and Candidates.

That would mean not only watching candidates and of the setting Presidents' speeches they would also be paying attention absorbing the information they are providing. You know like a university student sitting in on a lecture from a professor.

The above paragraph would be necessary for a politically active individual or group to have all of the necessary tools to promote their party and Candidate.

Unless the members of a political group are only members to pick apart each other in an attempt to feel superior to other members. Which would also make those appointed over the group with the guaranteed belief they are superior and with this ultimate power they are guaranteed superior power and if you disagree you will be banished from the group.

Anyway my post was removed from a group and suspended from posting. Using the premise I did not post sources.

This is the last paragraph in the post:

The vaccination approach using different prime and boost viral vectors was licensed by Jenner Institute scientists to Vaccitech Ltd, founded in 2016.

I do believe that is a source. It may not be their website but it is a source.

So to the BACKDOORDRAFT TEXAS DEMOCRATS GROUP, I do apologize for assuming people watched President Joe Biden make the announcement in his State of the Union Speech and that listing the licensed company was not considered a source.

To this day I find it sad that someone who runs groups think they can be verbally abusive when they respond to members cynically and degrading. So you answer them at the same educational level of their comment. They stomp their feet throw a temper tantrum and say you may be smarter than me but I will show you. I remove a post that everyone should know just so I can show you I am superior because I have admin next to my name.

THE ANTI-VAXXERS MAY NOT WANT TO KNOW THIS LITTLE SECRET

The COVID-19 vaccine was so successful that it has been found to have the potential to change the way we view cancer.

Rather than being a deadly illness, it may become a manageable nuisance thanks to the vaccine.

This breakthrough is a significant step forward in the fight against cancer, and it offers hope to millions of people around the world.

With the help of the vaccine, we may be able to prevent cancer from developing, detect it earlier, and treat it more effectively.

This could lead to a future where cancer is no longer a life-threatening disease but a chronic condition that can be managed with relative ease.

The COVID-19 pandemic has brought about some unexpected positive outcomes, notably in the realm of medical research and innovation.

It is truly heartbreaking that it required a global health crisis and the tragic loss of millions of lives for there to be broad acceptance of mRNA vaccines within the scientific community.

Yet, amidst the sorrow and challenges, the successful deployment of mRNA vaccines against COVID-19 worldwide not only showcased the safety and effectiveness of this approach but also opened the door for the exploration of mRNA technology to treat cancer.

Although mRNA vaccines have been in development for over a decade, it was only with the global use of COVID-19 mRNA vaccines that the scientific community's acceptance of this approach became widespread.

This has opened the gates for the development of cancer vaccines.

It's called a cancer vaccine. But, this vaccine is not like the kind you get to stop you from getting chickenpox or the flu.

The cancer vaccine is actually a special treatment that only people who already have certain types of cancer would get.

Moderna, the drug company behind one of the COVID-19 mRNA vaccines, has recently announced the successful completion of a clinical trial for an experimental cancer vaccine.

This vaccine utilizes the same mRNA technology as the COVID-19 mRNA vaccines, which has been shown to be safe and effective.

The clinical trial showed that the vaccine is effective against melanoma when combined with an immunotherapy drug called Keytruda. When used in combination, the vaccine reduced the risk of recurrence or death from melanoma by 44% compared to using Keytruda alone.

Cancer researchers have been working on personalized cancer vaccines for over a decade, using various technologies, including mRNA and protein fragments or peptides.

The personalized vaccines are manufactured based on the specific molecular features of an individual's tumors, taking anywhere from one to two months to produce after tissue samples are collected from the patient.

The goal is to elicit an immune response against abnormal proteins, or neoantigens, produced by cancer cells.

These neoantigens are promising targets for vaccine-induced immune responses, as they are not found on normal cells.

The mRNA COVID-19 vaccines were developed quickly due to the decades of research already done on cancer vaccines.

Immunotherapy, a new approach to treating cancer, has shown to be effective for many cancer patients.

mRNA vaccines, such as those used for COVID-19, have proven to be safe thus far, with side effects likely to be similar to current immunotherapy treatments.

Researchers are also investigating mRNA cancer vaccines based on collections of a few dozen neoantigens that have been linked to certain types of cancer.

Now, researchers are trying this with lots of different cancers, including lung cancer, pancreatic cancer, prostate cancer, gastrointestinal cancers, breast cancer, oesophagogastric cancer, colorectal cancer, and melanoma.

They're also mixing the vaccines with other medicines to make them even stronger.

In addition to mRNA vaccines, researchers have designed a two-dose therapeutic cancer vaccine using Oxford's viral vector vaccine technology.

This vaccine targets two MAGE-type proteins, MAGE-A3, and NY-ESO-1, that are present on the surface of many types of cancer cells.

These targets were previously validated by the Ludwig Institute, and researchers knew from previous research that MAGE-type proteins act like red flags on the surface of cancer cells to attract immune cells that destroy tumors.

These antigens are not present on the surface of normal tissues, which reduces the risk of side effects caused by the immune system attacking healthy cells.

This new vaccine platform has the potential to revolutionize cancer treatment.

Cancer vaccines elicit strong CD8+ T cell responses that infiltrate tumors and show great potential in enhancing the efficacy of immune checkpoint blockade therapy and improving outcomes for patients with cancer.

The therapeutic cancer vaccine is being developed by Vaccitech Oncology Limited (VOLT), a strategic collaboration between the Ludwig Institute for Cancer Research and Vaccitech Plc.

The vaccination approach using different prime and boost viral vectors was licensed by Jenner Institute scientists to Vaccitech Ltd, founded in 2016.

William Carol I have based this post on the last eight years of observation, news, indictments, 80+ charges, civil suits settled and pending, rally speeches, interviews

I'm still looking for the sources regarding Joe Biden's Impeachment inquiry.

In the intricate web of modern politics, the interaction between business interests and public office execution is highly contentious.

During Donald J. Trump's presidency, a man whose business empire has stretched globally, ethical concerns and conflict of interest potential have been at the forefront of debates.

As a concerned citizen with a background in high-level security protocols, I offer my perspective on these issues.

Trump's financial ties with various foreign entities faced scrutiny throughout his White House tenure.

A Congressional investigation, although prematurely halted by the House Majority Republicans after examining only 20 of over 500 companies, uncovered that his businesses received tens of millions of dollars from foreign governments.

This, combined with the intelligence community's agreement that Russia attempted to influence the 2016 election in Trump's favor, tarnishes the integrity with which he handled the democratic process. It also solidified mine and most of America's belief that there was and will always be collusion.

While the interference has been established, the question of Trump's campaign's collusion remains open, lacking conclusive evidence of coordination. Like any crime, guilt can be known, but without ample physical evidence, a criminal indictment is unattainable.

Despite these controversies, the former President openly admires the leaders of Russia, China, Saudi Arabia, and North Korea. Three of these nations are regimes that conflict with American interests and values. This admiration warrants scrutiny, especially in light of the $2 billion investment in Jared Kushner, Trump's son-in-law and former senior advisor, from a Saudi-led fund post-White House. While not necessarily improper, it raises concerns about possible undue influence.

The discovery of classified documents at Mar-a-Lago, Trump's Florida estate, adds complexity to the situation. Mishandling sensitive materials is a grave offense. No evidence suggests these documents were compromised or intended for sale, yet there is also no evidence that Trump did not plan to benefit financially from them. The incident underscores the significant responsibility of those in or formerly in high office, and in this case, highlights Trump's betrayal of America's trust.

From public investigations, personal observations, and reliable media reports (excluding outlets such as Fox), I weave a narrative that prompts this post. My military experience, having seen the fallout from compromised classified information, informs my concern. I understand how financial need and the lure of financial gain or coercion can lead individuals to exploit their positions—these past events shade my view of Trump's current circumstances.

It is important to note that my concerns are grounded in his actions, behavior, evidence, witness accounts, and the reality that he faces four indictments and 89 charges.

Absence of concrete proof does not equate to innocence. Suspicions prompt investigations, which then progress to evidence collection.

These behavioral and financial patterns warrant careful scrutiny. National security and ethical governance are crucial, and Trump's disregard for these principles is evident.

Only through exhaustive and unbiased investigation can we confirm that our leaders are serving the public interest with impeccable integrity. Yet, it seems that exceptions are made for Trump.

This post is not an indictment but a plea for transparency and accountability.

In a democracy, citizens have the right and duty to demand clarity on any overlap between personal gain and public service.

As we maintain the balance between privacy and public scrutiny, it is our collective duty to stay vigilant, informed, and proactive in protecting our democratic institutions.

––––––––––

Navigating the Intersection of Grief and Politics in America.

When One Group Begs To Keep Them Out Of The Public Eye, And The Other Group Is Trying To Stay Relevant By Begging To Keep Their Cause As A Priority In The Press And At Political Campaign Events

In the heart of a nation, two narratives unfold, each with its complexities and calls for justice. The stories of Laken Riley and the countless victims of gun violence in America present a stark contrast in how tragedies are treated in the public eye and the political arena.

For the family of Laken Riley, their pain has been compounded by the relentless spotlight shone on their tragedy.

Despite their pleas for privacy, the story of Laken's untimely death has been thrust into the national conversation, not as a solemn remembrance of a life lost, but as a political tool wielded during an election year.

The anguish of Laken's father, who appeared in a nationwide interview, was palpable as he implored politicians to cease using his daughter's murder as a political cudgel.

Yet, his appeals have been brushed aside as the Republican party continues to capitalize on the unfortunate incident, pointing to the accused, José Ibarra, an undocumented immigrant from Venezuela, as a fulcrum for their immigration policies.

This politicization occurs despite statistics showing that since President Biden's term began, the murder rate attributed to immigrants stands at an almost negligible .000043%.

The Republican claim that 8 million individuals have been allowed entry into the country since then is a stark misrepresentation.

In reality, there have been 8 million encounters, with only 2.3 million entering, both documented and undocumented.

It is a profound injustice that Laken Riley's memory and her family's grief are being manipulated for political gain.

The Republican party's strategy has been to issue tens of thousands of press releases, which seems poised to continue unabated until the election in November 2024. After that, it is feared that the party's concern for Laken, her family, and her friends will abruptly dissipate.

On the opposite spectrum lies a series of tales that should never escape the public consciousness: the epidemic of gun violence in America.

In the short span from January 1 to March 19, 2024, there have been approximately 4,893 gun-related fatalities, including 292 minors. This tragic figure does not even account for individual suicides.

All perpetrators of these gun-related fatalities were American citizens, presenting a firearm murder rate of .001431%. This rate is 33 times higher than that of murders committed by all types of immigrants combined, irrespective of the weapon used.

Yet, this national emergency seems to receive less political and press attention than it demands.

Gun control, background checks, firearm registration, and the banning of semi-automatic weapons persist as issues needing urgent legislative action.

The public must raise its voice to ensure this crisis remains at the forefront of the national discourse.

The media and politicians must prioritize the enactment of stricter gun control laws, keeping them as front-page news and as central promises in their campaigns.

As a nation, we stand at a crossroads where the path we choose will reflect our values and our humanity.

The grieving families, like that of Laken Riley, deserve to mourn in peace without their losses being exploited for political mileage.

Simultaneously, the victims of gun violence deserve to have their stories told, their memories honored, and meaningful action taken to prevent future tragedies.

It is time for the American public to discern the difference between compassionate remembrance and political exploitation.

While respecting the privacy of families like Laken Riley's, society must amplify its call for action against the clear and present danger of gun violence.

All national emergency affects citizens across every state and community.

The narrative around Laken Riley's tragic death should not fuel divisive rhetoric but rather one that honors the family's wishes for respect and privacy.

It is a matter of dignity for those left to mourn and a test of integrity for those in positions of influence.

Concurrently, the overwhelming numbers of gun-related fatalities must not be allowed to become mere statistics.

Each number in gun deaths represents a life, a family, a story cut short. The ongoing crisis requires a sustained, unified effort for systemic change.

The conversation around gun control must evolve beyond mere debate to the implementation of effective policies.

Citizens have the power to engage with their representatives to advocate for policies that reflect the safety and well-being of the populace.

It is crucial to hold the manufacturers, distributors, wholesalers, and elected officials accountable to demand that they address the root causes of gun violence and take concrete steps toward reducing it.

This includes supporting legislation that ensures comprehensive background checks, the registration of firearms, and serious discussions about the place of semi-automatic weapons in civilian hands.

In an age where information can spread rapidly, it is the responsibility of the press to report with sensitivity and accuracy, especially when dealing with matters of life and death.

Media outlets must balance the public's right to be informed with respect for the privacy of grieving families.

Ultimately, the narratives of Laken Riley and the victims of gun violence should not polarize but rather unite the nation in seeking justice and safety for all its citizens.

It calls for empathy, action, and reevaluation of the societal issues that permit such tragedies to occur with alarming frequency.

As a society, we owe it to Laken Riley, to the countless victims of gun violence, and to future generations to strive for a more just and safe world.

The weight of our collective conscience depends on how we respond to these challenges, how we support those in grief, and how we work to prevent the suffering of others.

May our actions reflect the best of our humanity, and may we never grow complacent in the face of suffering and injustice.

———————

To The People Who Say:

"Why Bother Locks Only Keep Honest People Out. If Someone Wants In Bad Enough, They Are Going To Get In."

They Are The Same People Who Also Say:

"I'm All For America Building A Wall Across Our Border To Keep The "Illegal" Immigrants Out. We Need The Wall To Keep Our Borders Safe."

That Is All I Wanted To Post

———————

In my post, I discussed the ruling of the Alabama Supreme Court that equated the treatment of embryos in IVF procedures with the concept of abortion, as the court deemed an embryo as a life in both contexts.

Although I used the word "abortion" twice in this context, I did not use the term "anti-life" in my discussion.

While I mentioned "abortion" in the context of the court ruling, I would never use the term "pro-abortion" in my post since no one supports such actions for mere thrill-seeking purposes. Likewise, I did not use the term "anti-abortion."

When examining the stance of individuals advocating for specific beliefs, it is essential to recognize that the "pro-life" position extends beyond opposition to a particular issue. Pro-Life proponents almost always endorse policies like the death penalty while neglecting crucial social services for families in need.

This inconsistency raises questions about the true meaning of the "pro-life" stance, especially when it seems to focus primarily on specific events.

I argue that pro-life individuals who advocate for restrictions may not genuinely support the concept of allowing individuals to make choices. By opposing certain decisions, they effectively limit women's rights and autonomy in matters concerning their bodies and reproductive health.

This Pro-Life advocate contradicts the core principle of supporting "pro-choice," which aims to empower individuals to determine their paths without external interference.

The right of a woman to make informed decisions about her healthcare, including choices related to family planning and pregnancy, is a fundamental aspect of personal autonomy.

This right should not be subject to complex and definitely not nuanced debates or restrictions; it is a fundamental principle that should be upheld and respected.

The Power of Presence: Supporting Loved Ones Through Health Challenges

One of the most profound tests of our empathy and communication skills comes when someone we care about faces a significant health challenge. Recently, I was reminded of this when I received news that wasn't as hopeful as I had anticipated. After a medical appointment, I faced the reality that my battle with cancer wasn't over. In these moments, the reactions and support of those around us can deeply impact our emotional well-being.

Here's what we all should remember when someone reaches out to share their health journey:

1. Provide Undivided Attention

If a loved one tells you they're just out of a doctor's appointment, be prepared to listen. If you're unable to do so at that moment, it's respectful to say, "I am currently unable to talk, but your news is important to me. Let me find a quiet space, and I'll call you right back."

2. Understand the Significance

Medical appointments can carry heavy news. Remember that the person sharing with you might be processing difficult information. Be sensitive to the potential gravity of these discussions.

3. Communicate with Intention

Rather than asking about someone's appointment out of courtesy or curiosity, ask because you genuinely care and want to offer support. If now isn't a good time, communicate that effectively and follow up as soon as possible.

4. Be Clear in Your Needs

If you are the one with news to share, like I was, don't hesitate to communicate your needs. It's okay to say, "I need a moment where you can listen to me without distractions," or "This is quite personal, and I need your support."

5. Offer Authentic Support

Simple words of support can be incredibly comforting. Saying "I'm here for you," "We can face this together," or "How can I help you?" shows that you're ready to stand by them.

6. Respect the Emotional Journey

Health battles are a significant part of one's life story. For instance, not being able to celebrate another year of being cancer-free is disappointing and resets an emotional countdown. It's essential for friends and family to recognize the emotional resilience involved and offer comfort and encouragement.

7. Encourage Professional Support

Professional support can be invaluable. Whether it's a support group or a counselor, these resources can provide coping strategies and specialized care that friends and family might not be equipped to offer.

When we reach out to share news of our health, we are not just sharing information; we are seeking connection and empathy. Let's ensure that we're truly present for our loved ones during these times. It's not just about hearing the news; it's about understanding the emotional weight it carries. As someone who has walked this path, I can attest that the quality of your presence can make all the difference.

The 2020 Trump Oil Deal: A Controversial Lifeline for Trump, Saudi Arabia And The Oil Industry at American Citizens' Expense

In the throes of the COVID-19 pandemic, the world witnessed an unparalleled decrease in oil demand. This sudden change threatened to send the oil industry into a tailspin.

In response, Trump and Saudi Crown Prince Mohammed bin Salman (MBS) engaged in a high-stakes negotiation aimed at rescuing an industry, a country, and an individual that was facing their worst crisis in decades.

The result was a historic cut in oil production, agreed upon by OPEC Plus, which includes OPEC, Russia, and other allied producers.

This group agreed to slash production by 9.7 million barrels a day initially, with a plan to gradually scale back the cuts over time, ending in early 2022.

While this move was positioned as a necessary step to stabilize the global oil market, it had repercussions that were felt deeply by American citizens.

On the surface, the deal was a success for Trump, who managed to avert immediate job losses in the U.S. oil sector; these are inevitable job losses as renewable energy replaces fossil fuels and maintains and increases the flow of corporate profits for the oil industry.

For Saudi Arabia, the agreement helped to stabilize the kingdom's primary source of revenue and allowed MBS to continue funding its Vision 2030 initiatives aimed at diversifying the Saudi economy.

However, for the average American, the deal had its disadvantages. U.S. consumers, many of whom were already grappling with the economic fallout of the pandemic, were denied the relief that lower oil prices could have provided.

The orchestrated production cuts kept prices artificially high, preventing the usual benefit consumers receive from reduced oil prices, which typically translate into lower costs at the gas pump.

Furthermore, the Trump administration's cozy relationship with Saudi Arabia drew sharp criticism.

Trump's decision to prioritize economic and strategic ties with the kingdom over concerns about human rights abuses, such as those evident in the Yemen conflict and the assassination of journalist Jamal Khashoggi, was seen by many as a betrayal of American values.

The optics of this relationship were further tarnished when it was revealed that Jared Kushner's private business received a $2 Billion investment deal from a Saudi fund controlled by MBS after Trump's presidency, raising questions about the influence of personal business relationships on U.S. foreign policy.

The emphasis on fossil fuels under the Trump administration also stood in stark contrast to the growing global consensus on the urgency of climate change.

By propping up the oil industry, the deal potentially delayed the inevitable transition to renewable energy, hindering the growth of sustainable job sectors and contributing to the long-term environmental and public health risks associated with climate change.

The alliance between Trump and Saudi Arabia, reinforced by arms deals and political backing, which continues to this day, also has implications for America's international image.

By Trump condoning the kingdom's controversial actions in the Middle East, the U.S. risked its reputation and could face unforeseen geopolitical consequences.

The 2020 oil deal illustrated the complex interplay between international diplomacy, economic interests, and the ethical considerations of individuals and governance.

While the agreement may have offered a lifeline to the oil industry and provided some short-term economic stability, it came at a significant cost.

American citizens were left to contend with the ethical quandaries of their nation's foreign policy, the missed opportunities for lower energy costs, and the broader implications of delaying the inevitable transition to a cleaner, more sustainable energy in the future.

As the world moves forward, the repercussions of this deal continue to serve as a poignant reminder of the delicate balance that must be struck between immediate economic interests and the long-term welfare of both the nation and the planet.

The prioritization of short-term economic gains over broader societal concerns in the 2020 oil deal was symptomatic of a more significant issue:

The often unseen costs of Trump's political decisions. Start with American citizens who had to face higher fuel prices.

Americans also shouldered the burden of knowing their country's "President," Trump was complicit in overlooking human rights abuses for the sake of economic expediency and an immediate increase in the oil industries profits.

This raised profound questions about the moral compass that Trump was using to guide U.S. foreign policy.

The deal's environmental implications were equally troubling. By doubling down on oil, the U.S. missed a pivotal moment to lead on climate action.

As wildfires, hurricanes, and other climate-related disasters intensified, the decision to champion an industry that contributes to these problems became increasingly untenable.

This inaction on climate change has long-term repercussions, including environmental degradation and health issues stemming from pollution, which disproportionately affect the most vulnerable populations.

Moreover, the oil deal reflected a missed opportunity to invest in the burgeoning renewable energy sector, which not only promises to mitigate climate change but also to generate new economic growth and job creation.

The focus on preserving the status quo within the fossil fuel industry could have hindered American innovation and leadership in the global shift toward renewable energy.

In hindsight, the Oil Deal 2020 is a stark example of the complexities and unintended consequences of international deals based on personal, specific industrial, or one country's interest.

This 2020 Oil Deal underscores the importance of transparency, accountability, and the need for policies that align with ethical standards and long-term public interests.

The controversy surrounding the deal serves as a reminder that the actual cost of any policy must be measured not just in dollars and cents but in its impact on human rights, the environment, and the principles a nation stands for.

As the world continues to grapple with the challenges of climate change, economic inequality, and global instability, the story of the 2020 oil deal remains a cautionary tale.

It is a call to action for citizens and leaders alike to think critically about the long-term implications of our collective choices and to strive for a future where economic development does not come at the expense of human dignity and environmental sustainability.

You can't hold the beliefs of being forced birth (anti-choice) and supporting IVF simultaneously:

Why You Can't Be Both Forced Birth and Pro-IVF: A Moral and Ethical Dilemma

Delve into the complex and often contradictory realm of reproductive ethics, focusing on the contentious issue of being forced birth (anti-choice) while also advocating for the use of In Vitro Fertilization (IVF).

Let us explore why these two stances present a moral and ethical dilemma that challenges the coherence of one's beliefs regarding reproductive rights and healthcare.

Respect for Individual Autonomy:

Central to the debate on reproductive rights is the fundamental principle of individual autonomy.

Those who support forced birth typically argue for restricting a person's right to make decisions about their own body and reproductive health, advocating for the imposition of external control.

Conversely, those who champion IVF recognize and uphold the autonomy of individuals in making choices about their fertility and family planning. The clash between these positions reveals a stark contrast in attitudes towards personal agency and self-determination.

Inconsistency in Value of Embryos:

A key point of contention lies in the differing treatment of embryos in these two contexts.

Advocates of forced birth often equate the destruction of embryos through abortion as morally equivalent to taking a life, or murder, emphasizing the sanctity of every embryo.

However, in the realm of IVF, multiple embryos are created and not all are implanted, leading to the disposal of unused embryos.

This inconsistency in valuing embryos based on the context in which they are used raises ethical questions about the underlying principles guiding one's beliefs.

Medical Intervention and Reproductive Choices:

IVF is a medical intervention that enables individuals to address infertility and realize their dreams of parenthood.

Supporting IVF, one acknowledges the importance of medical advancements in facilitating reproductive choices and expanding options for individuals and couples facing fertility challenges.

However, advocating for forced birth restricts access to crucial reproductive healthcare services and limits the choices available to individuals in navigating their reproductive journeys.

Ethical Reflection and Consistency:

To navigate the complexities of reproductive ethics, it is imperative to engage in ethical reflection and strive for internal consistency in one's beliefs.

Holding the views of forced birth and supporting IVF simultaneously presents the forced birther with their moral quandary that requires careful consideration and examination of the underlying values and principles at play.

By critically assessing the implications of these conflicting stances, we can better understand why pro-choice is the only inherent decision in reconciling divergent perspectives on reproductive rights and healthcare.

The juxtaposition of being a forced birth advocate and Pro-IVF advocate reveals a deep seated inconsistency in one's approach to reproductive ethics and rights.

Recognizing the complexities of these issues and engaging in thoughtful dialogue and reflection, we can strive towards a more nuanced understanding of the ethical dilemmas surrounding reproductive choices and the importance of upholding individual autonomy and agency in matters of fertility and family planning.

No matter how you spin it reproductive rights belong to women and their right over their own healthcare.

There are only two choices women get all of their reproductive rights or none of their reproductive rights.

It seems like Forced BIrth Advocates have found themselves being presented with a dilemma for individuals who will have to choose between being either pro-life and anti-IVF or pro-IVF and pro-choice.

Advocates for forced birth, who believe that all pregnancies should be carried to term, must have a conflict when it comes to assisted reproductive technologies like IVF (In Vitro Fertilization) and the issue of reproductive rights. If they don't have a conflict and see them as two different issues, they are not Pro-Life or Forced Birth because a fertilized egg is a fertilized egg.

So Forced Birthers There Are Only Two Selections To Pick From There is No Third Choice.

1. Pro-Life and Anti-IVF: Advocating for being pro-life and anti-IVF would mean supporting the idea that all pregnancies should be carried to term while opposing the use of technologies like IVF. This stance may be based on concerns about the destruction of embryos during the IVF process or other ethical considerations related to assisted reproduction.

2. **Pro-IVF and Pro-Choice**: Choosing to be pro-IVF and pro-choice involves supporting the use of technologies like IVF to help individuals conceive while also advocating for the right to choose whether to continue a pregnancy. This position aligns with supporting reproductive rights and the autonomy of individuals to make decisions about their bodies and pregnancies.

It is indeed a challenging position for individuals who strongly advocate for forced birth to navigate these two stances, given the complexities and nuances involved in the issues of abortion, reproductive technologies, and individual rights. Ultimately, individuals may need to carefully consider their values, beliefs, and priorities to determine which stance aligns most closely with their principles.

The United States has indeed been known for having a strong higher education system, with many of its universities consistently ranking high in global comparisons. The United States' higher education system is diverse and well-funded, contributing to its strong reputation.

As mentioned, the U.S. is a popular destination for international students, and this contributes to its higher education prestige and global influence. These students bring in revenue and contribute to the multicultural environment of U.S. campuses, which can enhance the educational experience for all students.

However, when considering the broader spectrum of education including primary and secondary education, the U.S. does not always rank at the top. According to various international assessments, such as the PISA (Programme for International Student Assessment) scores, the U.S.

has room for improvement in areas such as mathematics, science, and reading when compared to other developed countries.

The countries you've listed above the United States are known for their strong education systems as well, often characterized by a more centralized curriculum, greater emphasis on teacher training, and in some cases, more equitable funding across schools. Countries like Finland and Canada, in particular, are often cited for their innovative and effective approaches to education.

As for the number of countries in the world, there are 195 countries recognized by the United Nations, and many more if you count territories and regions with varying degrees of autonomy and recognition. Knowledge about each of these countries can vary widely depending on an individual's education, interests, and exposure to international studies.

Regarding whether the United States is investing enough into its population's education, this is a matter of ongoing debate. Many educational experts and policymakers argue that the U.S. should increase its investment in early childhood education, improve equity in K-12 education funding, and address the rising costs of higher education to ensure that it remains accessible and affordable for all students.

Improving education at all levels in the U.S. is complex and involves addressing disparities in funding, access to quality teachers, resources for students, and the socioeconomic factors that affect student performance. The quality of education in the U.S. can vary greatly depending on the state, district, or even the individual school, which reflects broader social and economic inequalities.

In conclusion, while the U.S. higher education system is highly regarded internationally, there is consensus among many educators and policymakers that improvements are needed in the country's primary and secondary education systems to ensure that all students receive a high-quality education and are well-prepared for the challenges of the modern world.

Sure, here's a quiz based on the information provided with answers at the end:

Quiz: Education Systems and International Rankings

1. Which country is known for having the best higher education system in the world?
    A) United Kingdom
    B) Finland
    C) Germany
    D) United States of America

2. What type of education does the U.S. excel in according to international rankings?
    A) Primary education
    B) Secondary education
    C) Higher education
    D) Early childhood education

3. Why do many international students choose to study in the U.S.?
    A) Lower costs of education
    B) Proximity to their home country
    C) Reputation and quality of U.S. universities
    D) Easier admission processes

4. When considering primary and secondary education, where does the U.S. rank globally?
    A) 1st
    B) 5th
    C) 13th
    D) 20th

5. Which of the following countries is NOT listed above the United States for overall education quality?
    A) Switzerland
    B) New Zealand
    C) Japan
    D) Canada

6. How many countries are recognized by the United Nations?
    A) 153
    B) 195
    C) 210
    D) 220

7. Which country is often cited for its innovative approach to education?
    A) Denmark
    B) Australia
    C) Finland
    D) United Kingdom

8. What is a key area for improvement in the U.S. education system?
    A) Increasing the number of international students
    B) Improving higher education rankings
    C) Improving primary and secondary education quality
    D) Reducing the diversity in schools

Answers:

1. D) United States of America
2. C) Higher education
3. C) Reputation and quality of U.S. universities
4. C) 13th
5. C) Japan
6. B) 195
7. C) Finland
8. C) Improving primary and secondary education quality

When MAGA Republican Cultist Members Tell You The Economic Outlook Is Horrible Just Look How Expensive Everything Has Become.

So They Claim We Are In A Slump, Recession Or Depression.

Don't Call Them Stupid. That's Not Nice.

Remember This:

A $17 **Bardsey Apple** Is Not A $17 **Bardsey** Apple Because No One Is Buying It.

A $17 **Bardsey Apple** Is A $17 **Bardsey Apple** Because The Economy Is Good, And More People Want That $17 **Bardsey Apple** Than They Have $17 **Bardsey** Apples.

If MAGA Was Correct That $17 **Bardsey Apple** Would Be A $1 **Bardsey Apple**. Because In A Poor Economy, It Is Better To Get Something Than Nothing.

RULE OF THUMB:

Democratic Control
Prices Higher = More Jobs Robust Economy

Republican Control
Lower Prices = Fewer Jobs Poor Economy

When Oil Companies Double Our Gas Prices In August 2024 In An Attempt To Influence The Election.

Here Is The Information You Will Need To Protect Yourself And Promote Biden, Including The Democratic Party.

When a MAGA Cultist throws it in your face, say, 'Thank you. I agree the President is doing a great job with the economy.

Although this post is factual, there are two things I want to mention:

Our country does not own our natural resources. We receive royalties, based on a percentage of sales price, for resources extracted on government land, so high prices bring higher government revenue.

Private entities ultimately set prices, and they are the only ones interested in Profit, Profit, Profit, Profit, so any idea they put out about public interest and not being responsible for high prices is just for show.

Misconception of Presidential Control over Gas Prices:

Gas And Housing High = A Robust Economy.

If Gas And Housing Is Low = A Slumping Economy Or Recession.

There is a widespread belief that the President sets gasoline prices, but this is incorrect.

This misconception, promoted by Republicans and oil companies, leads to blame on the incumbent administration for rising fuel costs, especially during elections.

So, I guess technically, it's true, but not the way their narrative portrays it.

Everything We Thought We Knew About Gas Prices Was Wrong

"Have you ever considered the intriguing relationship between gasoline prices and the state of the economy? It's a common misconception that high gas prices always indicate economic hardship. However, a closer look reveals a different story.

When gasoline prices are high, it's often a sign of a robust economy. Increased economic activity leads to higher gasoline consumption, increasing demand and prices.

Conversely, when gas prices drop, it can reflect a weaker economy. Reduced economic activity results in lower gasoline consumption, leading to decreased demand and lower prices to manage inventory levels.

So, next time you see gas prices fluctuating, remember that they are not just about what's happening at the pump.

They are intertwined with the ebb and flow of economic conditions, reflecting a dynamic relationship between supply, demand, and the economy's overall health."

When the country is under Democratic control, the economy is better, and gas prices are higher.

When Republicans are in control, the economy and gas prices dip.

The price of gasoline is influenced by various factors, interacting in complex ways to determine the final cost at the pump.

Speculators who invest in crude oil futures in the global market essentially bet on future oil prices, which sets how oil is priced.

Futures buyers commit to receiving oil at a set price in the future, regardless of market fluctuations.

This system creates an artificial market for oil, deviating from traditional supply and demand dynamics.

Artificial markets are volatile, challenging to predict, and can change rapidly.

Speculators, often conservative and right-leaning, fund conservative causes and candidates, influencing public opinion through gasoline prices.

The conservatives push the notion that high gas prices are a result of the current President's popularity is a false narrative the way they promote it. That needs to be debunked and corrected.

It is misleading to suggest that gas prices are based solely on the performance of the President in office

A strong economy leads to higher demand and higher gas prices, while a weak economy leads to lower demand and lower gas prices.

This means that both the government and its constituents play a role in determining the price of gas.

It is essential to recognize this relationship and consider the state of the economy when assessing gas prices.

Good Economy = High Gas Prices

Poor Economy = Lower Gas Prices.

Here's a simplified breakdown of factors influencing the pricing of a barrel of Crude Oil:

1. Crude Oil Prices:

Global market dynamics, geopolitical events, and OPEC decisions impact crude oil prices.

2. Refining Costs:

Refining processes, operational costs, and crude oil prices affect gasoline pricing.

3. Distribution and Marketing:

Logistic costs, marketing, distribution expenses, and profit margins influence the final price at retail stations.

4. Taxes:

Federal taxes have an insignificant effect on the price of gasoline. Federal taxes include excise taxes of 18.3 cents per gallon on gasoline and 24.3 cents per gallon on diesel fuel and a Leaking Underground Storage Tank fee of 0.1 cents per gallon on both fuels.

It is important to note that this has not changed since 1920, so the President does not affect gas prices unless they decide to up the tax, which hasn't changed in 104 years.

The government's role in energy markets is often to facilitate research and development, manage reserves, and sometimes influence prices through subsidies, not taxes.

5. Regulations:

Environmental regulations can raise gasoline production costs in certain regions.

6. Seasonal Demand:

Summer demand and the need for specialized gasoline blends can increase prices.

7. Exchange Rates:

Currency exchange rate fluctuations can influence oil and gasoline prices due to global trading in U.S. dollars.

8. Inventory Levels:

Crude oil and gasoline inventory levels can impact prices based on supply and demand dynamics.

9. Speculation:

Traders' actions in oil futures markets set crude oil prices through speculation.

10. Economic Conditions:

Economic health affects oil demand, with strong economies boosting demand and weak economies reducing it.

11. Real Estate:

Gasoline prices can indirectly impact real estate markets by reflecting economic conditions and influencing consumer behavior and location preferences.

Higher gasoline prices signify a robust income and will increase disposable income, commuting costs, and the desirability of specific locations (e.g., suburbs vs. city centers), impacting the property value increase in the real estate market.

Conversely, lower gasoline prices mean a weaker economy, so less disposable income, and we do not stimulate economic activity. We tend to hold our money and not take risks, which includes a drop in investment in real estate.

The shift to renewable energy and energy-efficient technologies aims to reduce oil dependence, enhance environmental outcomes, and foster a sustainable energy economy. This transition will impact sectors like transportation, manufacturing, and housing, shaping the evolving energy-economy relationship.

While speculators set crude oil prices, the gasoline market is shaped by global costs, taxes, regulations, and speculation.

The government plays a role through activities such as subsidizing alternative energies and managing strategic reserves, which can indirectly impact gasoline prices.

The government's push towards alternative energy sources aims to create a more sustainable energy future, reduce the environmental impact and reducing gas prices of fossil fuels, and potentially stabilize energy markets by reducing reliance on volatile oil prices.

How We Reduce Gasoline Prices

The shift towards renewable energy sources, such as wind and solar, as well as the increasing adoption of electric vehicles (EVs), can lead to reduced demand for oil and gasoline over time. Here's how these initiatives might affect the market:

1. Reduced Demand:

As more consumers and businesses turn to renewable energy and EVs, the demand for oil and gasoline will decrease.

This reduced demand will lead to lower prices for gasoline, assuming supply remains constant or increases.

2. Technological Advancements:

Improvements in renewable energy technology and battery storage could make these alternatives more cost-effective and reliable, further encouraging the shift away from fossil fuels.

3. Policy Incentives:

Government incentives, such as tax credits for renewable energy projects or subsidies for EV purchases, can accelerate the adoption of alternative energy sources and reduce the consumption of oil and gasoline.

4. Infrastructure Development:

Investment in renewable energy infrastructure, like wind farms, solar panels, and EV charging stations, can facilitate the transition to a less oil-dependent economy.

5. Economic Diversification:

As the economy becomes less reliant on oil, it may become more resilient to oil price shocks, which can have a broad range of economic consequences, including impacts on the real estate market.

6. Environmental Regulations:

Stricter environmental regulations can increase the costs of extracting and refining oil, which may make renewable energy sources more competitive.

7. Consumer Behavior:

Growing environmental awareness and changing consumer preferences can lead to lifestyle changes that reduce oil consumption, such as using public transportation, car sharing, or driving fuel-efficient vehicles.

8. Global Commitments:

International agreements and commitments to reduce carbon emissions can lead to policies that favor renewable energy over fossil fuels, influencing the global energy mix leading to lower oil demand.

In conclusion, the gasoline market is influenced by a complex set of factors that include global supply and demand for oil, refining and distribution costs, taxes, regulations, and market speculation, among others. The government's role is multifaceted, including regulation, subsidization of alternative energies, and strategic reserve management, all of which can indirectly affect gasoline prices.

Since The Election Of Donald Trump And His Supreme Court Appointments, The Separation Of Church And State Is Almost 99% Eradicated.

Just One More Ruling With The Right Case They Are Looking For, And We Will Be A Forced Theocratic Rule. With White Christian Nationalists Being Required Membership And Attendance By Everyone.

Does Project 2025 Almost Have Its Foundation Finished?

Since the founding of this country, the Religion Clauses of the First Amendment which are the Establishment Clause and the Free Exercise Clause and have been rightly understood to demand government neutrality to religion jointly.

Establishment Clause:

This clause prohibits the government from establishing or favoring any official religion. It ensures that the government does not show a preference for one religion over another or for religion over non-religion. It also ensures that religion does not participate in politics, candidates, or government. This helps maintain the principle of religious neutrality in government activities.

Free Exercise Clause:

This clause protects the right of individuals to practice their religion freely without government interference. It ensures that individuals are free to believe and worship as they choose without facing discrimination or persecution for their beliefs.

The majority of the current MAGA Trump-appointed Supreme Court now believes that the two clauses are inherently at odds with each other and that the Establishment Clause was long-settled and gets in the way of today's anti-establishment interests prohibiting the government from being involved in any form of funding for religion, to name just one or get in the way of the free exercise of religion.

The MAGA Supreme Court Justices have made clear that, to them, the Free Exercise Clause is all that matters because they threw out the Lemon v Kurtzman law that solidified the ruling and interpretation of the Establishment Clause.

June 21, 2022, the Court concluded for the first time that a state is required to allow vouchers (that is, taxpayer dollars) to be used for religious education.

In the Carson v. Makin case, One of the religious schools in Maine that was at issue teaches students to reject Islam. Another religious school requires teaching that "homosexuals and other deviants" are "perverted."

Forbidding forced taxpayer subsidy of religious education is one of the very reasons that the Establishment Clause exists in the first place.

By striking down Maine's program, the Court has required Islamic taxpayers to fund education denigrating their religion, forced LGBTQ families to pay for students to learn that LGBTQ people are perverted, and enlisted every Maine taxpayer of the financing religious ministry all in support of a supposed free exercise right.

Whether you realize it or not, your dollars are also being used because the state education budget includes federal tax dollars.

Before the 2022 Supreme Court rulings, these clauses were equally important because they helped uphold the separation of church and state, preventing the government from promoting or inhibiting any particular religion or religion influencing government.

They safeguarded individuals' rights to practice their religion without government intrusion. They protected the government from any religious intrusion in political campaigns or participating in the Executive,

Legislative, and Judicial Branches of any US government, including state, county, and local political agencies.

The Establishment Clause and the Free Exercise Clause played a crucial role in preserving religious freedom and ensuring that all individuals could worship according to their beliefs without fear of government interference.

As Justice Sotomayor wrote in dissent, this decision "continues to dismantle the wall of separation between church and state." Under this Court, the separation "that the Framers fought to build" has become a constitutional violation. Most justices believe that free exercise is so vital that it must supersede all other rights including equal protection, due process, and the whole panoply of constitutional and statutory protections against unfair discrimination.

The Federal Supreme Court did not uphold the star of Philadelphia's refusal to contract with a religious foster care agency that would not certify same-sex couples as foster care parents. The Court held that because the city's anti-discrimination policy allowed for some nonreligious exemptions, it was not neutral toward religion.

The Federal Supreme Court doesn't stop there. They have ruled religious organizations do not have to follow Civil Rights laws like Title VII and the Americans with Disabilities Act. For instance, they can discriminate against their "ministers," anyone employed by their organization, without having to prove that their actions were based on religious beliefs.

This means ministers lose protection from important civil rights laws like Title VII and the Americans with Disabilities Act. The right to apply this exception applies to employees who play a significant role in the organization's religious mission, such as teachers or musicians, even if their job duties are not religious. Some Supreme Court judges even suggested letting contracts and handbooks let all employees be listed as ministers, regardless of their jobs.

And, of course, it doesn't stop there.

In a 2020 court case called Bostock v. Clayton County, a big win for civil rights said that it's not okay to discriminate against people at work because of their sexual orientation or gender identity.

However, the Supreme Court also ruled that religious groups, organizations, churches, and even any private business employer could avoid following this anti-discrimination ruling by using a law called the Religious Freedom Restoration Act (RFRA).

The RFRA law says that the government must have an excellent reason if their actions get in the way of someone refusing employment because it is against the employer's religion.

The Supreme Court supporting RFRA shows that they believe a person's religious beliefs are more important than the government's efforts to stop discrimination.

In the past, the Constitution was understood to protect religious freedom and equal rights for everyone.

For example, in the 1968 case Newman v. Piggie Park Enterprises, the Court rejected a restaurant owner's argument that his religious beliefs justified refusing service to Black customers. This was ruled in favor of Newman.

However, At this time MAGA-appointed Supreme Court Judges ruled in favorof almost all religion and religious exemptions and allowed them the right to ignore and violate all Civil Rights and nondiscrimination laws.

These rulings towards religious exceptions suggest a shift away from the principles of the Constitution and the Civil Rights Act.

This change indicates that if the Piggy Park case were argued today, the outcome would favor the restaurant owner's discriminatory stance, which goes against the principles of equal rights and religious freedom enshrined in the Constitution.

Let's all hope that shortly we can dissolve this Fucked Up MAGA trend and when we VOTE OUT ALL OF THE MAGA CULTIST THAT HAS BEEN ELECTED AND GET RID OF THOSE APPOINTED BY MAKING CONGRESS DO THEIR JOB AND CHARGE THESE SUPREME COURT JUSTICES THAT ARE SO BLATANTLY VIOLATING THE CONSTITUTION THAT EVEN AN UNEDUCATED NOVICE CAN SEE IT.

Then, that of religious favoritism is only a short detour, and we return to our constitutional underpinnings.

Misconception of Presidential Control over Gas Prices:

If you don't want to read the article here is a simple breakdown:

Gas And Housing High = A Robust Economy.

If Gas And Housing Is Low = A Slumping Economy Or Recession.

There is a widespread but incorrect belief heavily marketed and spread by Republicans and oil companies that the President directly sets gasoline prices.

This false narrative has led to public discourse and expectations that the incumbent administration is responsible for rising fuel costs, especially during election cycles.

Everything We Thought We Knew About Gas Prices Was Wrong

"Have you ever considered the intriguing relationship between gasoline prices and the state of the economy? It's a common misconception that high gas prices always indicate economic hardship. However, a closer look reveals a different story.

When gasoline prices are high, it's often a sign of a robust economy. Increased economic activity leads to higher gasoline consumption, increasing demand and prices.

Conversely, when gas prices drop, it can reflect a weaker economy.

Reduced economic activity results in lower gasoline consumption, leading to decreased demand and lower prices to manage inventory levels.

So, next time you see gas prices fluctuating, remember that they are not just about what's happening at the pump.

They are intertwined with the ebb and flow of economic conditions, reflecting a dynamic relationship between supply, demand, and the economy's overall health."

When the country is under Democratic Control, the economy is better, and gas is higher.

When the Republicans have control, the economy and gas prices dip.

The price of gasoline is influenced by many factors, which interact in complex ways to determine the final cost at the pump.

Speculators who invest in crude **oil futures** in a world market essentially bet on how much oil will cost later, affecting how other people think oil should be priced.

Once locked into a contract, a futures buyer would receive a barrel of oil for the price dictated in the future agreement, even if the market price was higher when the barrel was delivered.

This means that the laws of supply and demand are no longer applied in the oil markets. Instead, an artificial market was developed.

Artificial markets are volatile; they're difficult to predict and can turn on a dime.

Spectators are generally conservative right-leaning and contribute significant funds to conservative causes and candidates.

So they can influence public opinion of Political Candidates through gasoline prices. By pushing the false narrative that gas prices are high because of presidential control.

If you're interested:

Here's a breakdown of some key factors contributing to how speculators determine the pricing of a barrel of Crude Oil.

1. Crude Oil Prices:

The most significant factor in the cost of gasoline is the price of crude oil, which is determined by the global oil market. This is not influenced by supply and demand: the dynamics, geopolitical events, OPEC's production decisions, and other factors.

2. Refining Costs:

Once crude oil is extracted, it must be refined into gasoline. The costs associated with refining, including the cost of crude oil, operating the refinery, and the complexity of the refining process, all contribute to the price of gasoline.

3. Distribution and Marketing:

After refining, gasoline is transported to distribution points and retail stations. Costs for logistics, marketing, and distribution, as well as the profit margins for these entities, are factored into the final price.

4. Taxes:

Federal taxes have an insignificant effect on the price of gasoline. Federal taxes include excise taxes of 18.3 cents per gallon on gasoline and 24.3 cents per gallon on diesel fuel and a Leaking Underground Storage Tank fee of 0.1 cents per gallon on both fuels.

It is important to note that this has not changed since 1920, so the President does not affect gas prices unless they decide to up the tax, which hasn't changed in 104 years.

The government's role in energy markets is often to facilitate research and development, manage reserves, and sometimes influence prices through subsidies, not taxes.

5. Regulations:

Environmental regulations can also impact the cost of gasoline. For instance, in regions where unique formulations are required to reduce pollution, gasoline may be more expensive to produce and distribute.

6. Seasonal Demand:

Gasoline prices often increase in the summer due to higher demand from travel and the need for unique summer blends of gasoline, which are designed to reduce smog and are more expensive to produce.

7. Exchange Rates:

Because the global oil market trades in U.S. dollars, fluctuations in currency exchange rates can impact the price of oil and, thus, gasoline. A weaker dollar makes oil more expensive.

8. Inventory Levels:

The levels of crude oil and gasoline inventories can influence prices. If inventories are low and demand is high, prices tend to rise. Conversely, if inventories are high, prices may drop.

9. Speculation:

Traders who buy and sell oil futures contracts based on their expectations for future oil prices mainly impact the crude oil market. If traders believe prices will rise, their activity can increase prices, and vice versa.

10. Economic Conditions:

The overall health of the economy can affect oil demand. In a strong economy, gasoline demand may increase as businesses and consumers use more energy. In a weak economy, demand may fall, leading to lower prices.

Real Estate:

Regarding the relationship between gasoline prices and the real estate market, there is a correlation; it's not a direct causation.

Higher gasoline prices signify a robust income and will increase disposable income, commuting costs, and the desirability of specific locations (e.g., suburbs vs. city centers), impacting the property value increase in the real estate market.

Conversely, lower gasoline prices mean a weaker economy, so less disposable income, and we do not stimulate economic activity. We tend to hold our money and not take risks, which includes a drop in investment in real estate.

However, the dynamics of the real estate market are complex and also depend on factors such as interest rates, employment levels, housing supply, demographic trends, and more. While energy costs, including gasoline, can have an impact, they are just one of many variables that influence real estate prices.

The transition to renewable energy and adopting more energy-efficient technologies are part of a broader strategy to reduce dependency on oil, improve environmental outcomes, and create a more stable and sustainable energy economy.

This transition will likely have far-reaching effects across various sectors, including transportation, manufacturing, and housing, as the interplay between energy and the economy continues to evolve.

Even though Speculators set the price of a Barrel of Crude Oil, the gasoline market itself is influenced by a complex set of factors that include global refining and distribution costs, taxes, regulations, and market speculation, among others.

The government's role is multifaceted, including subsidization of alternative energies and strategic reserve management, all of which can indirectly affect gasoline prices.

Chronology and Educational Overview of the U.S. Oil Industry and Economic Impact.

Under The Biden Administration:

The United States emerged as the world's largest producer of crude oil, surpassing traditional oil giants like Russia and Saudi Arabia.

Energy Independence and Strategy:

The U.S. holds a significant strategic oil reserve, which is separate from its commercial oil reserves estimated at 55.2 billion barrels.

Economic and Energy Interplay:

Oil production and profitability are deeply connected with the broader economy, influencing inflation, product pricing, and service costs.

The oil industry aims for record profits, which affects various sectors, including transportation and manufacturing.

Global Influence:

The U.S.'s status as a leading crude oil producer has major implications for global energy policy, supply chains, and trade relationships.

Future Projections:

The Energy Information Administration (EIA) projects that U.S. crude oil production will reach record levels in 2023 and 2024.

Energy Policy and Consumer Well-being:

Decisions in oil production impact the economy at large, affecting gas prices and the cost of goods and services.

Presidential Election Year Dynamics

The upcoming Presidential Election Year is critical, with gas prices expected to double by August, placing energy policy at the forefront of national discourse.

Market Speculation

Speculators in crude oil futures trading can distort market dynamics, affecting the price and availability of oil.

These investors bet on future oil prices, which introduces volatility into the oil market.

Oil Pricing and Production:

The average price per barrel of crude oil has risen due to speculative trading.

A barrel of crude oil (42 gallons) yields about 0.47 to 0.67 gallons of gasoline after refining.

Governmental Energy Initiatives:

Government efforts to promote alternative energy sources and fuel-efficient vehicles aim to reduce oil reliance and demand.

As clean energy adoption increases, oil demand may decline, potentially lowering gasoline prices.

Navigating the Energy Sector:

Stakeholders must stay informed about speculative trading, market conditions, and the shift towards sustainable energy to understand the impact on oil prices and consumer outcomes.

Twenty churches supported political candidates during the Texas 2022 Election. Experts say they violated federal law.

You may not be interested in the Johnson Amendment that bars churches from politics or the differences between tax-exempt and tax-deductible organizations and tax-exempt but not tax-deductible organizations. You can scroll down. I included four churches, or if you want to see all 20, I included the article link.

Are churches exempt from having to pay taxes? The short answer is "yes." For purposes of U.S. tax law, churches are considered public charities, also known as Section 501(c)(3) organizations. As such, they are generally exempt from federal, state, and local income and property taxes.

Churches aren't supposed to endorse political candidates, according to IRS rules.

The Johnson Amendment, passed in 1954, prohibits church leaders from intervening in political campaigns.

The law prohibits pastors from endorsing candidates during official church functions such as sermons.
Violations can lead to the revocation of a church's tax-exempt status.

The amendment affects nonprofit organizations with 501(c)(3) tax exemptions, which are subject to absolute prohibitions on engaging in political activities and risk loss of tax-exempt status if violated. Expressly, they are prohibited from conducting political campaign activities to intervene in elections for public office.

The Johnson Amendment applies to any 501(c)(3) organization, not just religious 501(c)(3) organizations.
The benefit of 501(c)(3) status is that in addition to the organization itself being exempt from taxes, donors who itemize may also take a tax deduction for their contributions to the organization.

According to the Internal Revenue Service, contributions to political campaign funds or public statements of position in favor of or in opposition to any candidate for public office are disallowed. However, certain voter education activities, including voter registration and get-out-the-vote drives, if conducted in a non-partisan manner, are not prohibited.

To be tax-exempt as a social welfare organization described in the Internal Revenue Code (IRC) section 501(c)(4), an organization must not be organized for profit. It must be operated exclusively to promote social welfare.

Under the Internal Revenue Code, all section 501(c)(3) organizations are prohibited from directly or indirectly participating in or intervening in any political campaign on behalf of (or in opposition to) any candidate for elective public office.

A 501(c)(4) nonprofit organization is a "social welfare group" that can advocate for causes and propositions like 501(c)(3)s. However, 501(c)(4) s can also endorse candidates and parties– one of the most substantial differences. **This status includes political action groups to advance reproductive or civil rights.** While nonprofit organizations with this status are also tax-exempt, **donations to 501(c)(4) groups are not tax-deductible**.

So, with a 501(c)(4), although tax-exempt, their donations are not. Example: A $100 donation to a church they don't pay taxes on, and I take a $100 deduction on my taxes. I donate $100 to a PAC, and they don't pay Taxes on my money, but I do. So there isn't a double exemption on the same $100.

Across the country, churches appear to be doing so anyway.

The endorsement of political candidates by religious leaders from the pulpit has grown increasingly brazen, aggressive, and sophisticated in recent years.

20 Churches That Violated Their Tax-Exempt Status During The 2022 Texas Election

The experts agreed that the cases below violate the law. The experts were Lloyd Hitoshi Mayer, a tax and election law expert at the University of Notre Dame; Ellen Aprill, an emerita tax law professor at Loyola Marymount University's law school; and Sam Brunson, a law professor at Loyola University Chicago.

In these cases, pastors said they were not endorsing candidates, but their actions equated to an endorsement, according to the experts. Some acknowledged that the law did not allow them to endorse before making their statements.

Mercy Culture
Location: Fort Worth
Pastors: Landon Schott, Heather Schott, and Steve Penate
Context: Pastors at Mercy Culture expressed support for political candidates in at least three sermons.

During one such instance on Feb. 6, the Schotts and Penate spoke in favor of Nate Schatzline, who is running for a seat in the state House. "Now, obviously, churches don't endorse candidates, but my name is Landon, and I'm a person before I'm a pastor. And as an individual, I endorse Nate Schatzline," Landon Schott said. Schatzline's appearance ended with Schott stating: "We declare Mercy Culture Church is behind you. We declare Mercy Culture Church is praying for you. We declare Mercy Culture Church is supporting you."

Early voting for the March 1 primary began eight days after the church service. Schatzline qualified for a runoff, which he won on May 24.

Church and candidate response: Mercy Culture, Landon Schott, and Heather Schott did not respond to questions or requests for comment.

<u>Unite Church</u>
Location: Anchorage, Alaska
Pastor: Josh Tanner
Context: On Jan. 16, Tanner introduced his congregation to Kelly Tshibaka, a Republican candidate for the U.S. Senate, and let her speak about how she expressed her faith during her career in government. "OK, so I want you to know that we're not just gonna be doing an endorsement for Kelly today, even though I am endorsing Kelly for U.S. Senate. And you can vote for whoever you want. I'm just letting you know who I'm voting for. It's gonna be her."

Tshibaka was among the top candidates to advance to the November general election.

Church and candidate response: Unite Church, Tanner, and Tshibaka did not respond to requests for comment.

"Uncle bill": a new "family"-based strategy

Some churches coordinated with one another to provide their congregations with a list that singled out specific candidates and omitted others.

Gateway Church
Location: Southlake
Pastor: Robert Morris
Context: Morris is among a group of Dallas-area pastors who have coordinated to highlight specific candidates running for public office. Since 2021, Morris has shown his congregation the names of particular candidates for office at least three times. (Morris also revealed the names during an Oct. 23 service.)

During an April 18, 2021, sermon, a day before early voting, Morris displayed the names of nine candidates running in nonpartisan races for school board and City Council on a screen.

"And so we're not endorsing a candidate," Morris said. "We're not doing that. But we just thought because they're a member of the family of God, that you might want to know if someone in the family and this family of churches is running."

All but one of the candidates whose names were shown either won their race or qualified for a runoff.

Church response:
Lawrence Swicegood, Gateway Media executive director, said in an emailed statement: "At Gateway Church:

We DON'T:
Support any specific political party
Endorse political candidate

We DO:
INFORM our church family of other church family members who are seeking office to serve our community.
ENCOURAGE our church family to vote as God leads them.
PRAY for our elected officials regardless of their political party or affiliation."

https://www.texastribune.org/2022/11/07/churches-list-violations-johnson-amendment/

The country's economic and energy landscape is intricately tied to the production and profitability of oil. This vital resource not only impacts gas prices but also ripples through various sectors, influencing inflation, product pricing, and service costs. From the cost of extracting petroleum to the myriad byproducts derived from it, the ramifications are far-reaching, extending to everyday essentials such as clothing.

In recent years, the United States has emerged as a global powerhouse in crude oil production, outstripping rivals like Russia and Saudi Arabia. Since 2018, the nation has held the title of the world's largest producer of crude oil, a testament to its robust energy sector. Projections from the Energy Information Administration (EIA) indicate that US crude oil production is poised to scale new heights in 2023 and 2024, setting the stage for record-breaking output levels.

Amidst these developments, it is worth noting that the substantial oil reserve of approximately 55.2 billion barrels in the United States does not encompass the Strategic Oil Reserves. This reserve, while substantial, underscores the nation's strategic positioning in the global energy landscape, offering a buffer to meet domestic demands and navigate market fluctuations.

As the nation navigates the complexities of energy production, political dynamics, and economic imperatives, the interplay of oil production, profitability, and the pursuit of record profits continues to shape market forces, consumer prices, and the broader economic outlook.

The quest for record profits within the oil industry not only drives production but also exerts a pervasive influence on inflation, product pricing, and service costs across the board. The economic ramifications of this pursuit echo far beyond the confines of the oil sector, casting a shadow over industries ranging from transportation to manufacturing and beyond.

The United States' status as a leading producer of crude oil has far-reaching implications, extending beyond the realm of energy policy. This dominance on the global stage underscores the nation's strategic positioning in the face of evolving geopolitical landscapes and shifting market dynamics. As the largest producer of crude oil since 2018, the US wields significant influence over global energy markets, shaping supply chains and trade relationships worldwide.

Looking ahead to 2023 and 2024, the Energy Information Administration (EIA) anticipates a surge in US crude oil production to unprecedented levels, charting a course toward record highs. This anticipated uptick in production underscores the nation's commitment to bolstering its energy independence and fortifying its position as a key player in the global energy arena.

As discussions surrounding oil reserves and production levels take center stage, it is essential to acknowledge the intricate interplay between energy policy, economic stability, and consumer well-being. The decisions made in the realm of oil production reverberate throughout the economy, influencing everything from gas prices to the cost of everyday goods and services.

In the midst of this dynamic landscape, the upcoming Presidential Election Year presents a pivotal moment for the nation, with gas prices poised to double come August. As Americans navigate the intersection of politics, economics, and energy policy, the role of oil production and profitability emerges as a central theme shaping the contours of the national discourse and the trajectory of the country's energy future.

Oil production and the pursuit of record profits play a pivotal role in shaping various facets of the economy, from inflation to product pricing and service costs. This symbiotic relationship underscores the intricate interplay between energy policy, market forces, and consumer outcomes.

A notable factor influencing the pricing and availability of oil on the global stage is the involvement of speculators who engage in crude oil futures trading. These investors essentially wager on the future price of oil, thereby influencing market perceptions and dictating the quantity of oil released by petroleum companies. Through futures contracts, buyers commit to purchasing oil at a predetermined price in the future, irrespective of the prevailing market rates at the time of delivery. This practice introduces an element of artificiality into the oil markets, bypassing traditional supply and demand dynamics and fostering market volatility.

In this context, the average price per barrel of crude oil has experienced an upsurge due to the impact of speculative trading and artificial market conditions. Each barrel of crude oil contains 42 gallons (159 liters), with approximately 1 gallon (about 3.8 liters) of crude oil yielding between 0.47 and 0.67 gallons (1.78 and 2.54 liters) of gasoline, contingent upon the refining process and crude oil quality.

Simultaneously, governmental efforts to promote the adoption of alternative energy sources like wind and solar power, alongside the promotion of fuel-efficient and electric vehicles, aim to reduce the reliance on oil and curb demand. As the transition towards cleaner energy sources gains momentum, the demand for oil is expected to diminish, potentially leading to a decline in gasoline prices. By diversifying energy portfolios and encouraging sustainable practices, the government seeks to mitigate the impact of oil market fluctuations and foster a more stable and resilient energy ecosystem.

In navigating the complex landscape of oil production, speculation, and market dynamics, stakeholders must remain attuned to the evolving forces shaping the energy sector. By understanding the nuances of speculative trading, the implications of artificial market conditions, and the imperative of transitioning towards sustainable energy solutions, individuals and policymakers can navigate the intricate web of factors influencing oil prices and consumer outcomes.

This is a long post I'm open to suggestions on what can be reworded or omitted.

It Is Important To Remember That Democrats And Republicans Held Different Beliefs That Switched In 1964 During The Civil Rights Movement

The Shared Legacy of Eugenics Across the American Political Landscape.

PAST, PRESENT AND FUTURE

The eugenics movement, with its dark history of promoting "racial purity," "racial improvement," and "planned breeding" through selective breeding, casts a long shadow over the 20th century.

This pseudo-scientific endeavor, which sought to improve the human population by preventing the reproduction of those considered "unfit," including ethnic and religious minorities, people with disabilities, the urban poor, and LGBTQ individuals, found support across the political spectrum in the United States.

Both Democrats and Republicans, influenced by the prevailing attitudes of their times, played roles in advancing eugenic policies.

This post explores the bipartisan responsibility for the eugenics movement in American history and acknowledges the complex shift in party ideologies, particularly during the civil rights movement.

In the late 19th and early 20th centuries, eugenics gained traction among intellectuals and political leaders.

It was an era when scientific racism and a misguided interpretation of Darwinian theory melded to justify inequality and discrimination.

Democrats and Republicans alike were not immune to the allure of eugenics, which was often framed as a progressive solution to societal problems.

Democrats of the early 20th century, particularly in the Southern states, were still influenced by the legacy of slavery and the Jim Crow laws that enforced racial segregation. Some viewed eugenics as a means to maintain racial hierarchies and purity.

In the early 20th century, there was a considerable exchange of eugenic ideas between the United States and Germany. American eugenics research was well-respected internationally, and many of its ideas were disseminated through books, papers, and conferences.

The Eugenics Record Office in the United States, established by Charles Davenport with funding from the Carnegie Institution and later the Harriman family, was a hub for eugenic thought and research.

American eugenicists such as Harry H. Laughlin and Madison Grant were influential, with Grant's book "The Passing of the Great Race" particularly impactful. This book was even praised by Adolf Hitler as his "bible," highlighting the direct line of influence.

American eugenicists pioneered the development of eugenic laws, including those mandating the forced sterilization of individuals deemed "unfit." By 1933, 29 U.S. states had passed sterilization laws, and these served as a model for the Nazis' own Law for the Prevention of Hereditarily Diseased Offspring, which led to the forced sterilization of hundreds of thousands of people.

The relationship between American eugenics and Nazi Germany's policies, including those that led to the Holocaust, is a complex and disturbing aspect of history. American eugenicists played a significant, albeit indirect, role in shaping some of the ideologies that the Nazi regime would later adopt and take to their most extreme conclusions.

Hitler and other Nazi officials took note of these policies and the pseudoscientific justifications behind them. They admired the United States' efforts to "cleanse" and "improve" its population.

The Nazi regime's policies would go much further, however, as they moved from sterilization to the mass murder of individuals they deemed "life unworthy of life," including LGBTQ+ people, people with disabilities, Romani people, Slavs, and, most notoriously, Jews.

The Holocaust was the systematic, state-sponsored persecution and murder of six million Jews by the Nazi regime and its collaborators. While the Holocaust was influenced by a variety of factors, including longstanding anti-Semitism, German nationalism, and the political conditions of the time, eugenics played a role in the ideological underpinning of the genocide.

The Nazis believed in the concept of racial purity and the superiority of the "Aryan" race, and they saw Jews and other groups as a threat to this purity. This twisted application of eugenic principles helped to justify the Nazis' policies of extermination, which also targeted homosexuals, political dissidents, and others.

The United States supplied Hitler with the Blueprints for Eugenics, and to add insult to injury, we refused asylum to the Jewish community because they were on our Eugenics list of unfit religious minorities.

After World War II, the full horrors of the Nazi regime's atrocities came to light, and eugenics as a movement was largely discredited. The Nuremberg Trials brought some of the leading figures of the Nazi regime to justice, and the world grappled with the ethical and moral failures that had allowed such crimes to occur.

The American eugenics movement faced a reckoning as well, as it became clear that the ideologies it had promoted had contributed to the justification of the Holocaust.

While the American eugenics movement did not directly cause the Holocaust, its influence on Nazi racial policies is an indelible part of the history

At the state level, eugenic laws often received bipartisan support. Forced sterilization laws were enacted in over 30 states, and politicians from both parties endorsed these measures.

The infamous Buck v. Bell case of 1927, which upheld the constitutionality of forced sterilization, was supported by Justice Oliver Wendell Holmes Jr., an appointee of Republican President Theodore Roosevelt. The decision indicated the broad acceptance of eugenic thought during that period.

White supremacy, critical race theory (CRT), and "The Great Replacement" conspiracy theory — each relates to discussions of race, power, and demographics, but in very different ways. It's important to differentiate between these concepts and how they intersect with ideas related to eugenics.

White supremacy is an ideology that holds white people as superior to those of all other races and, therefore, deserving of dominating society.

Historically, eugenics has been used as a pseudo-scientific justification for white supremacist beliefs. The idea that certain "races" are genetically superior to others is a concept that has been thoroughly discredited by modern science.

Still, it was a core belief of eugenicists in the past. While overt eugenics-based policies may no longer be legal or socially acceptable, the underlying racist ideologies can persist in more covert forms within white supremacist circles.

It's important to note that the White Supremacy Groups have endorsed Trump and the MAGA Movement.

CRT, or Critical Race Theory, is a framework developed by legal scholars that examines the relationship between race, law, and power in society.

It is an academic discourse that acknowledges the role of systemic racism in American history and its ongoing impact on present-day society.

CRT itself does not promote eugenics; instead, it provides tools to understand and dismantle racist structures, including those that historical eugenic policies have influenced.

So Now You Know Why Trump And MAGA Followers Do Not Want CRT In Schools.

The Great Replacement conspiracy theory, which is rooted in white supremacist rhetoric, falsely alleges that there is a deliberate plot to replace white populations with non-white immigrants for political or cultural reasons.

Proponents of this theory often express unfounded fears about demographic changes leading to the loss of white dominance in society.

This theory can share some thematic parallels with eugenic ideas in that it centers on preserving specific racial demographics, often framed as the "survival" of a preferred group.

The "Great Replacement" theory and the xenophobic rhetoric have gained prominence in some political circles, including during the Trump presidency.

However, it's a baseless and racist conspiracy that has no foundation in reality.

Oh, But It Isn't baseless, and it came to fruition Thanks To Donald Trump's Four Years Of Presidency And The MAGA Movement.

In any case, it's crucial to counter such harmful ideologies with factual information, education about the history and consequences of eugenics and racism, and policies that promote equity and protect human rights.

The lessons learned from the history of eugenics should be a reminder of the need for vigilance against any ideologies or narratives that devalue the lives of individuals based on their race, ethnicity, or any other characteristic.

It is crucial to note that party platforms and ideologies have evolved.

The Democrats and Republicans of the early 20th century do not neatly align with their contemporary party counterparts today.

During the mid-20th century civil rights movement, a significant realignment occurred, often referred to as a "party switch," where the Democratic Party became associated with civil rights and social equality. At the same time, the Republican Party attracted the conservative elements that were once at home in the Democratic Party.

Despite the decline of eugenics as a reputable science after World War II and the horrific revelations of the Holocaust, forced sterilization and eugenic ideologies persisted in various forms.

Policies founded on concerns about population control and welfare costs continued to target marginalized populations, with bipartisan negligence or even active support.

These practices were not the exclusive domain of any political party and reflected broader societal attitudes that transcended party lines.

The history of eugenics in the United States started as a bipartisan issue, one that should remind us of the dangers of pseudoscience and the importance of ethical policymaking.

As we move forward, we must recognize this shared legacy and how Democrats and Republicans have contributed to and can work to alleviate past injustices.

Acknowledging the evolution of party ideologies over time, especially during the civil rights movement, is crucial in understanding the current political landscape.

It serves as a reminder that political parties are not monolithic and that their values and priorities can shift significantly over time.

This understanding is vital for ensuring that past mistakes, such as those related to eugenic policies, are not repeated.

Unless You Are Donald Trump And Part Of the MAGA Movement

The Trump administration's strict immigration policies, including the "zero tolerance" policy that resulted in family separations and forced sterilization, have been the subject of intense scrutiny and criticism.

The theory propagates a conspiracy of deliberate cultural and demographic displacement, which can create an environment where eugenic-like ideas find support among specific individuals or groups.

Fear of the "Great Replacement" theory and the xenophobic and racist anxieties that have historically fueled eugenic movements gave Trump and MAGA the fodder they needed to put into place their solution for this theory.

It was done secretly from 2017 until September 2020, which did not stop until Biden was sworn in.

In September 2020, a whistleblower, nurse Dawn Wooten, brought to light that forced, Without Consent or with uninformed consent, gynecological procedures were being performed at the Irwin County Detention Center.

The complaint brought to everyone's attention that immigrant women were subjected to forced hysterectomies, sterilizations, and other unwarranted medical treatments, raising fears of a modern manifestation of eugenics based on race, poverty, and immigration status.

Forced sterilizations at the Irwin County Detention Center (ICDC) in Georgia have cast a long shadow over the United States, drawing parallels with the country's dark history of eugenic practices.

Whistleblowers brought to the public attention of coerced sterilizations at an ICE detention facility in Georgia. If it was happening at one ICE Detention Center, it was happening at all of them.

The specter of eugenics that hangs over the ICDC is a stark reminder of the need for vigilance in protecting reproductive rights and justice.

Today, as we face new challenges in genetics and bioethics, it is more important than ever to learn from the past and advocate for policies that respect human rights, diversity, and the complexity of human genetics.

The bipartisan history of eugenics in America teaches us that vigilance is necessary to prevent the misuse of scientific ideas, regardless of political affiliation.

As we confront these issues, Democrats and Republicans can champion legislation that protects individuals from discrimination and upholds the dignity of all people.

By working together, the two parties can address the lingering effects of eugenics and ensure that all individuals have the freedom and opportunity to contribute to society without the stigma of past pseudoscientific beliefs.

The history of eugenics in America is not a story of one political party's failings but a broader societal issue that transcended party lines and reflected the pervasive prejudices of the time.

It is a powerful reminder that political parties and their policies are subject to change and that the work of building a just and equitable society is an ongoing endeavor that requires bipartisan commitment and action.

Building upon this commitment, the present-day political climate presents a unique opportunity to address the underlying biases that still influence health, science, and policy.

Both Democrats and Republicans can unite around the common cause of rectifying the inequalities of the past by supporting robust education about the history of eugenics, its discredited theories, and its lasting impact on marginalized communities.

Moreover, current policymakers need to engage with communities that have historically been the targets of eugenic practices.

Listening to and learning from these communities can guide the development of more equitable policies. This engagement can also foster trust in medical and scientific institutions, which historical abuses have strained.

In genetics and reproductive rights, clear ethical guidelines and regulations must be established to prevent discrimination based on genetic information.

Both parties have a role in crafting legislation that safeguards against genetic profiling and ensures that advancements in genomics benefit all without repeating the eugenic goal of shaping the population based on flawed criteria of worthiness.

Healthcare reform is another area where the lessons of eugenics are relevant. Ensuring access to quality healthcare for all, regardless of genetic conditions or socioeconomic status, is a direct counter to the eugenic idea of valuing individuals based on perceived genetic "fitness."

Democrats and Republicans can find common ground in improving the healthcare system to serve everyone equitably.

The education system is pivotal in dismantling the remnants of eugenic thinking. By incorporating comprehensive science and history curricula that address the eugenics movement and its fallacies, future generations can be inoculated against the allure of such harmful ideologies. A bipartisan effort to support such educational initiatives can help ensure that the lessons of the past are not forgotten.

The legacy of eugenics is a stark reminder of how science can be misused to justify exclusion and inequality. It is a reminder that crosses party lines and decades of political change. But it also serves as a call to action for Democrats, Republicans, and all policymakers to work together to create a society where every individual is valued and has the opportunity to thrive.

By acknowledging past mistakes and actively working to prevent them recurring, both parties can contribute to a future that truly reflects the ideals of justice and equality for all.

Today, responsibility for addressing the legacy of eugenics and preventing its recurrence does not fall on any single individual, group, or political party. Instead, it is a collective responsibility shared by various sectors of society, including:

Both major political parties, as well as independents and smaller parties, bear the responsibility to enact and uphold laws that protect individuals from discrimination based on genetics or disabilities. Lawmakers at the federal, state, and local levels must ensure that the mistakes of the past are not repeated in any form.

The Republicans have taken the stance that Birth Control and Abortions are a form of Eugenics and should be outlawed. It is not for several reasons, but the primary reason is that they are a choice of the party involved, and neither is forced sterilization.

Researchers, geneticists, and healthcare providers must conduct their work ethically and educate the public about the complexities of genetics. They must also advocate for policies that promote equality and prevent discrimination.

Teachers, professors, and educational institutions are responsible for accurately conveying the history of the eugenics movement and its discredited theories, as well as promoting critical thinking about the ethical implications of science.

Judges and the judicial system must protect the rights of individuals, particularly those in vulnerable populations, and ensure that justice is served for violations of these rights. The legal system also plays a role in interpreting and enforcing laws related to discrimination and genetics.

Organizations dedicated to civil rights, disability rights, and genetic advocacy have a role in raising awareness, supporting affected individuals, and lobbying for policy changes that address the injustices of eugenics.

Journalists and media outlets must report accurately and responsibly on genetics-related issues, ensuring that the public receives factual information and that sensationalism does not contribute to misunderstanding or fear.

Every individual has a responsibility to be informed about the history and science of genetics, to reject discriminatory beliefs and practices, and to support policies and initiatives that promote inclusivity and genetic diversity.

Collective responsibility also means acknowledging that while the eugenics movement is a historical phenomenon, its underlying prejudices can manifest in new forms. Modern issues such as genetic privacy, reproductive rights, and access to genetic therapies present new ethical challenges that society must navigate carefully.

The responsibility for ensuring that eugenics does not find a foothold in modern society is a shared one, requiring vigilance, education, and ethical consideration from all corners of society. Only through a united effort can we ensure that the future of genetics and human improvement celebrates diversity and respects the intrinsic value of every individual.

In the modern era, advancements in genomics and biotechnology have opened up incredible possibilities for understanding and treating genetic diseases. However, they have also reignited ethical debates about the potential for new forms of eugenics. Some individuals and groups express interest in using genetic information to make selective reproductive choices, enhance human traits, or even design "perfect" babies, often referred to as "designer babies."

Here are some of the contemporary issues where echoes of eugenics can be heard:

With the advent of technologies like preimplantation genetic diagnosis (PGD), prospective parents undergoing in vitro fertilization (IVF) can screen embryos for specific genetic conditions. While this can help prevent serious genetic diseases, it raises concerns about where to draw the line.

Some fear the same technology could be used to select non-medical traits, such as physical characteristics or intelligence, which can veer into eugenic territory.

CRISPR-Cas9 and other gene-editing technologies can potentially correct genetic mutations at the embryonic stage, which could be a powerful tool against hereditary diseases.

However, the possibility of "enhancing" genes for certain desired traits brings up eugenic implications, particularly if these technologies become accessible only to the wealthy, potentially exacerbating social inequalities.

The idea of using biotechnology to "improve" or "enhance" human beings beyond what is considered "normal" raises ethical questions reminiscent of eugenic ideals.

The pursuit of enhancement could lead to a society where genetic "haves" and "have-nots" are further divided by their engineered abilities or attributes.

Even without explicit eugenic policies, societal pressures can create a coercive environment where people feel compelled to make confident reproductive choices.

For example, stigmas attached to disabilities can lead to fewer people choosing to carry a pregnancy to term if a genetic abnormality is detected.

The use of genetic data by insurance companies or employers could lead to a form of economic eugenics, where individuals with certain genetic predispositions are discriminated against in terms of insurance premiums or employment opportunities.

It's important to note that these technologies and practices do not inherently constitute eugenics. They become eugenic only when used to control who gets to reproduce or which traits are deemed acceptable in society.

The ethical use of genomics is focused on providing individuals with choices and improving health outcomes, not on enhancing or "cleansing" the gene pool.

The scientific community, ethicists, and policymakers have been working to address these concerns by establishing guidelines and regulations that ensure the ethical use of genomic technologies.

This includes emphasizing informed consent, protecting individual privacy, promoting equitable access to genetic services, and prohibiting genetic discrimination.

As we move forward, society must engage in open, informed discussions about the ethical use of genomics, taking lessons from the past to ensure that the future of genetic science benefits all of humanity without repeating the mistakes of eugenic ideologies.

Considering the historical context of the eugenics movement in the early 20th century, it is worth noting that opposition to eugenics was not strictly divided along liberal or conservative lines.

However, there were individuals and groups from various political backgrounds who voiced concerns about eugenics and its implications.

Progressive and liberal thinkers, as well as individuals associated with civil rights movements, were among the early critics of eugenics. They raised ethical concerns about the discriminatory and coercive practices advocated by some eugenicists.

In the United States, for example, civil rights activists and organizations, such as the NAACP (National Association for the Advancement of Colored People), were critical of eugenics due to its potential to perpetuate racial discrimination and inequality.

While there were individuals from both liberal and conservative backgrounds who supported eugenics, opposition to the movement often stemmed from concerns about human rights, individual autonomy, and the potential for eugenics policies to lead to systemic discrimination and abuses.

Ultimately, the critique of eugenics was based more on ethical, human rights, and social justice grounds for Republicans before the Civil Rights Movement and Democrats after the movement began.

The Republican Party's Unrecognizable Transformation

As a Democrat, I have watched with increasing alarm as the party across the aisle has undergone a series of metamorphoses that have left it virtually unrecognizable from its original incarnation.

The Republican Party, as it stands today, seems to be a far cry from its historical roots, and it is high time we address this transformation head-on.

Let's be clear: the Republican Party has only existed in its current form since 1964, after the seismic political realignment triggered by the Civil Rights Movement.

Prior to this, the GOP had a very different platform and demographic makeup. However, it seems that some modern Republicans are keen to retroactively claim credit for historical achievements to which they have no legitimate connection.

This revisionist approach to history does a disservice to the American people, who deserve a truthful account of political legacies.

Before 1964 The Republican Party was once a coalition with diverse viewpoints, which included progressive leaders who fought for civil rights and equality.

However, since 2015, there has been an even darker transformation. The rise of divisive rhetoric and the embrace of extremist ideologies have led to a Republican Party that, in my view, only exists in name.

It has been hijacked by elements that appear to eschew the fundamental principles of democracy and civil discourse that should define a political party.

Today's GOP, as I see it, has more in common with fringe groups that thrive on fearmongering and division, some terrorist groups, than with the Republican Party of Dwight D. Eisenhower or even Ronald Reagan.

This shift became particularly pronounced during and after the 2016 election cycle, which catalyzed a further departure from traditional conservative values toward a brand of politics that, in my opinion, often borders on demagoguery.

The original shift began when the Democrats, my party, took a definitive stand on social issues and civil rights in the 1960s, culminating with the passage of the Civil Rights Act.

In response, those who could not abide by this commitment to equality and justice defected to the Republican Party, reshaping its composition and values. It was an opportunistic move that has led to a long-term association of the GOP with regressive policies and ideologies.

The party that once stood for certain conservative principles now seems to prioritize power over policy, conflict over consensus, and division over unity. Such a trajectory is profoundly concerning, and it betrays the legacy of Republicans who once fought for important causes and sought to build a stronger, more inclusive America.

As Democrats, we are certainly not without our flaws, and we must also engage in introspection and growth.

However, the transformation of the Republican Party into an entity that seems to advocate for the superiority of a particular race or class is something that should concern all Americans, regardless of political affiliation. Bigotry, hate, and division have no place in any political party, and they certainly should not be the hallmarks of one of our nation's two major political entities.

It is not the label "Democrat" or "Republican" that defines a party's virtue or vice, but the values and actions of its members. Nonetheless, as a Democrat, I yearn for a return to a political landscape where both parties can engage in healthy debate, grounded in mutual respect and a shared commitment to the public good.

A hijacked Republican Party, one that strays far from the noble aspects of its past, is not only a loss for the GOP itself, but a loss for the American political system as a whole.

A functioning democracy thrives on the competition of ideas, on the balance of differing viewpoints, and on the possibility of compromise.

When one party veers towards extremism, it disrupts this balance and erodes the foundations of our democratic process.

It's crucial to remember that political parties are living entities, shaped by the people who inhabit them. They evolve and change with the times, responding to new challenges and the shifting sentiments of their constituents.

This is healthy and necessary. However, when these changes are fueled by the worst aspects of human nature—by fear, by prejudice, by a desire for domination rather than a desire for good governance—the party loses its legitimacy as a representative body in a democracy.

What we need now, more than ever, is for Republicans of good conscience to reclaim their party, to steer it back to a course that values truth, justice, and the principles upon which the United States was founded.

We need a Republican Party that contributes meaningfully to the national dialogue, that offers constructive, not destructive, criticism, and that works alongside Democrats to solve the real issues facing our nation.

The polarization of politics has led many to believe that bipartisanship is a relic of the past. I refuse to accept that. I believe in the possibility of a Republican Party that stands for something noble, that can join Democrats in the fight against inequality, climate change, and for a stronger, more unified country.

To those in the Republican Party who feel alienated by its current trajectory, I extend an invitation to work with us.

To those who are working to restore integrity and decency within the party, your efforts are recognized and appreciated. Our democracy is at its best when we have strong, principled parties that can disagree without descending into acrimony.

The future of the Republican Party—and indeed, the future of our nation—hangs in the balance. It's time to move away from the politics of division and toward a future where all voices can be heard and respected.

It's time for the Republican Party to find its way back to the core American values that once defined it. Only then can we all move forward, together, as a nation undivided.

In 2024, the United States will have a presidential election year, and the Democratic incumbent will run for election. Therefore, be prepared for gasoline prices to double starting in August.

Although it is underwater, the United States has annexed over 400,000 square miles of territory that is rich in oil and natural resources.

Currently, the United States is pumping more oil than at any other time in its history, with a reserve of approximately 55.2 billion barrels of oil, making it the sixth-largest oil reserve in the world. If the US stopped drilling and buying oil, we would have enough oil to meet our needs for five years. The US government charges a fixed price of 18.4 cents per gallon, regardless of what companies charge at the pump.

The primary reason for the high prices of gasoline at the pump is the profits of oil companies. As oil companies lean to the right and Republican, they increase the prices considerably during the election time when a Democratic candidate is in power. This is because Republicans and oil companies have successfully marketed the idea that the President sets gasoline prices.

Extensive research has unequivocally shown that immigrant workers have no negative impact on the wages of native-born workers. In fact, they play a vital role in complementing the existing workforce. It is important to recognize the indispensable contribution that employment-based immigrants make to the U.S. economy by fulfilling the temporary and permanent needs of employers across diverse industries.

It is a well-established fact that deporting undocumented immigrants does not benefit the American economy in any way. On the contrary, research has clearly demonstrated that immigrants are essential to the country's economic growth. They bring a unique set of skills and expertise that complements the existing workforce and helps create jobs for native-born workers. Therefore, it is crucial to acknowledge and appreciate the significant contributions that employment-based immigrants make to the U.S. economy.

There was a time before the MAGA Republican Cult.

That Democrats and Republicans got along and even shared lives. Our social views, although different, did not cause an end to relationships.

We were able to debate our beliefs with a calm conversation civilly. We all understood that without a bipartisan effort, nothing will pass.

We used to have the two parties to make sure with compromise that all Americans get some concessions.

Now, the MAGA Cult will not be satisfied until everyone who isn't a MAGA Cult Member is no longer a citizen or is eradicated, not just the left. They want to include the traditional Republicans in the eradication list. MAGA Cult thinks it is time for an American Citizen Cleansing.

Jay Jell pointed out in a comment when I posted this in mind one of my groups. His observation and reasoning made perfect sense, and looking through those eight years, I agree with him. So, I updated my post, deleted the old one, and included his comment.

I hate to be cynical, but I think, ultimately, the trigger that broke the camel's back on that one was the election of Obama because the MAGA freaks that have always been here found it an unforgivable thing to elect a black man. It was so unforgivable to them that they chose the least competent, loudest mouth, objective moron that they could find to replace him.

It's almost like they chose to shoot themselves in the stomach with Trump just to try and push this idea that the worst possible human being would be better than Obama so long as the skin is white

Before the MAGA Cult Republicans, the Americans who lived on the fringe of the United States and tended to keep a low profile. They tried not to bring attention to themselves. They prepared, preached, and hated groups, nationalities, and liberals quietly. They found their "false god."

The MAGA Cults Rhetoric gave the fringe a voice. MAGA is preaching and campaigning against everything that is not about or part of a Democracy.

A fringe theory is neither a majority opinion nor a respected minority.

They consider themselves sovereign citizens.

MAGA Cult hates everyone who, according to the MAGA Cult, doesn't consider themselves white.

Looking for any chance or excuse to kill. The Doomsday preppers.

The survivalists are a group that spends their lives consumed with being prepared for the inevitable end they believe is coming.

White Christian nationalism wants to cleanse the country of the blood they think is poisoning theirs.

People who believe a spiritual war is coming.

The anti-establishment.

Those who think women have no right to make their own decisions and have a place they belong in society.

The Victim America believers are those who think the rest of the world has taken advantage of America. So the victim America believers want us to shut down our borders, allow no immigration, and not help anyone—basically North Korea.

The Oath Keepers, The League of the South, Proud Boys, Fraternal Order of Alt-Knights.

Groups <u>organized</u> around the belief that they are preparing to counter an overreaching federal government.

Groups are heavily armed and refer to themselves as "constitutionalists" or "patriots."

Accelerationists are White supremacist groups who endorse violence to <u>hasten the downfall</u> of the government and pluralistic society and the establishment of a white ethnostate in its place.

Accelerationists are small cells and like to plan domestic terrorist acts.

The American Family Association hates giving women autonomy and the right to decide their health care and promotes the abolition of LGBTQ+.

They have accepted into their fold people who will commit domestic terrorism in the name of MAGA.

The MAGA Cult has taken the Republican Party hostage.

MAGA Cult has changed the Republican Party platform so much that it isn't even a party with conservative values.

MAGA Cult Republicans are about violence, eradicating anything that doesn't fit in their playbook, deporting any nonwhite nationality, or rounding them up for camps or slavery.

MAGA Cult Republicans Are The Largest White Supremacy Hate Group In The World.

MAGA Cult Republican Hate Group is Anti Democracy and Pro Totalitarianism.

There should be some law, policy, or procedure to stop allowing this group or party to run or hold office.

This article is just a short list of anti-American groups, to name a few.

POCs may have what some people perceive as equal rights on the books, but they are not treated equally in the US.

POC are constantly discriminated against. The laws are not enforced.

White people can not project that POC have equal rights. You are not a POC.

Prejudice is not limited to just one nationality. Every nationality has racist people in their demographic. People tend not to call minority groups as racist. POC racism usually stems from the way the majority treats them.

Most black individuals assume, based on my appearance as a bald white baby boomer, that I'm a bigot.

I completely understand why, based on white history.

I don't try to verbally convince them I'm not, you know, the adage "I'm not prejudiced; I have a black Friend." instead, I'm willing to start from the bottom and prove my acceptance through actions.

The Supreme Court even set back POC being treated equally when Affirmative Action was overturned. I would not want to work for or make money for a bigoted company.

There is some fentanyl being brought across the Southern Borders. However, the large bust is of white Americans that do not enter through the Southern Border. It is brought in through ports of call, hidden in imported products, or through Airports.

The impoverished immigrants coming through the southern border don't have a pot to piss in. They couldn't afford to buy or have the means to produce any product.

I do agree that we need a better plan and system to break up and end the cartels like we did and are doing with American Organized Crime.

There are multiple reasons POCs get longer and stronger sentences, but none of them are based on your biased reasons.

You keep eye contact when you pass a group of blacks; you make eye contact and memorize what they are wearing because predators go after the weakest.

That proves how racist you are. You are delusional if you think you aren't.

It may be illegal to discriminate based on POC when hiring. However, it is done in many ways. An excuse may be that you think they won't work well with staff, but it is not illegal. Break it down: they are black, and I'm uncomfortable with the individual. That is discrimination that can't be proven.

Companies may hire someone black but will pay less, and they won't be considered for promotions.

You keep referring to POC that they are less educated. You are a racist.

I live in a predominantly black city now. I have lived in Los Angeles, Cambridge, Boston, Dallas, Houston, Galveston, and Several towns in Germany, and I was raised in Mississippi.

I spent my 20s and 30s Protesting for equal treatment of everyone.

Just so you know some areas of the US are more segregated, which is illegal, but no one stops it.

A few years back a group of white men in Jasper, Texas tied a black man to the back of their truck and dragged him down a dirt road until his body parts fell off along the way.

Once upon a time in the bustling streets of colonial America, there lived a man of many talents and secrets—Benjamin Franklin. Though known to many as a founding father, inventor, and statesman, few were privy to the fact that Benjamin Franklin had a secret alter ego: Silence Dogood, his drag name.

Silence Dogood was a persona that Franklin had adopted during his younger years, a guise that allowed him to express thoughts and opinions that society otherwise would not have accepted from a man of his stature. This alter ego gave him the freedom to explore different facets of his personality, a freedom he cherished dearly.

As fate would have it, Franklin's dual life would intersect in ways he never could have imagined. One day, a gay man found himself in dire circumstances, facing persecution in a society that did not understand or accept him. Franklin, with his open mind and compassionate heart, came to the man's rescue, offering him refuge and a chance at a new life.

Little did Franklin know that this act of kindness would set in motion a chain of events that would change the course of history. The gay man, grateful for Franklin's intervention, revealed himself to be none other than a brilliant military strategist named Baron Friedrich von Steuben.

Franklin, now serving as an ambassador to France, saw an opportunity to not only save a man from persecution but also to secure a crucial ally for the American Revolution. He orchestrated von Steuben's escape from France and ensured his safe passage to George Washington at Valley Forge.

Von Steuben's military expertise proved to be invaluable to Washington and the Continental Army. His revolutionary military manual became the cornerstone of American military strategy, guiding soldiers through the darkest days of the Revolutionary War and beyond.

Thanks to Franklin's intervention, Washington's army gained a strategic advantage that ultimately led to victory in the war for independence. Franklin's role as a mediator between the French and the colonists had paved the way for this pivotal moment in history, solidifying his legacy as a hero of the Revolution.

As the smoke of battle cleared and the dawn of a new nation rose, Benjamin Franklin stood proud, his secret identity as Silence Dogood now a footnote in the annals of history. In the end, it was not just his inventions or statesmanship that defined him but his compassion, courage, and willingness to embrace all facets of humanity that truly set him apart. Benjamin Franklin, the man of many secrets, had become a legend in his own time.

Franklin's legacy as a pivotal figure in the American Revolution continued to grow as the newly formed United States navigated the challenges of building a nation from the ashes of war. His diplomatic skills and ability to forge alliances proved to be vital in securing international support for the fledgling country.

As the years passed, Franklin's influence extended far beyond the borders of the United States. His reputation as a progressive thinker and advocate for equality reached even the darkest corners of society, inspiring others to embrace diversity and acceptance.

Meanwhile, the friendship between Franklin and von Steuben deepened, their bond forged in the crucible of war enduring the test of time. The two men shared a mutual respect and admiration for each other, recognizing the role they had played in shaping the course of history.

Von Steuben's legacy as a military genius and mentor to generations of soldiers continued to grow, his name forever linked with the success of the American Revolution. His teachings and principles became the foundation upon which the United States Army built its traditions and values, ensuring that his contributions would never be forgotten.

As for Franklin, his role in the Revolution and his support for marginalized communities became a source of inspiration for future generations. His legacy as a champion of human rights and a defender of liberty lived on, a beacon of hope in a world fraught with division and discord.

In the end, Benjamin Franklin's story was not just one of a founding father or inventor but of a man who dared to embrace his true self and stand up for what he believed in. His journey from Silence Dogood to hero of the American Revolution was a testament to the power of compassion, courage, and acceptance in shaping the course of history. Benjamin Franklin's legacy would endure for generations to come, a reminder that true greatness lies not in wealth or power but in the ability to see the humanity in others and strive for a better world for all.

Which American Are You? I Know Who I Try To Be.

I hope 100% of the thousands of civilians heading to the Texas Border in the hopes of killing themselves as illegal immigrants will end up overwhelming the Texas Prison System. When Gregg Abbot asks for Federal Aid from Biden, he will laugh. Ignore him.

Are you still an American with concern for others, compassion for everyone who cares, will help a stranger, freedom, equality, justice, democracy, opportunity, liberty, individualism, civil rights, rights, founded on immigration, encourage immigration, belief in ending racism?

Or do you belong to the group that is selfish, greedy, will take, not willing to share, feel they are superior, will step on others' rights if it benefits them, and will let innocent people die just because they want a weapon? If you Want to close our borders and let people we don't know die with no concern. Some may even let the probe they know die.

So when you read below, you can tell by what bothers you which American and which party you belong to.

Mass School and church shootings against children and minority groups; bomb threats against state capitols for laws passed; murder threats against judges and lawmakers; a legislative war against women's health and children.

The Legislation attacks women's health, forcing women to carry a pregnancy (even if the fetus is not viable) but then virtually ignoring the needs of those children once they are born.

The refusal to greet with open arms and offer a safe place to stay and the chance and opportunity for immigrants with no concern of who they are or where they are from. Get back to the days of open borders.

The mass killings of immigrants, including men, women, and children, indiscriminately because we refuse to share what we have.

Pew Charitable Trust study shows most immigrants hold jobs such as food product inspectors/agricultural workers, plasters and stucco masons, drywall workers, sewing machine operators, tailors and dressmakers, and household workers such as housekeepers, gardeners, and nannies. These are generally low-paying jobs, with most workers employed in the private sector.

When did America become such a hate-filled country? When did we start to ignore the ideals of life, liberty, and the pursuit of happiness for everyone? Or is that an ideal for only a few?

It seems to have kicked into full gear about ten years ago when minority groups began to emerge as a vocal force in this country. Because the ruling majority did not understand them, the backlash became loud and clear: We don't want you.

Yet it was Republican President Ronald Regan who said one minority, immigrants, are the backbone of American business interests. Immigrant labor is willing to do the work so many American citizens were unwilling to do, but is necessary for profitability.

On the surface, it appears that both the United Kingdom and the United States Conservative Parties are the same.

However, looking deeper, the United States Conservatives are monetarily and self-gratification driven.

The United Kingdom Conservative Party is more policy-driven.

What has happened is that due to the actions of the MAGA Republican Party, the United States has moved even farther from conservatisms to liberalism.

The UK conservative party has held onto most of its position.

Conservative Parties in both countries are measured as the American government is "a republic with the form of a monarchy," and the United Kingdom is "a monarchy with the form of a government" to express these fundamental differences.

The UK has a state executive, Prime Minister, who maintains control because they hold a majority in Parliament. The state figurehead is a monarchial position, a birthright not elected or appointed, and technically plays no political role.

The US has a State President who holds executive office, commander in chief, and state figurehead. The president may or may not hold the majority of Congress.

American Conservatives are anti-freedom of the press and news. They call all adverse reporting in mainstream media fake news. They only approve and tell constituents to trust MAGA Conservative Republican

Approved Propaganda Reporting. You know I don't care what proof you have. Believe me, because I said it, so it is true.

UK Conservatives took on the media to force them to report the truth in reporting the news.

There is a direct contrast between these two incidents. American Conservatives argue against public policies from political criticism and then fight them economically by branding the negative political backlash. Whereas, in this example, the British Conservatives go directly for public policy to redress their grievances with the British mainstream media, putting the responsibility on policy and not markets.

UK Conservatives have held power for the last 120, one hundred and twenty years

The US Conservatives have only been able to maintain around eight years.

The significant difference here is that British Conservatism appears to be driven by policy, whereas American Conservatism is driven by brand. From the outsider's perspective, American Conservatism and the GOP are defined by their "anti-policies' ' perhaps even above those things it stands in favor of.

The apparent devotion to building party structure in today's British conservatism comes after the historical implosion of the party

The British conservatives have successfully corrected the issues of disunity and ideological conflict. This may be partly due to a "reimagination" of British conservatism. The exchange of power from the government to the citizens has been described as the "Big Society."

British conservatives had even gone so far as to adapt to "compassion" and a transfer to "progressivism," making their approaches adaptable and organizationally different from the thinking of America's conservative counterpart.

American Conservatism holds a major organization over American politics, but it lacks adaptability and centralization of its policy solutions. It also appears to lack a separation from public policy and marketplaces and exercises politics that blend the two as mutually inclusive.

If I were a candidate, my political platform would revolve around addressing the pressing humanitarian needs of our society.

My platform would almost certainly work against me in an election campaign. Still, it is necessary to bring several crucial issues our country faces to the forefront and out of the shadows.

I have prepared an extensive outline of what my political platform would be if I were running that aligns with the principles of the Democratic Party. As a liberal, progressive, and left-leaning party, we are committed to upholding democracy and ensuring equal treatment for all.

I can't condense all of my revolutionary ideas on civil rights, government, and policy into one single post.

Let me try to rewrite it to sound more assertive:

"Let me be clear - any form of sexual abuse is unacceptable and will not be tolerated on this platform. Do not even attempt to push a false narrative or engage in harassment. You should know that such abhorrent behavior will never be granted any protection under this platform, and those found engaging in such actions will be dealt with swiftly and decisively."

Our government must grant statehood to Puerto Rico and Washington, DC. The reason why these territories have faced difficulty in gaining statehood could be attributed, in part, to the fact that a significant portion of their population consists of people of color. This issue has often been a point of contention between the political parties, and it is crucial to approach this matter with fairness and objectivity.

The issuance of Executive Orders on various issues is being considered.

I propose that I implement everything by executive order and let Congress and the Courts be left to decide on the implications on their respective jurisdictions.

One proposed order would recognize the principle of body autonomy as an inalienable right of every individual, irrespective of gender or age. In this regard, the government would not interfere with personal healthcare decisions, as such interference could be seen as an affront to individual liberty and choice.

As a matter of urgency, I would sign an executive order to fortify the dollar by reinstating the policy abolished by Nixon, which mandates by law that we produce only money supported by natural minerals such as gold, silver, Rhodium, Osmium, Platinum, Ruthenium, Palladium, Indium, and other natural resources, including but not limited to oil reserves.

Education plays a pivotal role in shaping the future of our nation. And one of our topmost priorities should be to make sure that it is factual, fair, and balanced. This means we should not shy away from teaching all aspects of American history - the good and the bad - in public and private schools. It's time to introduce the facts of our country, including our successes and failures, and work towards making amends for past injustices. So, let's join hands and take a step towards creating a brighter future for our nation by educating ourselves and future generations.

The annexation of Mexican land by the United States through a declared war was a regrettable event in our shared history. The Treaty of Guadalupe Hidalgo, signed in 1848, resulted in the transfer of more than half of Mexico's territory, including present-day states of California, Nevada, Utah, Arizona, New Mexico, Texas, Colorado, and parts of Oklahoma, Kansas, and Wyoming to the United States.

While the treaty's terms were legally binding, it is essential to acknowledge that the acquisition of Mexican land was a deeply contested and controversial issue. The United States offered Mexico $37 million for the land north of the Rio Grande River, which Mexico refused. However, the decision to resort to war and forcibly annex a large portion of Mexican territory was both regrettable and unfortunate.

It is essential to learn from our past mistakes and strive for greater understanding and cooperation between our two nations. We acknowledge the significance of this event in our shared history and reaffirm our commitment to building a solid and respectful relationship with Mexico based on mutual trust and cooperation.

One potential proposal for making restitution towards the American Indigenous peoples is to grant their descendants automatic entrance into the United States. This could be achieved by providing them with legal immigration status and facilitating an accelerated process for acquiring legal citizenship and all its associated benefits. The EU has already implemented a similar policy for all their countries, resulting in minimal conflict. This approach may merit further consideration as a means of addressing the historical injustices suffered by the American Indigenous peoples.

We must outlaw credit interest rates that exceed 15% for credit cards, 9% for personal and auto loans, and 5.5% for mortgages. It is unacceptable to allow loans that target and exploit people experiencing poverty and those in desperate situations, such as Payday loans and Car Title Loans. Therefore, we must immediately eradicate these practices and protect vulnerable individuals from financial exploitation.

Imagine a future where the issue of restitution for slavery has been resolved. The value of paid wages for labor at that time, the number of years held, and the current dollar value have been determined to provide restitution to the descendants of enslaved people. The funds have been selected, and the distribution plan has been implemented.

In this scenario, surviving descendants will receive the restitution they deserve, and the trust will disseminate the funds to support future descendants. For example, imagine a direct descendant who was owned by someone and started working when they were 12. They worked until 1865, when they were freed at 50, which amounts to 38 years of employment for which they were unpaid. Let's say they worked on a farm. In 2024, the average farmhand earns $38852 a year in the US. So, the restitution, which is now being distributed over the direct descendants alive, is $1,476,376, and it continues supporting future direct descendants.

Shortly, there may be a legal requirement for politicians to provide proof to back up their campaign accusations. This could mean that the days of politicians making baseless claims without consequences may be numbered. If politicians fail to comply with this requirement, they could face prosecution and imprisonment for a minimum of one year and a maximum of ten years per incident if found guilty.

Moreover, it is also possible that a disclaimer for speeches or interviews may be required when trigger words are used while running for office or in office. This would mean that politicians must provide trigger-word translations, which could lead to greater transparency and accountability in political discourse. For example, Illegal Aliens means People Of Color from Mexico, Central America, and South America. Crime translates to people of color. Crime rate rising = there has been an increase of people of color moving into the area.

In addition, the possibility of dissolving the Electoral College for any election and replacing it with a majority vote system may also be on the horizon. This could lead to more excellent representation and equality in the voting process, with every citizen's vote counted equally. It's an exciting time for democracy, and we may see significant changes in the future.

It's time to take action and outlaw all of the Jim Crow laws that are still on the books. Felons who have served their time must be granted the right to vote, and we need to make it happen now.

Congresspeople must retire after six terms, which amounts to 12 years of service. Additionally, Senators must retire after two terms, which equals 12 years of service.

Shortly, we will witness a remarkable transformation in the prison system.

A comprehensive evaluation of all prisoners and prisons will be conducted to ensure that justice is served and fairness is upheld.

A closer look at all sentences will be undertaken to eliminate racial bias during sentencing.

The federal and state governments will be urged to implement balanced sentences, and the party will continue to push for significant prison reform.

We eagerly anticipate a future where justice is accessible to all, and we will not rest until this goal is achieved.

Businesses with 25 or more employees must establish a club, union, or organization representing the employees and standing up for their rights against the company and management, including pay negotiations. Failure to comply with this requirement will result in severe consequences.

My proposal is a Medicare-for-All plan that can be implemented immediately upon taking office. With Medicare already in place, a few price adjustments would be all that's required. Under 65s would pay only $125 for Medicare Part A, and those aged 65 or over would receive it for free.

Imagine a future where the government has returned the two trillion dollars taken from Social Security and Medicare, and the programs are now solvent for 50 more years.

Additionally, with the implementation of tax reform, the tax rates for people and businesses making Under $125,000 will be 5% for those making $125 000 to $200,000, 15% for $200,000 to 300,000, 30% for $300,000 to $500,000 45% over $500,000 are now a flat rate of 60%, over $1,000,000 is 65%, over $1.5 million is 70%, $2.5 million and above is 75%. Those making more than $3 million are taxed at 80%. This is a significant improvement from the previous state of affairs and could lead to a more equitable distribution of wealth. It's exciting to think about the future if these changes come to fruition.

Effective immediately, all organized lobbies and lobbyists supported by profit or non-profit entities, including companies, organizations, and religious institutions, are declared illegal.

Our government is only for the people, and subsequently, only individual registered voters will be allowed to attempt to influence the government.

Furthermore, donations to political campaigns are strictly limited to a maximum of $200 per year per candidate. Any violation of this order will be met with severe consequences.

The provision of mental health treatment has been inadequate and almost non-existent in recent years. The decision by Ronald Reagan to terminate government-funded mental health treatment and discharge people under care by closing government-run facilities has plunged thousands of people in dire need of mental healthcare into homelessness.

It is, therefore, imperative that mental health is accorded equal priority as physical health. Every individual should have access to the necessary mental health treatment at no cost.

We must push through and enact gun control laws. Registering all firearms is a must, and there should be a yearly renewal of the registration at a cost that matches the value of each weapon. It is an absolute necessity that all gun owners pass strict requirements before being allowed to own firearms legally in the United States. Let me be clear: no one is interested in taking away your guns as long as you follow the law.

All individuals who own weapons must obtain certification, licensing, and an apparent mental health clearance and renew it every two years.

The cost evaluation and fee will be based on the number and types of weapons owned.

Possessing any rapid-fire weapons or accessories will be deemed illegal unless you are an active or reserve military personnel or are employed in some local, city, county, state, or federal agency that requires weapons for your line of duty.

Let us all work together to ensure the safety and security of our community.

Pass gun laws that will hold manufacturers and city, county, and state officials as responsible as the perpetrator of any gun violence in their jurisdiction.

Manufacturers will be held responsible for gun violence because they spend millions to make sure laws are lax to maximize profits.

Government officials who approve lax gun laws will also be held responsible because it is their job to implement and enforce federal, state, and local gun laws and to pass additional gun requirements to make sure no one who can't have weapons won't end up with weapons.

Clarify the second amendment by updating it in a new amendment.

A well-regulated Militia, being necessary to the security of a free State, the right of the people to keep and bear Arms, shall not be infringed.

The Second Amendment does not guarantee anyone or any individual the right to bear arms. When our founding fathers wrote The Constitution, it only covered white male landowners. Today, most of us, based on the founding father's beliefs, would be excluded under this requirement alone.

The second part is that you must be part of a well-regulated Militia. According to government standards, you must be between 17 and 45 and be a member of an organized sanctioned group such as local police, sheriff, state troopers, DEA, DOJ, CIA, FBI, National Guard, and military, to name a few.

The Second Amendment does not pertain to an individual; it only pertains to organized, sanctioned, and endorsed by government groups.

If someone's rhetoric causes injury, death, or harm to anyone or anything by a group or individual, the individual or group that spewed the rhetoric will be held responsible for the exact charges the perpetrator or perpetrators commit

Clarify that no political party allows the entry of illegal aliens. If the party will enable them to enter, they are immigrants

We Will Increase Legal Immigration Numbers From All Countries Regardless Of Nationality. Anyone who can Be Vetted will receive a welcome package explaining the steps and requirements to achieve citizenship.

Legal Immigration Will Increase Our Economy, Our GDP, Our Tax Revenue, and Our Need For Employment. However, Contrary To Republican Belief, Immigration Does Not Increase Our Legal Voters For Many Years To Come.

The Federal Government Will Work With The States On A Plan To End The Unhoused And Will Help Anyone who Can't Afford Housing. Each State Will Be Required To Build Or Provide Affordable Housing To The Low-income and Unhoused.

At Least 10% Of All New Structures built as residences Will Have To be built and donated as no-frills to code Two-, Three, Or four-bedroom homes built Provided To This Program.

Together, The Builders, States, City, and County Will All Benefit From This Program.

We will put through an amendment guaranteeing equality for everyone.

Religion and Religious Groups will have their Tax Exempt Status revoked.

Everyone Will Start Paying Their Fair Share Of Taxes.

It Is Quite Obvious That Based On How Church Members And Staff Fly Around And Live In Luxurious Estates, They Are For-Profit Companies.

Also, anyone who claims to be a religious group and so on is automatically Granted Tax-Free status Because They Were Supposed To Stay Out Of Government And Politics, you know, separation of church and state.

However, Since Roe V Wade Gave Women The Right To Choose, Jerry Falwell And His Evangelical Church Became Very Active In Government And Politics, And All The Rest Got Involved Right Behind Him. So Now It's Time To Pay Taxes Like Everyone Else.

Bipartisan work should be required, regardless of which party is the majority.

It will be a crime for Groups and religions that advocate hate, violence, murder, or the eradication of any group of people to fall under the same prosecution and jurisdiction as any Mafia, organized crime, or crime family.

Elected officials who push for or advocate violence towards any protected group should be removed from office immediately and charged with a terroristic threat

Our government operates by a legal system that protects facts, not hearsay or beliefs.

Companies must offer up to 180 paid days to their employees for paternity, maternity, or emergency family should be provided once every 24 months.

For-profit companies with products and services sold in the United States must contain at least 65% of the product or service assembled or manufactured in the US or a US territory.

Furthermore, all oil, chemical, and gasoline-based products must mandatorily contain at least 50% of America's resources.

It is indispensable to make price gouging illegal, and prices must be strictly kept under 300% of production cost because Americans should not be taken advantage of under any circumstances.

Government-funded daycare for children under twelve or disabled for working parents based on income eligibility must be provided without fail.

Additionally, the ADA, American Disability Act, must be expanded to include paid services for people who can't afford them so that they can have the same quality of life as everyone else.

Instead of a minimum wage, we will firmly establish a maximum wage gap, where the wage gap between the highest-paid executive and the lowest-paid employee will be set by law. For example, there can't be a gap of more than 20 times an hour.

Lastly, when companies give out bonuses, they must give the same percentage bonus to every employee. This will ensure that rewards are equal and businesses do not try to circumvent the wage gap while making back lost profits from tax increases or funds lost by no longer being able to buy stock since stock buyback will be illegal.

We must establish a Climate Planet Repair Plan that mandates the participation of every business operating in the US.

The level of contribution required from each organization should be commensurate with the extent of their contribution to the problem.

What are your thoughts on this? Is there anything you disagree with or want to see added or removed? Please share your feedback in the comments.

———————————

Make an argument for why the churches and religions should pay taxes in the United States.

There are several arguments that can be made for why churches and religious institutions should pay taxes in the United States:

1. Separation of church and state: The United States Constitution mandates the separation of church and state. Exempting churches from taxes can be seen as the government favoring religion, which goes against the principle of religious neutrality. Tax exemptions for churches can be seen as a form of government support for religion, which may infringe upon the principle of the separation of church and state.

2. Fiscal responsibility: Taxes are a primary source of revenue for the government to fund public services and infrastructure. By exempting churches and religious institutions from paying taxes, the government may be missing out on significant revenue that could be used to benefit the community as a whole. Requiring churches to pay taxes would ensure that they are contributing their fair share to support the society in which they operate.

3. Level playing field: Tax exemptions for churches can create an uneven playing field in the marketplace. Non-religious organizations, including businesses and other non-profits, are required to pay taxes on their income and property. When churches are exempt from taxes, they may have a competitive advantage over other entities that are subject to taxation. Requiring churches to pay taxes would help level the playing field and promote fairness in the marketplace.

4. Accountability and transparency: Requiring churches to pay taxes would also increase their accountability and transparency. Currently, churches are not required to disclose their financial information to the same extent as other non-profit organizations. By subjecting churches to taxation, they would be required to comply with tax laws and regulations, which would increase transparency and accountability in their financial affairs.

5. Public benefit test: Many tax-exempt organizations are required to demonstrate that they provide a public benefit in order to qualify for tax-exempt status. Requiring churches to pay taxes would subject them to a similar public benefit test, ensuring that they are contributing to the welfare of society in order to justify their tax-exempt status.

In conclusion, there are compelling arguments for why churches and religious institutions should pay taxes in the United States. Requiring churches to pay taxes would uphold the principles of separation of church and state, promote fiscal responsibility, ensure a level playing field, increase accountability and transparency, and subject churches to a public benefit test.

Incorporating the fact that religious institutions and churches make over $1.2 trillion in revenue per year further strengthens the argument for why they should pay taxes in the United States:

1. Revenue generation: With religious institutions and churches collectively generating over $1.2 trillion in revenue annually, they represent a significant economic force in the country. Requiring them to pay taxes on this substantial income would provide a substantial source

of revenue for the government, which could be used to fund essential public services, infrastructure projects, and social welfare programs.

2. Fair share contribution: Given the substantial revenue generated by religious institutions and churches, it is only fair that they contribute their fair share to support the society in which they operate. Requiring them to pay taxes would ensure that they are not only benefiting from the infrastructure and services funded by taxpayer dollars but are also actively contributing to their upkeep and improvement.

3. Level of public benefit: With such significant revenues, it is crucial to assess whether religious institutions and churches are providing a commensurate level of public benefit to justify their tax-exempt status. Requiring them to pay taxes would subject them to scrutiny regarding the extent of their public benefit activities and ensure that they are fulfilling their obligations to the broader community.

4. Fiscal responsibility and accountability: The substantial revenue generated by religious institutions and churches underscores the need for them to be held accountable for their financial affairs. Paying taxes would increase their financial transparency and accountability, ensuring that they are complying with tax laws and regulations like other entities operating in the country.

5. Economic fairness and competitiveness: With religious institutions and churches operating as significant revenue-generating entities, exempting them from taxes creates an uneven playing field in the marketplace. Requiring them to pay taxes would promote economic fairness and competitiveness by ensuring that all organizations, regardless of their religious affiliation, are subject to the same tax obligations.

Incorporating the fact that religious institutions and churches make over $1.2 trillion in revenue per year further underscores the importance of subjecting them to taxation in the United States. Requiring churches to pay taxes would not only provide much-needed revenue for the government but also promote fairness, accountability, and transparency in their operation.

Which System Do You Think Would Be Better For Our Working Class?

The choice between implementing a minimum wage and a maximum salary cap (The maximum wage top official can make without raising the wage for everyone) with a bonus system that ties bonuses to the percentage of an employee's salary can be influenced by various factors and considerations. Here are some points to consider for each scenario:

Minimum Wage:

Pros

I was unable to find Pros for the working class.

Cons:

Provides a guaranteed minimum income level for all workers, ensuring a basic standard of living.

It helps increase poverty and income inequality by keeping the wages of low-income workers below the poverty level

It was supposed to offer financial security and stability for workers and their families. However, it has only increased company profits while widening the income gap.

The government thought it would lead to increased consumer spending as low-wage workers should've had more disposable income.

Major Cons:

Minimum wages lower the value of the working class, which could lead to job losses as some businesses may struggle to increase profits so they can afford to reduce labor costs while increasing workload.

Corporate Greed will result in higher prices for goods and services as companies pass the blame on increased labor costs to consumers when asked for a raise in minimum wage. The increase in prices because of labor costs is a lie and is the excuse that companies use whether there is a minimum wage increase or not.

Minimum Wage does not directly address the issue of excessive profits, higher executive compensation, and income inequality within the working class within a company.

Maximum Salary Cap with Bonus System:

Pros:

The salary cap plan Limits income inequality by capping the ratio between the highest and lowest earners within a company.

Encourages fairer distribution of wealth by tying bonuses to a percentage of an employee's salary, and has to be paid to everyone, not just management.

Wage Caps Promote a sense of shared success and teamwork among employees.

Wage Caps Ensure that bonuses are distributed in a way that reflects the overall compensation structure of the company.

Cons

False: It may discourage top talent from joining or staying with a company if the salary cap restricts their earning potential.

Fact: Top Talent can make as much as they want. They have to remember when they give themselves a hundred percent raise, every employee in the company gets a hundred percent wage increase.

False: This could lead to complexities and challenges in calculating and administering bonuses based on a percentage of each employee's salary.

False: If The CEO gets A Five Million Bonus. That bonus equals 33.33% of their salary, and then everyone in the company receives a 33.33% of their salary bonus. After all, the Working Class has made the company and its products profitable.

True: It might not fully address broader societal issues of income inequality beyond the company level.

Also, Fact: Unfortunately, not every company is up and up. Many have unscrupulous business practices like paying lower wages under the table, maintaining two sets of books, and coming up with backdoor incentives to pay the rich while ignoring the working class.

The effectiveness of either approach would depend on the specific goals and values of the organization or society in question. Some may argue for combining strategies or other innovative solutions to achieve fair compensation and address income inequality while acting in a possessive manner with you, not trusting you, and frequently accusing you of cheating

Some causes that can contribute to controlling behavior

For some people, attempting to control certain situations is a way of coping with <u>anxiety</u>. Treating anxiety or the underlying condition causing it may improve their controlling behavior.

Some <u>personality disorders</u>, such as <u>borderline personality disorder (BPD)</u> and <u>narcissistic personality disorder (NPD)</u>, may increase the chances of someone using controlling behavior.

A person <u>may have</u><u>Trusted Source</u> learned controlling behavior and other forms of abuse from other people. For example, they may have grown up in a family with domestic violence or intimate partner violence or learned from caregivers to try to exert power over their partner.

It is crucial to note that although mental health conditions and past trauma <u>can contribute</u> to controlling behavior, they can never justify abuse.

How to deal with controlling people

Strategies for dealing with controlling people depend on whether the behavior is abusive and whether it occurs at home or in the workplace. If the behavior is not abusive, it may be best to begin by discussing it with the person. However, confronting a person with abusive behavior may flare up the situation and potentially be dangerous.

Communicate

A person can try communicating with a controlling person by:

using "I" statements, such as "I feel hurt," to speak in a way that reduces feelings of blame

discussing ways to divide responsibilities or share control

offering alternative courses of action to replace the behavior, such as making plans together rather than the person making plans for them If, after speaking calmly and openly with someone, they do not listen and continue the controlling behavior, a person may need to consider distancing themselves from the individual.

Set boundaries

It is impossible to influence how someone else behaves completely, but people can be clear about the treatment they expect and how they will respond if someone crosses the line.

A person needs to set boundaries, assertively share what they want with another individual, and say "no" when they are unwilling to do something. By setting boundaries, a person regains control and clarifies what they will and will not tolerate.

When someone is controlling, you can respond in ways to take a stand and diffuse the situation.

Ignoring them and walking away: If a person is trying to humiliate someone, quietly walking away will draw attention to their dysfunctional behavior rather than indulging them.

Creating a distraction or changing the subject: If a controlling person uses long, rehearsed speeches to wear a person down, interrupting them will make it more difficult for them to return to where they left off.

Asking them a question: If someone views a situation as only being able to go the way they want or the complete opposite, it can help to ask a question. A question can reinforce that there are more than two options available.

Counteracting with reason: If a parent uses the fact that they gave birth to someone as a way to control them, the person could ignore the attempt at guilt tripping and counteract with logic rather than emotion. They could remind the parent that people never have to do anything and have the right to choose.

Acknowledging their fear: If a controlling person is jealous about someone's relationship with another friend, it may be helpful to respond directly to their fear of abandonment. Acknowledging their fear that the person will leave them for someone else and discussing the topic may prevent them from making envious comments in the future.

To a degree, everyone wants to control what happens to them. However, if a person needs to control every part of their routine, situation, or environment, they may have anxiety or a mental health condition.

When someone tries to control or manipulate others, this can be a form of abuse.

It may be possible for a controlling person to change their behavior over time with psychotherapy if a relationship is unhealthy and not abusive. However, if a relationship involves abuse, a person's behavior could escalate to physical violence.

It is important for people living with a controlling or abusive person to create a safety plan to protect themselves. A safety plan can help them leave a threatening situation safely and be more independent once they have left.

We stole over half of Mexico's land just because we wanted it. We offered 37 million, but they said no because they liked it. So we took it by force.

Before the Americas existed, the natives of the continent had a nomadic lifestyle. They used to migrate with the changing seasons from one end of the continent to the other in search of food, water, and shelter. However, with the introduction of modern borders and territorial boundaries, this way of life has been disrupted and the free movement of people and resources has been greatly hindered.

One notable aspect of the colonizers who inhabited the land south of us was their tendency to integrate with the indigenous people. Despite cultural and linguistic differences, many colonizers sought to establish peaceful relationships with the native inhabitants and even intermarried with them. This integration was not without its challenges and conflicts, but it nevertheless allowed for a degree of cultural exchange and mutual understanding between the two groups. Unlike us, we committed near genocide, rounded up the few left, and put them on reservations.

It is worth noting that all individuals living south of our region are considered native to the Americas. Therefore, they should have the freedom to move to our area if they wish to do so. It is important to remember that approximately one-third of our country was once a part of Mexico, making it a shared history and heritage that we should respect and acknowledge.

Acting in a possessive manner with you, not trusting you, and frequently accusing you of cheating

Some causes that can contribute to controlling behavior

For some people, attempting to control certain situations is a way of coping with anxiety. Treating anxiety or the underlying condition causing it may improve their controlling behavior.

Some personality disorders, such as borderline personality disorder (BPD) and narcissistic personality disorder (NPD), may increase the chances of someone using controlling behavior.

A person may haveTrusted Source learned controlling behavior and other forms of abuse from other people. For example, they may have grown up in a family with domestic violence or intimate partner violence or learned from caregivers to try to exert power over their partner.

It is crucial to note that although mental health conditions and past trauma can contribute to controlling behavior, they can never justify abuse.

How to deal with controlling people Strategies for dealing with controlling people depend on whether the behavior is abusive and whether it occurs at home or in the workplace.

If the behavior is not abusive, it may be best to begin by discussing it with the person. However, confronting a person with abusive behavior may flare up the situation and potentially be dangerous.

How to deal with controlling people
Strategies for dealing with controlling people depend on whether the behavior is abusive and whether it occurs at home or in the workplace. If the behavior is not abusive, it may be best to begin by discussing it with the person. However, confronting a person with abusive behavior may flare up the situation and potentially be.

Communicate

A person can try communicating with a controlling person by:

using "I" statements, such as "I feel hurt," to speak in a way that reduces feelings of blame

discussing ways to divide responsibilities or share control

offering alternative courses of action to replace the behavior, such as making plans together rather than the person making plans for them If, after speaking calmly and openly with someone, they do not listen and continue the controlling behavior, a person may need to consider distancing themselves from the individual.

Set boundaries

It is impossible to influence how someone else behaves completely, but people can be clear about the treatment they expect and how they will respond if someone crosses the line.

A person needs to set boundaries, assertively share what they want with another individual, and say "no" when they are unwilling to do something. By setting boundaries, a person regains control and clarifies what they will and will not tolerate.

When someone is controlling, you can respond in ways to take a stand and diffuse the situation.

Ignoring them and walking away: If a person is trying to humiliate someone, quietly walking away will draw attention to their dysfunctional behavior rather than indulging them.

Creating a distraction or changing the subject: If a controlling person uses long, rehearsed speeches to wear a person down, interrupting them will make it more difficult for them to return to where they left off.

Asking them a question: If someone views a situation as only being able to go the way they want or the complete opposite, it can help to ask a question. A question can reinforce that there are more than two options available.

Counteracting with reason: If a parent uses the fact that they gave birth to someone as a way to control them, the person could ignore the attempt at guilt tripping and counteract with logic rather than emotion. They could remind the parent that people never have to do anything and have the right to choose.

Acknowledging their fear: If a controlling person is jealous about someone's relationship with another friend, it may be helpful to respond directly to their fear of abandonment. Acknowledging their fear that the person will leave them for someone else and discussing the topic may prevent them from making envious comments in the future.

To a degree, everyone wants to control what happens to them. However, if a person needs to control every part of their routine, situation, or environment, they may have anxiety or a mental health condition.

When someone tries to control or manipulate others, this can be a form of abuse.

It may be possible for a controlling person to change their behavior over time with psychotherapy if a relationship is unhealthy and not abusive. However, if a relationship involves abuse, a person's behavior could escalate to physical violence.

It is important for people living with a controlling or abusive person to create a safety plan to protect themselves. A safety plan can help them leave a threatening situation safely and be more independent once they have left.

We stole over half of Mexico's land just because we wanted it. We offered 37 million, but they said no because they liked it. So we took it by force.

Before the Americas existed, the natives of the continent had a nomadic lifestyle. They used to migrate with the changing seasons from one end of the continent to the other in search of food, water, and shelter. However, with the introduction of modern borders and territorial boundaries, this way of life has been disrupted and the free movement of people and resources has been greatly hindered.

One notable aspect of the colonizers who inhabited the land south of us was their tendency to integrate with the indigenous people. Despite cultural and linguistic differences, many colonizers sought to establish peaceful relationships with the native inhabitants and even intermarried with them. This integration was not without its challenges and conflicts, but it nevertheless allowed for a degree of cultural exchange and mutual understanding between the two groups. Unlike us, we committed near genocide, rounded up the few left, and put them on reservations.

It is worth noting that all individuals living south of our region are considered native to the Americas. Therefore, they should have the freedom to move to our area if they wish to do so. It is important to remember that approximately one-third of our country was once a part of Mexico, making it a shared history and heritage that we should respect and acknowledge.

From my perspective, the current issue at the border is not about the number of immigrants coming into the country, but rather how we are treating them. There are reports of overcrowded detention centers, separated families, and inadequate access to basic necessities such as food, water, and medical care. These conditions are unacceptable and do not align with the values of fairness and compassion that our country stands for. It's important that we address this crisis and find a humane solution that respects the dignity and rights of all individuals, regardless of their background or immigration status.

Again, if they were not brown we would process all of them into the US.

Better yet if they were white, we would process all of them into the US.

"Unveiling the Dirty Truth: How Our Obsession with Cleanliness Is Making Us Sick and Species Disappear"

Did you know that over 70 species have vanished from our planet, leaving us poorer in biodiversity and more vulnerable to the consequences of our actions? It's a sobering thought that echoes the impact of our lifestyle choices on both the environment and our health.

In our pursuit of cleanliness, are we unknowingly harming ourselves? The rise of allergic, autoimmune, and inflammatory diseases in Western societies has raised eyebrows and sparked conversations about the price we pay for our obsession with hygiene.

While hygiene is crucial for public health, could it be that we've taken it too far? Long gone are the days when working outside with our hands kept us healthy, and only the privileged few fell ill. Today, our immune systems seem to be struggling in the face of our sanitized surroundings.

Researchers point to a combination of factors, including our improved sanitation practices, as potential culprits behind the surge in inflammatory diseases. By reducing our exposure to germs and environmental triggers, have we inadvertently weakened our body's defenses against diseases?

But it doesn't stop there. The overuse of antibiotics, changes in our diets, and the ever-rising levels of pollution play their own sinister roles in this health drama. It's a complex web of interactions that demands our attention and action.

Could it be that our quest for cleanliness has backfired, causing our immune systems to go haywire? Some studies suggest that our squeaky-clean habits and reliance on antibacterial products may be disrupting the delicate balance of our immune system, paving the way for allergies, asthma, eczema, and autoimmune disorders.

As we navigate this landscape of health challenges, it's essential to strike a balance between cleanliness and exposure to the natural world. Perhaps it's time to rethink our approach to hygiene, embrace a more holistic view of health, and work towards a future where both humans and species thrive in harmony with the environment.

Imagine a world where our well-being is not at odds with the survival of countless species that call our planet home. A world where our health is not compromised by our fear of germs but enriched by our connection to the natural world.

It's time to question the status quo and rethink our relationship with cleanliness. Perhaps it's not about avoiding dirt at all costs but about embracing the beneficial microbes that surround us, shaping our immune systems and keeping us healthy.

What if we could find a middle ground, where good hygiene practices coexist with a healthy dose of exposure to the outdoors? Where we understand that a little dirt might not be such a bad thing, and that our bodies are designed to interact with the environment in ways that promote resilience and well-being.

By raising awareness about the impact of our lifestyle choices on our health and the environment, we can pave the way for a future where both humans and species thrive. It's a journey that starts with a shift in perspective, a willingness to embrace the complexity of our interconnected world, and a commitment to making informed choices that benefit us all.

Let's challenge the notion that hygiene is always next to godliness and instead strive for a balance that honors both our health and the diversity of life on Earth. Together, we can create a world where our well-being is not a casualty of our pursuit of cleanliness but a testament to our harmony with the natural world.

As we stand at this crossroads of health and environmental impact, the choices we make today will shape the world we pass on to future generations. It's a responsibility that we cannot afford to ignore, a call to action to reevaluate our priorities and values.

What if we could learn from the wisdom of the past, when working in harmony with nature kept us healthy and resilient? What if we could strike a balance between modern conveniences and ancient practices, finding a path forward that honors both tradition and innovation?

It's a challenge that requires collective effort and individual commitment. By being mindful of the products we use, the foods we eat, and the environments we inhabit, we can make a difference in our own health and the health of the planet.

Let's not wait for more species to disappear or for our health to deteriorate further before we take action. Let's be proactive in reimagining a future where hygiene, health, and biodiversity coexist in a delicate dance of interconnectedness and mutual benefit.

Together, we have the power to shape a world where clean hands and a healthy immune system are not mutually exclusive but complementary aspects of a thriving ecosystem. It's a vision worth striving for, a journey worth embarking on, and a legacy worth leaving behind for generations to come.

In our quest for a healthier future, let's remember that every choice we make has ripple effects that extend far beyond ourselves. By reevaluating our relationship with cleanliness and embracing a more holistic approach to well-being, we can pave the way for a brighter, more sustainable tomorrow.

What if we viewed our bodies not as isolated entities to be shielded from the world but as intricate ecosystems deeply intertwined with the environment around us? What if we recognized that our health is intricately linked to the health of the planet and all its inhabitants?

It's time to break free from the confines of conventional thinking and explore new ways of living that honor the interconnectedness of all life. Let's embark on this journey of discovery and transformation together, forging a path that leads to a world where vitality, diversity, and harmony reign supreme.

As we navigate the complexities of modern life, let's not forget the wisdom of the past and the lessons nature has to teach us. By listening to the rhythms of the earth, respecting its delicate balance, and nurturing our connection to it, we can find the answers we seek to lead healthier, more fulfilling lives.

The time for change is now. Let's embrace this opportunity to redefine our relationship with cleanliness, health, and the world around us. Together, we can create a future where our well-being is inextricably linked to the well-being of the planet, where every shower we take and every product we use is a conscious choice that reflects our commitment to a brighter, more sustainable future.

Let's embark on a journey of rediscovery, reconnecting with the wisdom of our ancestors who lived in harmony with nature and understood the importance of balance in all things. By embracing a more balanced approach to hygiene, we can reclaim our health and vitality while protecting the delicate web of life that sustains us all.

Imagine a world where our actions reflect a deep respect for the natural world, where every decision we make is guided by a commitment to preserve the beauty and diversity of our planet for future generations. It's a world where cleanliness is not just about sterile surfaces and sanitized hands, but about a deep reverence for the interconnectedness of all living beings.

Let's be the change we wish to see in the world, starting with small steps in our daily lives that can have a profound impact on our health and the health of the planet. Whether it's choosing eco-friendly cleaning products, spending more time in nature, or supporting initiatives that promote sustainability, each choice we make matters.

Together, let's rewrite the narrative of cleanliness and health, forging a new path that leads to a future where thriving ecosystems and vibrant communities coexist in harmony. It's a journey of self-discovery, growth, and transformation that begins with a simple realization: that our well-being is intricately connected to the well-being of all life on Earth.

Join us on this journey of exploration and empowerment as we strive to create a world where health, hygiene, and biodiversity flourish hand in hand. Together, we can shape a future where our actions reflect our deepest values and aspirations, where every shower we take, every product we use, and every choice we make is a step towards a brighter, more sustainable tomorrow.

Pro-Life States + Anti-Women + Anti-Children = Death

52% Of Our Nation Is Pro-Choice
44% Of Our Nation Is Pro-Life

Pro-life is not about families. Pro-Life is not about supporting women. Pro-Life is not about the children. Pro-Life is about controlling women and misogyny. Period. End of story

In anti-abortion states, children were not being adopted instead More than 4 million children went into foster care during this time period. Black children disproportionately got placed in foster care.

It is concerning to note that the number of children being placed in foster care has increased, pro—life see it as a small acceptable seemingly small margin. While an 11% increase may not seem like a significant rise, it is important to consider the current state of the foster care system. The system is already overburdened, and the pandemic has only exacerbated the situation. A recent study has shown that in 2022, more than half of all states experienced a significant decline in the number of available foster care homes. This means that even a relatively small increase in the number of children seeking foster care could have a serious impact on the system's capacity to provide safe and stable homes for all those in need. Therefore, we must remain vigilant and proactive in addressing the challenges that the foster care system faces.

Pro-Life States only focus on the fetus. States that are anti-abortion are most committed to requiring women to carry pregnancies to term. Pro-Life states invest the least in the health and economic security of expectant mothers and children after they are born.

The disproportionate burden abortion restrictions place on racial and ethnic minority families. Mainly families from these communities had to put children into foster care not due to neglect or abuse, but because they didn't have adequate housing.

Pro-Life States are the poorest states with the most poverty stricken individuals and the lowest tax collections requiring tax money from Pro-Choice States in order to be able to provide the very basic needs for their constituents.

Maternal, fetal and infant mortality rates are higher in states that ban or restrict abortion

The rates of mothers and newborn babies dying during pregnancy, at birth, or postpartum are much higher in states that currently ban or restrict abortions

States that have restricted access to abortion services had maternal death rates 62% higher than in states preserving access to abortion services.

Death rates from any cause among women of reproductive age 15 to 44 were 34% higher in abortion-restriction states than in abortion-access states

Fetal or infant death rates in the first week of life occurred at a 15% higher rate, on average, in states with abortion restrictions than in states with broader abortion access.

More people in the US pro-life states die from complications of pregnancy and childbirth than all other developed nation combined and <u>most of the deaths could've been prevented with prenatal healthcare proper nutrition and regular</u> check-ups.

39% of the counties in states restricting abortion access fit the criteria to be labeled "maternity care deserts," meaning there is limited or no access to maternity health care services.

The infant and perinatal mortality rates were 6.2 deaths per 1,000 births in abortion-restriction states.

Infant mortality in the first year of life was higher in abortion-restriction states than in abortion-access states.

Women of reproductive age and birthing people in states with current or proposed abortion bans have more limited access to affordable health insurance coverage.

Pro-Life States have less access to insurance, higher teen pregnancy rates, and less access to sex education.

In general, the states that restrict abortions have more kids and more kids of color.

Many of these are states whose economies revolve around large numbers of low-wage jobs, and the vast majority of them suffer from elevated rates of poverty, particularly among children.

The anti-abortion states have the largest share of children living in poverty

Among the anti-abortion states, 16 also rank in the top half of states for the largest share of children living in "extreme" poverty (with incomes half or less of the national poverty level, or roughly $13,000 for a family of four). Fourteen of them fall in the top half of states for the most significant share of children reporting that they have experienced hunger.

The anti-abortion states have the most children who are born prematurely or with low birth weights or who die as infants.

Anti-abortion states have the highest share of low-income women of childbearing age with no health insurance.

Anti-abortion states have little or no systems set up to provide for children from birth through eighteen.

Anti-abortion states have refused to offer state Earned Income Tax Credits for low-wage families, requiring paid family leave and <u>expanding Medicaid eligibility</u> as allowed under the Affordable Care Act.

So we will end with Pro-Life also Pro Strong And extended prison sentences if they don't qualify for capital punishment.

I guess they think they're doing the religious and for God thing by protecting them for nine months so they won't feel guilty spending the rest of the fetus's lifetime pretending the children don't exist and trying to sentence them to death.

The only problem with the migration to the southern border is racism, bigotry, prejudice, and lack of appropriate funding.

Unfortunately, many people tend to disregard important information without even giving it a chance.

Some may think they already know everything to understand, while others might be too stubborn to learn anything new.

Additionally, some people might label crucial information as tedious or too lengthy despite its significance.

Listen up! It's time to stop relying on politicians or anyone else regarding matters that affect people's lives.

Yes, I did my research, but I wrote this post because I empathize with those impacted by these issues.

Full disclosure: I do vote Democrat. They do tend to, but not always, lean toward civil rights and equal humane treatment.

I would also like to point out that not all conservatives and Republicans are bigots and racists. I'm sure if you look, you can find some

Some liberals and democrats are bigots and racists. I'm sure if you look, you can find some.

However, neither party tends to believe in what I stand for regarding immigration. I don't think that any country that is founded on freedom and equality should have closed borders because no one who believes in freedom would want their country to be exclusive. They would wish freedom and equality to spread like a virus so that everyone on earth could have the same chance to experience freedom.

It doesn't matter if I'm persecuted; it doesn't matter if people mock me. It doesn't matter if people want to say nasty things to me; I have the truth on my side

I've made a couple of critical observations on the behavior of Americans.

Let's try to use a little common sense. As bad as most of us Americans think things are in the United States, the people Migrating at the moment think more like Americans than we do. They believe we have a great thing, and they want to participate in it.

American citizens tend to behave like spoiled rich kids who are not willing to share their resources and freedoms with others. Such behavior is driven by the belief that having more resources and wealth makes them superior. However, this attitude goes against the country's founding principles, which were not based on any particular religion or race. We must embrace the values of sharing, compassion, and kindness, which are essential for any society to thrive.

We should be concerned that some individuals in the United States want to turn it into a dystopian society similar to the one depicted in the book "1984".

A society where the government will dictate every aspect of people's lives, including their thoughts, beliefs, and even religion.

In this dystopian society, people will be forced to practice only one religion, which is a version of Protestant white nationalist Christianity. Those who do not want to practice any religion will be forbidden from doing so, and people who hold different beliefs will be marginalized and eradicated.

This dystopian vision is alarming, and it highlights the importance of upholding the values on which the country was founded, such as freedom, equality, and diversity.

It is essential to ensure everyone's rights and beliefs are respected and no one is forced to conform to any particular ideology or religion.

We must emphasize tolerance, acceptance, and inclusion of different cultures, religions, and beliefs to build a harmonious and peaceful society where everyone can live without fear of persecution or discrimination.

It's time to use your brain, research, check your facts, and educate yourself on American history, current events, and the world's history.

Stop listening to politicians or even me when it has anything to do with people's lives.

Yes, I did my research, but I wrote this post because I feel a lot of compassion for the people this affects. It is based on facts and studies from groups, studies, and legal departments that report unbiased facts

Use your brain, research, check your facts, and educate yourself on American history, current events, and the world around you.

All Political Parties have a vested interest in anything they campaign on or side they take. They will always take the side of the one with the most money thrown at them. They will choose the cause they can exploit to get votes. They will embellish, spin, and tell false narratives.

Also, please be more innovative when you come up with conspiracy theories.

When a kid can figure out, the a conspiracy theory can't be true. I always wonder why adults believe it. You're not trying very hard. Use your Common sense. It goes a long way.

Okay, let's see if we can figure out how absurd and irrational some of these conspiracy theories are:

One Conspiracy Theory because of The concern of the anti-immigration Republican Elected officials is that people between the ages of 18 and 35 crossing the Southern Border UNARMED into the United States of America UNARMED And are all military age and are UNARMED, so people believe they are coming here UNARMED to start a war against the US while UNARMED at the same time once they've entered UNARMED BECAUSE They came here UNARMED.

The general public has been convinced through another conspiracy theory that was spread by Republicans who are racist and bigoted. They claim immigrants are evil, and they claim that crime skyrockets and murders are commonplace with Immigrants, whether legal or illegal. This is a total lie. Let me see if you can use your common sense.

Scenario) I left my home filled with violence, and I'm starving with no place to live. I get to your border, and I cross it illegally. I find a job with either forged documents or because of someone's kindness. So, to keep what's going well for me, I have to stay low-key, under the radar, and make sure I don't draw any attention. What are the odds I will commit a serious crime and get my family sent back?

Yes, there are some bad apples, but far fewer than we have that are American-born bad apples. For everyone one immigrant bad apple, there are 5 American an-born bad apples. We can't deport the American-born, so what's your plan to take care of the American-born Bad Apple?

With that being said, I have some valuable insights about immigration that I believe most Americans are not aware of.

Various aspects of immigration policies and procedures are often overlooked or misunderstood.

These include the different types of visas, the rigorous screening process, and the various benefits and drawbacks of immigration for the country as a whole.

Understanding these nuances is crucial to having informed discussions about immigration and its impact on society.

I want to clarify that personal or familial factors do not influence my opinion on immigration.

Specifically, I don't have any immediate family members who are currently attempting to immigrate to a different country, nor do I have any relatives who are married to individuals with dual citizenship.

My stance on immigration is based solely on my values and beliefs, as well as my understanding of the policies and laws in place.

As a proud American citizen, it is my moral responsibility to ensure that every individual, irrespective of nationality, is entitled to the same rights and freedoms to pursue happiness.

Whether they are American citizens or not, if they find their way to the United States, they should be treated with respect and dignity and given equal opportunities to thrive and prosper.

It is not our job to persecute or ridicule them; instead, we must stand up for them and protect their rights.

We must not take their lives or use them as political pawns but rather treat them as fellow human beings who deserve our compassion and support.

As a society, we must consider every individual as equal, irrespective of their ethnicity, race, or religion.

Our responsibility is to help them find the right path to enter the United States as immigrants and provide them with all the necessary assistance to fulfill their aspirations of becoming American citizens.

It is not only a matter of justice and human rights, but it is also a fundamental principle that has made America a beacon of hope and opportunity for people worldwide.

Even if I face persecution or mockery for standing up for what is right, it doesn't matter. I have the truth on my side, and I will continue to advocate for the rights and dignity of every individual, regardless of their background or nationality.

It is only by upholding these values that we can ensure a better future for ourselves and for generations to come.

The United States does not have an illegal immigration problem.

The United States does have a problem, and it's with its people.

I want to express a concern that many people may not fully comprehend the rights of individuals from the regions south of the United States.

The History that predated our colonizing the Americas needs to be pointed out, and that is that the indigenous people of the Americas migrated throughout both continents and central America, often in sync with the changing seasons.

Therefore, it is crucial to recognize that the people crossing the US Southern Border are not "illegal aliens" but rather individuals with an inherent right to be on this land.

Additionally, it's essential to highlight the fact that over one-third of the land in the United States was initially owned by indigenous people who now reside south of the Southern Border. Yet, it was taken away from them by the United States forcibly.

Hence, it is crucial to acknowledge and respect the rights of our southern brothers and sisters.

The United States is facing several challenges relating to racism, stereotypes, and bigotry. Additionally, there is a shortage of funding for processing immigration and judges and counsel for immigration cases.

The lack of funding for immigration processing is forcing many individuals to cross the border illegally. If the processing were well-funded, this would not be necessary. However, due to the overwhelming number of cases, many are turned away without even having the opportunity to talk to an official to know if they may qualify for entry or if they are approved or rejected.

Most of the United States citizen's problems with immigration are based on racism, bigotry, prejudice, rhetoric, talking points, misinformation, and the beliefs of the political party they are affiliated with. Not one of the issues is based on facts. Then, the press that aligns with that party perpetuates and continuously spreads the rhetoric until people accept it as fact. Beliefs shouldn't matter when it comes to immigration.

Americans need to learn how vital all immigration is to this country's economy, taxes, safety, and labor force and increase the population required growth.

The facts on the negative impact issues with immigration into our country. Before I write a list, I must tell you that all of these negative issues affect the immigrants, not the citizens. They Must take jobs they're overqualified for, they're discriminated against, denied healthcare, and they are considered to be uninsurable

I'm open to constructive criticism and welcome anyone who wants to point out my mistakes. Any hateful or verbal attacks will be ignored.

However, simply stating that I'm wrong won't suffice. I would appreciate it if you could explain how and why I'm wrong and, if possible, provide evidence to support your argument.

But even if you don't have any proof, I'm confident in my ability to defend my position. So feel free to challenge me, and let's engage in a healthy debate.

It's important to understand that the issue of migration to the southern border of the United States is not something that any elected officials can control. Regardless of which political party is in power, they do not have the authority to determine who can migrate to the country.

Therefore, it is unfair to blame any particular office or political party for this issue.

Instead, policymakers must work together to address the underlying causes of migration and develop fair and compassionate solutions.

I want to highlight the issue of migration and suggest a possible solution to address it.

There is a political need for the United States to get more involved in the countries where people are migrating and help influence their governments or push for a fair and just society to promote positive economic growth and fundamental human rights.

By doing so, it can encourage the citizens to stay in their countries and reduce the number of people migrating.

I suggest that the United States should stop exploiting the resources of our southern neighbors and refuse imports produced from the forced labor of these countries for cheap imports.

The United States should also pressure governments of countries that benefit from illegal goods and work with the government and farmers who profit from unlawful agricultural products.

To help them transition from growing illegal crops, these farmers should be encouraged to grow specialty products that have a higher market value.

This would lower their security and transport costs while increasing their profit margins and making them legal with a decent living.

Just an example, Saffron has a higher profit margin than cocaine.

There is a need for more honest politicians to run countries that work for the people instead of their interests.

This needs to happen to both governments, theirs and ours. We need to have politicians with integrity and honesty to promote the welfare of their citizens.

Overall, I present a comprehensive approach to addressing the issue of migration by addressing the root causes of the problem and promoting sustainable development and human rights.

The Immigration and Nationality Act (INA) is a federal law that governs the immigration process to the United States.

Under this act, the country can grant approximately 675,000 permanent immigrant visas annually. These visas are awarded to individuals who wish to become permanent residents of the United States and eventually apply for citizenship.

The INA is designed to regulate and manage the flow of immigrants into the United States. It sets out specific criteria for eligibility and establishes various categories of visas available to applicants. The government determines the number of visas granted yearly and is subject to change based on the country's needs.

One of the reasons for granting permanent visas is to meet the need for a future labor force. The United States requires population growth to maintain a growing economy and a stable workforce. Therefore, the number of visas must increase exponentially to meet this growing demand.

As per the projections made by FWD.us, it has become imperative for the United States to increase its immigration levels to maintain a favorable senior-to-working-age ratio and expand its population to grow its economy.

According to the INA estimation, the U.S. must double its immigration levels to stay competitive globally and ensure the long-term viability of programs like Social Security.

Immigrants play a significant role in contributing to population growth in the United States, and without them, the population in 2050 would be the same as our current size.

Therefore, stimulating immigration is crucial for the growth and progress of the U.S. economy, as it will help maintain a healthy ratio of workers to retirees and contribute to the country's overall development.

If we calculate the number of legal immigrants that should be allowed to migrate into the US each year, based on the current population and expected growth rate.

According to the math, the number of immigrants we need to migrate to our border would be around 1,350,000 annually.

This number would need to be maintained until the current population of 56 million immigrants living in the US doubles to 112 million.

It is vital to ensure that the immigration system is fair and efficient to handle this influx of people while also considering the economic and social implications of such a considerable population growth.

It is widely acknowledged that immigrants are a crucial factor in driving entrepreneurship and innovation in the United States. Studies have shown that immigrants are twice as likely to start their businesses as native-born Americans, which creates many job opportunities for everyone, including native-born Americans.

Immigrants have been crucial in boosting wages and strengthening the middle class, especially in fields that are facing labor shortages.

It is essential to dispel the myth that immigrants take jobs away from Americans.

In reality, immigrants help grow the economy by filling critical labor needs, purchasing goods and services, and paying taxes.

When more people are employed, productivity increases, and as a result, the economy grows.

This is why, as more and more Americans retire in the coming years, immigrants will play a vital role in filling labor demand and maintaining the social safety net.

Immigrants' contributions to the U.S. economy cannot be overstated.

From Silicon Valley to Main Street, immigrants have brought their talents, skills, and entrepreneurial spirit to the United States, helping to create some of the most successful companies in the world.

They have also helped to shape the cultural fabric of the nation, bringing diverse perspectives and experiences that enrich the lives of all Americans.

In 2016, immigrants significantly contributed to the US economy by adding $2 trillion to the Gross Domestic Product (GDP).

This figure is a testament to their hard work and dedication to building a better life for themselves and their families in the United States.

Moreover, immigrants paid $458.7 billion in state, local, and federal taxes 2018.

This tax revenue is essential to fund government services, such as infrastructure, education, and healthcare. It also helps to ensure that public safety and security are maintained, which benefits everyone who lives in the United States.

Additionally, the spending power of immigrants in 2018 alone was $1.2 trillion. This massive purchasing power was used to buy goods and services, which boosted local business activity. This, in turn, created jobs and helped to stimulate economic growth in various sectors of the economy.

It proves that immigrants are a vital part of the US economy, and their contributions are invaluable to the nation's success.

It is crucial to understand the potential impact of any proposed cuts to our legal immigration system. Such decisions could have severe consequences for our economy, leading to a 2% decrease in GDP over two decades, a 12.5% shrink in growth, and the loss of 4.6 million jobs. The Rust Belt states, in particular, would be hit hard, as they depend heavily on immigration to stabilize their populations and revive their economies.

It is essential to recognize that immigrants bring valuable skills and education to the United States. Recent studies have shown that 43% of family and diversity-based immigrants who have arrived in the United States are college graduates, which is significantly higher than the 29% of native-born Americans who have attained a college degree. This means that immigrants are highly educated and skilled in their fields, making significant contributions to the U.S. economy and helping to drive innovation and growth in various industries.

Immigrants play a significant role in the American economy. Despite making up only 13% of the population, they constitute 30% of new entrepreneurs. Their contribution to the flexible workforce is invaluable as it allows companies to grow faster and increases the productivity of American workers. By bringing in individuals with diverse skill sets and new ideas, they contribute to developing a more innovative and competitive economy.

In addition, immigrants have founded 45% of Fortune 500 companies, which employ over 10 million people worldwide. This statistic is a testament to their entrepreneurial spirit, hard work, and ingenuity.

It is not surprising that the majority of Americans support immigration. According to a recent survey, over 75% of Americans are firmly against any reductions to our legal immigration system. They recognize that immigration benefits the U.S. by bringing in talent, innovation, and diversity.

The importance of immigrants for the American economy will only increase in the coming years. As the U.S. population ages, immigrants and their families will be crucial for our workforce. By 2050, the 65-and-older population will almost double, inevitably reducing the number of people in our workforce. However, immigrants are of working age, with a staggering 79% in the workforce. This is in stark contrast to only 61% of their native-born counterparts.

In conclusion, immigrants are an essential part of the American economy. Their contributions to entrepreneurship, innovation, and productivity are invaluable. As the U.S. faces demographic challenges, immigrants and their families will be crucial for our workforce and economy.

Extensive and rigorous research conducted by experts in the field has provided conclusive evidence that the presence of immigrant workers in the American workforce does not lead to negative consequences for the wages of native-born workers. In fact, immigration plays a vital and positive role in complementing the skills and abilities of the existing workforce and is an indispensable contributor to the U.S. economy. Employment-based immigrants, both temporary and permanent, are essential to fulfilling the labor needs of employers across diverse industries, as they bring with them a unique set of skills and expertise that is often in high demand.

Deporting undocumented immigrants, on the other hand, is not only inhumane but also counterproductive to the American economy. Empirical research has shown that immigrants are a crucial element of the country's economic growth, and their continued presence is necessary for the creation of new jobs and the expansion of existing industries. By bringing in a diverse range of talent and expertise, employment-based immigrants play a significant role in enhancing the productivity and competitiveness of the American workforce. Therefore, it is essential to acknowledge and appreciate their valuable contributions and to create a welcoming and inclusive environment that supports their continued presence and participation in the U.S. economy.

So we owe those that are native to the Americas. Native Americans have lived from the southern tip of South America To The Northern tip of Greenland and were here centuries before the colonization of the Americas. All of them are owed restitution and are entitled to US Citizenship.

My proposal and a way to make restitution is to give all of the American Indigenous peoples' descendants that we stole from automatic entrance into the United States. Granting them all legal immigration status and put them on a fast-track, accelerated process to acquiring legal citizenship with all of its benefits.

Let's try to use a little common sense. As bad as most of us Americans think things are in the United States, the people Migrating at the moment think more like Americans than we do. They believe we have a great thing, and they want to participate in it.

Now, if we want the migration to stop or at least slow down, we as a country need to get more involved in where these people are migrating from and help influence the governments and invest in their economies in a way that will encourage positive economic growth and get them to recognize fundamental human rights and make sure they receive fair treatment. Do what it takes so that it will encourage their citizens to want to stay in their countries.

We must stop stripping their resources and using forced or cheap labor to import more affordable products. Stop buying illegal goods.

That means working with the farmers. Yes, in our country, they are criminals who profit from illegal agricultural products. Please encourage them to grow products considered a specialty and sell for are and the price of the illegal products. This could end up making them higher profit margins on their products. Their security and transport costs would go down, while if they are growing specialty products, export costs would also go down, making them legal with a decent living.

We must push for more honest politicians running the countries that work for the people instead of the pocketbook. We need to do that for both governments, theirs and ours.

Stop listening to politicians or even me when it has anything to do with people's lives. Yes, I did my research, but I wrote this dialogue because I empathize with the people this affects.

Use your brain, research, check your facts, and educate yourself on American history, current events, and the world around you.

All Political Parties have a vested interest in anything they campaign on or side they take. They will always take the side of the one with the most money thrown at them. They will choose the cause they can exploit to get votes. They will embellish, spin, and tell false narratives.

Also, please be more innovative when you come up with conspiracy theories.

When a kid can figure out, a conspiracy theory can't be true. I always wonder why adults believe it. You're not trying very hard. Use your Common sense. It goes a long way.

Okay, let's see if we can figure out how absurd and irrational some of these conspiracy theories are:

One Conspiracy Theory because of The concern of the anti-immigration Republican Elected officials is that people between the ages of 18 and 35 crossing the Southern Border UNARMED into the United States of America UNARMED And are all military age and are UNARMED, so people believe they are coming here UNARMED to start a war against the US while UNARMED at the same time once they've entered UNARMED BECAUSE They came here UNARMED.

The general public has been convinced through another conspiracy theory that was spread by Republicans who are racist and bigoted. They claim immigrants are evil, and they claim that crime skyrockets and murders are commonplace with Immigrants, whether legal or illegal. This is a total lie. Let me see if you can use your common sense.

Scenario) I left my home filled with violence, and I'm starving with no place to live. I get to your border, and I cross it illegally. I find a job with either forged documents or because of someone's kindness. So, to keep what's going well for me, I have to stay low-key, under the radar, and make sure I don't draw any attention. What are the odds I will commit a serious crime and get my family sent back?

Yes, there are some bad apples, but far fewer than we have that are American-born bad apples. For everyone one immigrant bad apple, there are 5 American-born bad apples. We can't deport the American-born Born, so what's your plan to take care of the American-born Bad Apple?

Let me hear from you what you see and if anything is wrong.

The United States of America started with almost an entirely open border and encouraged immigration.

The first change made regarding immigration since our Inception was the ACT Prohibiting the Importation of Slavery of 1807. We did a great thing with this change. But it could have been better. If they showed up on our shore, we turned them away. What we should have done was confiscate their cargo and grant them freedom.

We followed that up with the Chinese Exclusion ACT of 1882, another significant sign our country is made up of a lot of bigoted assholes.

At this time, we still had open borders for everyone not of a shaded race.

America's first version of the Border Patrol was formed in 1904 in El Paso. It consisted of 75 people and was responsible for California to Texas. Did you notice the northern border patrol is missing?

In 1915, Congress authorized another group, The Mounted Guards, also known as "Mounted Inspectors," whose main objective was to round up the Chinese.

The National Origins Act authorized the formation of the US Border Patrol, and our borders closed on May 26, 1924.

Let's talk about the truth regarding Immigration. We need to do our best to disperse the truth. We need to save lives by breaking stereotypes, which has caused an increase in violence and death of our Southern Immigrants. We need to suppress and eradicate bigotry and racism through education

The immigration issue at the southern border is complex, and it requires a comprehensive solution that addresses the root causes of the problem.

We need to acknowledge that no President is responsible for the number of people migrating to our Southern Border, and it is caused by multiple factors from the immigrants' homes, such as government, starvation, safety, housing, persecution, war, violence, and crime.

Thus, we must get involved in the Southern Countries and help them with the issues causing the great migration, along with bringing modernization to their countries to the 21st century.

It is essential to remember that the issue of migration in the Americas is not new and has existed since the formation of the United States.

Therefore, instead of politicizing the matter, we need to find sustainable solutions that prioritize human dignity and safety.

This requires a bipartisan effort, where the government, NGOs, Non-Governmental Organizations. and other stakeholders work together to address the issue.

We need to focus on creating a comprehensive plan that would significantly reduce the number of illegal immigrants making it into the US.

This plan should consider the factors that fuel migration in the North and the Western Hemisphere, including violence, economic instability, and political persecution.

Moreover, we should learn from past immigration and our mistakes and avoid anti-immigration rhetoric that only fuels hate and division. Instead, we must create an environment that welcomes immigrants and provides them with the support they need to integrate into society.

In summary, we must approach the immigration issue at the southern border with compassion, empathy, and a willingness to find sustainable solutions that prioritize human dignity and safety. It is only by working together that we can achieve this goal.

So this is why we have a great migration at the Southern Border.

It is only because of Racism, and Bigotry are why it's considered a crisis.

We Can Fix What People Call The Invasion Of Illegal Immigrants Coming Over Our Southern Border.

We go back to the immigration policies that were in effect when our ancestors arrived starting in the 1600s

Explain to the immigrants coming now that they can't do what our ancestors did back in 1600 -1865 when they arrived.

Explain that they can't steal property from the citizens already living here, and they can't own anyone even if it does make their life easier.

Put additional trained immigration processing personnel at all the border entry points. This would help increase legal immigration, which would reduce illegal immigration.

Help everyone who wants to enter this country fill out their and their family's applications.

Have an expedited system to get everyone that wants to enter vetted and approved.

Give the immigrants a welcome package containing all the instructions on what they will need to complete and accomplish so that it will help them transition into living in the US as immigrants.

Stop caring what the Extreme anti-immigration people think regarding immigration. If you ignore them and do the right thing, they have no power.

Poke the stick so they will continue to throw temper tantrums over their belief in the excellent replacement theory.

Let The Idiots on the right keep thinking about those who are immigrating to the US so that they can vote.

Don't tell the right that if an immigrant attempts to vote or votes before they become a citizen, they will be imprisoned, deported, or both.

Don't tell the Republicans that immigrants have to pay income tax doing the jobs no one is willing to do, which reduces the deficit and increases funds for the federal budget.

Don't tell the MAGA Cult that the immigrants spend billions and billions of dollars on goods and services in the US.

Stop letting the MAGA Cult spread misinformation about Immigrants.

Statistically, Immigrants are more likely to be law-abiding citizens because they are grateful to the US for giving them the opportunity. On average, the crime rate decreases in high immigrant population communities.

The United States of America's Population Has Peaked And Will Start Decreasing Without Increasing Immigration And Promoting Bigger Families.

Let Me See If I Can Explain It An Easier Way.

The population of The United States right now is 339,996,563.

Seventy-six million four hundred thousand are baby boomers, which means they are past childbearing and are now the next generation to pass.

Our population growth last year was only .47%, a significant decrease.

For The United States to maintain its population and to get the increase we need to survive and maintain its workforce:

Every Woman In The United States Has To Produce An Average Of 2.1 Children Each.

As of this post, the average woman is only giving birth to 1.66 children each

The population growth rate for 2023 so far is only .09%

20% of our population is at retirement age.

If we don't increase immigration and the birthrate soon, The United States will have an economic meltdown because we won't have the working population to replace those who are retiring.

OKAY LET ME SAY IT AGAIN

We Are A Country Founded By Immigrants.

All Of The Americas Are Colonial Countries

There Is No Such Thing As A Race Of Americans. There Are Natives in the Americas who were here before we started colonizing our country and started calling this land the Americas. There were no borders, and natives in the Americas Stretched from the tip of South America and its islands to the tip of Greenland.

STOP BITCHING ABOUT IMMIGRATION LEGAL OR ILLEGAL.

THE ONLY REASON WE HAVE ANY ILLEGAL IMMIGRANTS IS THE MINORITY IS PREJUDICED, AND THESE IMMIGRANTS ARE PEOPLE OF COLOR and Native to the Americas.

History Of Immigration Into The United States

PART 1 FROM 1607-1864

A BRIEF HISTORY OF AMERICAN IMMIGRATION AND HOW WE WENT FROM HAVING AN OPEN-DOOR MIGRATION TO ALMOST A COMPLETE IMMIGRATION SHUTDOWN

Before the settling of Jamestown, the Americas.

The population of Natives in the Americas was 100%.

According to the 2020 census, the population of Natives in the Americas, in the United States of America is now a whopping 1.6%.

Individuals arrived in the British colonies via two very different paths. Some were forced to immigrate, either through transportation or slavery, while others came voluntarily. "Transportation," a criminal term for forced emigration, allowed Britain to expel its social undesirables, criminals, and others to populate its North American colonies.

In practice, criminals sentenced to death could either choose transportation or hanging, so forced emigration was a common choice since death was the only punishment for a felony conviction under English common law.

In North America, transported persons began landing in British colonies as early as 1615

There have been 4 million people who were involuntarily relocated or forced to immigrate to the United States.

More than 86 million people have legally immigrated to the United States between 1783 and 2019

From 1607-1776:

Britain fiercely protected citizenship by limiting naturalization and forcibly populating its colonies with criminals and other social pariahs that the British government deemed undesirable.

Naturalization was economically important because only British citizens, known as "subjects," could own real estate and bequeath it to their heirs under English common law.

Britain's unwillingness to naturalize immigrants relegated most of its alien residents to a legal position called "denizen," similar to the Athenian metic (a foreign resident of Athens), which gave them limited economic rights, reduced their political rights and placed restrictions on bequeathing their estates under English law.

Whereas European countries discouraged the interior migration of their citizens, they typically encouraged the immigration of skilled workers without encouraging naturalization.

European governments also encouraged immigration to their colonies, and colonial governments offered quick naturalization, land grants, and debt relief in North America.

British Crown's desire to settle its colonies caused it to ignore the lax naturalization processes in the colonies, which granted immigrants the rights of Englishmen within the colonies in which they resided.

1700 Parliament limited the colonies' ability to grant naturalization and other group rights because it believed colonial naturalization policies weakened English citizens' trading positions.

Plantation Act of 1740 Pact created a uniform naturalization system that granted new, non-Catholic colonial settlers English naturalization after seven years of residency contingent upon a religious test, a pledge of allegiance, and a statement of Christian belief to which some people, such as Jews, were exempt.

Ignoring the Plantation Act, the colonies preferred to rely on more rapid local naturalization processes to incentivize immigration further.

By 1717, the Transportation Act was passed and granted English courts the ability to sentence convicts to transportation, thus streamlining the process. The courts could banish convicts for up to 14 years and turn them into indentured servants.

Before the American Revolution, Britain transported about 50,000 convicts to the American colonies.10 While colonists opposed transportation, the colonies could not prevent the migration of British subjects exempted from many colonial immigration restrictions.

The largest population of displaced people to North America were not criminals from Britain but 388,000 enslaved Africans.

Slavery was different from the other forced migrations as, unlike in the case of convicts, there was no possibility of earning freedom. However, some enslaved people were emancipated in the centuries before the American Civil War.

Enslaved Africans and their descendants have comprised a substantial part of the population in the British colonies and the United States since the 1600s, but thinking of enslaved people as immigrants stretches the meaning of that word to its breaking point during this period.

Enslavement was an experience so radically different from what was experienced by other migrants that the story of slavery does not fit into this narrative.

Those who migrated to the colonies of their own volition were drawn by the allure of cheap land, high wages, and the freedom of conscience in British North America.

Many of these individuals financed their passage by entering into indentured servitude contracts. This arrangement meant that migrants exchanged future years of their labor for passage to North America.

At the end of their contracts, the indentured servants would be discharged with a small amount of cash and skills and sometimes land on the new continent.

During the 1700s, a significant share of Europeans coming to British North America were indentured servants.

While the colonies were eager to attract immigrants, colonial cities and towns still regulated immigration by barring entry of people experiencing poverty, applying head taxes, and using banishment.

However, these small and heterogeneous colonial communities were less meticulous than European governments in enforcing their immigration laws and generally granted equal rights to accepted foreigners.

Massachusetts applied its laws against pauperism equally to all members, regardless of citizenship status. Other states extended voting rights to aliens and, sometimes, to "servants, People of color, Aliens, Jews, and Common sailors."

By 1755, the colonial population had surpassed one million residents.

Seven Years' War and subsequently curtailed colonial naturalization authority in 1773.

Parliament's actions infuriated colonialists to such an extent that they complained about them in the Declaration of Independence.

There were 2.2 million residents in North America by the beginning of the American Revolution.

The Constitution gave Congress the power to establish a uniform rule of naturalization in Article I, Section 8. It made immigrants eligible for all federal offices except the presidency and, later, the vice presidency.

The Revolutionary War divided the population into three categories: former British citizens who supported the revolution and became

American citizens, British citizens who still supported the British government and became enemy aliens, and a murky middle ground of "fair-weather" residents.

After the war, the presence of former loyalists and those in the murky middle prompted the U.S. government to view citizenship as "both a matter of place of birth and one of consent."

Congress in 1789, almost 10 percent of all members of the House of Representatives and the Senate were foreign-born, compared to just 3 percent in 2021

In the beginning, North America had an open-door policy regarding immigration

The Constitution did not create an enumerated power to control free people's immigration into the United States.

At first, The Constitutional Convention's decision granted government authority over naturalization to the states, so they regulated immigration as part of their policing powers—banishing criminals and noncitizens, denying entry to the poor, and even attempting to ban whole races.

The Founders were concerned about Catholicism, alien voting rights, non-English languages, and cultural assimilation. Thomas Jefferson summarized their overall position when he stated, before listing his concerns, that "the present desire of America is to produce rapid population, by as great importations of foreigners as possible."

The desire to populate the United States was to pay the country's debts and the demand for new laborers.

1790 U.S. Census, which excluded Native Americans, revealed that the United States population had grown significantly since the 1770s, reaching roughly 3.9 million residents. The Census also showed that about 80.7 percent of the United States population was white, while the remainder (19.3 percent) were almost all enslaved Africans.

Congress passed the Naturalization Act of 1790, extending citizenship to free white persons of good character who had resided in the United States for two years and took an oath of allegiance. The law excluded indentured servants, non-whites, and enslaved people from naturalization.

The Naturalization Act of 1790, even with its exclusions, was arguably the most liberal naturalization law to date, as it created a short and uniform path to citizenship that lacked gender requirements, religious tests, skills tests, or country of origin requirements.

Some Congressmen were unsatisfied with the Naturalization Act of 1790.

They feared that a large foreign-born population with voting rights could undermine national security, especially when the United States faced the prospect of war.

So Congress passed the Naturalization Act of 1795.

This act increased the residency requirement for naturalization to five years and added a clause requiring prospective citizens to declare their intention to naturalize three years before doing so.

The Naturalization Act of 1795 also held a religious and moral subtext that changed "good character" to "good moral character."

Congress passed a series of bills in 1798 collectively known as the Alien and Sedition Acts that expanded the federal government's involvement in immigration policy. Together, these acts subjected aliens to the threat of national surveillance and arbitrary arrest and granted a new power to the president to deport noncitizens via decree.

Congress passed a series of bills in 1798 collectively known as the Alien and Sedition Acts that expanded the federal government's involvement in immigration policy.

These acts also subjected aliens to the threat of national surveillance and arbitrary arrest and granted a new power to the president to deport noncitizens via decree.

Although these acts empowered the federal government, much of the Alien and Sedition Acts expired by 1801.

Congress passed the Naturalization Law of 1802, which reverted the residency requirements for naturalization to five years. However, the 14-year waiting period remains the longest legally mandated residency time required for prospective citizens before becoming eligible for naturalization in American history.

Today's immigrants who entered on student visas, adjusted to H1B visas, and earned green cards may wait longer for citizenship. Still, those are not mandated wait times as they arise from a combination of different legal requirements.

By 1819, economic depression and the worry that Britain might ship their poor to the United States tempered Congress' pro-immigration position.

While Congress lacked power under the Constitution to control immigration.

Congress in 1819 indirectly regulated immigration under the guise of safety by limiting the number of passengers a ship could carry based on its cargo.

This legislation lowered the carrying capacity of passenger ships and increased the price of travel, consequently reducing the number of poor immigrants who could afford passage.

The bill also required ship captains to provide a passenger manifest to customs officials and allowed the federal government to track immigration flows for the first time.

The next wave of immigrants began to arrive around 1830 when the U.S. population was nearly 12.9 million.

In 1830, most immigrants relied on credit or family remittances to pay for their passage to the United States

This funding method caused the number of indentured servants to decline and nearly disappear.

The Irish Potato Famine, beginning in 1845, and the European political revolutions of 1848—helped push immigrants to the United States.

The number of immigrants jumped from 599,125 during the 1830s to 1,713,251 during the 1840s

In the Antebellum Period, immigrants were mainly German, Irish, English, Canadian, and French.

These immigrants had different cultures and religions, particularly German craftworkers and Irish Catholics, both of which created a political backlash and prompted the emergence of nativist political parties in the United States.

In 1855, in New York City, 51 percent of the population was foreign-born.

California had more than 63 percent of its population was foreign-born in 1855

Despite slowing immigration flows, between 1820 and 1860, the 30-year- a long wave of immigrants altered U.S. demography, increasing the foreign-born population to 13.2 percent by 1860

When the Civil War began in 1861, the demand for workers in war industries increased.

The Homestead Act in 1862 and the Act to Encourage Immigration of 1864, also known as the Contract Labor Act.

The Homestead Act offered land grants to both U.S. citizens and immigrants who were eligible for naturalization and who were willing to settle and develop the land for five years.

The last consequential immigration law passed during Lincoln's administration was the Contract Labor Act of 1864, which allowed private employers to recruit foreign workers, pay their transportation costs, and contract their labor.

Regionally, the proportion of the foreign-born population could be far higher. In New York City, 51 percent of the population was foreign-born, while in California, more than 63 percent was foreign-born in 1855.

Civil War and Postbellum Expansion

When the Civil War began in 1861, demand for workers in war industries increased. To fill the void, pro-immigration Republicans sought to discredit nativists. President Abraham Lincoln contended that "our immigrants [are] one of the principal replenishing streams appointed by Providence to repair the ravages of internal war and its waste of national strength and wealth." Under the Lincoln administration, Congress passed the Homestead Act in 1862 and the Act to Encourage Immigration of 1864, also known as the Contract Labor Act. The Homestead Act offered land grants to both U.S. citizens and immigrants who were eligible for naturalization and who were willing to settle and develop the land for five years. The last consequential immigration law passed during Lincoln's administration was the Contract Labor Act of 1864, which allowed private employers to recruit foreign workers, pay their transportation costs, and contract their labor.

The Lincoln administration had a more prolonged-term effect on American immigration policy when it appointed Anson Burlingame as the U.S. Minister to China in 1861. Burlingame negotiated the Burlingame-Seward trade treaty with China in 1868. Recognizing the "mutual advantage of the free migration and emigration of their citizens," the Burlingame-Seward Treaty ensured that Chinese citizens had the right to emigrate and enter the United States. Although the treaty didn't secure naturalization rights for Chinese immigrants, it secured their ability to emigrate legally, which had previously been illegal under Chinese law. In other words, the U.S. government negotiated a treaty where a significant provision required the Chinese government to allow emigration to the United States. As a result, Chinese immigrants joined an increasing flow that pushed the U.S. foreign-born population up to about 14.4 percent of the total in 1870.

With the Civil War concluded Congress set about reforming naturalization law to be consistent with the end of slavery.

However, Congress members disagreed on how far they should extend the rights afforded by naturalization.

Sen. Charles Sumner (RMA) wanted to liberalize existing naturalization legislation by striking out "the word 'white' wherever it occurs so that there shall be no distinction of race or color in naturalization."

Other members of Congress refused to extend naturalization rights to Asians and American Indians. Ultimately, the Naturalization Act of 1870 only granted naturalization rights to "aliens being free white persons, and to aliens of African nativity and persons of African descent."

The federal government even seemed to initially interpret the newly ratified Fourteenth Amendment, which stated that "all persons born or naturalized in the United States, and subject to the jurisdiction thereof, are citizens of the United States and of the State wherein they reside," to prohibit birthright citizenship for the descendants of Chinese immigrants.

The federal government held this position until the Supreme Court ruled otherwise in the 1898 United States v. Wong Kim Ark decision. In response to growing anti-Chinese sentiment nationwide, especially in California, Congress passed the Page Act of 1875.

The Page Act restricted the immigration of Chinese contract laborers, convicts, and many Chinese women, most of whom were the wives of male workers, on the spurious grounds that they were prostitutes. These restrictions violated the Burlingame-Seward Treaty.

Throughout the 1870s, the federal government adopted and began enforcing many state-level restrictions that had been on the books for decades but were rarely enforced. Congress also passed the Immigration Act of 1882 and the Chinese Exclusion Act in the same year. The former bill imposed a $0.50 federal head tax on each alien passenger to fund immigration enforcement. It also mandated that state officials identify and deny entry to "any convict, lunatic, idiot, or any person unable to take care of himself or herself without becoming a public charge."

The Chinese Exclusion Act emulated previous California legislation that attempted to impose blanket bans on immigrants from China. Although the Chinese Exclusion Act of 1882 only imposed a 10-year ban on Chinese laborers, Congress extended this ban through 1943.

While the Supreme Court initially ruled that states had the authority to regulate immigration, it expanded the federal government's immigration authority over time. For example, the Supreme Court found, in the case of Corfield v. Coryell (1823), that "[c]ommerce with foreign nations, and among the several states, can mean nothing more than intercourse with those nations, and among those states, for purposes of trade." However, the Supreme Court did not consider free immigrants as articles of commerce, so they were not subject to federal regulation. Similarly, the Supreme Court's 1837 New York v. Miln ruling noted that "[p]ersons are not the subjects of commerce, and not being imported goods, they do not fall within the reasoning founded upon the construction of a power given to Congress to regulate commerce and the prohibition of the states from imposing a duty on imported goods."

Thus, states could pass laws excluding various kinds of immigrants, reaffirming the lack of federal jurisdiction.

Twelve years later, however, the Supreme Court's rulings in the Passenger Cases struck down several state laws that restricted immigration because they interfered with the commerce clause and federal jurisdiction over taxation and indirect regulation of immigrants.

By 1875, the Supreme Court's Henderson v. Mayor of New York ruling struck down a New York state law that required both a bond for ship captains and an immigrant fee because it infringed on Congress's power to regulate commerce. In this case, the Justices noted that the power to regulate commerce ended when the passengers landed in the United States. In the 1884 Head Money Cases, the Supreme Court decided that Congress had "the power to pass a law regulating immigration as a part of the commerce of this country with foreign nations" and overrode state immigration policies. Although many of these cases expanded Congress' authority, they were minor encroachments relative to the Supreme Court's decision in Chae Chan Ping v. United States 1889.

Prompted by a provision of the Chinese Exclusion Act, the Supreme Court determined that Congress had an extra-constitutional plenary power over immigration based on the "incident of sovereignty" rather than any specifically enumerated power. The Court reached this conclusion even though the Constitution explicitly enumerates other powers that are unquestionably an "incident of sovereignty," such as regulating international commerce, raising an army, and declaring war. In the Court's opinion, Justice Stephen Field recounted California's constitutional convention, which had found that "the presence of Chinese laborers had a baneful effect upon the material interests of the state and public morals; that their immigration was in numbers approaching the character of an Oriental invasion, and was a menace to our civilization." Field then reasoned that the United States had the power to "preserve its independence, and give security against foreign aggression and encroachment," such as Chinese migration. The Supreme Court's decision created a "constitutional oddity" that subsequently decreased judicial oversight of immigration law.

The Progressive Era

Between 1861 and 1890, 10.4 million immigrants arrived in the United States, mainly of Southern and Eastern European descent.

Between 1861 and 1890, 10.4 million immigrants arrived in the United States, mainly of Southern and Eastern European descent. This wave was more than twice the size of the previous wave, with 4.9 million immigrants of primarily Northern European descent who migrated to the United States between 1831 and 1860—by 1890, decades of immigration increased the foreign-born portion of the U.S. population to 14.8 percent. In this new wave, many migrants desired to work temporarily in the United States before returning home. While return migration was not a new phenomenon, lower transportation costs made the option more viable.

Congress passed the Immigration Act of 1891 after a congressional investigation found "widespread violations and circumventions" of existing immigration laws. The new legislation expanded the list of excluded immigrants, enabled the deportation of immigrants present for less than a year if government authorities found them excludable, and established the Office of the Superintendent of Immigration within the Treasury Department—later reformed as the Bureau of Immigration. The act also made immigration inspectors' rulings final and ended the possibility of judicial review, although the Treasury Secretary could still review them. Twelve years later, the Immigration Act of 1903 expanded the list of excludable immigrants and excluded aliens from "due process protection hitherto provided by the Fourteenth Amendment to all 'persons' rather than 'citizens.'" In 1903, Congress also relocated the Bureau of Immigration to the Department of Commerce and Labor.

During the early 1900s, many Progressives argued that immigrants impeded the achievement of an ideal society, committed crimes, and abused welfare. Others proposed that the government had a duty to protect natives from immigrants who supposedly depressed innovation and lowered native-born American wages. Scholars of the era contended that certain ethnicities possessed immutable intrinsic characteristics that would prevent assimilation into American society. To combat these perceived ills, Progressives championed mandatory literacy tests, as well as various other eugenics-inspired racial and ethnic exclusions of Jews, Asians, and Africans.

The confluence of pseudo-scientific eugenic claims and a desire for an activist federal government engendered several immigration acts between 1890 and 1907, some of which have already been discussed, that increased the number of inadmissible classes of immigrants, expanded the power of deportation and raised the head tax on immigrants to $4. Anti-immigrant sentiment also prompted the United States to block the immigration of Japanese laborers via the informal Gentlemen's Agreement.77 Additional immigration restrictions were politically popular but divisive for the Republican Party.78

Dillingham Commission, World War I, and the National Origins Act:

1910–1930

Progressives and nativists bolstered their anti-immigration position by using the Dillingham Commission report as evidence that "'new immigrants' were fundamentally different from old immigrants who came from Western and Northern Europe."79 The Dillingham Commission was staffed with members who had previously supported immigration restrictions, except for one member named William S. Bennet of New York.80 Its members cherry-picked data to conclude that immigrants from Northern and Western Europe were innately superior to those from Southern and Eastern Europe. When data revealed large numbers of Northern and Western Europeans seeking welfare in American cities, the Dillingham Commission returned the data "for further information or corrections."81 Despite its methodological flaws, policymakers embraced the report and its recommendations because it confirmed their prejudices.

Citing concerns about the intelligence of new immigrants and how well they would assimilate, the Americanization movement started as a collective of private nonprofit organizations that backed civics classes, language lessons, and the destruction of the "hyphenated American." This movement eventually morphed into a series of government programs that wrote school curricula to push for immigrant assimilation, including banning the German language from being spoken in public schools.82 These anti-German laws slowed assimilation but were very popular, especially during World War I.83 Politically, anti-immigration sentiment prompted Congress to pass the restrictive Immigration Act of 1917—overruling President Woodrow Wilson's veto. This act sanctioned legal immigrants' detention and deportation if they committed a deportable crime within five years of their arrival. It also imposed literacy tests and other restrictive measures aimed at limiting immigration flows from African and Asian countries.84

After the end of World War I, the demobilization of four million soldiers and the anticipation of a wave of post-war migration caused Congress to consider further immigration restrictions.85 Restrictionists and eugenicists strengthened their position during this time by providing their dubious accounts of immigration's role in American history.86 Others misused administered intelligence tests to prove the intellectual inferiority of black Americans and new immigrants, biasing their results by intentionally surveying a disproportionate number of immigrants and blacks who were mentally disabled for their final report and then omitting that crucial detail in their conclusions.87 With support mounting, Congress passed restrictive legislation again in 1921.

Before 1921, immigration laws pertained primarily to which immigrants to exclude, while any immigrant not expressly excluded could migrate. However, beginning in 1921 and continuing until today, the opposite has been the status quo: federal agencies decide which immigrants to admit and deny entry to those not explicitly approved.
The Emergency Quota Act of 1921 broke with previous immigration laws by establishing a cap on quota admissions equal to roughly 358,000 for immigrants from the Eastern Hemisphere, exempting immediate relatives. This was the first American immigration law that substantially emphasized family-based immigration over economic immigrants. Of the total quota admissions, the bill allocated 55 percent to Northern and Western European countries. The bill's provisions favored family members of U.S. citizens by exempting admissions of certain immediate

relatives. Before 1921, immigration laws pertained primarily to which immigrants to exclude, while any immigrant not expressly excluded could migrate. However, beginning in 1921 and continuing until today, the opposite has been the status quo: federal agencies decide which immigrants to admit and deny entry to those not explicitly approved.

The Immigration Act of 1924, also known as the National Origins Act, refined the system established in 1921. The new law reduced the annual quota from roughly 358,000 to about 164,000. The law also established per-country cap allocations that awarded 82 percent of the world quota to immigrants from Western and Northern European countries, 14 percent to immigrants from Eastern and Southern European countries, and 4 percent to immigrants from the remaining Eastern Hemisphere.88 Like the 1921 Act, the 1924 Act did not restrict immigrants from the Western Hemisphere. The 1924 act also categorized wives and children as nonquota admissions, exempting them from the quota caps. Under the 1924 act, there were three categories of aliens: quota immigrants entering under immigration statutes as permanent residents, nonquota immigrants entering as spouses and unmarried children of quota immigrants, and nonimmigrants entering temporarily.89

Few politicians opposed the 1921 Emergency Quota and 1924 National Origins Acts. These laws were politically popular because of widespread notions of eugenics, nationalism, and xenophobia. For example, even popular books, such as The Melting Pot Mistake by New York University sociologist Henry Pratt Fairchild, defended the new restrictionist regime by using the crudest elements of nationalism, eugenics, and xenophobia.90 Former state senator Edwin E. Grant, a Democrat, summed up these sentiments when he wrote, "The prosperity made possible by our forefathers has lured the parasites of Europe—the scum that could have so well been eliminated from the melting-pot."91

Since eugenics was a significant motivation, it is initially perplexing that the Immigration Act of 1924 established quotas based on the country of origin rather than the immigrants' race or genetics, especially considering how the latter characteristics were most important to the progressive demographic central planners of the time. A proponent of the law, Fairchild noticed this peculiarity and commented that:

The question will probably at once arise: why, if this legislation was a response to a demand for racial discrimination, was it expressed in terms of nationality? The answer is simple. As has already been shown, our actual knowledge of the racial composition of the American people, to say nothing of the various foreign groups, is so utterly inadequate that the attempt to use it as a basis of legislation would have led to endless confusion and intolerable litigation. So Congress substituted the term nationality and defined nationality as country of birth. It is clear, then, that "nationality," as used in this connection, does not conform precisely to the correct definition of either nationality or race. But in effect, it affords a rough approximation to the racial character of the different immigrant streams.92

The 1924 Immigration Act did not place numerical quotas on immigrants from countries in the Western Hemisphere.93 As a result, immigration from Mexico and Canada spiked as immigrants from these regions replaced Asian and European immigrant laborers. In response, immigration restrictionists argued that Mexicans could not legally immigrate because they were ineligible for citizenship as "mixed breeds"—a legal argument based on a statute that limited immigration to only those who could naturalize.94 Specifically, economist Roy L. Garis reasoned that "to admit peons from Mexico... while restricting Europeans and excluding Orientals is not only ridiculous and illogical— it destroys the biological, social, and economic advantages to be secured from the restriction of immigration."95 Eventually, the federal government resolved this disagreement by classifying Mexicans as white.96 The Supreme Court, however, decided not to confer the racial status of "white" to high-caste Hindus, in United States v. Bhaghat Singh Thind, even though racial theorists deemed Asian Indians to be Aryans.97

Regardless of the motivations behind the 1924 Immigration Act, it created a complex quota system that was tough to impose and took years to establish, partly due to the Bureau of Immigration's lack of administrative capacity.98 For example, the 1924 Immigration Act required the prescreening of immigrants at embassies and consulates abroad, implementing a visa system, and deporting illegal arrivals.99 To enforce the law, Congress also created the U.S. Border Patrol. Additionally, Congress allowed Immigration Bureau agents to arrest unlawful border crossers without obtaining warrants, to board and search vessels, and to access private lands within 25 miles of the border.100 Despite these powers, an estimated 175,000 illegal entries occurred annually.101 When the act went into force as it was intended to be in 1929, Congress allowed unlawful immigrants who were eligible for naturalization and who were present since 1921 to regularize their status.102

The Great Depression, World War II, and Post-War Recovery:

1930–1965

The 1924 Act significantly reduced the number of legal immigrants entering the United States. Five years before the act, an average of 554,920 legal immigrants arrived each year; during the five years after the act, the average number of legal immigrants arriving each year dropped to 304,182. By 1932, the inflow of legal immigrants had fallen to 35,576. Throughout the entire decade of the 1930s, legal immigration averaged 69,938 annually. The number of immigrants arriving in the United States dropped by 90 percent from 1924 to 1940. The annual immigrant inflow in 1924 was equal to 0.63 percent of the total U.S. population. By 1940, that figure had collapsed to 0.05 percent of the population.

In 1933, an Executive Order merged the Bureau of Immigration and the Bureau of Naturalization into the Immigration and Naturalization Services (INS) with the Department of Labor. As the country entered the Great Depression, Secretary of Labor William N. Doak thought that deporting illegal immigrants would create jobs for natives.103 As a result, the federal government deported more than one million

Mexicans and persons of Mexican ancestry in what was euphemistically known as "repatriation," even though approximately 60 percent of the deportees were U.S. citizens, having been born in the United States to Mexican parents.104 Despite its intended goal, the repatriation efforts increased unemployment rates for native-born Americans.105 Although Congress passed no additional significant immigration restrictions during the Great Depression, President Herbert Hoover did establish new administrative barriers by instructing immigration officials to interpret existing public charge statutes to exclude non-wealthy immigrants.106

President Franklin D. Roosevelt issued Executive Order 9066, establishing concentration and detention camps for Japanese and Germans inside the United States.

Before World War II, politicians and bureaucrats applied immigration laws selectively to meet the demands of labor unions, denaturalize and deport political activists, and prosecute criminals.107 In 1940, Congress passed the Alien Registration Act that forced noncitizens to register with the federal government, provide fingerprints, and notify the government in the event of an address change. The law also made prior involvement in the Communist, Fascist, or Nazi political parties grounds for deportation.108 In the same year, the Department of Justice took over the INS.109 Congressman Thomas F. Ford (DCA) noted that "the mood in the House is such that if you brought in the Ten Commandments today and asked for their repeal, and attached to that request an alien law, you could get it."110 Under these conditions and just two months after the United States entered into World War II, President Franklin D. Roosevelt issued Executive Order 9066, establishing concentration and detention camps for Japanese and Germans inside the United States.111

World War II Refugee Policy and Reform

Historically, the United States was a refuge for displaced persons and those fleeing persecution. These refugees included but were not limited to, expelled British political and religious dissidents, Jews escaping the pogroms in Eastern Europe and Russia, and Europeans escaping nationalist uprisings. However, the 1920s immigration laws did not allow exceptions to the quotas for refugees.112 As Adolf Hitler rose to power in Germany in the 1930s, a refugee crisis mounted that Western countries mostly ignored or actively worsened. The lack of a humanitarian response caused the U.S. commissioner overseeing the League of Nations to resign in protest, stating, "When domestic policies threaten the demoralization and exile of hundreds of thousands of human beings, considerations of diplomatic correctness must yield to those of common humanity."113

Even after the Nazi government indicated at a meeting of the Intergovernmental Committee on behalf of refugees that it would allow 40,000 refugees to leave with some of their assets, thus reducing the likelihood that immigrants would become a public charge, few countries were eager to accept them.114 In the United States, Congress was so indifferent to the refugee crisis that it defeated a 1939 proposal that would have facilitated the migration of 20,000 children from Nazi Germany, even though all of the children had U.S. family sponsors.115

The federal government did allow about 127,000 German Jews to enter the United States between 1933 and 1940. However, the quota for German immigrants, as set by the 1920s immigration laws, was underfilled by about 110,000 for the entirety of the 1930s.116 That many more German Jews could likely have escaped Germany before World War II if the meager quota had been fully utilized. One estimate reported by author and Holocaust historian Henry L. Feingold was that 62,000 to 75,000 Jewish refugees could have left Europe between 1940 and 1942. Still, enforcement of the U.S. public charge rule blocked them.117 By the time World War II began in 1939, approximately three-fifths of the Jews in Germany, Austria, and Czechoslovakia had escaped, but about 250,000 to 300,000 people were still left behind.118 If the pre-1920s immigration laws had been in effect, then there is little doubt that virtually all German Jews—and many others from Eastern

Europe—could have escaped to the United States before the outbreak of the war.

The voyage of the St. Louis neatly summarizes the tragedy of U.S. immigration policy. The St. Louis sailed from Europe in 1939 with 900 Jewish passengers. The Cuban government denied the ships' passengers the ability to disembark, prompting St. Louis to sail to the United States, where the U.S. government rejected the refugee's entry. Without a port to dock at, the St. Louis returned to Europe, where European countries admitted some refugees. Ultimately, 254 of the 900 passengers perished during the war.119 The disconnect between the actions and words of Western governments prompted Hitler to remark that "it is a shameful example to observe today how the entire democratic world dissolves in tears of pity, but then, despite its obvious duty to help, closes its heart to the poor, tortured people."120

The postwar revelation of the Holocaust shamed the United States for its pre-war anti-refugee policy. It generated political support for the passage of the Displaced Persons Act of 1948 and the Refugee Relief Act of 1953. These two pieces of legislation helped facilitate the post-war immigration of refugees.121 As a result of these and other provisions, the United States admitted more than a half million refugees between 1945 and 1953.122 Another motivating factor for liberalizing refugee flows after World War II was the realization that the United States could use refugee policy to increase its international prestige relative to that of the Soviet Union to combat Soviet propaganda.123 Congress made the first moves in this direction during World War II when it lifted the ban on Chinese immigrants and established a meager quota in 1943 to limit the effectiveness of Japanese propaganda.124

The Bracero Program

Amid World War II, the federal government instituted the Mexican Labor Program, commonly known as the Bracero Program. The Bracero Program was similar to the temporary-worker programs of 1917 and 1922 that allowed for the entry of 50,000 to 80,000 Mexican laborers.125 This program gave farmers, who faced severe labor scarcity and wage controls during the war, access to Mexican laborers under certain conditions. Along with a minimum wage standard and housing protections, the program also established terms of return for Mexican workers who would labor in agriculture. At the same time, Americans were employed in war industries or serving in the military. The Mexican government was allowed to select participants for the program.

Some U.S. farmers refused to use the program because of the precedent it set for government control of the labor market. Other farmers hired lower-cost illegal immigrant workers. A third group paid braceros less than the mandated minimum wage.127 Enforcement remained lax, and many farmers abused bracero workers.128 Between 1942 and 1964, the Bracero Program facilitated roughly 4.5 million Mexican agricultural workers' legal entry.

During the Great Depression and World War II, few immigrants wanted to come to the United States illegally, and the program allowed some of those who might have otherwise come illegally to enter on a visa instead.130 During this period, immigration enforcement performed relatively well, but it quickly broke down in the face of sustained postwar immigration flows. In 1946, an INS report recorded a massive increase in illegal entries that were "riddling the country of aliens illegally in the United States," with more illegal entries than any previous year.131 In subsequent years, reports described a steady increase in the number of illegal immigrants as "virtually an invasion."

Illegal immigration increased substantially in 1947 when the Bracero Program temporarily ended.
Illegal immigration increased substantially in 1947 when the Bracero Program temporarily ended. This influx of illegal immigrants prompted the federal government to arrest 142,000 illegal workers between 1947 and 1949 before returning them to the border to grant them temporary work visas. This process eventually morphed into a revamped Bracero Program. However, the slight liberalization under the Bracero Program did not legalize the entire population of illegal workers and left two

million illegal Mexican immigrants living in the American Southwest in the early 1950s.

The federal government also responded to these inflows with two additional interrelated actions. The first was a legal reform and expansion of the bracero guest worker visa program in 1951.. The second was Operation Wetback in 1954, an ill-conceived immigration enforcement operation that removed almost a million illegal Mexican immigrants. Between 1953 and 1954, the federal government removed or returned more than two million illegal immigrants.136 It is important to note that the government legalized many of those apprehended in Operation Wetback and gave them bracero work visas as an extension of the 1947–1949 legalization program. The government derogatorily referred to this legalization process as "drying out."1

Some illegal immigrants took "a walk-around the statute" to gain a bracero worker visa—a process where they were driven down to the Mexican border by the INS or Border Patrol and made to take one step across the border and then immediately reenter the United States legally with a bracero work visa.138 The combination of a legal migration pathway with consequences for breaking immigration laws incentivized Mexican migrants to come legally. As a result, the number of removals in 1955 fell significantly, and those who had previously entered illegally instead signed up to become braceros.

Before the expansion and partial deregulation of the program in 1951, employers in the Rio Grande Valley referred to the Border Patrol as a "Gestapo outfit" that wrenched their willing illegal workers away from employment.140 The INS commissioner, Joseph Swing, realized that he would have to reduce both the demand for and supply of illegal immigrant workers to have any hope of success, which he accomplished by telling farmers that they could hire as many legal Mexican workers as they demanded if they followed the rules.141 Farmers who did not comply were punished, but this rarely happened because compliance was easy and cheap. Commissioner Swing characterized the success as an "exchange" of illegal workers for legal guest workers.

A Border Patrol official warned that if the Bracero Program was ever "repealed or a restriction placed on the number of Braceros allowed to enter the United States, we could look forward to a large increase in the number of illegal alien entrants into the United States."143 After Congress canceled the program in 1964 in response to political pressure from labor unions and labor organizers, illegal immigration jumped because Congress failed to replace it with another effective lower-skilled guest worker visa program.144 By the time Congress canceled the program in 1964, regulations promulgated by the Department of Labor had whittled the number of guest-worker visas down to just 200,000.145 The department's wage regulations and labor certification requirements raised costs for farmers and migrants, incentivizing them to move into the informal, underground economy.146 Ending the Bracero Program did not end temporary worker migration to the United States; it merely made such migration illegal.147

Shifting Perceptions and the Immigration and Nationality Act of 1952
Eugenicist, progressive, and nationalist justifications for the 1924 National Origins Act were less popular after World War II. However, immigration restrictionists still hoped to achieve "the preservation of whiteness" through the immigration system.148 The 1950s McCarran Report defended the National Origin Act's system of allocating quotas as the best way to "preserve the sociological and cultural balance of the United States."149 Despite Truman's veto, Congress passed the Immigration and Nationality Act of 1952. This bill increased the quota for Europeans from outside of Northern and Western Europe, granted the Department of State the ability to deny entry to those it thought would lower native wages, repealed the 1880s' prohibitions against contract labor, and set a minimum quota of a hundred visas for immigrants from every country. The bill promoted family reunification by continuing the exemption of children and spouses of citizens from the numerical caps.150

The 1952 act introduced four preference categories, allotting 50 percent of the quota admissions to immigrants with needed skills, 30 percent to parents of adult citizens, 20 percent to the spouses and children of legal residents, and any unused green cards to the siblings and adult children of citizens.151 Further, the act created nonimmigrant visa categories that are familiar to us today, such as treaty traders or investors (E), students (F1), temporary workers of distinguished ability or merit (H1), and others.152 The bill favored Europeans, and because few wanted to immigrate then, many available visas went unused between 1952 and 1965.

The 1950s McCarran Report defended the National Origin Act's system of allocating quotas as the best way to 'preserve the sociological and cultural balance of the United States.'

The Immigration and Nationality Act also removed the ban on Asian immigration and many due-process safeguards that protected immigrants from deportation abuses.153 Senators Hubert Humphrey (DMN) and Herbert Lehman (DNY) lamented that the act subjected deportees to the tyranny of bureaucrats and that deportations "without hearings or findings, and the possibility of judicial review, would be the beginning of a police state."154 In 1958, Congress expanded its 1929 regularization provisions to illegal entrants and overstayers eligible for naturalization who had resided in the United States since 1940.

Reopening the Immigration System: 1965–2000

Between 1952 and 1960, immigration rebounded from its World War II lows and averaged 257,000 immigrants annually, but the 1960 census revealed that only 5.4 percent of the United States population was foreign-born.155 The Civil Rights movement and the rejection of eugenics positioned public opinion against the national quota system, laying the groundwork for reform.156

The Immigration and Nationality Act of 1965

Sen. Philip Hart (DMI) and Rep. Emanuel Celler (DNY) championed the Immigration and Nationality Act of 1965, which would end the national quota system and replace it entirely with a preference system for immigrants from the Eastern Hemisphere.157 The 1965 act created categories of immigrants that included the unmarried and married sons and daughters of U.S. citizens; siblings of U.S. citizens; spouses and unmarried sons and daughters of green card holders; members of the professions that include, but are not limited to, architects, engineers, lawyers, physicians, surgeons, and teachers; scientists and artists of exceptional ability; skilled and unskilled workers in occupations for which labor was in short supply; and some refugees.158 Congress set aside 74 percent of the available green cards for family members, 20 percent for workers, and 6 percent for refugees.

Early versions of the Immigration and Nationality Act of 1965 allocated fewer green cards for family members and more for workers. Those who supported the national origins system and opposed non-European immigration pushed for the expanded family-based immigration system to maintain European favoritism in the law. Rep. Michael Feighan (DOH) introduced amendments that set aside 74 percent of the 1965 act's green cards for family members because he believed the current stock of European-American immigrants would use them to create and maintain ties with Europe.160 He did not anticipate, however, that Latin Americans and Asians would be the primary beneficiaries.

As with the 1921, 1924, and 1952 acts, the 1965 Immigration and Nationality (Hart-Celler) Act did not count spouses, minor children, or the parents of U.S. citizens over 21 against the numerical cap.161 The bill also mandated that employment-based immigrants must receive certification from the Department of Labor that "the employment of such aliens will not adversely affect the wages and working conditions of the workers in the United States similarly employed."162 Before the 1965 act, the government had to demonstrate that a new worker would depress American citizens' wages to deny the new worker a visa. Still, the new bill put the onus on the applicant to show that no adverse effect would result—this was a substantial burden shift that increased visa denial rates.163

Further provisions of the 1965 Immigration and Nationality Act limited immigration from both hemispheres to 290,000 annually—170,000 for the Eastern Hemisphere and 120,000 for the Western Hemisphere.164 The act limited immigration from any individual country in the Eastern Hemisphere to 20,000 annually. By 1976, this provision also applied to Western Hemisphere countries.165 Lastly, the act extended the administrative amnesty of 1929 to those who were illegally present in 1948, legalizing about 44,106 illegal immigrants by 1981.166

RELATED READ

Free to Move: Foot Voting, Migration, and Political Freedom

Immigration policy is the most debated and controversial issue of our time. Across the developed world, political parties have significantly diverged on this issue. In Europe, political parties with a nativist bent have won elections and governed in coalition with other mainstream parties. But even mainstream parties, such as the Danish Social Democrats, have adopted anti-immigration platforms as they adapt to the opinions of voters skeptical of immigration—and have maintained power.

Under the new system, the number of immigrants from the Western Hemisphere increased because the family-reunification portions of immigration law expanded chain migration from Latin America.167 Moreover, the 1965 act did not replace the Bracero Program with another functional guest worker program, guaranteeing increased illegal migration.168 Demographically, the removal of racial restrictions significantly increased the number of Asian immigrants and slightly increased the number of Hispanic immigrants. Geographically, Florida, California, New York, Texas, Illinois, and New Jersey received the bulk of new immigrants.

In 1968, Sen. Edward M. Kennedy (DMA) secured the federal government's agreement to the 1967 United Nations Protocol Relating to the Status of Refugees.170 From 1967 to 1980, waves of refugees fleeing communism arrived in the United States through a mixture of special legislative remedies and presidential parole power. Congress replaced this ad hoc system with a formal admission process in the Refugee Act of 1980. This bill restricted the use of presidential parole, temporarily raised the refugee limits from 17,600 to 50,000, and established a new category for asylum seekers. The bill mandated that the president, in consultation with Congress, determine the number of future refugees admitted annually. Moreover, this bill amended the Immigration and Nationality Act to conform with the 1967 United Nations Protocol Relating to the Status of Refugees, recognizing individuals with specific characteristics as refugees. From 1980 to 2000, the federal government accepted an average of 97,000 refugees annually.

Legal immigration expanded in the wake of the 1965 act. Between 1966 and 1980, the average annual number of immigrants increased by roughly 150,000, compared to the yearly averages between 1952 and 1965. By 1980, 6.2 percent of the 226 million U.S. population was foreign-born, and 524,295 immigrants entered legally that year.172 The number of illegal immigrants also grew, in part, because the 1965 act did not create a way for lower-skilled workers to enter the country and legally work. Estimates suggest that there were 28 million illegal immigrant entries to the United States from 1965 to 1986; these were offset by 23.4 million departures, yielding a net difference of about 4.6 million over 21 years.

The Immigration Reform and Control Act

The influx of illegal immigrants forged a contentious political alliance between Democrats who were interested in amnesty for illegal immigrants and Republicans who wanted to end illegal immigration. This overlap allowed Sen. Alan K. Simpson (RWY) and Rep. Romano Mazzoli (DKY) to submit immigration reform bills based on policy recommendations made by the 1980 Select Commission on Immigration and Refugee Policy. Despite being delayed by political posturing, a transmuted version of the bill called the Immigration Reform and Control Act (IRCA) passed in 1986.

This act consisted of two main components: amnesty for illegal immigrants who had lived continuously in the country since January 1,

1982, and penalties for employers who willingly hired illegal immigrants. The bill granted roughly three million illegal immigrants amnesty and created 109 new INS offices to enforce immigration laws.175 The act slightly lowered illegal immigrant wages. Still, it failed to dim the wage magnet entirely because employer sanctions incentivized unlawful immigrant workers to purchase fake documents on the black market, steal identity documents, and borrow valid documents from those with legal work authorization.

The legalization component of the law did succeed, however, as immigrants earned green cards and saw substantial wage gains in the years after legalization. The IRCA also attempted to deregulate and expand low-skilled guest worker visas, but it had virtually no effect on migration. Ultimately, IRCA did not create a way for future low-skilled migrants from Mexico and Central America to enter lawfully. Although IRCA boosted the number of Border Patrol agents along the southwest border to roughly 3,350 agents by 1988, illegal immigration nevertheless increased.

The Anti-Drug Abuse Act of 1988 created a category of offenses called aggravated felonies that subjected noncitizens to deportation after completing their prison sentence.178 Although the bill defined aggravated felonies as murder, drug trafficking, and illicit trafficking in arms, Congress has since increased the number of crimes that are considered aggravated felonies. By 2016, more than 30 types of offenses were deemed aggravated felonies, including minor crimes with a sentence of one year or more.179 An aggravated felony conviction subjects a noncitizen to deportation, removes all possibility of deportation relief, and bans them from the United States for life, even if the immigrant committed the crime before it was considered an aggravated felony.

The Reforms of the 1990s

Legal immigration flows surpassed one million in 1989, the first time since 1914. By 1990, the immigrant stock was 19.8 million, accounting for 7.9 percent of the U.S. population. In 1960, 84 percent of the U.S.

foreign-born population in the United States were either from Europe or Canada. In 1990, about 7 percent of green cards were issued to those from Europe, 22 percent to those from Asia, and 59 percent to those from either Mexico, Central America, or South America. Legislation was partially responsible for the change in origin regions, but much of the shift was due to economic development globally. Whereas Europe and Canada were wealthy regions relative to the rest of the world, developing nations were affluent enough that their citizens could emigrate but not yet wealthy enough to entice them to stay.

Following the expansion of legal immigration after 1968, Congress passed the Immigration Act of 1990 to liberalize the immigration of skilled workers and increased the number of green cards issued annually to 675,000. Similar to earlier legislation, the law allowed immediate relatives—children, spouses, and parents of U.S. citizens—and a few other classes of immigrants to immigrate outside the direct numerical limits. It provided, at minimum, another 226,000 green cards for family reunification and 140,000 green cards to employment-based immigrants divided among five preference categories. The 1990 act also raised the annual per-country ceilings to 7 percent (25,620) of the total familial and employment-based allowance. Lastly, the Immigration Act of 1990 added and reformed nonimmigrant visas for skilled workers, such as the H1B visa for skilled workers in specialty occupations and the O1 visa for individuals with extraordinary ability or achievement.

Finally, the bill allocated 55,000 immigration visas to a Diversity Visa program that awarded visas to nationals from countries with low immigration levels to the United States. Despite the program's name, Congress created it not to increase immigrant flows from Africa and Asia but rather from Ireland. Members of Congress began to realize that the 1965 reforms, which allocated the majority of green cards on a family reunification basis, favored recent non-European immigrants over others. The program was an attempt to accommodate these newly disfavored European immigrants.

Unsurprisingly, given congressional intent and a temporary allocation of 40 percent of the diversity visas to the Irish, in 1994, almost all diversity visa recipients were from European countries.185 From 1995 to 2000, an average of 42 percent of diversity visas were issued to European countries, but over time the composition of recipients shifted.186 In 2016, the percentage of diversity visas issued to European countries fell to 24 percent, while the rate of diversity visas issued to Africans and Asians increased to 40 percent and 31 percent, respectively.187

Despite the 1990 act, the illegal immigrant population increased from about 3.5 million in 1990 to 5.7 million in 1995.188 Restrictionists argued that immigrants had adverse economic effects, failed to assimilate culturally, used an abundance of welfare, and amplified the perceptions of lawlessness and social chaos along the border with Mexico caused by illegal immigration.189 Restrictionists also introduced a new argument based on a relatively new concern regarding immigrants' supposed environmental damage.

Politicians and activists of the era havehed out many immigration debates at the state level, California Propositions 187 and 227 being the two most well-known examples.190 The former curtailed welfare for illegal immigrants and required every state employee to report suspected illegal immigrants to the INS, while the latter eliminated bilingual education in public schools.191 Both passed by wide margins. At the federal level, the Clinton administration attempted to reduce illegal immigration administratively via border operations such as Operation Hold the Line in 1993 and Operation Gatekeeper in 1994.

Similarly, Congress passed the Antiterrorism and Effective Death Penalty Act and the Illegal Immigration Reform and Immigrant Responsibility Act in 1996. These bills increased the penalties for illegal entry, created mandatory detention for many classes of noncitizens, and expedited deportation procedures for some instances. The bills also limited judicial review of certain types of deportations and allowed secret evidence in removal proceedings for noncitizens accused of terrorist activity.192 Additionally, the Illegal Immigration Reform and Immigrant Responsibility Act increased the interior deportation apparatus in the United States. It prevented illegal immigrants from using the legal system to earn a green card through the so-called three-and-ten-year bars, which prevented illegally present immigrants who leave the United States from legally returning for any reason, thus guaranteeing that the number of illegal immigrants would grow more rapidly than in the pre-IRCA period.193

Congress also passed the Personal Responsibility and Work Opportunity Reconciliation Act. The act made most noncitizens ineligible for means-tested welfare, authorized the states to deny providing welfare such as Medicaid to immigrants, and delayed the possibility of receiving welfare for most immigrants for five years.194 While initially impactful, the act became less effective as the federal government backed some of its welfare restrictions and states started providing social services to ineligible immigrants.

By 1997, the number of Border Patrol agents along the southwest border increased to 6,315—roughly double the number employed in 1987. The additional enforcement measures increased the cost of crossing the border illegally, increased illegal immigrants' use of smugglers, inflated smugglers' fees, and decreased the incentive for illegal immigrants to return home after successfully entering the United States.195

Immigration Policy in the 21st Century: 2000–2020

In 2000, Republican presidential candidate George W. Bush appealed to Hispanic voters by supporting expanded legal immigration and legalization for illegal immigrants, a lesson he learned after winning two gubernatorial elections in Texas.196 Bush's pro-immigration tactic in Texas was at odds with that of California Republican Governor Pete Wilson, who devastated his party's popularity among Hispanic voters.197 The Bush administration hoped to create an extensive guest worker program and legalize illegal immigrants even after the 9/11 attacks.

Congress passed the USA Patriot Act shortly after the 9/11 attacks. The Patriot Act reduced the rights of immigrants by expanding deportation powers to suspected terrorists and allowed the attorney general to detain aliens without charge or recourse to due process.198 In 2002, after the INS issued visa extensions to two of the deceased 9/11 terrorists, Congress passed the Homeland Security Act, which consolidated 22 federal departments and agencies into the new Department of Homeland Security.199 This act moved many federal agencies responsible for immigration enforcement under the department's purview. It restructured them as Customs and Border Protection, Immigration and Customs Enforcement, and Citizenship and Immigration Services.

During Bush's terms in office, he signed both the Enhanced Border Security and Visa Entry Reform Act of 2002 and the Secure Fence Act of 2006 and renewed the USA Patriot Act. These laws reaffirmed the government's power to detain immigrants without trial, authorized about 850 miles of fencialong the southwest border, and expanded the size of Border Patrol.200 Congressional actions also increased nonimmigrant visa security screening through reforming or implementing various programs, such as the Automated Biometric Identification System, the Student and Exchange Visitor Information System, and the Electronic System for Travel Authorization.201

On the nonsecurity side of immigration, Congress passed the H1B Visa Reform Act of 2004, which provided 20,000 additional H1B visas to high-skilled temporary workers with advanced degrees from American universities. This act came only four years after Congress passed the American Competitiveness in the Twenty-First Century Act in 2000, which temporarily raised the annual H1B cap and permanently exempted universities and nonprofit research institutions from the visa cap. In 2006, the Republican-led Senate passed the Comprehensive Immigration Reform Act, which, among other things, would have legalized illegal immigrants and expanded legal immigration. Still, the House of Representatives did not ratify the act. Similar bills also died in the Senate in 2007 and 2008.

The Pew Research Center estimated that the illegal immigration population peaked at 12.2 million in 2007, and the issue moved to the forefront of the 2008 presidential election. Democratic presidential candidate Barack Obama ran on a platform of increased employer sanctions and earned legalization for noncriminal immigrants. His Republican opponent, John McCain, who had recently helped write the failed 2007 immigration bill, supported comprehensive immigration reform.202 After Obama's victory, Congress reintroduced the DREAM Act in 2009 to legalize many illegal immigrants who entered the country as children, but it ultimately failed in the Senate after passing in the House of Representatives.203

In 2012, Obama announced the Deferred Action for Childhood Arrivals program (DACA), which granted a two-year work permit and a reprieve from deportation to illegal immigrants who met many of the latest DREAM Act requirements.204 By the 2012 presidential election, Republican presidential candidate Mitt Romney rejected a pathway to citizenship, opposed DACA, and argued that strict enforcement of existing laws would lead to illegal immigrants' self-ddeportation.205 Conversely, Obama continued to support comprehensive immigration reform and the targeted deportation of illegal immigrants.206 Obama's administration removed more illegal immigrants than any other administration, earning him the nickname "Deporter-in-Chief."207 Obama removed 1,242,486 illicit immigrants from the interior of the United States during his entire eight years, averaging 155,311 removals per year. President George W. Bush removed 819,964 illegal immigrants from the interior of the United States during the last six years of his administration, equal to an average of 136,661 removals per year. Estimating the number of illegal immigrants deported in 2001 and 2002, based on those deported during 2003–2006, shows that Bush's administration would have deported 1,000,653 illicit immigrants from the interior of the United States, with an annual average of 125,082. In comparison, President Trump only managed to remove 325,660 people from the interior of the United States during his entire term in office. On average, Trump removed an average of 81,415 illegal immigrants per year

In 2013, eight senators—including John McCain (RAZ), Charles Schumer (DNY), and Lindsey Graham (RSC)—introduced the Border Security, Economic Opportunity, and Immigration Modernization Act, colloquially known as the "Gang of Eight" Bill. This bill proposed a myriad of immigration reforms. Among these was that it allowed many illegal immigrants to obtain Registered Provisional Immigration status, which would eventually permit them to naturalize. It also created a W visa program that provided temporary work visas for less-skilled immigrants. The bill exempted the families of immigrants who obtained employment-based green cards from the numerical cap, established a merit-based system for admitting low-skilled and high-skilled workers, and ended the diversity visa program. Congressional Budget Office estimates indicated that the bill would decrease the federal deficit, increase legal immigration, and reduce illegal immigration.209 However, despite passing the Senate 68 to 32, the bill languished and died in the House.

In 2014, Obama issued the Immigration Accountability Executive Action, which granted three years of temporary revocable relief and work authorization to four to five million illegal immigrants by expanding DACA to cover the parents of U.S. citizens. This order increased and redirected enforcement resources to the southern border. The memo also prioritized deportation for "national security threats, serious criminals, and recent border crossers."210 The executive action altered administrative procedures to allow visa processing for illegal immigrant spouses of U.S. citizens without needing to leave the country, help high-skilled workers on H1B visas change their jobs more accessible, and reduce barriers to foreign-born entrepreneurs' immigration. The courts blocked Obama's executive action in late 2014, and in 2016, the Supreme Court deadlocked at a 4–4 decision, thereby defaulting to the lower court's decision.

By 2016, the illegal population receded to 10.7 million, and in 2016, there were 17,000 Border Patrol agents and 654 miles of primary fencing on the southwest border.212 During the 2016 presidential elections, immigration became a focal point. Democratic presidential candidate

Sen. Bernie Sanders (IVT) criticized open borders as "a Koch brothers' proposal."213 Sanders acknowledged that a liberal U.S. immigration policy would improve immigrants' well-being but stated that his first obligation was to U.S. children, whom he argued would be injured by immigration. Republican presidential candidate Donald Trump said that he would "put America first" by denying entry to immigrants who, he claimed, take Americans' jobs, commit crimes, and pose national security threats.214

Trump won the Republican nomination—beating Republicans who held more traditional positions on immigration—by calling for a wall on the southern border, ending birthright citizenship, banning Muslim entry into the United States, and terminating DACA.215 Conversely, the Democratic presidential nominee, Hillary Clinton, advocated almost the opposite approach. Instead of increased enforcement, Clinton promised that, in her first 100 days, she would introduce comprehensive immigration reform, defend DACA, and expand the Affordable Care Act subsidies to all immigrants.216

Upon taking office, Trump issued multiple executive orders to stop the issuance of visas to immigrants and nonimmigrants from several primarily Muslim-majority countries based on the assertion that they would be detrimental to national security.217 The Trump administration also halted DACA and lent support to the RAISE Act in 2017, which would have cut legal immigration by half.218 There was little congressional action on immigration under the Trump administration, but various federal agencies utilized the regulatory state to reduce legal immigration.219 For example, the Department of Justice and the Department of Homeland Security have attempted to expand immigration enforcement in the interior of the United States and along the border. Similarly, the Citizenship and Immigration Services issued a final rule that altered the public charge grounds of inadmissibility, which could substantially reduce the number of new green cards issued.220 Trump campaigned on building a wall across the length of the southern border. Despite Trump's efforts, the number of lawful permanent residents entering the United States had not declined much by the end of 2019.

Trump issued his most significant immigration executive actions after the COVID-19 pandemic and the recession. In April 2020, Trump practically ended issuing green cards to people abroad, which usually accounts for about half of new green cards issued annually. In the last six months of the 2020 fiscal year (April to September), the federal government only issued about 29,000 green cards. During the same period in 2016, it had issued approximately 309,000 green cards. Compared to the last half of 2016, the number of green cards issued in the 2020 fiscal year fell by 90.5 percent (Figure 4).221 from January 2017 to February 2020, the average number of green cards issued per month to immigrants abroad was down about 0.5 percent under Trump compared to the January 2013 to February 2016 period under Obama, with cumulative numbers down just over 3.2 percent.222 In other words, Trump's lasting impact on issuing green cards to immigrants abroad was minimal before his COVID-19 executive orders.

As with immigrant visas, Trump significantly reduced the issuance of nonimmigrant visas (NIVs) in response to the recession and the COVID-19 pandemic (Figure 5). In the last six months of the 2020 fiscal year (April to September), the federal government issued 397,596 NIVs. In the same period in 2016, during Obama's last full year in office, it issued more than 5.6 million NIVs. Compared with the previous half of the 2016 fiscal year, the number of nonimmigrant visas issued in the last half of the 2020 fiscal year fell by almost 93 percent.223 During the period from January 2017 to February 2020, before the COVID-19 pandemic, the average number of monthly NIVs issued was down about 12 percent under Trump compared to the January 2013 to February 2016 period under Obama, and the cumulative numbers were down by just over 14 percent. Beginning in mid to late March, the Trump administration virtually halted the issuance of NIVs to people abroad. Comparing the decline in the number of visas issued abroad under Trump through November 2020 with the second term of the Obama administration, Trump reduced the number of green cards issued by approximately 418,453 and the number of NIVs by about 11,178,668. That's roughly an 18 percent decline in the number of green cards issued abroad and approximately a 28 percent decline in NIVs compared to Obama's second term. The COVID–19–related restrictions were the most severe and impactful immigration policies adopted by the Trump administration.

Refugee admissions sharply declined during the Trump administration, from 84,995 in 2016 to a mere 11,841 in 2020.225 This decline was steep and occurred annually due to Trump's orders. Under the Refugee Act 1980, the president sets worldwide and regional refugee numbers. Every year, Trump cut the numbers, and refugee admissions fell. Trump's control over legal immigration and the reduced number of refugee admissions exposed just how much power the executive branch of government has over immigration.226 Congress has given an enormous amount of energy to the president to set immigration policy. The most significant institutional change in immigration policy is that Congress' importance is shrinking while the executive branch's power is growing. How this will affect future immigration policy and the political debate over the issue remains to be seen.

Conclusion

In 2019, the United States issued just over one million green cards. Of these green cards, 63 percent were based on familial relationships (81 percent of which went to immediate family relatives of U.S. citizens and green card holders); 5 percent were based on employment; and the remainder were based on various humanitarian concerns or the diversity green card lottery.227 More than half of those obtaining a green card were adjustments of status, meaning that they were already in the United States, as opposed to new arrivals from abroad. The demand to immigrate to the United States, combined with numerical limits and per-country caps on family and employment-based migration, has created a backlog of individuals who have been approved for green cards but cannot yet receive them. As of 2019, roughly one million foreign workers and family members were awaiting employment-based green cards in the

United States, while another 3.6 million prospective immigrants were awaiting their visas.228 For immigrants from some countries, such as those from India, they will not receive their employment-based green cards for roughly a decade.

While estimates of the size of the illegal immigrant population continue to fall, the demand for nonimmigrant visas continues to rise. In 2018, the Department of State issued nearly 196,409 H2A visas for temporary agricultural workers, compared with the 11,004 visas it issued in 1996. Similarly, the issuance of H2B visas for temporary nonagricultural workers has grown significantly, increasing from 12,200 in 1996 to 97,623 in 2018.231 Demand for high-skilled workers has been so high "that the annual H1B cap was reached within the first five business days on eight occasions" between 2008 and 2020.232 Since the academic year 2008–2009, more than 600,000 international students have enrolled in American educational institutions each year. Many of those students have been unable to obtain green cards, given the current numerical constraints. Overall, the U.S. immigration system remains fragmented as of early 2021. Relative to a system that prioritizes economic contributions and creates pathways for immigrants to work in the United States legally, the current system constrains economic growth. Path dependency and politics preserve the status quo and make it difficult to reach a consensus on immigration despite seemingly straightforward opportunities to harness prospective immigrants' desire to live and work in the United States. Although regulatory changes can generate meaningful improvements to the United States immigration system, congressional reform is likely necessary to replace the patchwork of current immigration policies with a coherent system that channels the constructive powers of immigration rather than disrupting them.

Here are some examples illustrating the difference between respectful cultural inclusion and disrespectful cultural appropriation:

Respectful Cultural Inclusion:

This means attending a traditional cultural festival, such as a Chinese New Year celebration, with an open mind and genuine interest in learning about the customs and traditions.

Help by collaborating with members of a particular cultural community to create a project or event that honors and celebrates their heritage respectfully and authentically.

When you choose to take part in a workshop or seminar led by individuals from a different cultural background than what is your background, you gain a deeper understanding of their experiences and perspectives.

Disrespectful Cultural Appropriation:

When someone chooses to wear a sacred religious symbol, such as a Native American headdress, either as a fashion accessory or as part of a costume without taking the time to understand its cultural significance or obtaining permission from the originating community, it is a type of disrespectful cultural appropriation.

When individuals or groups use elements of a particular culture, such as traditional designs or patterns, to mass-produce merchandise for profit without acknowledging the cultural origins or providing any benefit to the original community.

When groups adopt specific cultural practices or rituals superficially for personal gain or as a trend, without understanding their meaning or the historical context the practices and rituals stand for, it is also a type of disrespectful cultural appropriation.

In essence, respectful cultural inclusion involves genuine engagement and appreciation for different cultures, while disrespectful cultural appropriation involves superficial, uninformed, or exploitative adoption of cultural elements.

It's essential to approach cultural exchange with sensitivity, empathy, and a willingness to learn and respect the origins and significance of the traditions and practices.

decades, and by 2040, the United States will have over 6 million fewer working-age people than in 2022,"

"Announcements of high-profile layoffs and concerns about the impact of artificial intelligence (AI) obscure America's continuing need for additional workers at the top and bottom of the skill distribution. International migration is the only potential source of growth in the U.S. working-age population in the coming years."

"The U.S. will need workers with specialized skills that are in short supply and take years of education and training to acquire. Now and in the future, the U.S. will still need workers, and it risks not having enough of them, particularly those with desired skills, absent additional immigration." Many Americans in the working age show no desire to seek any education that will help them meet this demand.

A lack of workers has already hampered plans to increase semiconductor manufacturing in the United States. "TSMC Chairman Mark Liu said construction [of a new plan] in Arizona is hampered by a shortage of skilled workers and that the company might have to bring in experienced technicians temporarily from Taiwan," reported the _Wall Street Journal_. "He said this would delay the mass production of 4-nanometer chips in the first factory until 2025."

The Semiconductor Industry Association (SIA) has warned that "the United States faces a significant shortage of technicians, computer scientists, and engineers." Economists and business analysts have concluded it is difficult to "restore" operations in any industry without sufficiently educated and trained employees.

Zavodny notes a falling U.S. population will mean fewer workers to produce goods and services. However, an aging population will keep demanding goods and services that require labor. The result is likely to be shortages and price pressures, including inflation.

"A shrinking population means fewer people to generate new ideas that lead to technological progress and long-run growth," writes Zavodny. A recent NFAP study concluded immigrants founded or cofounded 65% of the top AI companies in the United States. In comparison, 70% of full-time graduate students in AI-related fields are international students.

Immigrants have supported U.S. population growth during the past half-century. The role of immigrants will become more pronounced as baby boomers continue to leave the labor force and U.S. births fall, according to the data. The numbers show only through sustained or increased immigration can the U.S. working-age population continue to grow.

"A shrinking working-age population can easily lead to economic stagnation or even falling living standards for a nation," concludes Zavodny.

United States Immigration System Isn't The Problem.

AMERICA'S CITIZENS ARE THE PROBLEM.

TO MAKE IT SIMPLER, IT IS THEIR PREJUDICE AGAINST PEOPLE OF COLOR THAT IS THE PROBLEM.

The Only Place American Citizens Seem To Have A Problem With Immigration Is From The Southern Border.

As a settler colonial society, the United States owes much of its population growth and cultural develop. ment to immigration. Except for those few individuals who are 100% Native American, every American is either an immigrant themselves or directly descended from immigrants.

The United States has the highest immigrant population in the world at 50.6 million (as of mid-2020), which equates to approximately 15.3% of the total U.S. population and 18% of international immigrants worldwide.

The U.S. immigrant population is also notably diverse, welcoming new arrivals from more than 200 countries and territories.

The U.S. is one of the easiest countries to immigrate to, but the process for People Of Color is now more difficult.

Tracking U.S. immigration trends across the decade from 2011-2020, the U.S. welcomed nearly 10.3 million immigrants, of which almost 1.5 million (14.3%) were from Mexico.

Americans Need To Grow Up And Welcome All Immigrants With Open Arms.

WE ARE ALL TRANSPLANTS OR DECENDENTS OF TRANSPLANTS.

REMEMBER, MEXICANS HAVE A BIGGER RIGHT HERE THAN WE DO. AFTER ALL, THEY ARE THE DESCENDANTS OF INDIGENOUS PEOPLE.

The USA's History of Immigration.

Although it has always been regular, it used to be welcoming. So, new regulatory changes bringing us back to treating others humanely can generate meaningful improvements to the United States immigration system. Congressional reform is likely necessary to replace the patchwork of current immigration policies with a coherent system that channels the constructive powers of immigration rather than disrupting them.

Are MAGA Cult Members So Lost In Reality That They Believe What The Elected MAGA Republicans Are Saying About What They Claim

Is Happening At The Southern Border Is Something New And Has Not Exited Since The Formation Of The United States?

Number of Immigrants living in the United States That Crossed The Southern Border Legally and illegally:

Biden: Has 46.2 million immigrants, Foreign-born, living in the US during his presidency.

Trump: He had 44.8 million immigrants, foreign-born, living in the US during his presidency.

Biden has done no marketing advertising or pushed any plan to encourage immigration from any country south of the US.

Trump did no marketing, advertising, or push any plan that would encourage any immigration from any country south of the US.

The reality is that no President is responsible for the number of people migrating to our Southern Border.

Why has this increase started occurring, and what could happen next?

Regardless of who is elected President in November 2024, it's likely the number of border crossings will continue to increase, and there are multiple reasons why this is happening right now:

Their government, starvation, safety, housing, persecution, war, violence, and crime are some reasons people uninvited are showing up at our southern border

Many of those migrants are from Venezuela, where a socioeconomic crisis – fueled by President Nicolás Maduro's authoritarian government and worsened by the global pandemic and US sanctions – has led one in four Venezuelans to flee the country since 2015.

Both migrants and smugglers keep a close eye on US policies, Ruiz says, and many adjust their plans accordingly. "If smugglers figure out that families are making it through, more families will come."

Increases in violence in some areas of Mexico have also fueled more migration.

It's important to remember that a complicated mix of factors fuels migration in the Western Hemisphere.

"These are only some of the levers in play right now. And regardless of what any presidential administration does today or tomorrow, the people on the way already will continue, unless something else happens in their Countries to stop it."

This one MAGA Cult Republicans Southern Border Ploy Has Been In The Making Since Biden Took Office in 2021.

Looney Toon MAGA Cult Republican Texas Governor Who Has Been in Office Since 2015. Although Trump had a bigger immigration problem than any President before he was elected. Both Trump and Abbott took office at the same time. Not one complaint about the Southern Border that was blamed on Trump.

In 2021, Biden took office, and Abbott started his second term simultaneously. Biden was barely finished with his inauguration, and Abbott began his antiimmigration campaign through regular press conferences.

As the press would start Dying down, Abbott would increase his rhetoric and his extreme antics.

Biden and the Senate came up with a comprehensive southern border plan. This plan won't stop immigration but will significantly reduce the number of illegal immigrants making it into the US.

Trump, who is trying to stay out of prison and doesn't care about anything, not even his MAGA Cult Followers, wants to use the problem Abbot himself started by his inhumane treatment of Humans for his campaign platform.

Trump informed the House of Representatives that they are MAGA Cult Republicans who were elected to work for the people by the people. The House MAGA was not elected to follow a leader who is not in power, and they should all be impeached.

Anyway, The House MAGA was instructed to kill the bill that would solve the problem.

MAGA Abbott was instructed to ignore the Supreme Court Ruling. MAGA informed all of the MAGA Governors to Back MAGA Texas Governor and turn this into the most significant shit show anyone has seen.

This whole ordeal is to help take a giant step toward a totalitarian government.

Suppose we were serious and wanted to stop the problem on the Southern Border. We must get involved in the Southern Countries and help them with the issues causing the great migration, along with bringing modernization of their countries to the 21st Century.

Everything wrong on the southern border for 2024 falls flat at the MAGA-CULT REPUBLICANS FEET.

Since June 2022, LGBTQ+ And The Southern Border Have Been Put Back On The Radar Of The Extreme Right And Are Marked As Evil And Being Persecuted Like It Is 1969 Again.

WHY?

The Moral Majority, Christian Right, Christian Nationalists, And The Evangelicals Collected Billions Every Year, From Small Cash Donations To Battle Overturning Roe V Wade And To Abolish Abortions.

After the landmark Supreme Court decision in Roe v. Wade was overturned, several advocacy groups that had been working towards abolishing abortions for women faced a significant crisis. The decision significantly impacted their funding, with donations decreasing rapidly and almost drying up completely. Many of these groups were heavily reliant on the support of individual donors who had been motivated to abolish abortions for women. In the aftermath of the decision, however, many of these supporters either stopped donating or shifted their focus towards other causes. This left the groups in a precarious financial situation, with many struggling to maintain their operations, sustain their staff, and line their pockets. In the face of this challenge, some groups resorted to adopting new fundraising strategies

So, These Morally immoral groups looked for specific individuals or groups of people who are not well-known or popular in mainstream society and are therefore more vulnerable to being targeted or persecuted without causing outrage or concern from the general public. These individuals will have unique beliefs, lifestyles, or identities that are not widely accepted or understood, making them easy targets for those who seek to enforce their moral standards. They can be "persecuted against," which means the following is acceptable in the groups above God's eyes. This mistreatment will be deliberate and systematic and will involve harassment, discrimination, or even violence. By framing this behavior as a form of "moral justice," those who perpetrate it will justify their actions as necessary to uphold their values or beliefs, regardless of the harm it may cause.

So These Four Religious Fanatic Groups Decided On Targeting The LGBTQ+, More Specifically, The Trans Community And Drag Queens. The Other Community Would Be The People Migrating Up From The Countries South of Us To Our Southern Border, You Know

Because They Are Supposedly Evil And Everything Because They're Brown.

The "religious" groups listed above stand for Perpetrating hate, and they have nothing to do with God. It is essential to remember that the groups or individuals who claim to represent or stand for God or religion do not necessarily reflect the true essence or teachings of these beliefs. It is crucial to differentiate between the actions of such groups and the core principles of the respective faiths, as they may not align with each other. Therefore, it is advisable to always approach any religious or faith-related matter with an open mind and without being influenced by the actions of extremist or radical groups.

The Moral Majority, Christian Nationalists, Christian Right, and Evangelicals prioritize money, power, and control over everything else. They are always very vocal about their beliefs and have accumulated much wealth, which they use to influence political officials. Specifically, they have developed a close relationship with Republican officials who they have bought out, making them their puppets. This gives them a significant amount of control over the political landscape. In addition to owning politicians, they also have a large following of uniformed individuals who support them financially. Through these means, they can maintain their hold on power, continue to push their agenda forward and amass wealth.

We, as individuals, have been consumed by the idea of defending ourselves and our actions, as well as justifying our existence to others. We have always played by the Anti-LabBTQ+ Bible Thumper rules. We have been conforming to societal norms and expectations rather than stepping out of our comfort zones and taking risks. It's time to change our approach and adopt a new mindset, prioritizing taking the offensive rather than always playing defense. In other words, we should be proactive and assertive rather than constantly reacting to outside influences...

We should turn the tables and do this scenario where we start promoting extreme stereotypes. As a result, they would be struggling to defend themselves in public speaking and press releases.

This could be a challenging situation since promoting extreme stereotypes could be considered an offensive act and could damage one's reputation.

Until they learn that that is what they do to us, hopefully, they will realize that it's important to be mindful of the impact of our words and actions on others and to apologize and make amends when necessary.

We need to get the IRS to conduct official audits of these four religious groups by the government. Since these groups operate as non-profit organizations (NPOs), to maintain their tax-free status, they must adhere to specific rules and regulations. For instance, they cannot participate in political activities or engage in any commercial enterprise to make a profit. Therefore, it is important to ensure that these groups are following the laws and regulations set forth by the government to maintain their status as NPOs and continue to receive tax benefits.

I want to bring to everyone's attention a topic that may not be very popular, but it is important to discuss because facts are facts. It's about a specific issue that has been bothering me for a while now, and I'd like to share my thoughts on it.

So, let me see if I understand this correctly. There is a situation or a problem that I'm going to address, and I want to make sure I have a clear understanding of what is happening. What follows is my understanding.

It is important to emphasize that everyone is of equal value and worth, regardless of their religion, gender, sex, lifestyle, nationality, or any other distinguishing characteristic. This includes individuals who have committed crimes, people with disabilities, members of governments, governmental agencies, political subdivisions, labor unions, partnerships, associations, corporations, legal representatives, mutual companies, joint-stock companies, trusts, unincorporated organizations, trustees, and individuals of all races, colors, national origins, ages (40 and over), sexual orientations, gender identities, heights, weights, marital statuses, genetic information, and veteran statuses (including qualified individuals whom the contractor knows to be spouses or other associates of a protected veteran).

It is crucial to understand that individuals of different races and colors, such as Whites, Blacks, Asians, Latinos, Arabs, American Indians, Alaska Natives, Native Hawaiians, Pacific Islanders, persons of more than one race, and all other persons, whatever their race, color, or ethnicity, are entitled to the same level of human value and respect as anyone else. No one should be discriminated against or mistreated due to their race, color, or ethnicity, and it is our responsibility as human beings to ensure that this basic principle is upheld and respected at all times.

Individuals should be free to choose their religion and practice it as they see fit. However, I do not believe this freedom extends to certain practices within religious beliefs. In my opinion, practices such as sacrifice, having multiple spouses, genocide, or promoting hatred towards individuals with different lifestyles or races should not be allowed. When a church or religion engages in such practices, they are no longer a religion but rather a hate group. It is essential to recognize and differentiate between religious freedom and harmful practices that have no place in society.

Throughout history, there have been instances where countries have taken over land inhabited by a particular nationality and given it to another group based on their religious beliefs, customs, and traditions. Some nations have carried out this act of land theft, and it has resulted in displacement, conflict, and devastation for the people affected. Despite being a civilized world, such actions have caused significant damage to humanity and have raised questions about the morality of such decisions.

The decision to grant a specific country to a particular group of people was not based on any tangible evidence, historical record, or proof of ownership. Instead, it was rooted in a belief system that hinged on an ancient book, which lacked any concrete evidence to support its claims.

This belief system had been passed down from generation to generation and had become an integral part of their cultural identity. According to this belief system, their God had chosen them to be the rightful owners of the land thousands of years ago.

Despite the lack of objective evidence to support this claim, this belief had become so deeply ingrained in their culture that it ultimately led to the decision to grant them the land in question.

According to the history of this exchange, we will be discussing the treatment of the nationality and the group of people that was already occupying the country in question. The people in question were not given special treatment and were left in their place.

The reason for this was that the group of people who were given the country had just survived a holocaust and were believed to be peaceful. It was assumed that they would welcome the nationality with open arms and incorporate them into their community without any issues.

However, the way things went and what goes on makes you question the peacefulness of this nationality by examining the mythology and religious beliefs that form the basis of their culture. It is suggested that by looking at their teachings, it may be possible to gauge how peaceful they are.

Throughout history, there have been many archaeological discoveries that have shed light on the ancient civilizations that existed in Egypt and Israel. These discoveries have included thousands of artifacts, bones, homes, and towns that date back thousands of years.

Interestingly, as researchers have dug deeper into the history of these regions, they have found no, no, zero evidence to support the biblical account of the Jewish people's escape from Egypt and their subsequent journey to the land of Canaan. Despite extensive excavations and studies, there have been no bones, artifacts, or related people found to suggest that the Jewish people existed in these areas at that time.

According to the Bible, the Jewish people fled Egypt and eventually settled in the land of Canaan, but archaeological evidence does not support this account. The area now Israel was still part of Egypt during this time and was ruled by the same pharaoh whom the Jewish people supposedly escaped from. Therefore, based on the artifacts, homes, and items found, if the Jewish community had been present in this region, they would still have been under the Pharaoh's rule.

According to Jewish Mythology, the Jewish Practice maintains that the Exodus, as described in the Book of Exodus, took place in real-time history. The Exodus is believed to have been a significant event that led to the liberation of the Israelites from slavery in Egypt. According to the book, the Exodus resulted in the death of thousands of Egyptians and the wiping out of hundreds of thousands of the Israelites who wandered the desert. The Exodus is considered a cornerstone of Jewish theology, and its celebration, Passover, is one of the most important religious festivals in the Jewish calendar.

Following Jewish teachings, it is believed that throughout their history, the Jewish People slaughtered hundreds of thousands of individuals residing in more than 300 towns. They claim to have committed over 300 genocides. While there is no concrete evidence to support their occurrence, they are still celebrated and taught with great pride within the Jewish religion. This belief is a testament to the rich and complex history of the Jewish People and their enduring cultural traditions.

According to the Biblical account, the Jewish people wandered the desert for forty years after their exodus from Egypt. However, despite extensive research and exploration, no concrete evidence has supported this claim. To put things into perspective, the area the Jewish people supposedly wandered in was roughly the size of Arizona, making it difficult to comprehend how they could have remained lost for such a prolonged period. Nonetheless, this historic account continues to be a topic of fascination and debate among scholars and religious communities alike.

According to historical accounts, during the great exodus, approximately twenty-two million Jewish people reportedly remained in Egypt. However, despite extensive research and various archaeological excavations, there is no concrete evidence to suggest that the Jewish community was ever present in ancient Egypt at the time of the exodus, let alone enslaved. The lack of evidence has led many scholars to question the accuracy of these historical accounts, and the true extent of the Jewish community's involvement in ancient Egyptian society remains a topic of debate and speculation.

It's hard to understand why we ever expected that the Israelis would coexist peacefully with the Palestinians. Despite the numerous attempts at peace talks and diplomatic efforts, the conflict between the two groups persists, with violence and bloodshed becoming all too common. It's a complicated and profoundly entrenched issue with no easy solutions, and it's a tragedy that innocent people on both sides continue to suffer.

The lack of historical evidence and proof has been a subject of interest for individuals who question the authenticity of the Bible. This has sparked a debate over whether the Bible is based on purely fictional stories or whether it has some elements of truth to it. Despite various attempts to prove the historical accuracy of the Bible, some individuals have maintained their stance that the Bible is not a reliable historical source. This has led to further investigations and discussions on the topic.

The United States of America was founded on the separation of church and state, which means that the government should not interfere with religious beliefs or practices, and no particular religious institution should be given preference or authority over others. This principle has been enshrined in the First Amendment of the US Constitution, which prohibits the establishment of a state religion and guarantees the freedom of religion, as well as freedom of speech, press, assembly, and petition. The separation of church and state is a cornerstone of American democracy, promoting pluralism tolerance, and protecting individual rights and liberties.

We should have never got involved in a religious war

We need to correct our mistake by removing and relocating one of the two nationalities from Israel. I say we remove the Jewish community because the Palestinians were already there. When they bitch they need to understand it is because of their actions that they lost their country. And they lied about it being theirs. Or the nations that support Israel need a new way to force the Israelites into a treaty of acceptance and equality.

We need to hold the Israelites and Hamas accountable for their war crimes

The Bible has been a topic of discussion for centuries and has been widely used to support various beliefs and practices. However, some argue that the Bible is nothing more than a book of fictional stories with no factual basis. Many people believe that the Bible has been proven to be incorrect and that its stories are merely for entertainment value.

Using the Bible as a basis for granting, giving, or awarding anything is misguided and wrong. According to this perspective, the land belongs to those who have settled it now and does not belong to anyone who claimed ownership of it thousands of years ago.

The influx of people migrating to the southern border cannot be blamed on elected officials, American citizens, or political parties.

Instead, the responsibility lies with the countries from which they are escaping. It is essential to recognize that those individuals are seeking refuge and a better life, and they deserve our empathy and support.

However, The MAGA Republican Party and the American Citizens who voted for them are solely responsible for the overwhelming influx of illegal immigrants coming across our southern border. To address this issue, we must increase the number of individuals processing these immigrants. Many of these individuals would qualify for legal status, but the number of people crossing the border makes it difficult to process them all legally.

We cannot solely blame ourselves for this issue. The root cause of this problem is the countries they are coming from, not taking care of their citizens. It is clear that these individuals are fleeing their own countries in search of a better life, and their civil rights are being violated.

To truly end this crisis, we must take a more active role in the countries these individuals are fleeing from. We must work with these countries and find a way to replace corrupt governments. Help end the tide of marketing, production, and trade of illegal substances, eliminate forced labor, and stop importing cheap goods. Encourage their governments to take responsibility for their citizens.

Rather than focusing our efforts solely on the Middle East, we must also prioritize working with the southern border countries.

If we can bring our Southern Countries into the 21st century instead of many of them operating like third-world nations, immigration may not stop, but it would decrease significantly.

Death rates from any cause among women of reproductive age -- 15 to 44 -- were 34% higher in abortion-restriction states than in abortion-access states

Fetal or infant death rates in the first week of life occurred at a 15% higher rate, on average, in states with abortion restrictions than in states with broader abortion access.

More people in the US die from complications of pregnancy and childbirth than any other developed nation, and <u>most are preventable.</u>

39% of the counties in states restricting abortion access fit the criteria to be labeled "maternity care deserts," meaning there is limited or no access to maternity health care services.

The infant and perinatal mortality rates were 6.2 deaths per 1,000 births in abortion-restriction states.

Infant mortality in the first year of life was higher in abortion-restriction states than in abortion-access states.

Women of reproductive age and birthing people in states with current or proposed abortion bans have more limited access to affordable health insurance coverage.

Pro-Life States have less access to insurance, higher teen pregnancy rates, and less access to sex education.

In general, the states that restrict abortions have more kids and more kids of color.

Many of these are states whose economies revolve around large numbers of low-wage jobs, and the vast majority of them suffer from elevated rates of poverty, particularly among children.

The anti-abortion states have the largest share of children living in poverty

Among the anti-abortion states, 16 also rank in the top half of states for the largest share of children living in "extreme" poverty (with incomes half or less of the national poverty level, or roughly $13,000 for a family of four). Fourteen of them fall in the top half of states for the most significant share of children reporting that they have experienced hunger.

The anti-abortion states have the most children who are born prematurely or with low birth weights or who die as infants.

Anti-abortion states have the highest share of low-income women of childbearing age with no health insurance.

Anti-abortion states have little or no systems set up to provide for children from birth through eighteen.

Anti-abortion states have refused to offer state Earned Income Tax Credits for low-wage families, requiring paid family leave and expanding Medicaid eligibility as allowed under the Affordable Care Act.

So we will end with Pro-Life is also Pro Strong And extend prison sentences if they don't qualify for capital punishment. I guess they think they're doing the religious and for God thing by protecting them for nine months so they won't feel guilty spending the rest of the fetus's lifetime trying to sentence them to death.

————————

Please share by spreading the truth about Immigration.

We need to do our best to disperse the truth.

We need to save lives by breaking stereotypes, which has caused an increase in violence and death in our Southern Immigrants at our Southern borders.

The immigration issue at the southern border is complex, and it requires a comprehensive solution that addresses the root causes of the problem.

We need to acknowledge that no President is responsible for the number of people migrating to our Southern Border, and it is caused by multiple factors such as government, starvation, safety, housing, persecution, war, violence, and crime.

Thus, we must get involved in the Southern Countries and help them with the issues causing the great migration, along with bringing modernization to their countries to the 21st century.

It is essential to remember that the issue of migration is not new and existed during the formation of the United States.

Therefore, instead of politicizing the matter, we need to find sustainable solutions that prioritize human dignity and safety.

This requires a bipartisan effort, where the government, NGOs, and other stakeholders work together to address the issue.

We need to focus on creating a comprehensive plan that would significantly reduce the number of illegal immigrants making it into the US.

This plan should consider the factors that fuel migration in the Western Hemisphere, including violence, economic instability, and political persecution.

Moreover, we should learn from past immigration and our mistakes and avoid anti-immigration rhetoric that only fuels hate and division. Instead, we must create an environment that welcomes immigrants and provides them with the support they need to integrate into society.

In summary, we must approach the immigration issue at the southern border with compassion, empathy, and a willingness to find sustainable solutions that prioritize human dignity and safety. It is only by working together that we can achieve this goal.

So this is why we have a great migration at the Southern Border.

Racism and Bigotry are why it's considered a crisis.

LIKE IT OR NOT WE NEED TO INCREASE OUR IMMIGRATION OR GET OUR KIDS TO GET OFF THEIR ASSES AND GET EDUCATED.

U.S. Risks Decline And Stagnation Without Immigrants

The U.S. labor force will shrink, and America risks stagnation and declining living standards without immigrants.

"Without continued net inflows of immigrants, the U.S. working-age population will shrink over the next two decades, and by 2040, the United States will have over 6 million fewer working-age people than in 2022,"

"Announcements of high-profile layoffs and concerns about the impact of artificial intelligence (AI) obscure America's continuing need for additional workers at the top and bottom of the skill distribution. International migration is the only potential source of growth in the U.S. working-age population in the coming years."

"The U.S. will need workers with specialized skills that are in short supply and take years of education and training to acquire. Now and in the future, the U.S. will still need workers, and it risks not having enough of them, particularly those with desired skills, absent additional immigration." Many Americans in the working age show no desire to seek any education that will help them meet this demand.

A lack of workers has already hampered plans to increase semiconductor manufacturing in the United States. "TSMC Chairman Mark Liu said construction [of a new plan] in Arizona is hampered by a shortage of skilled workers and that the company might have to bring in experienced technicians temporarily from Taiwan," reported the _Wall Street Journal_. "He said this would delay the start of mass production of 4-nanometer chips in the first factory until 2025."

The Semiconductor Industry Association (SIA) has warned that "the United States faces a significant shortage of technicians, computer scientists, and engineers." Economists and business analysts have concluded it is difficult to "restore" operations in any industry without sufficiently educated and trained employees.

Zavodny notes a falling U.S. population will mean fewer workers to produce goods and services. However, an aging population will keep demanding goods and services that require labor. The result is likely to be shortages and price pressures, including inflation.

"A shrinking population means fewer people to generate new ideas that lead to technological progress and long-run growth," writes Zavodny. A recent NFAP study concluded immigrants founded or cofounded 65% of the top AI companies in the United States, while 70% of full-time graduate students in AI-related fields are international students.

Immigrants have supported U.S. population growth during the past half-century. The role of immigrants will become more pronounced as baby boomers continue to leave the labor force and U.S. births fall, according to the data. The numbers show only through sustained or increased immigration can the U.S. working-age population continue to grow.

"A shrinking working-age population can easily lead to economic stagnation or even falling living standards for a nation," concludes Zavodny.

Stop listening to politicians or even me when it has anything to do with people's lives. Yes I did my research but I wrote this dialogue because I feel a lot of empathy for the people this affects.

Use your brain do your own research check your facts and educate yourself on American history and current events and the history of the world around you.

All Political Parties have a vested interest in anything they campaign on or side they take. They will always take the side of the one with the most money thrown at them. They will choose the cause they can exploit to get votes. They will embellish spin and tell false narratives.

Also, please be more innovative when you come up with conspiracy theories.

When a kid can figure out a conspiracy theory can't be true. I always wonder why adults believe it. You're not trying very hard. Use your Common sense it goes a long way.

Okay, let's see if we can figure out how absurd and irrational some of these conspiracy theories are:

One Conspiracy Theory is because of The concern of the anti-immigration Republican Elected officials is that the UNARMED people between the ages of 18 and 35 crossing the Southern Border into the United States of America UNARMED And are all military age and are UNARMED, so people believe they are coming here UNARMED to start a war against the US while UNARMED. At the same time once they've entered UNARMED BECAUSE They came here UNARMED.

The general public has been convinced through another conspiracy theory that was spread by Republicans that are racist and bigoted they claim immigrants are evil and they Claim that crime skyrockets and murders are commonplace with Immigrants, whether legal or illegal. This is a total lie. Let me see if you can use your common sense.

Scenario) I left my home filled with violence, and I'm starving with no place to live. I get to your border, and I cross it illegally. I find a job with either forged documents or because of someone's kindness. So, to keep what's going well for me, I have to stay low-key, under the radar, and make sure I don't draw any attention. What are the odds I will commit a serious crime and get my family sent back?

Yes, there are some bad apples but far fewer than we have that are American-born bad apples. For everyone one immigrant bad apple there are 5 American-born bad apples. We can't deport the American Born so what's your plan to take care of the American Born Bad Apple.

Let me hear from you what you see and if anything is wrong.

Full disclosure: I do vote Democrat. They do tend to, but not always, lean toward civil rights and equal humane treatment.

I would also like to point out not all conservative and republicans are bigots and racist. I'm sure if you look you can find some

I would also like to point out some liberals and democrats are bigots and racist. I'm sure if you look you can find some.

However, neither party tends to believe in what I stand for regarding immigration. I don't believe that any country that is founded on freedom and equality should have closed borders because no one free and that believes in freedom would want their country to be exclusive. They would want freedom and equality to spread like a virus so that everyone on earth could have the same chance to experience freedom.

The United States of America started with almost an entirely open border and encouraged immigration.

The first change made regarding immigration since our Inception was the ACT Prohibiting the Importation of Slavery of 1807. We did a great thing with this change. But it could have been better. If they showed up on our shore we turned them away. What we should have done was confiscate their cargo and grant them freedom.

We followed that up with the Chinese Exclusion ACT of 1882, another significant sign our country is made up of a lot of bigoted assholes.

At this time, we still had open borders for everyone that was not of a shaded race.

America's first version of the Border Patrol was formed in 1904 in El Paso. It consisted of 75 people and was responsible for California to Texas. Did you notice the northern border patrol is missing.

In 1915, Congress authorized another group, The Mounted Guards, also known as "Mounted Inspectors," whose main objective was to round up the Chinese.

The National Origins Act authorized the formation of the US Border Patrol, and our borders closed on May 26, 1924.

Let's talk about the truth regarding Immigration. We need to do our best to disperse the truth. We need to save lives by breaking stereotypes, which has caused an increase in violence and death of our Southern Immigrants. We need to suppress and eradicate bigotry and racism through education

The immigration issue at the southern border is complex, and it requires a comprehensive solution that addresses the root causes of the problem.

We need to acknowledge that no President is responsible for the number of people migrating to our Southern Border, and it is caused by multiple factors from the immigrants home such as government, starvation, safety, housing, persecution, war, violence, and crime.

Thus, we must get involved in the Southern Countries and help them with the issues causing the great migration, along with bringing modernization to their countries to the 21st century.

It is essential to remember that the issue of migration in the Americas is not new and has existed before the formation of the United States.

Therefore, instead of politicizing the matter, we need to find sustainable solutions that prioritize human dignity and safety.

This requires a bipartisan effort, where the government, NGOs, Non-Governmental Organization. and other stakeholders work together to address the issue.

We need to focus on creating a comprehensive plan that would significantly reduce the number of illegal immigrants making it into the US.

This plan should consider the factors that fuel migration the North and the Western Hemisphere, including violence, economic instability, and political persecution.

Moreover, we should learn from past immigrations and our mistakes and avoid anti-immigration rhetoric that only fuels hate and division. Instead, we must create an environment that welcomes immigrants and provides them with the support they need to integrate into society.

In summary, we must approach the immigration issue at the southern border with compassion, empathy, and a willingness to find sustainable solutions that prioritize human dignity and safety. It is only by working together that we can achieve this goal.

So this is why we have a great migration at the Southern Border.

It is only because of Racism and Bigotry are why it's considered a crisis.

We Can Fix What People Call The Invasion Of Illegal Immigrants Coming Over Our Southern Border.

We go back to the immigration policies that were in effect when our ancestors arrived starting in the 1600's

Explain to the immigrants coming now that they can't do what our ancestors did back in the 1600 -1865 when they arrived.

Explain that they can't steal property from the citizens already living here, and they can't own anyone even if it does make their life easier.

Put additional trained immigration processing personnel at all the border entry points. This would help increase legal immigration wich would reduce illegal immigration.

Help everyone who wants to enter this country fill out their and their family's applications.

Have an expedited system to get everyone that wants to enter vetted and approved.

Give the immigrants a welcome package containing all the instructions on what they will need to complete and accomplish so that it will help them transition into living in the US as an immigrant.

Stop caring what the Extreme anti immigtation people think regarding immigration. If you ignore them and do the right thing they have no power.

Poke the stick so they will continue to throw temper tantrums over their belief in the great replacement theory.

Let The Idiots on the right keep thinking about those who are immigrating to the US so that they can vote.

Don't tell the right that if an immigrant attempts to vote or votes before they become a citizen, they will be imprisoned, deported, or both.

Don't tell the Republicans that immigrants have to pay income tax doing the jobs no one is willing to do. Which reduces the deficit and increases funds for the federal budget.

Don't tell the MAGA Cult that the immigrants spend billions and billions of dollars on goods and services in the US.

Stop letting the MAGA Cult spread misinformation about Immigrants. Statistically, Immigrants are more likely to be law-abiding citizens because they are grateful to the US for giving them the opportunity.

On average, the crime rate decreases in high immigrant population communities.

The United States of America's Population Has Peaked And Will Start Decreasing Without Increasing Immigration And Promoting Bigger Families.

Tragedy Is That Republicans Can Only Survive As A Party With False Narratives That Focus On Fear, Hate, Division, Racism, Discrimination, Untrue Women's Issues, Censorship, And Empty Promises.

Tragedy Is Republicans Using Individuals' Personal Stories For Political Gain.

Tragedy Is Laken Riley's Horrific Brutal
    Murder

Tragedy Is Republicans Politicizing Laken Riley's Murder.

Tragedy Is Republicans Using Karla Jacinto Romero's Story From 2008 For Political Gain By Lying About Her Tragic Story.

Tragedy Is Republicans Not Caring About The Pain Their Lies Has Caused Ms. Romero

Tragedy Is Republicans Using Such A Horrific Crime To Advance Their Political Agenda Without Considering That The Survivors Have To Relive The Incident Every Time Their Stories Are Told.

Tragedy Is Republicans Wanting 46,200,000 Immigrants To Be Found Guilty And Deported Because Of Any Murder.

Tragedy Is Republicans Can't Do Simple Math. According To Them, 8,000,000 Immigrants Entered The United States In 2023. An Undocumented Immigrant Brutally Murdered Laken Riley.

Tragedy Is That Republicans Can't Figure Out Why It's Newsworthy. It Is Because Murder Committed By Immigrants Is So Rare That People Are Shocked, And That Is Why The Press Gives It National Coverage.

Tragedy Is That Republicans Blame Most Murders In The USA On Undocumented And Documented Immigrants.

Tragedy Is That Republicans Know The Statistics Of Crime And Murder But Choose To Ignore Them And Instead Spread False Propaganda

Tragedy Is Republicans Know, The Number Of American Citizens That Commit Murder In The USA Is 3.7%.

Tragedy Is That Republicans Contribute To Hate Crimes Committed Because They Ignore The Fact That The Number Of Undocumented And Documented Immigrants Combined That Commit A Murder Is .000063%.

Tragedy Is That Republicans Are The Problem To The USA, It's Citizens And The Immigrants In America With Their False Narratives.

Tragedy Is Republican Math Is So Far Off They Should Be Held Accountable For Any Violence That Occurs Stemming From Their Rhetoric.

Tragedy Is That Republicans Believe In A Different Set Of Laws For Immigrants, And They Should Not Be Allowed The Same Rules, Rights, And Laws Set Out In Our Judicial Process.

Tragedy Is Republicans Thinking That Someone Being Arrested For Non-Violent Crimes Should Be Held Without Bond Because They Are Undocumented, Even If, At the Time Of Their Arrest, Their Record Showed They Pose No Risk To The Community.

Tragedy Is The Republicane Misinformation That Leads To Fear And Hatred Towards A Whole Group Based On The Actions Of A Few.

Tragedy Is Republicans Ignoring The Contributions Of Immigrants, Both Documented And Undocumented, To Our Society And Economy.

Tragedy Is Republicans Overlooking The Fact That Many Immigrants Come To The US Seeking Safety And Opportunity, Not To Commit Crimes.

Tragedy Is Republicans Forgetting That We Are A Nation Of Immigrants And That Diversity Strengthens Our Communities.

Tragedy Is Republicans' Loss Of Humanity When They Fail To Empathize With The Plight Of Others, Regardless Of Their Legal Status.

Tragedy Is When Republicans Pass Policies Driven By Fear Override The Values Of Justice And Compassion That Are Supposed To Define Our Society.

Tragedy Is Republicans Perpetuating Harmful Stereotypes And Discrimination Against Marginalized Groups Instead Of Promoting Understanding And Acceptance.

Tragedy Is When Republicans Deny Individuals Basic Human Rights And Dignity Simply Because Of Their Immigration Status.

Tragedy Is When Republicans Tear Families Apart Due To Harsh Immigration Policies That Lack Compassion And Empathy.

Tragedy Is The Republicans Missed Opportunity To Embrace Diversity And Learn From Different Cultures And Backgrounds That Immigrants Bring To Our Society.

Tragedy Is When Republicans Lose Sight Of Our Shared Humanity And Fail To Recognize The Inherent Worth And Potential Of Every Individual, Regardless Of Nationality Or Background.

Tragedy Is When Republicans Allow Fear And Ignorance To Drive Us Apart Instead Of Coming Together To Find Solutions That Benefit Everyone In Our Diverse Communities.

Tragedy Is When Republicans Prioritize Division And Exclusion Over Unity And Understanding, Missing Out On The Richness And Strength That Diversity Can Bring.

Tragedy Is When Republicans Fail To Recognize The Interconnectedness Of Humanity And The Shared Responsibility We Have To Support And Uplift One Another. Including Refugees And Immigrants Seeking A Better Life

Tragedy Is When Republican Policies And Actions Dehumanize And Marginalize Individuals, Creating Barriers To Their Full Participation In Society And Denying Them The Opportunities They Deserve.

Tragedy Is When Republcans Turn A Blind Eye To The Suffering And Struggles Of Those Most Vulnerable In Our Society.

Tragedy Is When Republican Policies And Actions Dehumanize And Marginalize Individuals, Creating Barriers To Their Full Participation In Society And Denying Them The Opportunities They Deserve.

Tragedy Is When Republicans Turn A Blind Eye To The Suffering And Struggles Of Those Most Vulnerable In Our Society.

Tragedy Is When We Allow Republican Rhetoric And Misinformation To Drive A Wedge Between Communities And Perpetuate Harmful Stereotypes And Prejudices.

Tragedy Is When Republicans Fail To See The Potential And Talents That Immigrants Bring To Our Society.

Tragedy Is That Because Of Republicans, Immigrants Are Missing Out On The Opportunities for Mutual Growth And Enrichment.

Tragedy Is When Republicans Prioritize Fear And Xenophobia Over Compassion And Solidarity, Leading To A Society That Is Divided And Fragmented.

Tragedy Is When Republicans Pass Discriminatory Policies And Practices To Undermine The Fundamental Values Of Equality And Fairness That Should Guide Our Society.

Tragedy Is When Republicans Fail To Recognize The Inherent Worth And Dignity Of Every Individual, Regardless Of Their Background Or Circumstances.

Tragedy Is When Republicans Lose Sight Of The Fact That We Are All Interconnected And Their Actions Have Real And Lasting Impacts On Others.

Tragedy Is When Republicans Prioritize Division And Exclusion Over Unity And Solidarity, Perpetuating Cycles Of Injustice And Inequality.

Tragedy Is When Republicans Fail To Recognize The Humanity In Every Individual And Only Treat People As Mere Statistics Or Labels Rather Than As Complex, Unique Human Beings With Their Own Stories And Aspirations.

Tragedy Is When Republicans Perpetuate Fear And Ignorance To Overshadow Empathy And Compassion, Leading To The Marginalization And Mistreatment Of Those Who Are Most In Need Of Support And Understanding.

Tragedy Is When Republicans Prioritize Short-Term Gain Over Long-Term Well-Being, Sacrificing The Values Of Justice, Equality, And Respect In The Process.

Tragedy Is When Republicans Perpetuate Cycles Of Discrimination And Exclusion, Perpetuating Harm And Hindering The Potential For Positive Change And Progress In Our Society.

Tragedy Is When Republicans Push For Divisions Based On Race, Ethnicity, Nationality, Or Immigration Status To Overshadow Our Shared Humanity And Common Values.

Tragedy Is When Republicans Ignore The Stories Of Resilience, Courage, And Hope That Many Immigrants Carry With Them.

Tragedy Is That Republicans Reduce Immigrants Identities To Stereotypes And Misconceptions.

Tragedy Is When Republicans
Fail To Recognize The Richness And Vibrancy That Diversity Brings To Our Communities.

Tragedy Is That Republicans Stifle The Immigrant's Potential For Growth, Innovation, And Mutual Understanding.

Tragedy Is When Republicans Turn A Blind Eye To The Voices Of Those Who Are Marginalized And Oppressed, Perpetuating Cycles Of Discrimination And Exclusion.

Tragedy Is Republicans Can't Recognize Their Actions Have Far-Reaching Consequences For Individuals And Society As A Whole.

Tragedy Is When Republicans Allow And Spread Fear And Misinformation To Drive Us Apart For Political Gain.

Tragedy Is Republlicans Continues To Creating Barriers To Empathy, Understanding, And Collaboration Among Diverse Communities.

Tragedy Is When Republicans Fail To Recognize The Shared Aspirations And Dreams That Unite Us As Human Beings, Regardless Of Our Backgrounds Or Circumstances.

Tragedy Is When Republicans Prioritize Exclusion And Discrimination Over Inclusivity And Acceptance.

Tragedy Is Republicans Denying Individuals The Opportunity To Participate In And Contribute To Society Fully.

Tragedy Is When Republicans Perpetuate Systems Of Oppression And Inequality That Limit The Potential And Well-Being Of Individuals And Communities, Perpetuating Cycles Of Suffering And Hardship.

Society Needs to Take On The Republicans And Dismantle These Barriers, Challenge Prejudice And Injustice.

Society Needs To Push Out Antiquated Republican Beliefs And Foster A Culture Of Respect, Solidarity, And Mutual Support By Embracing The Majority Of Societies Shared Humanity, Celebrating Our Differences, And Working Together toward a More Equitable And Harmonious World.

Society Can Overcome Tragedy And Build A Future Where Compassion, Understanding, And Unity Prevail.

Republicans must Listen, Learn, And Empathize With Society As A Whole, Including Immigrants.

Everyone In Society, Including Republicans, Should Be Standing Up For Justice, Equality, And Human Rights.

Republicans Have To Learn To Work With Everyone In America, Not Just MAGA.

We Can Come Together And Work Toward A More Just, Inclusive, And Compassionate World Where Tragedies Born Out Of Ignorance And Intolerance Can Be Replaced With Harmony, Respect, And Unity.

Everyone, Including Republicans Must Stand Up Against MAGA, Injustice, Advocate For The Rights Of All Individuals, And Work Towards Building A More Compassionate And Inclusive World Where Everyone Is Valued, Respected, And Given The Opportunity To Thrive. Together.

Everyone And Republicans Should Be Striving To Create A Society Where Tragedy Is Replaced By Empathy, Solidarity, And A Commitment To Upholding The Dignity And Rights Of All.

The Entire Population, Including Republicans, Must Challenge Systemic Barriers and Advocate For Social Justice.

The USA, Including Republicans And MAGA, Should Strive To Be The Model Country And Create A More Inclusive And Equitable World Where Everyone Has The Opportunity To Thrive And Contribute To The Common Good.

If Everyone Plus Republicans And MAGA Promoted Empathy And Understanding. Our Nation Would Be A Model For The World To Emulate.

If Our Nation Had Respect For All Individuals, We Would Be Working Towards A Society Where Tragedy Is Replaced With Hope, Compassion, And Unity.

America needs to Stand Up Against MAGA And Republicans For Their Promotion Of Injustice.

America As A Whole Should Advocate For The Rights Of All Individuals And Foster A Culture Of Empathy And Inclusivity.

By Recognizing The Majorities Shared Humanity And Embracing The Diversity That Surrounds Us, We Can Create A More Compassionate And Equitable World For Everyone.

Everyone must Challenge Prejudices, Advocate For Fair And Just Immigration Policies, And Work toward a More Inclusive And Compassionate Society Where Everyone Is Valued And Respected.

Even Without The Republicans, We Have The Numbers To Build A World Where Tragedy Is Replaced By Empathy, Justice, And Genuine Appreciation For The Diversity That Enriches Our Lives.

We need to Strive For A More Inclusive And Compassionate Society Where We Acknowledge The Humanity And Contributions Of All Individuals, Regardless Of Their Immigration Status.

Every Murder Is A Tragedy

Laken Riley's Murder Was A Tragedy.

Tragedy Is Republicans Politicizing Laken Riley's Murder.

Tragedy Is Using Such A Horrific Crime To Advance Your Political Agenda Without Considering That The Survivors Have To Relive The Incident Every Time Ms. Riley's Story Is Told

Tragedy Is Wanting 46,200,000 People To Be Found Guilty Of Any Murder.

Tragedy Is Republicans Can't Do Simple Math. According To Them, 8,000,000 Immigrants Entered The United States In 2023. An Undocumented Immigrant Brutally murdered Laken Riley. It's News Worthy Because It Is So Rare That People Are Shocked, And The Press Gives It National Coverage.

Tragedy Is That Most Murders In The USA Are Blamed On Undocumented And Documented Immigrants.

The Number Of Undocumented And Documented Immigrants Combined That Commit A Murder Is .000063%. The Number Of American Citizens That Commit Murder Is 3.7%.

Tragedy Is That American Citizens Are The Problem To Ourselves And The Immigrants.

Tragedy Is Republican Math Is So Far Off They Should Be Held Accountable For Any Violence That Occurs Stemming From Their Rhetoric.

Tragedy Is That Republicans Believe In A Different Set Of Laws For Immigrants, And They Should Not Be Allowed The Same Rules, Rights, And Laws Set Out In Our Judicial Process.

Tragedy Is Thinking That Someone Being Arrested For Non-Violent Crimes Should Be Held Without Bond Because They Are Undocumented, Even Though They Are In The System With An Immigration Court Date.

Jose was arrested by the NYPD in August 2023 and charged with riding a gas-powered moped with Franco's girlfriend's son on the back without any head protection or restraint for the child.

Jose was then arrested a month later for stealing from a Walmart store.

It Is A Tragedy That On February 22, 2024, Riley fails to return home after going for a run near her campus.

Jose was arrested and charged a day later with concealing the death of another, false imprisonment, felony murder, malice murder, kidnapping, aggravated assault, and aggravated battery in connection with the death of Riley.

It Is A Tragedy That Two Kids Lost Their Lives That Night. Ms. Riley's Loss Of Life Is Significantly More Tragic Than Jose's. She Was An Unwilling Participant.

It Should Be Noted Even In The Case Of Murder. In The United States, The Accused Is Entitled To A Bond Hearing, And Unless They Are Deemed A Flight Risk, A Bond Will Be Set.

Tragedy Is Wanting 8,000,000 People To Be Found Guilty Of A Murder.

Tragedy Is Republicans Can't Do ASimple Math. According To Them, 8,000,000 Immigrants Entered The United States In 2023. An

Undocumented Immigrant Brutally murdered Laken Riley. It's News Worthy Because It Is So Rare That People Are Interested.

During the 1870s and 1880s, discussions of "human improvement" and the ideology of scientific racism became increasingly common. So-called experts determined individuals and groups of people to be either superior or inferior. They believed biological and behavioral characteristics were fixed and unchangeable, and placed individuals, populations and nations inside of that hierarchy.

Eugenics is a set of beliefs and practices that aim to improve the genetic quality of a human population by promoting the reproduction of individuals with desirable traits and limiting or preventing the reproduction of individuals with perceived undesirable traits. This concept is based on the idea that certain traits are hereditary and that the human population can be improved through selective breeding.

Eugenics is the scientifically inaccurate theory that humans can be improved through selective breeding of populations.

Eugenicists believed in a prejudiced and incorrect understanding of Mendelian genetics that claimed abstract human qualities (e.g., intelligence and social behaviors) were inherited in a simple fashion. Similarly, they believed complex diseases and disorders were solely the outcome of genetic inheritance.

The implementation of eugenics practices has caused widespread harm, particularly to populations that are being marginalized.

Eugenics is not a fringe movement. Starting in the late 1800s, leaders and intellectuals worldwide perpetuated eugenic beliefs and policies based on common racist and xenophobic attitudes. Many of these beliefs and policies still exist in the United States.

The genomics communities continue to work to scientifically debunk eugenic myths and combat modern-day manifestations of eugenics and scientific racism, particularly as they affect people of color, people with disabilities and LGBTQ+ individuals.

Eugenics is the scientifically erroneous and immoral theory of "racial improvement" and "planned breeding," which gained popularity during the early 20th century. Eugenicists worldwide believed that they could perfect human beings and eliminate so-called social ills through genetics and heredity. They believed the use of methods such as involuntary sterilization, segregation and social exclusion would rid society of individuals deemed by them to be unfit.

The eugenics movement first gained popularity in the late 19th and early 20th centuries, particularly in the United States and Europe.

In the United States, the eugenics movement began to gain traction in the early 20th century, with the founding of the Eugenics Record Office in 1910 by biologist Charles Davenport.

From the turn of the century, German eugenicists formed academic and personal relationships with the American eugenics establishment, in particular with Charles Davenport, the pioneering founder of the Eugenics Record Office on Long Island, New York, which was backed by the Harriman railway fortune. A number of other charitable American bodies generously funded German race biology with hundreds of thousands of dollars, even after the depression had taken hold.

German readers still closely followed American eugenic accomplishments as the model: biological courts, forced sterilisation, detention for the socially inadequate, debates on euthanasia. As America's elite were describing the socially worthless and the ancestrally unfit as "bacteria," "vermin," "mongrels" and "subhuman", a superior race of Nordics was increasingly seen as the answer to the globe's eugenic problems. US laws, eugenic investigations and ideology became blueprints for Germany's rising tide of race biologists and race-based hatemongers.

One such agitator was a disgruntled corporal in the German army. In 1924, he was serving time in prison for mob action. While there, he spent his time poring over eugenic textbooks, which extensively quoted Davenport, Popenoe and other American ethnological stalwarts. And he closely followed the writings of Leon Whitney, president of the American Eugenics Society, and Madison Grant, who extolled the Nordic race and bemoaned its "corruption" by Jews, Negroes, Slavs and others who did not possess blond hair and blue eyes. The young German corporal even wrote one of them fan mail.

In The Passing of the Great <u>Race</u>, Grant wrote: "Mistaken regard for what are believed to be divine laws and a sentimental belief in the sanctity of human life tend to prevent both the elimination of defective infants and the sterilisation of such adults as are themselves of no value to the community. The laws of nature require the obliteration of the unfit and human life is valuable only when it is of use to the community or race."

One day in the early 1930s, Whitney visited Grant to show off a letter he had just received from Germany, written by the corporal, now out of prison and rising in the German political scene. Grant could only smile. He pulled out his own letter. It was from the same German, thanking Grant for writing The Passing of the Great Race. The fan letter called Grant's book "his Bible". The man who sent those letters was <u>Adolf Hitler</u>.

Hitler proudly told his comrades how closely he followed American eugenic legislation. "Now that we know the laws of heredity," he told a fellow Nazi, "it is possible to a large extent to prevent unhealthy and severely handicapped beings from coming into the world. I have studied with interest the laws of several American states concerning prevention of reproduction by people whose progeny would, in all probability, be of no value or be injurious to the racial stock."

It gained further momentum in the 1920s and 1930s, leading to the passage of laws that allowed for the forced sterilization of individuals deemed "unfit" to reproduce.

The eugenics movement in the United States reached its peak in the 20th century

The Supreme Court's decision in Buck v. Bell upheld the constitutionality of a Virginia law allowing for the forced sterilization of individuals deemed "unfit," thereby sanctioning the practice of eugenics.

Following the Buck v. Bell decision in 1927, many states enacted laws that allowed for the forced sterilization of individuals considered mentally ill, intellectually disabled, or otherwise "unfit" to reproduce. This marked a dark period in American history when thousands of individuals were involuntarily sterilized under the guise of eugenics.

American eugenics refers *inter alia* to **compulsory sterilization laws adopted by over 30 states** that led to **more than 60,000 sterilizations of disabled individuals**. Many of these individuals were sterilized because of a disability: they were **mentally disabled or ill**, or belonged to **socially disadvantaged groups** living on the margins of society. American eugenic laws and practices implemented in the first decades of the twentieth century influenced the much larger National Socialist compulsory sterilization program, which between 1934 and 1945 led to approximately 350,000 compulsory sterilizations and was a stepping stone to the Holocaust.

In the United States, slavery and its legacies, fears of "**miscegenation**" and eugenics were deeply connected in the early 20th century. Prominent American eugenicists expounded on their concerns of "race suicide," or the increasingly differential birthrates between immigrants, the non-whites and the poor whites compared to native-born educated and wealthy whites.

Eugenicists used these concerns to promote discriminatory policies like anti-immigration and sterilization.

American eugenicists from a variety of disciplines declared certain individuals unfit, "feebleminded" or anti-social, which resulted in the involuntary sterilization of **at least 60,000 people** through 30 states' laws by the 1970s.

These eugenicists disproportionately targeted Latinxs, Native Americans, African Americans, poor whites and people with disabilities during the entirety of the 20th century.

Eugenicists were also crucial to the enactment of discriminatory immigration legislation that was passed in 1924 (the Johnson-Reed Act), which completely excluded immigrants coming into the United States from Asia.

It wasn't until the mid-20th century that the eugenics movement began to decline due to changing social attitudes, scientific advancements, and the association of eugenics with the holocaust. The practice of forced sterilization for eugenic purposes gradually fell out of favor, and by the 1970s, the era of state-sanctioned eugenic sterilizations supposedly came to an end in the United States.

It was not until Nazi Germany adopted American eugenic theory and practice came to the attention of the general public that public opinion about eugenics ultimately shifted in the United States. The counter-movement against eugenic sterilization culminated in the Supreme Court's 1942 decision in *Skinner v. Oklahoma*. While *Skinner* rejected eugenic sterilization as a valid state goal and recognized that procreation is a basic civil right, to this day the Supreme Court has never explicitly overruled *Buck v. Bell*.

Although support for eugenics-based sterilization laws waned, new justifications for coerced sterilization arose. Following World War II, concerns about population control, immigration, and welfare costs emerged as new rationales for targeting marginalized populations. By the 1960s, a new era of sterilization abuse was born, which once again focused on the poor, immigrants, and people of color.

For example, in the 1974 case of *Relf v. Weinberger*, a federal court found that poor people in the South were being forced to agree to sterilization when doctors threatened to withhold welfare benefits or medical care, including for childbirth. *Relf* involved the forced sterilization of two Black sisters, just 12 and 14 years old, who were sterilized by a federally-funded family planning clinic in Alabama. Their mother signed an "X" on a consent form she could not read, discovering too late that she had inadvertently "consented" to the permanent sterilization of her daughters Mary Alice and Minnie Relf.

Doctors were even withholding pain medication from women, that met the sterilization standard, during childbirth until they signed papers allowing the doctor to sterilize them.

By the mid-20th century, eugenics had largely fallen out of favor as a mainstream scientific theory, and the practice of forced sterilization began to decline. Laws permitting involuntary sterilization were gradually repealed or became unenforced. Additionally, the civil rights movement and changing societal values contributed to the rejection of eugenics-based policies.

While there was no single court case that ended the practice of eugenics in the United States, the shift in public opinion, along with changing scientific understanding and ethical considerations, played a significant role in discrediting and ultimately abandoning eugenics as a legitimate practice.

The 1978 Federal Sterilization Regulations were implemented to prevent abuses and protect individuals from being coerced or forced into sterilization procedures. However, as mentioned, enforcement of these regulations has been inconsistent in some cases, leading to continued violations and abuses, particularly in vulnerable populations such as prisoners and individuals in underfunded healthcare settings.

The cases of female prisoners in California being sterilized without their full and informed consent are particularly troubling examples of violations of human rights and medical ethics.

It is essential for policymakers, healthcare providers, and advocates to remain vigilant in ensuring that individuals are fully informed and empowered to make decisions about their own reproductive health, free from coercion or manipulation.

The passage of legislation like California's Bill SB1135 to ban sterilization in correctional facilities without proper consent is a step in the right direction towards protecting the reproductive rights and autonomy of individuals, especially those in vulnerable and marginalized populations.

Continued efforts to raise awareness, enforce regulations, and hold accountable those responsible for abuses already done are crucial in preventing eugenic practices and upholding human rights for all individuals.

With the completion of the Human Genome Project (HGP) and, more recently, advances in genomic screening technologies, there is some concern about whether generating an increasing amount of genomic information in the prenatal setting would lead to new societal pressures to terminate pregnancies and to reinstate eugenics.

When the HGP began in 1990, there was widespread concern that genomics would lead to a new era of eugenics. Many bioethicists were aware of how past eugenic movements used genetic information to ostracize historically marginalized groups and believed that people would use the outcomes of the HGP and subsequent developments in genomics to further marginalize and stigmatize certain groups. People were also concerned that the HGP would usher in a new era of behavior genetics, where genes would be used to explain certain behaviors. Many discussions about the HGP revolved around whether employers or insurance companies could use genomic information to discriminate against specific individuals.

As far back as 2018 under Trump's Immigration policy news that a for-profit ICE detention center in Georgia was doing forced sterilization procedures on immigrant women.

Decades later in 2020, this practice of forcibly sterilizing minority women is still taking place. However, these forced sterilizations are now being done by ICE authorities.

One nurse at a facility in Ocilla, Georgia filed a whistleblower complaint alleging concern over the high number of hysterectomies performed on ICE detainees.

Multiple women shared their experiences with these procedures taking place inside the immigration facility.

One woman stated that when she questioned what treatment she was receiving, she received three different answers by three different people: the doctor, a corrections officer, and a nurse at the detention center.

By December of 2020, more than forty women had come forward with written testimonies stating they received invasive and unnecessary medical procedures while under ICE's care.

After speaking with their clients, attorneys discovered women had complained to ICE since 2018 regarding this misconduct, but ICE "continued a policy or custom of sending women to be mistreated and abused."

All of the victims were lower-income immigrant women who had an extremely minimal grasp of the English language, which left them vulnerable to coercive authority figures.

Republicans today claim that legalized abortions is eugenics.

In his April 2023 ruling aiming to suspend the FDA's approval of the abortion drug mifepristone, the Texas-based federal judge Matthew Kacsmaryk cited Justice Clarence Thomas's efforts to link abortion to eugenics. Thomas devoted over a dozen pages to this theme in his 2019 opinion on the Supreme Court's decision about two abortion laws. He warned of "the potential for abortion to become a tool of eugenic manipulation" and argued that "the use of abortion to achieve eugenic goals is not merely hypothetical." He harked back to the Supreme Court's upholding the constitutionality of Virginia's forced-sterilization law in *Buck v. Bell* in 1927, which many consider one of the Court's worst mistakes. He reflected that "[t]echnological advances have only heightened the eugenic potential for abortion, as abortion can now be used to eliminate children with unwanted characteristics, such as a particular sex, mixed-race, or disability."

At the same time conservatives believe eugenics has a positive role to play in society. They feel it is the cure to the great replacement theory.

Anti-abortion advocates typically have no problem with state efforts to control reproduction based on racist and bigoted ideas. This is not just a historical phenomenon of forced sterilization under explicitly eugenic laws; recent and current practices also bespeak eugenic intentions. The debate over welfare policy in the 1990s was deeply racialized and some conservative lawmakers tried to control the birth rate of single mothers, particularly Black single mothers, through the Aid to Families with Dependent Children (AFDC) program. They introduced family caps, which denied incremental increases to benefits for families after they had a certain number of children.

One Department of Health and Human Services official spoke in favor of family cap policies by saying that the government should not reward "irresponsible" behavior.

77,254,048 Registered Voters That Are Neither Democrat Or Republican.

35,739,952 Registered Republicans And If We Win It's A Fair And Honest Election.

48,426,000 Registered Democrats And If We Win, We Cheated And Did Election Manipulation.

At best, Republicans Start Negative 12,686,048 Votes They Need From The Undecided Or 3rd Party Voters To Tie.

Leaving 64,568,000 Undecided And 3rd Party Voters, both Democrats And Republicans Will Need To Compete To Get The Majority To Elect Their President.

Ultimately, It Is The Electoral Votes That Decide. Which Needs To Be Changed.

It would help if you stopped trying to take credit for anything that happened back in US History.

You have only existed since 1964.

So you still weren't happy, so you completely changed again. You are no longer the party you were until 2015.

From 2015 to the present, the Republican party only exists in name. Today's Republican party has been hijacked. It has completely changed into nothing that a political party stands for and everything terrorist groups stand for.

The Republican Party before 1964 had a platform that had zero in common with today's republican platform. (The only thing the party today has in common with the party before 1964 is the word "Republican.")

The only reason you all jumped ship and took over the Republican Party was because the Democratic Party adopted more social issues and sponsored the Civil Rights Act.

You were solidifying your bigotry. You thought with the southern Republicans you would have a majority, but so bad wasn't true. You did become the party known for the perseverance in maintaining the perception of whites being superior and that bigotry is an honor and a right.

It doesn't matter whether it was Democrat or Republican if the party stood for or was for something with a horrific outcome.

You can bet it was the so-called "conservative" who was in charge, and it is their side to blame.

Scientific racism is an ideology that appropriates the methods and legitimacy of science to argue for the superiority of white Europeans and the inferiority of non-white people whose social and economic status have been historically marginalized.

Like eugenics, scientific racism grew out of:

The misappropriation of revolutionary advances in medicine, anatomy and statistics during the 18th and 19th centuries.

Charles Darwin's theory of evolution through the mechanism of natural selection.

Gregor Mendel's laws of inheritance.

Eugenic theories and scientific racism drew support from contemporary xenophobia, antisemitism, sexism, colonialism and imperialism, as well as justifications of slavery, particularly in the United States.

I feel like either Republican Leaders are Idiots or they take their constituents for idiots.

It Could Be Both.

Just Because Russia And Nazis had Socialist in their names they had nothing to do with socialism they were anti-socialist.

In simple terms it was a deceptive marketing ploy that still works when talking to right leaning people.

The reality is Marxism, Communism, Natzism and Totalitarianism are actually in reality anti socialism.

In American political discourse, "socialism" is sometimes used by members of the Republican Party, and indeed by some political commentators more broadly, as a pejorative term to describe policies that involve government intervention or expansion of social services. While this usage can be part of a legitimate debate about the role of government in society, it can also be a rhetorical strategy to frame such policies as inherently negative, suggesting a slippery slope toward an authoritarian or dysfunctional state.

This usage might oversimplify or misrepresent what socialism is, according to its academic or theoretical definitions. Socialism, as traditionally conceived, involves the collective ownership of the means of production, not merely government intervention or the provision of social safety nets. In the context of American politics, many policies labeled as "socialist" by critics are, in fact, examples of social democracy or welfare state policies, which are typical features of many capitalist societies.

The United States, like many other capitalist countries, operates with a mixed economy, which means it combines elements of free markets with social programs and government regulations. Some of these social programs have roots in or share characteristics with socialist ideals, such as providing for the common welfare and reducing economic inequality, but they operate within a fundamentally capitalist framework. Here are a few examples:

1. **Social Security**: A program designed to provide financial assistance to retirees, the disabled, and survivors of deceased workers. It is funded through payroll taxes and is a form of social insurance.

2. **Medicare**: A national health insurance program primarily for people aged 65 and older, but also available to some younger people with disabilities.

3. **Medicaid**: A program that assists with medical costs for some people with limited income and resources. It is jointly funded by the federal government and the states.

4. **Public Education**: Free access to K-12 education is a hallmark of the American system, and public funding for education can be seen as a socialist principle in that it is meant to benefit the entire community and is funded through taxation.

5. **Public Infrastructure**: Roads, bridges, public parks, and utilities are often provided by the government, which can be seen as a form of socialism in that the infrastructure is owned and maintained for public use and benefit.

Critics who label these programs as "socialist" often do so to suggest that they are steps towards a more comprehensive socialist system that could threaten individual freedoms or the free market economy. Proponents of these programs, on the other hand, argue that they are necessary components of a modern society that ensure a minimum standard of living, contribute to economic stability, and provide for the common good.

It is also worth noting that the use of the term "socialism" in American political dialogue can be historically and culturally loaded, reflecting Cold War era sentiments where socialism was directly equated with the ideologies of countries like the Soviet Union. This historical backdrop contributes to the emotional weight of the term and can sometimes overshadow objective discussion of policy.

In summary, the misuse of the term "socialism" in political rhetoric can serve to stigmatize certain policies or political opponents rather than foster a nuanced discussion about the actual content and merits of those policies. It's important for a healthy democracy to have accurate and honest discourse around economic systems and policies.

It's important to understand that the terms "socialism," "Marxism," "communism," "Nazism," and "totalitarianism" have specific historical and ideological meanings, but these meanings can be distorted in political discourse. Each of these terms represents complex ideas and systems that have been interpreted and implemented in various ways throughout history. Here's a breakdown of each:

1. **Socialism**:
Socialism is an economic and political system where the means of production (like factories, resources, and land) are owned or regulated by the community as a whole or the state. The goal of socialism is to reduce class disparities and promote a more equitable distribution of wealth and power. Socialism encompasses a broad spectrum of theories and practices, ranging from democratic socialism, where political democracy is combined with social ownership, to more authoritarian forms where the state has a central role in planning and control.

2. **Marxism**:
Marxism is a socio-economic theory and method of socioeconomic analysis that views class relations and social conflict using a materialist interpretation of historical development. It originates from the works of 19th-century German philosophers Karl Marx and Friedrich Engels. Marxism posits that capitalism, through its inherent exploitation and inequality, will inevitably lead to a proletarian revolution, after which a classless and stateless society (communism) will emerge.

3. **Communism**:
Communism, in its ideal form, is a classless, stateless society where all property is communally owned, and each person contributes and receives according to their ability and needs. Marxism is often seen as a theoretical foundation for communism, which has been the goal of various political movements, most notably in the 20th century. However, in practice, states that have claimed to be communist (like the Soviet

Union or China under Mao) often diverged significantly from Marxist theory, resulting in authoritarian regimes with centralized control.

4. **Nazism**:
Nazism, or National Socialism, is a far-right, fascist ideology and movement founded and ruled by Adolf Hitler and the Nazi Party in Germany. Despite having «Socialism» in its name, Nazism is fundamentally opposed to Marxist socialism and communism. Nazis co-opted the term «socialism» to attract workers and to represent their (false) claim of supporting the common German (excluding those they deemed as «others,» such as Jews, whom they persecuted and murdered in the Holocaust). Nazism is characterized by extreme nationalism, racism, xenophobia, and the expansionist doctrine of Lebensraum. It is a totalitarian ideology, which means it seeks to control all aspects of public and private life.

5. **Totalitarianism**:
Totalitarianism is a political system where the state recognizes no limits to its authority and strives to regulate every aspect of public and private life. This term is broad and can apply to various ideologies that seek total control, whether it›s far-right, like in Nazi Germany, or far-left, like in Stalin›s Soviet Union. Totalitarian regimes are often characterized by strong central rule, an extensive use of propaganda to maintain the personality cult of the leader, and the suppression of freedom.

In the American political context, sometimes terms like socialism and communism are used by some political figures and commentators as catch-all terms to criticize policies or politicians they view as too interventionist or redistributive. This usage can sometimes be more about political rhetoric than accurate ideological or economic analysis.

It's worth noting that political language is highly context-dependent and can be used in a variety of ways, not always strictly adhering to the original or academic definitions of these terms. Political labels can be misused to mischaracterize opponents or policies, which can lead to confusion about the true nature of these ideologies.

Regarding cancer. Protect the Penis. Please like and share.

The Cancer You Suffer Through Alone Because No One Is Willing To Talk About It

Men and boys after reading this I hope all of you get tested and vaccinated for human papilloma virus (HPV).

Urethral cancer is a type of cancer affecting the male urethra. Although some people with urethral cancer do not complain of any symptoms, most do. What are these symptoms? How should this malignancy be treated? What is the chance of recovery? A layer of cells called epithelium lines the urethra. In men there are several glands located along the length of the urethra. A supportive network of connective tissue, elastic and muscle fibers and blood vessels surrounds the urethra.

What causes urethral cancer?

The exact cause of urethral cancer is not known. However, chronic inflammation and infection have been identified as factors that may increase the risk for developing this condition. Many men with urethral cancer have previously been treated for urethral stricture disease or sexually transmitted infections (STI's) chronic urinary tract infection. In men the presence of human papilloma virus (HPV) has been linked to urethral cancer. Human papilloma virus (HPV) can also cause cancer in women.

What are the symptoms of urethral cancer?

In its early stages, there are usually few symptoms associated with urethral cancer. As the cancer grows, some patients may notice a lump or growth on the urethra. Others may notice pain or bleeding that accompanies urination. If the tumor grows so that it narrows the diameter of the urethra, patients may have difficulty urinating or pass blood from their urethra.

How is urethral cancer diagnosed?

The diagnostic investigation begins with a thorough medical history and physical examination. The urologist will ask the patient about medical conditions that may be associated with urethral cancer, such as urethral stricture, STIs, bladder cancer, and urinary tract infection. The urologist will examine the urethra, feeling for any abnormalities. An important diagnostic instrument that the urologist will use is the cystoscope, which is a thin, lighted scope that allows the urologist to view the inside of the urethra. Cystourethroscopy is most commonly performed as an office procedure under local anesthesia. If the urologist observes any abnormalities, the patient will require a biopsy.

A tissue biopsy is essential to diagnose urethral cancer. It is difficult to perform this procedure under local anesthesia, so the patient is usually scheduled to return for biopsy. Under general anesthesia or regional anesthesia, the urologist will biopsy any suspicious areas identified. Certain patients may also require a biopsy technique that involves passing a needle through the skin or urethral growth. The biopsy tissue is then sent to the pathologist for examination under a microscope to confirm the diagnosis. Before the patient awakens from anesthesia, the urologist will perform a thorough examination to determine the local extent of the tumor.

Once urethral cancer is found, the extent of disease is categorized (i.e. staged) based on how deeply the tumor has penetrated the tissues surrounding the urethra. More tests will be performed to find out if cancer cells have spread to other parts of the body. A CT scan of the abdomen and pelvis may be performed in order to examine the lymph nodes that collect drainage from the urethra. An MRI may be performed in order to examine the local extent of the tumor. A chest X-ray is usually obtained to ensure that the tumor has not spread to the lungs, and select patients may require a bone scan to look for bony metastases. If the urethral cancer is classified as transitional cell carcinoma, the patient will undergo either excretory urography or retrograde pyelography to image the lining of the kidney and ureter to ensure there are no other sites of cancer.

In men, the part of the urethra that is closest to the bladder and prostate is more likely to originate from the cells that line the urinary tract (urothelial or transitional cells), whereas the part of the urethra inside the penis is more likely to originate from cells more like the skin (squamous cells), This difference may impact the way the disease is treated.

How is urethral cancer treated?

There are treatment options for all patients diagnosed with urethral cancer. These options may be divided into three categories: surgery, radiation and chemotherapy. Surgery is the most common treatment for cancer of the urethra. There are several surgical techniques that may be used. For so-called "superficial" cancers, where the tumor has not invaded into surrounding tissues, the tumor may be removed by inserting an instrument such as a cystoscope into the urethra and using a loop electrocautery to remove the tumor, thereby avoiding an incision. For tumors that demonstrated invasion, some patients may require conventional surgery to remove the affected area. Certain men with a tumor that involves only part of the urethra inside the penis (anterior urethra) may require removal of part of the penis that contains the tumor (partial penectomy) or even removal of the entire penis (penectomy). A decision about whether to remove part or all of the penis depends on the location of the tumor and whether the entire tumor can be removed (with an adequate margin of normal tissue (usually 1-2 centimeters) to still allow a man to stand to urinate. In addition, if the tumor is invading into the erectile tissues of the penis itself, the entire penis may need amputation. If this procedure is done, a small hole on the underside of the scrotum is created (perineal urethrostomy) that allows urination. Of course, this procedure results in a situation where the patient must sit to void. For patients with tumors that involve the part of the urethra that connects to the bladder and prostate (posterior urethra) more extensive surgery may be required. In men with this type of tumor the bladder and prostate, part of the bony pelvis, as well as the penis, may be removed.

If this surgery is done, a piece of bowel is utilized to create a pouch into which the kidneys drain. This pouch can either be incontinent (thus, requiring wearing a stoma bag) or continent (requiring that the patient pass a small catheter 3-4 times a day to drain the pouch). Determining which type of reconstruction is right for you depends on what other medical conditions you have and your personal preference. For the men undergoing these extensive surgeries lymph nodes in the pelvis are often removed as well. When this is done, some patients may experience leg swelling owing to the fact that the lymphatic nodes that are removed are responsible for the drainage of fluid that seeps out of the blood vessels into the legs. Radiation therapy destroys cancer with high-energy radiation. Radiation therapy may be used alone or in conjunction with surgery or chemotherapy. Although radiation therapy may allow the patient to retain his or her urethra and surrounding organs, this method of treatment is not without complications. Radiation to this region can result in bladder irritation, incontinence, or bleeding, rectal pain and bleeding, as well as stricture to the urethra, causing obstructive urinary symptoms. Chemotherapy kills cancer cells with drugs. Chemotherapy is generally reserved for situations where the cancer has escaped the urethra, so called metastatic tumors. Usually it is utilized either before surgery or radiation or after to help kill cells outside of the area targeted by the surgery or radiation. The type of drugs used for the treatment of each cancer depends on the risk that patient has for having metastasis, the burden of metastatic disease, and the specific histologic subtype of the tumor (urothelial or squamous). Each chemotherapy drug has a different side-effect profile, but most patients are monitored very closely by an oncologist during and after treatment with these drugs to prevent major problems with the medications.

What to expect after treatment?

Despite aggressive therapy with chemotherapy, radiation therapy and surgery, recurrence of urethral cancer following treatment is not uncommon. For this reason, patients with this condition require life-long follow-up with a physician. Follow up generally entails having a physical exam, lab work, CT scan and a chest x-ray on a semi-annual or annual basis. Only with early recognition of recurrence and prompt initiation of appropriate therapy in such cases is prolonged survival possible.

Frequently asked questions:

What determines if urethral cancer can be treated with local excision vs. a more radical surgical procedure?

In general, urethral cancers that involve the anterior urethra (part of the urethra closest to the outside) are more often successfully treated with local surgery. Tumors that involve the posterior urethra (part of the urethra closest to the bladder) often require more radical surgery to ensure optimal outcome.

What are the chances of urethral cancer coming back following treatment?

The likelihood of urethral cancer recurring following treatment depends on both the stage and location of the initial tumor. For patients with low stage disease, the five-year disease specific survival rate approaches 90 percent; patients with high stage disease have a survival rate of 33 percent. For patients with tumor located in the anterior urethra (the portion of the urethra in the penis for men) regardless of stage, the five-year disease specific survival is 60 to 70 percent, whereas for patients with tumor located in the posterior urethra (the area that traverses the prostate in men) regardless of stage, the five-year survival rate is less than 25 percent.

I, Todd Emerson, have been lucky so far. They have only removed an inch of my urethra. I now urinate and ejaculate from a hole on the underside of my penis. I have been able to keep my entire penis so far. Please like and share. You may save a life.

Causing Harm To Millions Because Of The Ignorance And Not Being Educated As How Sensationalized Rhetoric Causes Violence Towards Others.

First, I want to stress that It is essential to emphasize the treatment of all victims of any crime with dignity and respect rather than exploiting them as tools to advance a political agenda.

If a particular incident is widely reported on national news, it is always an uncommon occurrence.

Cases that are commonplace or occur frequently will not get national news coverage.

Sensationalizing rare events for political campaigns and network ratings causes harm to the lives of countless individuals simply because of your personal biases, bigotry, prejudices, racism, homophobia, and segregation.

It is crucial to refrain from spreading hysteria and fear without concrete evidence that the statistics and occurrences are not embellished. Then, using your hysteria, calling for retribution will be justified.

When you have actual verifiable proof, your calls for mass deportation and the apprehension of the guilty class become relevant.

Until then, Rather than rushing to judgment, unfairly implicating entire groups based on the actions of a few, and causing harm, it is essential to focus on making a positive impact.

Research and participation in positive changes that will increase tolerance and acceptance can be achieved through educating oneself, promoting tolerance and acceptance, understanding immigration issues, advocating for equality among all nationalities, engaging with different generations, embracing diverse genders, and fostering constructive dialogue among opposing political factions.

Let us redirect our energies toward initiatives that foster unity, empathy, and mutual respect instead of perpetuating divisions and prejudice.

Racism is attached or an extension of the emotion of fear. Whether it is fostered or vanishes are due to a number of factors.

One: the more positive exposure you have to your surroundings and others you "think" are not like you then racism is only a word with a vague definition.

Two: When you're young and you're sheltered or kept from everything surrounding you that people that are your authority are uncomfortable with or had a perceived or real negative experience with promotes and nurtures racism.

Neither of these conditions the negative side nor the positive side are permanent with influential education that promotes and actively recruits with a program that glorifies their beliefs, makes promises, and has an active, visual, and literature that is well produced and readily available.

Inclusivity: Benefits and Potential Losses

Benefits of Inclusivity:

1. **Enhanced Understanding:** Positive interactions with people from diverse backgrounds can decrease prejudicial beliefs. Understanding and appreciating cultural differences can lead to more harmonious communities.

2. **Educational Growth:** Inclusive education can promote a broader worldview and appreciation for diversity, helping to prevent the establishment of racist attitudes.

3. **Diverse Representation:** Seeing diverse groups in media, literature, and leadership roles can challenge stereotypes and foster a sense of belonging and acceptance for everyone.

Potential Losses with Inclusivity:

1. **Social Changes:** Embracing inclusivity might lead to changes in social circles. Individuals may lose connections with friends or family who do not support or understand the importance of inclusivity.

2. **Identity Questions:** Some individuals might struggle with their own identity as they embrace inclusivity, especially if they feel pressure from their traditional social group to resist change.

Racism: Detriments and Opportunities for Change

Detriments of Racism:

1. **Social Division:** Racism can cause deep societal divides, leading to discrimination and social injustices that affect the quality of life and opportunities for the targeted groups.

2. **Wasted Talent:** It prevents individuals from reaching their full potential because of barriers to education and employment opportunities based solely on race.

3. **Cultural Loss:** A lack of diversity can result in a narrower cultural perspective, stifling innovation and creativity.

Opportunities for Change:

1. **Diverse Environments:** Exposing young people to diversity can prevent the development of racist beliefs, fostering a more inclusive mindset from an early age.

2. **Challenging Prejudices:** Encouraging individuals to question and challenge racist ideas, even when they come from authority figures or within their own social circles, can lead to personal and societal growth.

3. **Accessible Information:** Providing well-crafted educational resources that advocate for equality and celebrate diversity can help shift perspectives and reduce racism.

In summary, while inclusivity promotes a more understanding and cooperative society, it can also lead to the loss of social connections if one's existing network does not support these values. Racism, on the other hand, breeds division and limits both individual and collective progress. However, it is not an unchangeable state; through diverse experiences, education, and challenging existing prejudices, society can move towards greater inclusivity.

Multi-infarct dementia (MID) Is Not The Same As Alzheimer's

There isn't a cure for MID. Brain damage from MID is permanent.

Instead, treatment focuses on preventing any additional damage.

A person with Multi-infarct dementia has two or more of these specific difficulties, including a decline in:
Memory.
Reasoning.
Language.
Coordination.
Mood.
Behavior.

MID typically affects people between the ages of 60 and 75

What are the risk factors that cause multi-infarct dementia?

Smoking

Alcohol Abuse

Drug Abuse

High blood pressure (hypertension)

Conditions like atherosclerosis, coronary heart disease, heart valve disease, and carotid artery disease cause MID.

Management and Treatment

Physicians recommend lifestyle changes, such as regular exercise, eating a healthy diet high in B1 or thiamin, stopping smoking, and STOP ABUSING ALCOHOL and STOP ABUSING STREET and PRESCRIPTION DRUGS.

(MID) symptoms may begin suddenly and remain permanently or for short periods.

They include:

Confusion or problems with memory.

We are wandering or getting lost in familiar places.

I was walking with rapid, shuffling steps.

Loss of bladder or bowel control.

I was laughing or crying at inappropriate times.

Difficulty following instructions.

Issues counting money and making monetary transactions.

Unable to keep up with conversations

Unable to follow the storyline in entertainment

Some people with MID seem to have an improvement in their symptoms for short periods but then decline.

Multi-infarct dementia results from several small strokes that the individual and those around them are unaware of.

What causes multi-infarct dementia?

Many people who have MID and the people around them don't realize they've had strokes.

However, these very tiny strokes can still damage your brain tissue. Several tiny strokes can cause enough brain damage to lead to dementia.

What are the risk factors for multi-infarct dementia?

Diagnosis and Tests

How is multi-infarct dementia diagnosed?

There's no test to diagnose multi-infarct dementia, so that the diagnosis can be challenging.

If you have symptoms of MID, your provider will ask about your health history and perform physical test including neurological exams.

They'll also assess your risk for stroke, which may point to a diagnosis of MID.

Imaging tests of your brain, such as <u>MRI</u> or <u>CT scans</u>, can help diagnose MID if they show areas of brain damage.

Your provider may also refer you to a specialist for <u>neuropsychological testing</u> so they can assess your cognitive symptoms, like memory issues.

They'll also recommend lifestyle changes, such as regular exercise, eating a healthy diet high in B1 and thiamin, stopping smoking and STOP ABUSING alcohol and STOP ABUSING STREET, and PRESCRIPTION DRUGS.

What can I expect if I or my loved one have multi-infarct dementia?

Multi-infarct dementia often gets worse over time. MID's course is usually more like a staircase with sudden periods of decline (sometimes followed by some improvement) and then more sudden periods of decline,

Dementia from MID results from brain damage due to a lack of blood flow from a series of strokes.

Alzheimer's disease causes dementia from an abnormal build-up of proteins in your brain.

How Slavery, Racism, Prejudice, Language, And Customs Kept Mexico A Country After The Mexican-American War Or How A Little Known Man Stopped The Complete Annexation

After the Mexican-American War, the USA had the opportunity to acquire the entire nation of Mexico based on our belief in Manifest Destiny. It was the idea that white Americans were divinely ordained to settle throughout the American Continents.

The ideology of Manifest Destiny inspired a variety of measures designed to remove or destroy the native population. US President James K. Polk was a firm believer.

However, factors like race, slavery, language, and customs influenced the desires of the South and the North's views on slavery as to whether the US annexed all of Mexico.

The aftermath of the war presented complex challenges for the United States regarding the potential annexation of Mexican territories.

Divergent opinions, especially in the Southern states, emerged regarding land acquisition and slavery expansion.

While some supported territorial growth to promote slavery, others grappled with the difficulties of integrating Mexican territories into the Union.

The Southern states, driven by a desire to expand slavery, saw Mexican territories as potential areas for growth.

The South believed that acquiring new land in the southern regions would lead to the creation of more slave states, according to federal law, giving them the majority power between free and enslaved states in Congress. This perspective highlighted the economic and political motivations behind the Southern push for territorial expansion. It also made northern states unwilling to approve the annexation of the entire country of Mexico.

Despite their ambitions for growth, many Southerners held deep-seated racist views towards Mexicans and other non-white groups. This racial prejudice influenced their perception of Mexicans as inferior and incompatible with American society.

The cultural differences between Mexicans and Anglo-Americans further heightened these biases, fostering a sense of cultural superiority among specific segments of the American population.

The vast size and diverse demographics of Mexico presented significant challenges for the United States in terms of governance and administration. Integrating Mexico into the Union would have required a monumental effort to assimilate the Mexican population, establish effective governance structures, and address existing social and economic disparities.

The debates over annexing Mexican territories following the Mexican-American War revealed the complex blend of political, economic, racial, and cultural factors that influenced American expansionism in the 19th century.

The divergent views within the Southern states highlighted the intricate considerations, ranging from slavery expansion to the governance and assimilation challenges. These discussions emphasized the multifaceted nature of American territorial ambitions and the nuanced issues of race, culture, and governance inherent in the expansion process.

The conflicting perspectives of the Southern states regarding the annexation of Mexican territories exposed the deep-seated tensions within American society in the post-war era. The push for expansion to support slavery clashed with racial prejudices and cultural barriers, complicating the vision of integrating Mexican lands into the Union.

While some Southern voices supported acquiring new territories to strengthen the power of slave states, others wrestled with the ethical and practical consequences of such expansion.

Racial prejudices among certain Southern groups not only influenced the views of Mexicans but also brought attention to broader problems of inequality and discrimination in American society.

Additionally, the logistical hurdles governing a large and varied territory like Mexico posed significant challenges for those advocating annexation. The difficulties of integrating a distinct culture, setting up efficient governance systems, and tackling socio-economic gaps raised severe doubts about the viability and long-term success of such a venture.

Nicholas Trist, a lesser-known figure in the debate over the Mexican annexation, took matters into his own hands. He made the final decision for the United States.

He played a crucial role in saving half of Mexico's territory by negotiating a treaty, being an opponent of the Mexican-American War.

President Polk fired Trist while negotiating the treaty, for not wanting to negotiate the surrender of all of Mexico's land.

Trist didn't care that he was fired. He defied the order and completed the treaty, giving 55% of Mexico's land to the United States and allowing Mexico to keep 45% of its land.

The Treaty of Guadalupe Hidalgo, which officially ended the Mexican-American War (1846-48), was signed on February 2, 1848, at Guadalupe Hidalgo.

Like always, the United States did not honor all of the treaties.

While the Treaty of Guadalupe Hidalgo formally ended the Mexican-American War in February 1848, tensions between the Governments of Mexico and the United States continued to simmer over the next six years.

The two countries each claimed the Mesilla Valley as part of their own country.

The Mexican Government demanded monetary compensation for Native American attacks in the region because, under the Treaty, the United States had agreed to protect Mexico from such attacks.

However, the United States refused to comply, insisting that while they had agreed to protect Mexico from Native American attacks, they had not agreed to financially compensate for attacks that did occur because we were not protecting them.

These continuing tensions between Mexico and the United States complicated U.S. efforts to find a southern route for a transcontinental railroad as the only viable routes passed through Mexican territory.

Mexico, however, had already granted Mexican Don José de Garay the right to build colonies for Americans on the isthmus with capital from the New Orleans Company.

In 1853, Mexican officials evicted Americans from their property in the disputed Mesilla Valley.

When the U.S. Government did not act, Governor William Lane of New Mexico declared the Mesilla Valley part of the U.S. territory of New Mexico.

Mexican President Antonio de Santa Anna responded by sending troops into the valley.

Attempting to defuse the situation, U.S. President Franklin Pierce sent James Gadsden, the new U.S. Minister to Mexico, to negotiate with Santa Anna. Secretary of State William Marcy instructed Gadsden to renegotiate a border that provided a route for a southern railroad, arrange for a release of U.S. financial obligations for Native American attacks, and settle the monetary claims between the countries related to the Garay project.

The persistent efforts of private American citizens to enter Mexico illegally and incite rebellions to gain territory exacerbated tensions between the governments. (see any irony looks like what we accuse the Mexicans of doing)

In the new treaty, the US was to pay the amount to Mexico of $10 million, and the land purchased was 29,670 square miles, and removed any mention of Native American attacks and private claims.

And again the United States reneged on payment.

After the Gadsden's Purchase, a new border dispute caused tension over the United States' lack of payment, and the treaty failed to resolve the issues surrounding financial claims and border attacks.

Why Don't We Have Delayed Broadcasts of Debates With Fact Check

In an era defined by the rapid dissemination of information and the prevalence of false narratives, the need for accuracy and truthfulness in political discourse has never been more critical.

Political debates, as platforms for candidates to articulate their ideas and policies, play a pivotal role in shaping public opinion.

To ensure the integrity of these debates and combat the spread of misinformation, a forward-looking approach involves broadcasting political debates on a delay with real-time AI-powered fact-checking.

By harnessing the capabilities of AI for instant fact-checking, broadcasters can provide viewers with accurate information in real-time, effectively countering false or misleading statements as they arise during debates.

This approach not only promotes truth and accuracy but also empowers viewers to engage with debates in a more informed and discerning manner.

The utilization of AI-driven fact-checking serves as a powerful tool in combating misinformation, which can quickly permeate public discourse and sway opinions.

By promptly identifying and correcting falsehoods, broadcasters can mitigate the impact of misinformation and uphold the integrity of political discussions, fostering a climate of transparency and accountability.

Moreover, the integration of AI technology enables instant verification of statements made by politicians and candidates, holding them accountable for the accuracy of their claims.

The knowledge that their remarks will be swiftly fact-checked incentivizes speakers to uphold truthfulness and integrity, contributing to a more honest and responsible exchange of ideas.

In addition to promoting truth and accountability, real-time AI fact-checking during debates serves to educate the public and enhance media literacy.

By displaying corrections on-screen where false statements are identified, viewers not only receive accurate information but also learn to critically evaluate political rhetoric, fostering a more discerning and engaged citizenry.

By leveraging AI for instant fact-checking in delayed broadcasts of political debates, broadcasters can instill greater trust in the political process and media coverage.

The transparency and reliability afforded by this approach demonstrate a commitment to accuracy and truth, reinforcing the credibility of information presented to viewers.

In conclusion, the convergence of delayed broadcasts, real-time AI fact-checking, and the display of facts where false statements are made offers a transformative approach to enhancing political discourse.

By leveraging technology to promote truth, combat misinformation, hold politicians accountable, educate the public, and foster trust, this innovative strategy sets a new standard for informed, responsible, and democratic dialogue in the political arena.

The Declining Influence of Organized Religion In Politics and the Rise of Secularism Has The Christian Nationalists, Christian Right, Federalists, And Republicans Desperately And Aggressively Trying To Maintain Power Through Any Avenue Possible.

In recent years, there has been a noticeable shift in religious beliefs and affiliations, with traditional forms of religion losing ground to secular beliefs and ideologies.

This post examines the patterns and potential reasons behind the decline in organized religion, the growth of non-religious populations, and the rise of evangelical megachurches.

Data indicates that religious faith has significantly decreased over the past 15 years, with a drop from 77% to 65% in those who identify with a religion, and these numbers are falling more rapidly with each passing year. Among younger generations, the decline is even starker, with only 46% of Millennials and a mere 23% of Generation Z reporting religious beliefs.

Projections suggest that by the year 2100, traditional religions might become less popular than alternative beliefs such as paganism, which would mark a considerable shift in societal norms and values. This could lead to a landscape where religion no longer wields the power to influence political decisions or societal norms to the extent it does today.

Many traditional religious institutions have been resistant to recognizing LGBTQ+ rights, including gay marriage. The perception of these institutions as intolerant has alienated many, especially younger generations, who tend to be more supportive of these rights.

Some religious groups have been accused of using fear tactics to control or target marginalized groups, often leading to labels such as "deviant" or "groomer," which has caused pushback from those who advocate for a more inclusive and loving approach to spirituality.

The denial of women's autonomy, particularly in healthcare and holding leadership roles, has been a point of contention, with many religious doctrines advocating for traditional gender roles that are increasingly seen as outdated.

Some have used religion to justify racism, hatred, and even violence, which has led to a critical reevaluation of religious teachings and their applications in modern society.

Allegations made against religious leaders for making false claims, such as having direct conversations with God or healing incurable diseases, have undermined the credibility of spiritual authority for many.

There are also criticisms against religious institutions urging followers to give up wealth in the name of faith, which has caused some to question the motives behind such teachings.

Countries with high levels of atheism often provide substantial economic, political, and existential stability.

Studies suggest that "security in society seems to diminish religious belief."

When people's basic needs are met and they feel secure, they are less likely to seek comfort or answers in religion. This trend is observable in nations with robust educational systems, social security, and low inequality.

Despite the decline in religious affiliation, evangelical megachurches have seen growth, though not at a rate that offsets the numbers leaving traditional churches.

Megachurches often engage in extreme public practices and verbally abusive public displays to attract attention, performing public spectacles to draw attention to attract publicity that will attract disillusioned individuals who are easily manipulated and seek a sense of community or excitement.

The shifting landscape of religious belief is complex and multifaceted. While traditional religious institutions may be losing their hold on large segments of the population for various reasons, including their stance on social issues, use of fear, and perceived lack of authenticity, there are still pockets of religious growth and transformation.

Evangelical megachurches are one such example. They capitalize on modern media and marketing techniques to create a sense of community and spectacle that appeals to specific demographics.

Megachurches often provide a sense of belonging and an energetic atmosphere that can be appealing to those disillusioned from traditional worship that has adopted a more liberal view and, with their need for public approval, to feel superior and seek acceptance of the like-minded are drawn to the church even though it has a more contemporary form of worship.

Their services often include modern music, multimedia presentations, and messages that resonate with Christian Rights everyday concerns.

This approach contrasts with the more traditional and sometimes austere services of conventional churches, making megachurches particularly attractive to younger churchgoers.

As traditional congregations dwindle, remaining believers may feel a sense of insecurity about the future of their faith.

This can drive them towards larger congregations, where the sheer number of attendees provides a sense of reassurance and communal strength.

The growth of megachurches can then be seen as a response to the need for a fortified religious identity in an increasingly secular world.

The rise of the internet and social media has exposed individuals to various ideas and beliefs, challenging traditional doctrines and dogmas.

Additionally, globalization has brought people of diverse backgrounds and faiths into closer contact, promoting a more inclusive and pluralistic worldview. As a result, many people are reevaluating their religious beliefs and often finding that secular humanism or other philosophies align more closely with their values.

As society progresses, the role and influence of religion will likely continue to evolve.

The decline in traditional religious affiliation may not necessarily signal the end of spirituality or the quest for meaning and purpose in life.

Instead, people may find new ways to express their spirituality outside the confines of organized religion.

Society must foster respectful dialogue between the religious and non-religious.

Understanding and respecting different beliefs can help bridge the divide and promote a more harmonious coexistence, regardless of the religious landscape of the future.

The decline of traditional religious affiliation is a multifaceted phenomenon influenced by social progress, changing norms, and the rise of secularism.

While some religious institutions face challenges in retaining their congregations, others, like megachurches, adapt and thrive in new ways. The trend towards a more secular society does not negate the human search for meaning; instead, it reflects a transformation in how people connect with the divine and each other.

As beliefs evolve, the conversation about faith and spirituality remains an essential part of the human experience.

"Why We Should Teach History And Events The Way They Happened, Not as We Pretend"

Think about history like a big, old family photo album. Inside, some pictures make us smile, some that make us wince, and others that might even make us cry. But we can't just rip out the pages we don't like.

Every photo tells a story of where we came from and can teach us something important for our lives today.

Now, some folks are arguing about what kids should learn in school.

They're worried that if we teach them about the darker parts of our history, it will make white kids feel bad like they did fix something wrong.

That's not the point of learning history. It's not about making anyone feel guilty; it's about understanding the whole story, not just the happy parts.

As an example, put my family history in the picture. My family history includes two famous religious leaders—Brigham Young and William Penn.

They did some great things, bad things, and everything in between, but they lived in times when not everything was fair or proper.

Now, just because you come from them doesn't mean you have to feel proud or ashamed of everything they did. You're your own person, and history should not make you the same as the past but make you better because of what you learn so the negative isn't repeated.

People should be frustrated because some people are using religion to divide us, not bring us together like our ancestors didn't want and came to America to escape religious persecution. Everyone should see this, and it doesn't sit right with anyone.

So when we hear, "Don't teach the bad stuff; it'll make white kids feel guilty," that's like saying you should get a trophy or a timeout for things your great-great-grandparents did. It doesn't make sense.

Instead, we should look at history like a lesson book. The bad stuff? Let's learn from it so we don't repeat the same mistakes. The good stuff? Let's make sure we keep doing those things. And the horrible stuff we can't change? Let's learn, understand, and empathize with those who were wronged to know how much better we need to be going forward.

So, let's keep it accurate when we talk about the past. No sugar-coating, no blame games—just the true story of how we all got here, warts and all. That way, we can all learn and do better together.

It's like telling kids the truth about their origins—it might be challenging, but it helps them grow up strong and intelligent. That's the kind of history lesson we all deserve.

Remember that history is not just a collection of facts and events; it is a living narrative that shapes our identities and influences our perspectives. By confronting the uncomfortable truths of our past, we can foster empathy, promote understanding, and work towards healing the wounds of history.

As we navigate the complexities of our shared story, let us strive to build bridges instead of walls, to seek common ground rather than sow division. By embracing our diversity and learning from our past, we can create a more inclusive and equitable society where everyone is valued and respected.

So, let's continue the conversation, ask questions, listen to diverse perspectives, and engage in meaningful dialogue.

Together, we can write a new chapter in our history—one that reflects our shared humanity, our commitment to justice, and our determination to create a better world for future generations.

For any political party to be successful, it must demonstrate social understanding and the ability to function effectively within a democratic republic.

Here are 15 areas where the Democratic Party Excels and the Republican Party could improve to serve the United States of America better:

Active Listening:

Engaging with constituents' ideas and perspectives fosters collaboration and prevents misunderstandings.

Effective Communication:

Clear and truthful communication is crucial for building trust and avoiding confusion or conflict within the democratic process.

Reliability:

Meeting deadlines and honoring campaign promises is essential for maintaining trust and credibility with the electorate.

Openness to Feedback:

Accepting constructive criticism and feedback is vital for personal and party growth, as well as ensuring successful reelection.

Respectful Discourse:

Encouraging civil discourse and avoiding hostility towards differing viewpoints promotes a healthy political environment and encourages bipartisan cooperation.

Delegating Authority:

Allowing for autonomy among politicians and embracing diverse perspectives can lead to innovation and stronger decision-making processes.

Decisiveness:

Making timely decisions and sticking to a consistent narrative helps maintain momentum and demonstrates leadership to constituents.

Adaptability:

Embracing change and new ideas is crucial for staying relevant and addressing the evolving needs of society.

Transparency:

Being open and honest about intentions, actions, and decision-making processes builds trust and credibility with the public.

Empathy:

Understanding and considering the needs and concerns of all citizens fosters inclusivity and ensures policies are equitable and just.

Collaboration:

Working across party lines and seeking common ground fosters unity and effective governance for the benefit of all Americans.

Accountability:

Taking responsibility for actions and decisions, as well as being willing to learn from mistakes, builds integrity and trust with the electorate.

Innovation:

Embracing new ideas and approaches to problem-solving leads to progress and better outcomes for society as a whole.

Respect for Institutions:

Upholding and respecting the institutions of democracy and the rule of law is essential for maintaining a stable and functioning government.

Long-Term Vision:

Developing and implementing policies that consider the long-term well-being of the nation and future generations ensures sustainable progress and prosperity.

I apologize for any confusion. To clarify, the classification of Hispanics as white on official U.S. documents before the 1970s did not exempt them from discrimination. Instead, this classification often failed to capture the distinct cultural, social, and economic challenges faced by Hispanic communities, which could be quite different from those faced by people considered white within the societal context of the time.

The evolution of racial and ethnic classifications in the United States government documents reflects the nation's complex attitudes towards race and ethnicity. To summarize and clarify:

Blacks were classified as "Black" or "Negro," which historically subjected them to systematic discrimination and segregation. The categorization of the Irish as "Black" or "Negro" during the 19th and early 20th centuries was a tool to discriminate against them, similar to the discrimination faced by African Americans. This practice diminished as the Irish assimilated and were later accepted as white by the mid-20th century.

Hispanics, before the 1970s, were often classified as white by the government, which obscured the unique challenges they faced and did not always reflect their lived experiences. With the introduction of "Hispanic" as an ethnicity in the 1970 Census, there was a formal recognition of the Hispanic identity, allowing for a more accurate representation of the group's demographics and the discrimination they encountered.

This change was significant because it acknowledged that Hispanics, despite being classified as white, often experienced discrimination and social disparities that were not adequately addressed by being lumped together with the white majority. The introduction of the "Hispanic" identifier was an attempt to better understand and address these issues.

The push to remove race from government documents comes from a desire to dismantle the historical systems of oppression tied to these classifications. Critics argue that these systems are based on unscientific notions of race and perpetuate discrimination. They believe that eliminating racial categories could lead to a more equitable society.

Nonetheless, others argue that racial and ethnic data are essential for identifying and rectifying social inequalities. They maintain that such information helps policymakers address systemic discrimination in areas like health care, education, and employment.

The debate continues, highlighting the need to reconcile the historical misuse of racial classifications with the ongoing need to address inequality. A more nuanced approach to using racial data could involve collecting this information in a way that promotes inclusivity and equality, while still recognizing and addressing the historical and current impacts of racial discrimination.

Cinco de Mayo can be interpreted and celebrated in different ways, and it can indeed be seen as both an opportunity for cultural inclusion and a potential example of cultural appropriation.

On one hand, Cinco de Mayo is a significant date in Mexican history, commemorating the Mexican army's victory over the French at the Battle of Puebla in 1862. For many Mexican-Americans and others, celebrating Cinco de Mayo can be a way to honor and showcase Mexican culture, history, and heritage. It can serve as an opportunity for cultural inclusion, education, and appreciation, fostering understanding and unity among diverse communities.

Cinco de Mayo has been commercialized and reduced to stereotypes, often involving the appropriation of Mexican culture for profit or entertainment. This can involve the trivialization of cultural symbols, reinforcement of negative stereotypes, and the perpetuation of shallow, inaccurate representations of Mexican culture. When this occurs, it can be seen as cultural appropriation, as aspects of a marginalized culture are taken and used by members of a dominant culture without proper understanding, respect, or acknowledgment of their significance.

Blacks Were Black, The Irish Were Black, And Hispanics Did Not Exist Until The 1970s, According To The United States of America Government.

The history of racial classification on official documents in the United States is marked by its use as a tool for discrimination, a practice that dates back to colonial times.

Originally, these classifications were implemented to reinforce a social hierarchy that privileged European colonizers and oppressed non-European groups.

Over time, this racial categorization became entrenched in social practices and legal frameworks, impacting various immigrant populations, including the Irish and, later, Hispanic individuals.

Blacks were classified as "Black" or "Negro," which historically subjected them to systematic discrimination and segregation.

The categorization of the Irish as "Black" or "Negro" was a tool to discriminate against them, similar to the discrimination faced by African Americans.

The Irish, during the 19th and early 20th centuries, found themselves misclassified upon arrival in the U.S.

During the peak of Irish immigration, particularly during the Great Famine in the mid-19th century, many Irish were not considered white and were labeled as "Black" or "Negro" on official documents, which subjected them to discrimination and exclusion similar to other marginalized groups.

This was not an isolated incident but part of a larger system of racial hierarchies and prejudices.

As the Irish assimilated into American society, their racial classification changed, and by the mid 20th centuries, they were generally accepted as white, which underscores the fluidity and constructed nature of racial categories, influenced more by socio-economic and political factors than by any inherent biological traits.

Hispanic individuals have also faced changing racial classifications within the U.S. For much of the 20th century, Hispanics were often classified as white on official documents, reflecting the binary view of race that dominated the United States' perspective at the time.

This classification obscured the diverse experiences and backgrounds of Hispanic people and did not account for the discrimination and social disparities they faced.

The official classification of Hispanics changed with the introduction of the term "Hispanic" as an ethnicity in the 1970 Census, With the introduction of "Hispanic" as an ethnicity there was a formal recognition of the Hispanic identity, allowing for a more accurate representation of the group's demographics and the discrimination they encountered albeit still within the confines of the broader racial categories established by society.

This change was significant because it acknowledged that Hispanics, despite being classified as white, often experienced discrimination and social disparities that were not adequately addressed by being lumped together with the white majority. The introduction of the "Hispanic" identifier was an attempt to better understand and address these issues.

It did not work because this new term broadened the discrimination instead of magnifying their abilities and attributes.

The historical misuse of racial classifications has led to calls for the removal of race from government documents.

I am a critic and in the category of the push to remove race from government documents comes from a desire to dismantle the historical systems of oppression tied to these classifications.

Critics argue that these systems are based on unscientific notions of race and perpetuate discrimination. They believe that eliminating racial categories could lead to a more equitable society.

They suggest that eliminating race from official documents could help dismantle systems of oppression and lead to a society where individuals are recognized for their individual attributes rather than their racial identity.

Proponents of retaining racial information, however, argue that it is essential for monitoring and addressing social inequalities.

They claim that racial data is necessary to understand and combat disparities in health, education, and employment, and that without it, policy makers would be unable to effectively address systemic discrimination.

The debate continues, highlighting the need to reconcile the historical misuse of racial classifications with the ongoing need to address inequality. A more nuanced approach to using racial data could involve collecting this information in a way that promotes inclusivity and equality, while still recognizing and addressing the historical and current impacts of racial discrimination.

The history of race as a classification on official documents is a testament to its role in perpetuating discrimination and inequality, rather than serving as a simple acknowledgment of one's skin color.

The categorization of race originated in colonial times as a means to enforce a social hierarchy, legitimizing the oppression of non-European groups for the benefit of European colonizers.

This system entrenched itself in laws and social practices, and it expanded to affect various immigrant groups, including the Irish during the 19th and early 20th centuries.

The Irish, fleeing the Great Famine and seeking refuge in the United States, encountered a racial classification system that did not initially recognize them as white. Instead, they were often labeled as "Black" or "Negro" on official documents, subjecting them to the same prejudice and exclusion faced by other marginalized groups.

While there isn't a specific range of years when this practice was universally applied, it was more common during the peak of Irish immigration to the United States, which occurred in the mid-19th century during the time of the Great Famine in Ireland. This discrimination and racial categorization were part of a larger pattern of racial hierarchies and prejudices that existed in American society during that time and the selection of race for discrimination and hierarchy against people of color still exist today.

This misclassification was not an isolated practice but part of a broader strategy to maintain a racial hierarchy. It was a clear illustration of how race, as a social construct, was manipulated to justify unequal treatment.

The practice of categorizing Irish individuals as "Black" or "Negro" on official forms or in society occurred primarily during the 19th and early 20th centuries in the United States. This was a time when racial classifications were often used to justify discrimination, segregation, and unequal treatment of various ethnic and racial groups.

As the Irish assimilated and societal attitudes evolved, so too did their racial classification. By the late 19th and early 20th centuries, they were generally accepted as white, highlighting the arbitrary and changeable nature of racial categories, which are influenced by socio-economic and political contexts rather than biological facts.

Given this history, there is strong justification for reevaluating the use of race on government documents. Critics of racial classification argue that its historical use as a tool for discrimination and its lack of a scientific basis make it both harmful and obsolete. They contend that eliminating race from official documents would help dismantle the remnants of a system designed for exclusion and oppression. Furthermore, doing so could move society towards a more equitable future where individuals are not judged or categorized based on perceived racial identities but rather on their merits and individual characteristics.

However, proponents of retaining racial data argue that it is necessary for identifying and addressing disparities in areas such as health, education, and employment. They believe that without this data, it would be challenging to measure progress towards racial equality or to implement policies that target systemic discrimination.

Ultimately, the debate about whether to remove race from government documents balances the need to confront the historical misuse of racial classifications with the contemporary requirements to track and address inequality. A possible compromise could involve the use of race-related data in a more nuanced and responsible manner, ensuring it supports equality and inclusion while recognizing the complex legacy of race in government and society.

Human beings have a tendency to form immediate impressions about others, often based on visible differences such as race, gender, age, and other characteristics.

These preconceived notions are influenced by a complex web of factors including our evolutionary history, societal teachings, personal experiences, and emotional responses.

Even the oppressed can have preconceived judgments. I am an older man who is white and naturally bald who lives in the South.

People make judgments about me all the time. However, I understand the reason. It's because many like me are exactly what the suppressed expect. I live and love everyone and hope that by example, people will learn I'm not the same as those who are extreme.

Let's explore these influences in more detail to understand why we might harbor these perceptions and how we might overcome them:

Evolutionary Instincts:

Historically, being able to quickly assess whether someone was a friend or foe was crucial for survival. Our ancestors relied on visual and behavioral cues to make these judgments. While modern society is vastly different, some of these instinctual behaviors linger, prompting us to make snap judgments based on appearance.

Cultural and Social Teachings:

From a young age, individuals are often taught to view the world in certain ways, which includes beliefs about other groups of people. These beliefs can be based on stereotypes that are perpetuated by family, media, and society at large.

Fear of the Unknown:

When encountering someone we know nothing about, fear can take hold. This fear might stem from uncertainty about the other person's intentions or from a lack of understanding about their background and experiences.

Personal Insecurities:

Sometimes, individuals project their own insecurities onto others, which can manifest as prejudice. This can be a defense mechanism to cope with feelings of inadequacy or vulnerability.

Unacknowledged Biases:

Many people harbor biases they are not aware of or do not want to acknowledge. These unconscious biases can influence behavior in subtle ways, despite a person's conscious efforts to be fair and open-minded.

Confusion:

When confronted with customs or ways of life that are significantly different from our own, confusion can arise. This lack of understanding can lead to misconceptions about other people.

Explicit Bigotry:

Some individuals hold strong negative beliefs about certain groups, often rooted in hatred or a desire to maintain power and privilege. This can lead to overt discrimination and hostility.

Feeling Of Superiority:

A person might feel that their own culture, race, or group is superior to others, which can lead to dismissive, violence or condescending attitudes towards those who are different.

Misguided Religious Beliefs:

In some cases, individuals might interpret religious texts in ways that justify prejudice against certain groups, using these interpretations to support their biased views.

Understanding that these preconceptions can be present even in those who consider themselves accepting is important. It's also critical to recognize that marginalized or oppressed groups can have their own biases, as no one is immune to the influence of their environment and experiences.

The path to overcoming these prejudgments is through education and exposure. By learning about different cultures, nationalities, and ways of life, individuals can broaden their understanding and reduce the impact of unfounded biases. It's also through meaningful interactions and relationships with diverse groups that people can challenge their own prejudices.

Regarding the personal anecdote, it highlights a valuable point: individuals are often judged based on the actions of others who share superficial similarities with them, such as race, age, or geographic location. It demonstrates the importance of individual actions in challenging stereotypes and preconceptions.

It's vital to remember that affirming a lack of prejudice can inadvertently confirm its presence. True intent is shown through actions rather than words (someone saying I'm not prejudice or I have black friends, many times confirms their prejudice). To truly combat prejudice, one must actively demonstrate open-mindedness, compassion, and a willingness to engage with and learn from those who are different from oneself. This can involve a variety of actions, such as:

Engaging in Dialogue:

Having open and honest conversations with people from diverse backgrounds can help break down barriers and correct misconceptions. This requires active listening and a willingness to understand different perspectives.

Self-Reflection:

Taking the time to reflect on one's own beliefs and behaviors can reveal hidden biases and prejudices. Once recognized, individuals can work to change these patterns of thought and action.

Seeking Out New Experiences:

Actively putting oneself in situations where one is exposed to different cultures and communities can foster a greater appreciation for diversity. Travel, attending cultural events, or volunteering for organizations that work with diverse populations can be enriching experiences.

Education and Continuous Learning:

Seeking out information about the histories, traditions, and experiences of different groups can provide context and understanding that dispel stereotypes. This can include reading books, watching documentaries, or taking courses on social justice and cultural studies.

Championing Inclusivity:

Advocating for policies and practices that promote diversity and inclusivity in one's community, workplace, or social circle can lead to broader societal change.

Being an Ally:

Standing up against discrimination and prejudice when you witness it sends a powerful message. This can involve intervening when someone is being treated unfairly,supporting initiatives that combat inequality, and amplifying the voices of those who are marginalized.

It's important to recognize that overcoming prejudice is not a one-time act but a continuous process of growth and learning. The goal is to cultivate an environment where diversity is celebrated, and where individuals are evaluated based on their character and actions, rather than on superficial attributes or the actions of others who may look like them.

In the context of the personal anecdote shared, it is clear that the individual is aware of the stereotypes associated with his demographic and strives to demonstrate through his actions that he does not fit those stereotypes. By living a life of love and acceptance, he hopes to serve as an example that challenges the preconceived ideas others may have about him. This approach reflects the understanding that we all have a role to play in creating a more inclusive and understanding society.

A Little History Of Why Race As A Required Selection On An Official Document Is Used For Discrimination And Not Just To Know Color

The practice of categorizing Irish individuals as "Black" or "Negro" on official forms or in society occurred primarily during the 19th and early 20th centuries in the United States. This was a time when racial classifications were often used to justify discrimination, segregation, and unequal treatment of various ethnic and racial groups.

While there isn't a specific range of years when this practice was universally applied, it was more common during the peak of Irish immigration to the United States, which occurred in the mid-19th century during the time of the Great Famine in Ireland. This discrimination and racial categorization were part of a larger pattern of racial hierarchies and prejudices that existed in American society during that time.

As attitudes towards race and ethnicity evolved and as laws and societal norms changed, the practice of categorizing Irish individuals as "Black" or "Negro" became less common and eventually faded away. Today, the Irish are generally considered as part of the broader category of white Americans in terms of racial classification in the US.

Harnessing Technology for Truth Telling In Political Campaigns:

Real-time Fact-Checking in Delayed Political Debates And Facts Displayed By Scrolling At The Bottom Of Campaign Ad Before They Can Air

In the ever-evolving landscape of political discourse, the demand for accuracy and accountability has never been more pressing. As the battle against misinformation rages on, I propose a solution to enhance transparency in political debates that involves broadcasting debates on a delay to allow for comprehensive fact-checking by individuals or artificial intelligence (AI) systems.

The concept of delaying the broadcast of political debates to facilitate thorough fact-checking represents a significant step towards ensuring the veracity of information presented to the public.

By providing fact-checkers - whether human experts or AI algorithms - with the necessary time to research and verify statements made during debates, this approach aims to elevate the quality of public discourse and empower viewers with reliable, fact-based information.

The implementation of a delayed broadcast for political debates introduces a strategic pause that allows for a more in-depth and rigorous verification process. This additional time window enables fact-checkers to delve into the complexities of statements, cross-reference information with reliable sources, and provide audiences with a comprehensive analysis of the accuracy of claims made by candidates.

Moreover, leveraging technology such as AI for fact-checking purposes can enhance the efficiency and accuracy of the verification process. AI systems can quickly sift through vast amounts of data, identify patterns, and detect inconsistencies in real-time, offering a valuable tool to streamline fact-checking operations and deliver timely and precise assessments of the information presented in debates.

While the introduction of a delayed broadcast for political debates poses logistical challenges, such as coordinating the timing of fact-checking activities and maintaining the integrity of the broadcast schedule, the potential benefits far outweigh the complexities. By prioritizing accuracy, truthfulness, and transparency, this approach holds the promise of fostering a more informed and engaged electorate and promoting a culture of accountability in political communication.

The adoption of a delayed broadcast model for political debates, coupled with robust fact-checking mechanisms powered by human expertise and AI technology, represents a transformative leap towards a more trustworthy and reliable public discourse.

By embracing innovation and collaboration, we can fortify the foundations of democracy, empower citizens with accurate information, and uphold the principles of truth and integrity in the political arena.

In the realm of political communication, the integration of delayed broadcast and real-time fact-checking stands as a beacon of hope in the fight against misinformation and deceptive narratives. By harnessing the combined power of technology and human expertise, we have the opportunity to elevate the standards of public discourse, hold leaders accountable for their statements, and empower citizens to make informed decisions based on verified facts.

As we navigate the complexities of the digital age and the fast-paced nature of political communication, embracing innovative solutions like delayed broadcast for fact-checking offers a path towards a more transparent, honest, and trustworthy democratic process. This approach not only serves to safeguard the integrity of political debates but also fosters a culture of critical thinking, civic engagement, and informed citizenship.

The road ahead may be fraught with challenges and uncertainties, but by committing to the principles of accuracy, transparency, and accountability, we can pave the way for a more resilient and robust democracy. Let us seize this moment to champion truth, combat falsehoods, and champion a future where facts reign supreme, and the voice of the people resonates with clarity and integrity in the political arena.

In embracing the convergence of technology and truth, we embark on a journey towards a more enlightened and empowered society where the pursuit of knowledge, honesty, and fairness guides our collective path forward. Together, let us harness the transformative potential of delayed broadcast and real-time fact-checking to build a brighter future founded on the pillars of integrity, transparency, and trust in our democratic institutions.

The relationship between a love for comedy, political engagement, and mental health is complex and can vary from person to person. Here are some possible reasons why these connections might exist:

1. **Satirical Nature of Comedy**: Comedy often involves satire and social commentary, which can naturally lead comedians and comedy lovers to engage with political and social issues. Satire is a way to critique societal norms and challenge authority, making it a common tool for addressing political topics.

2. **Coping Mechanism**: Comedy can serve as a coping mechanism for individuals dealing with stress, anxiety, or depression. Humor can provide a temporary escape from negative feelings and help people navigate difficult emotions or situations.

3. **Sensitivity to Social Issues**: People who love comedy may have a heightened sensitivity to social injustices and inequalities, which can lead them to be more politically engaged. Comedy can be a way to shine a light on societal issues and provoke thought and discussion.

4. **Intellectual Stimulation**: Comedy often requires critical thinking and analysis of social dynamics and human behavior. People who enjoy comedy may also be intellectually engaged with political issues, leading to a higher likelihood of political involvement.

5. **Existential Angst**: Some comedians and comedy lovers explore deep existential questions and grapple with the absurdity of life through humor. This introspection can sometimes lead to feelings of existential angst or depression.

It's important to remember that these are general observations and may not apply to every individual who loves comedy, is politically engaged, or experiences depression. Each person's relationship with humor, politics, and mental health is unique and influenced by a variety of factors. If you or someone you know is struggling with depression or any mental health issue, it's essential to seek professional help and support.

The Building Blocks Of a Fulfilling Democracy: How 15 Key Traits Shape Individuals And Align With Democratic Ideals

As we navigate the complex tapestry of society, our individual personalities play a pivotal role in shaping our interactions, beliefs, and political affiliations. Certain key traits contribute to our personal development and can often align with the values upheld by political entities, such as the Democratic Party. Here's a closer look at 15 personality traits that not only shape us as individuals but also reflect the principles that often draw people to the Democratic Party.

Gratitude: A Foundation for Positive Policy

Gratitude, the act of recognizing and valuing what we have, is a trait that encourages a positive outlook and community spirit. For Democrats, this might translate into policies that acknowledge progress and work to protect the achievements of past social reforms.

Generosity: The Spirit of Social Programs

Generosity, the desire to help others, aligns with Democratic advocacy for social welfare programs designed to support those in need, reflecting a commitment to the well-being of the broader community.

Humility: The Basis of Public Service

Humility in leadership can be seen as a willingness to put public interest above personal gain, a trait that resonates with the Democratic ideal of serving the community and being open to diverse perspectives.

Empathy: The Heart of Inclusive Politics

Empathy, the ability to understand and share the feelings of others, is vital in crafting legislation that considers the experiences of all citizens, a key aspect of Democratic policy-making.

Compassion: The Drive for Equitable Change

Compassion, caring for those who suffer, drives humanitarian efforts and policies aimed at reducing inequality and injustice, core tenets of the Democratic agenda.

Acceptance: The Fabric of a Diverse Coalition

Acceptance is crucial in embracing diversity and fostering an inclusive society, a fundamental principle of the Democratic Party as it seeks to represent a wide array of cultures, identities, and beliefs.

Tolerance: The Art of Democratic Discourse

Tolerance, the respect for differing viewpoints, is essential in a democracy and a value that Democrats emphasize as they advocate for free speech and civil debate.

Integrity: The Keystone of Trustworthy Governance

Integrity in politics means adhering to ethical standards and transparency, qualities that the Democratic Party strives to uphold in its quest for accountability and public trust.

Kindness: The Touchstone of Community Relations

Kindness, the simple act of being considerate and caring, is reflected in community outreach and constituent services that Democratic representatives often prioritize.

Patience: The Tempo of Progressive Change

Patience is required to see long-term policy initiatives through to fruition, a trait that Democrats must harness as they work toward gradual and sustained social progress.

Forgiveness: The Path to Reconciliation

Forgiveness, letting go of past grievances, is necessary for healing divisions within a society, a process that Democrats often facilitate through restorative justice and reconciliation efforts.

Resilience: The Fuel for Overcoming Adversity

Resilience is the ability to withstand and recover from setbacks, a quality that underpins the Democratic narrative of hope and recovery in the face of social and economic challenges.

Optimism: The Vision for a Better Future

Optimism, the belief in a brighter tomorrow, is what drives the Democratic Party's pursuit of progressive policies aimed at improving the nation's future, from environmental protection to education reform.

Open-mindedness: The Gateway to Innovative Solutions

Open-mindedness, the readiness to consider new ideas, is crucial for adapting to changing circumstances and solving complex problems, a concept often embraced by Democrats as they seek to address the evolving needs of society.

Authenticity: The Core of Genuine Representation

Authenticity, being true to oneself and one's values, is a trait that resonates with voters and is something Democratic candidates often strive to convey, demonstrating commitment to their constituents' needs and interests.

These 15 personality traits not only contribute to a fulfilling personal life but are also mirrored in the values and actions of the Democratic Party.

By promoting policies that reflect these qualities, Democrats aim to create a society where every individual can thrive, emphasizing the importance of community, empathy, and integrity.

As individuals, embodying these traits can lead us to engage more meaningfully in the democratic process, supporting leaders and initiatives that align with our vision of a compassionate, inclusive, and forward-thinking society.

Ultimately, these traits serve as the building blocks of both our individual character and the ideals of a democratic society.

By nurturing these qualities within ourselves, we contribute to the collective effort to build a more just, equitable, and resilient nation. As members of a democracy, our personal growth and the political choices we make are interconnected, each influencing the other in profound ways. Through our daily actions, advocacy, and voting decisions, we have the power to shape not only our own lives but also the direction of our country and its policies.

So, if you don't want us to teach critical race theory, why don't we teach true history and all the facts, The good, the bad, and the ugly? The ugly that we cannot fix. The bad is this stuff that we can fix, and the good is that things we should repeat.

The reason those who oppose teaching actual history is because they want to take us back there. Please! If you don't believe me, it's in their name, MAGA, make America great AGAIN.

When we use the excuse that makes today's white kids feel guilty for our past.

Based on That logic, that would mean that I should be held responsible, reap the benefits, and get the credit for two religious leaders in our past. I had a multiple great-grandparent, Brigham Young, on my mother's side and a multiple great-grandparent, William Penn, on my father's side.

Two count them two prominent religious leaders from the past, and here I sit without guilt, disillusioned by religion because of all the hatred it stands for today.

So stop pissing in your Cheerios and teach the actual truth of history the way it happened.

A Brief History Lesson As To Why We Still Call Minority, Especially Black, Neighborhoods Are Referred To As Wards:

The phenomenon referring to neighborhoods as Wards is related to historical practices of segregation and discrimination that were formalized under the Jim Crow laws in the United States.

These laws, which were enacted in the late 19th and early 20th centuries, enforced racial segregation in the Southern United States and created a legal basis for discriminating against African Americans in various aspects of life, including housing, employment, education, and public accommodations.

While Jim Crow laws themselves did not specifically mandate the naming of neighborhoods as "wards" or otherwise, the segregation they enforced contributed to the creation of racially homogenous neighborhoods.

These policies, along with other discriminatory practices such as redlining (wherein areas were mapped out and rated on the perceived financial risk, often based on racial composition), led to the underinvestment in minority neighborhoods and a lack of recognition or formal naming that might be more common in white communities.

Over time, the economic and social impacts of these policies contributed to stark disparities between white and minority neighborhoods in terms of infrastructure, amenities, and public perception.

The reference to minority areas without specific names, and instead by terms like "wards" or numerical designations, can perpetuate a sense of otherness and contribute to stigmatization.

Additionally, the use of "Wards," impersonal or administrative terms for certain areas also serves as a coded language or dog whistle to signal "unsafe" or less desirable neighborhoods, often reinforcing racial stereotypes and biases.

It's essential to recognize that the names and terms used to refer to different areas can carry significant weight and reflect historical and ongoing inequalities.

Making the efforts to rename and rebrand neighborhoods should be part of broader initiatives to address these issues and promote inclusivity and equity.

However, such efforts must be sensitive to the history and wishes of the residents, ensuring that changes are not merely cosmetic but part of a genuine commitment to improving the lives of all community members.

I am very sorry people feel the way they do about Biden. I'm sad that they never got a candidate that suited them.

I was not happy to find out that Bill Clinton, the first Democrat I voted for, was a sexual predator or that Hillary didn't divorce him and follow her dreams.

I thought Obama did not have enough experience when he ran, but he had rock star appeal. Yet he proved himself. My husband and I wouldn't be married today had he not been President.

Biden should have stood up for Anita Hill.

All candidates and Presidents make mistakes.

Donald Trump, In my opinion, whether he is in or out of office, is a danger to democracy and will take away all citizens what was supposed to be guaranteed: their American Freedoms

Trump poses a security risk, an actual danger, an end to world democracy, and quite possibly an end to earth's sustainable environment, ending everyone and everything's chances at survival.

At least give Biden the credit he is due with another term in office if you can't, at least vote for the continuation of democracy by not voting for Trump.

Biden Successes

1. Passed the $1.2 trillion bipartisan infrastructure package to increase investment in the national network of bridges and roads, airports, public transport, and national broadband internet, as well as waterways and energy systems.

2. Helped get more than 500 million life-saving COVID-19 vaccinations into the arms of Americans through the American Rescue Plan.

3. Stopped a 30-year streak of federal inaction on gun violence by signing the Bipartisan Safer Communities Act that created enhanced background checks, closed the "boyfriend" loophole, and provided funds for youth mental health.

4. Made a $369 billion investment in climate change, the largest in American history, through the Inflation Reduction Act 2022.

5. Ended the longest war in American history by pulling the troops out of Afghanistan.

6. Provided $10,000 to $20,000 in college debt relief to Americans with loans who make under $125,000 a year. The Supreme Court struck down College Dept Relief. However, the administration has announced a new plan to forgive billions in loans that were qualified under special programs but not done due to DOE mismanagement in previous years. Read the article above)

7. Cut child poverty in half through the American Rescue Plan.

8. Capped prescription drug prices at $2,000 per year for seniors on Medicare through the Inflation Reduction Act.

9. Passed the COVID-19 relief deal that provided payments of up to $1,400 to many struggling U.S. citizens while supporting renters and increasing unemployment benefits.

10. Achieved historically low unemployment rates after the pandemic caused them to skyrocket.

11. Imposed a 15% minimum corporate tax on some of the largest corporations in the country, ensuring that they pay their fair share, as part of the historic Inflation Reduction Act.

12. Recommitted America to the global fight against climate change by rejoining the Paris Agreement.

13. Strengthened the NATO alliance in support of Ukraine after the Russian invasion by endorsing the inclusion of world military powers Sweden and Finland.

14. Authorized the assassination of the Al Qaeda terrorist Ayman al-Zawahiri, who became head of the organization after the death of Osama bin Laden.

15. Gave Medicare the power to negotiate prescription drug prices through the Inflation Reduction Act while reducing government health spending.

16. Held Vladimir Putin accountable for his invasion of Ukraine by imposing stiff economic sanctions.

17. Boosted the budget of the Internal Revenue Service by nearly $80 billion to reduce tax evasion and increase revenue.

18. Created more jobs in one year (6.6 million) than any other president in U.S. history.

19. Reduced healthcare premiums under the Affordable Care Act by $800 a year as part of the American Rescue Plan.

20. Signed the PACT Act to address service members' exposure to burn pits and other toxins.

21. Signed the CHIPS and Science Act to strengthen American manufacturing and innovation.

22. Reauthorized the Violence Against Women Act through 2027.

23. Halted all federal executions after the previous administration reinstated them after a 17-year freeze

---

I Propose A New Law That, If Passed, Would Protect The Firearm Owners, The Second Amendment, And At The Same Time Protect All US Citizens.

When a crime is committed with a firearm, the perpetrator and the owner should be charged for the crime. The crap that the owner can't be charged if the weapon was stolen is bullshit.

I call bullshit because the owners must properly store any potentially lethal weapons safely so that theft isn't even possible. If you buy a firearm, you assume all the risks of that purchase. You, as a gun owner, must protect the general public from harm caused by it.

The idea that both the perpetrator of a crime and the owner of a firearm used in that crime should be charged covers legal and ethical considerations.

Implementing such a law would likely require legislative action and a shift in legal principles regarding responsibility and ownership.

Here's a breakdown of how this could theoretically be approached and some reasons why proponents might argue it should be done:

How The Law Could Be Implemented:

Legislation:

To hold firearm owners criminally liable for crimes committed with their stolen or loaned firearms. The following new laws would need to be enacted. These laws would have to clearly define the circumstances under which an owner would be liable, the nature of the required safe storage, and the penalties for non-compliance.

Safe Storage Requirements:

This law would need to specify what constitutes "safe storage." This could mean mandating specific types of gun safes, locks, or other security measures that are considered reasonably impenetrable.

Mandatory Reporting:

Laws could require gun owners to report a stolen or loaned firearm within a 24-hour timeframe. Failure to report the theft or loan promptly would result in liability if the gun is used in a crime.

Burden of Proof:

The legal system would not need to determine the burden of proof to show that the owner did not store the firearm safely. This would involve being charged with negligence by the owner in civil or criminal court.

Education and Training:

Implementing mandatory licenses and training for gun owners on proper firearm storage and safety would be a part of this approach, ensuring owners know their responsibilities and the legal consequences of non-compliance.

Why Proponents Argue It Should Be Done:

Accountability:

Proponents will argue that increased accountability will encourage gun owners to take the responsibility of owning a firearm more seriously and to implement robust security measures to prevent theft and mass shootings.

Prevention of Crime:

By holding owners accountable for the secure storage of their firearms, the law will deter potential thieves because the more challenging they are to steal, the less likely they are to commit the theft. The law will reduce the number of firearms that are available to be used in crimes.

Reducing Gun Violence:

The ultimate aim of such laws would be to reduce gun violence and mass shootings by ensuring that fewer firearms fall into the wrong hands through theft or loaning weapons.

Public Safety:

Proponents will argue that gun ownership comes with a societal responsibility to ensure that firearms do not pose an undue risk to public safety.

Pro Firearm And Anti Having Responsibilities For Owning Their Firearms Will Argue:

Feasibility of Theft Prevention:

It may be argued that no security measures are foolproof, and it could be unreasonable to expect that theft can be made "impossible." I say that's the risk you take for your 2nd amendment right. My response: I would rather you, as a firearm owner, run the risk of ending up in prison for negligence than someone innocent ending up in a grave.

Rights of Gun Owners:

There is a balance to be struck between holding gun owners accountable and respecting their rights. Any new legislation would need to navigate this carefully to avoid infringing on constitutional rights, such as the Second Amendment in the United States. My response is that there is no balance to be struck. Gun owners being responsible and accountable is respecting their rights. If you own a gun, you must protect everyone in society from harm caused by your ownership. No one is stepping on a gun owner's constitutional right. These laws would protect societies' constitutional rights from gun ownership.

Legal Precedents:

The principle of mens rea (guilty mind) is central to many legal systems, and holding someone criminally liable for actions they did not commit or intend presents a significant shift in legal thinking. Response: Legal thinking is if you're in a car and your passenger goes inside and robs a bank, everyone in the vehicle robbed the bank. Owning a weapon used by someone else, you did the crime.

Enforcement:

Enforcing such laws could be challenging, and determining the level of security that constitutes "safe storage" could be subjective and contentious. Response: it's simple: if it's locked away in a hidden safe and you're not bragging about all your firearms, people won't know you have them or where they are.

The bottom line is that whoever bought the weapon is responsible for the firearm. Who or how it is used is the owner's responsibility.

American Citizens Are Responsible For 7.2 Million Crimes In The United States In 2023.

The Immigrants that have arrived in the United States, both legal and illegal, committed 15,267, including both violent and nonviolent, crimes in 2023.

Republicans are right; immigrants are our most significant threat to the well-being of American Citizens. What Dumbasses.

The reason they can focus on a crime and nationalize it and use it against immigrants is because there are so few immigrant crimes they are easy to remember and publicize.

Could you imagine Republicans trying to remember millions of American Citizen's crimes in detail?

Republicans take the immigrant's honesty and being law-abiding visitors against them.

The Republicans exploit the immigrants like the coyotes and human traffickers do.

You know, use them like they are disposable for their benefit.

Let's try to break this down in a simpler way while correcting some misconceptions:

Imagine you're at school, and there is a big group of kids who were born and grew up in your town (let's call them "locals").

There's also a smaller group of new kids who have come from different places (let's call them "newcomers").

Now, if someone checked and found out that the "locals" got into trouble 7.2 million times in one year, while the "newcomers" got into trouble 15,267 times, you might look at those numbers and think, "Wow, the 'newcomers' don't get into trouble nearly as much as the 'locals.'"

But let's say there's a group at school, a club, that has prejudices and that thinks the "newcomers" are a big problem.

They might say, "See, these 'newcomers' are causing trouble, and that's bad for our school." But if you really look at the numbers, the "locals" are the ones getting into trouble way more often.

Now, why would this club focus on the fewer troubles caused by the "newcomers"? It is called deflection. It's because those troubles are rarer and might stand out more, just like if something unusual happens at school, it's what everyone talks about. It's easier to remember and talk about the few incidents involving "newcomers" than to try to remember all the incidents involving the "locals."

This club is picking on the "newcomers," saying they're a big problem, even though the numbers show they actually get into trouble less often.

It's like saying a couple of bad apples in a basket means all the apples are bad, which isn't fair or true.

So, when this club says, "newcomers are our biggest problem," it's not really accurate according to the numbers. In fact, most "newcomers" are trying to do their best, just like most "locals" are.

It's not nice or fair to treat the "newcomers" like they're only here to cause problems, especially when most of them are following the rules.

It's important to remember that everyone is an individual, and making big judgments about any group of people without looking at the whole picture isn't the right thing to do.

Like I said, "That makes you a dumbass!"

Let's explore the financial, societal, and ethical implications of banning abortions in the poorest states in the United States; these are predominantly red states that are already receiving more federal subsidiaries than blue states. Now, because of the ban in red states, they want more with no exceptions:

Financial Impact:

$105 billion

The estimated annual cost to American states with abortion bans is no exception.

Healthcare Costs:

Banning abortions in the poorest states will lead to a significant increase in unplanned pregnancies and high-risk pregnancies.

The abortion ban will result in higher healthcare costs for both individuals and the government, including expenses related to prenatal care, delivery services, and postnatal care.

Medicaid, which covers many of these costs, will substantially increase spending.

Social Services Costs:

Children born due to the ban need additional support from social services, such as welfare, food assistance, healthcare programs, and educational services. In the poorest states, where resources are already limited, this could strain government resources and increase public spending in these areas.

Economic Productivity:

Restrictions on abortion access have impacted the workforce in the poorest states, as women may face challenges in pursuing education, maintaining employment, and contributing to the economy. The ban has led to a decrease in overall economic productivity and growth in these regions.

Societal Implications:

Women's Rights:

Banning abortions in the poorest states without exceptions has disproportionately impacted women living in poverty, limiting their access to reproductive healthcare services and infringing upon their reproductive rights and autonomy.

Health Inequalities:

Restrictions on abortion access have done nothing but exacerbate existing health disparities in the poorest states, particularly for women who may not have access to safe and affordable reproductive healthcare services. The ban did lead to adverse health outcomes and widened the gap in health inequalities.

Social Welfare:

The ban has done nothing but place additional strains on social welfare systems in the poorest states, as families may require more support due to the financial burden of unplanned pregnancies and extra children. The abortion ban has further stretched limited resources and impacted vulnerable populations.

Ethical Implications:

Reproductive Justice:

Banning abortions without exceptions in the poorest states has raised ethical concerns about reproductive justice and equity. It restricted individuals' ability to make informed decisions about their reproductive futures and perpetuated inequalities in access to healthcare services.

Healthcare Ethics:

Today, with the ban in place, it has caused severe ethical dilemmas for healthcare providers practicing in the poorest states; they have to choose between conflicting obligations, whether to follow the law or provide ethical, evidence-based care to their patients. Today, with the passing of the no-exceptions abortion ban, we are daily challenging the principles of patient-centered care and autonomy.

Poverty and Choice:

Limiting access to abortion services in the poorest states further entrenchs cycles of poverty and has restricted individuals' choices and opportunities for economic advancement. It disproportionately impacted those already facing socioeconomic challenges

So, In conclusion, a ban on abortions in the poorest states in the US with no exceptions has created profound financial, societal, and ethical implications.

It is crucial to consider the unique challenges and vulnerabilities of these regions when discussing policies that impact reproductive healthcare access and individual rights.

When Most Of Us Hear Rhetoric, We Immediately Accept It As A Lie. I Thought I Would Share What Political Rhetoric Is And How We Can Bring It Back To A Positive Meaning.

The understanding of "rhetoric" in everyday language, especially in the context of politics, has indeed taken on a largely negative connotation, often being equated with deceit, manipulation, or empty talk. However, this interpretation strays significantly from the academic and historical understanding of rhetoric. Let's delve into the nuances of rhetoric, its importance, and how it manifests within political discourse, using examples to illustrate these points.

Understanding rhetoric within the framework of politics and political parties involves examining how both major parties in the United States—the Democrats and Republicans—use persuasive communication to promote their platforms, criticize their opponents, and ultimately try to win elections. The misuse of rhetoric, where it becomes synonymous with dishonesty or manipulation, is a significant concern in political discourse.

Rhetoric, as initially conceptualized in ancient Greece, particularly by philosophers like Aristotle, is the art of persuasion. Aristotle defined rhetoric as "the faculty of observing in any given case the available means of persuasion." It is not inherently about deceit or lies but about convincing or persuading an audience using effective communication strategies.

Improving political rhetoric and encouraging bipartisan collaboration are crucial to fostering a healthier democracy. The importance of truth in election campaigns should be a priority. Misinformation can significantly harm the democratic process, leading to distrust and polarization among the electorate.

The concept of ensuring "truth" in political campaigns, however, presents several challenges. First, determining what constitutes "truth" can be complex, as politicians often deal in interpretations of facts, promises about the future, and opinions on policies. Regulatory efforts must distinguish between preventing outright falsehoods and preserving freedom of speech.

With the influence of MAGA (Make America Great Again), it's essential to understand that political movements often reflect deeper societal divisions.

While MAGA is being described as separatist and challenging the two-party system, those within the MAGA movement claim they are simply advocating for what they think is their version of what America should be.

MAGA, although they are a cult acting group, unfortunately they highlight the broader challenge of political polarization in the U.S.

MAGA has proven that the Bipartisan Legislature is not possible as long as they have elected officials that have any influence.

After MAGA has been voted out or has lost majority influence, we can address these issues. It may be beneficial to focus on common ground and areas where bipartisan cooperation is possible.

History shows significant legislative achievements often involve compromise and collaboration across party lines. Here are a few strategies that could help improve political rhetoric and encourage bipartisan efforts:

It emphasizes honesty, transparency, and ethical behavior in political discourse and campaigns. It's a call to action for individuals and elected officials to prioritize integrity in the political process. Below are some further thoughts and considerations building upon your suggestions:

Promoting Civil Discourse:

Encouraging politicians and citizens alike to engage in respectful and constructive dialogue, even in disagreement, can help de-escalate tensions and foster understanding.

Fact-Checking and Accountability:

Fact-checking is critical in ensuring that political statements and campaign promises are grounded in truth. The rise of independent fact-checking organizations has made strides in this area, but political parties adopting these practices could further enhance credibility. Accountability mechanisms, such as penalties for disseminating false information, could deter dishonesty, but they must be designed to respect free speech while combating misinformation.

Media Literacy and Critical Thinking:

Equipping the electorate with the skills to critically evaluate political messages and distinguish between credible information and misinformation can reduce the impact of false or misleading campaign rhetoric.

Electoral and Campaign Finance Reform:

Implementing reforms that encourage transparency, limit money's political influence, and promote electoral competition could help create a more level playing field and reduce incentives for divisive tactics.

Campaign finance is a contentious issue, with concerns about "dark money" and the influence of super PACs clouding electoral integrity. Legislation requiring full disclosure of campaign contributions and spending could mitigate these issues. However, such measures face significant legal and political hurdles, especially in jurisdictions prioritizing free speech in political expenditures.

Encouraging Bipartisan Initiatives:

Actively supporting politicians and organizations that work on bipartisan initiatives can demonstrate the value of cooperation and help build momentum for collaborative efforts.

Ethical Communication:

Committing to ethical communication involves a shift in the culture of political campaigning, where the emphasis moves from winning at any cost to engaging in honest discourse.

This requires leadership and a willingness from political figures to prioritize long-term democratic health over short-term electoral gains.

Civic Education:

A well-informed electorate is less susceptible to manipulation through misleading rhetoric. Enhancing civic education in schools and through public campaigns can help citizens better understand political processes, fact-check claims independently, and engage in the political system more effectively.

Educational Efforts:

Education programs that emphasize the importance of democracy, the responsibilities of citizenship, and the value of diversity and inclusion can lay the groundwork for a more engaged and understanding electorate.

Public Disclosure:

Beyond financial aspects, requiring disclosure about campaign strategies, data use, and advertisement targeting can help demystify political campaigning and allow voters to understand how they are being approached and influenced.

Enforcement of Regulations:

Existing regulations often suffer from weak enforcement mechanisms. Strengthening these, possibly through independent oversight bodies with real power to sanction violations, could significantly improve campaign integrity.

Integrity Codes:

Internal integrity codes could serve as a pledge to voters, promising adherence to ethical standards. While voluntary, these codes, if publicly promoted and adhered to, could become a point of competitive advantage, encouraging more honest campaigning.

Challenges and Considerations:

While these suggestions are commendable, their implementation faces numerous challenges. Political will is a significant factor; reforms that could potentially disadvantage incumbents or powerful interests are difficult to enact. Moreover, the line between regulating honesty and infringing on free speech is delicate. Care must be taken to ensure that efforts to improve rhetoric and campaign integrity do not stifle legitimate political debate.

In a polarized political environment, accusations of bias in fact-checking or regulatory enforcement can further entrench divisions. Finding common ground, as suggested in the bipartisan laws for truth in election campaigns, requires cooperation and trust, which are currently lacking in many political contexts.

Ultimately, improving the honesty of political discourse and the integrity of election campaigns is not just a matter of enacting policies or regulations. It requires a cultural shift within political parties, the media, and the electorate toward valuing truth, transparency, and democratic principles above partisan victory.

So Everyone Thinks They Know "WOKE," And I'm Sure Some Do.

At least they Know The Version Of "WOKE" They Have Been Taught. So What They Know Is True To Them.

So, I Thought I Would Share What It Means To Republicans To Democrats And What It Originally Meant In Our History

In the United States, the term "woke" has become a focal point of contrasting rhetoric between the two major political parties, the Republicans and the Democrats. Here's an analysis of how each party approaches and interprets "woke," followed by an in-depth exploration of the facts and truth underlying the concept.

REPUBLICAN PERSPECTIVE:

Critique of "Woke" Culture:

Republicans often criticize "woke" culture as overly politically correct, divisive, and a threat to traditional values. They see it as an ideology that prioritizes identity politics and social justice causes over individual freedoms and unity.

Legislative Reactions:

Some Republicans have taken legislative action against what they perceive as "woke" excesses. For example, the introduction of bills like the "Stop WOKE Act" aims to counter what they view as divisive teachings and policies associated with the concept.

Political Weaponization:

Republicans frequently use "woke" as a pejorative term to denigrate Democrats and progressives, framing them as out of touch with mainstream values and overly focused on identity politics.

DEMOCRATIC PERSPECTIVE:

Embrace of "Wokeness:

Democrats generally embrace "wokeness" as a commitment to addressing social injustices, systemic racism, and inequality. They view it as a necessary tool for advancing social progress and advocating for marginalized communities.

Policy Support:

Democrats often back policies and initiatives that aim to rectify historical injustices and promote equity and inclusion. This includes advocating for diversity, equity, and inclusion measures in various sectors and supporting educational efforts highlighting social justice issues.

Criticism of Misuse:

While supporting the core principles of being "woke," some Democrats criticize the co-optation and misrepresentation of the term, emphasizing the importance of substantive action and genuine awareness rather than performative gestures.

FACTS AND TRUTH ABOUT "WOKE":

Evolution of the Term:

Over time, "woke" has evolved beyond its original context and been embraced by a wider audience, leading to diverse interpretations and applications.

Today's Core Principles:

At its core, "woke" underscores the importance of awareness, empathy, and action in combating inequality and discrimination. It advocates for recognizing and addressing structural inequities in society.

Complexity and Nuance:

The discourse surrounding "woke" reflects broader societal debates about social justice, equity, and the legacy of historical injustices. While political parties may frame "woke" differently based on their ideologies, the fundamental truth about "woke" lies in its advocacy for a more just and equitable society.

In essence, the concept of "woke" embodies a complex and evolving conversation about social awareness, justice, and equity. While political parties may diverge in their interpretations and uses of the term, the underlying truth of "woke" lies in its call for recognizing and addressing systemic injustices to create a more inclusive and equitable society.

HOW WOKE BEGAN AND INSTRUCTIONS ON HOW IT WAS USED:

During the Jim Crow era in the United States, the term "woke" was used as a call to heightened awareness and vigilance among African Americans and other marginalized groups to protect themselves from the pervasive racial discrimination and violence of the time. It served as a reminder to be cautious, alert, and proactive in navigating a society marked by segregation, prejudice, and threats to personal safety.

Example:

Imagine a scenario during the Jim Crow era where a Black family is traveling through a town known for its hostility towards African Americans. As they go about their day, the parents instruct their children to "stay woke" before leaving the safety of their home.

In this context, "stay woke" serves as a powerful message to the children, emphasizing the importance of staying aware of their surroundings, being cautious in their interactions, and avoiding places or situations that could endanger them due to racial discrimination. The parents may advise their children to avoid certain establishments or areas where they could face harassment, violence, or unjust treatment based on their race.

By heeding the advice to "stay woke," the children are better equipped to navigate the challenges and dangers posed by the discriminatory Jim Crow laws and societal attitudes of the time. This guidance underscores the necessity of remaining alert, informed, and prepared to protect oneself in an environment where racial prejudice and injustice are pervasive.

Overall, during the Jim Crow era, the concept of being "woke" was a vital tool for marginalized communities to safeguard themselves against systemic racism, discrimination, and violence, highlighting the resilience and resourcefulness of individuals striving to protect themselves and their loved ones in the face of adversity.

Complexity and Nuance:

The discourse surrounding "woke" reflects broader societal debates about social justice, equity, and the legacy of historical injustices. While political parties may frame "woke" differently based on their ideologies, the fundamental truth about "woke" lies in its advocacy for a more just and equitable society.

In essence, the concept of "woke" embodies a complex and evolving conversation about social awareness, justice, and equity. While political parties may diverge in their interpretations and uses of the term, the underlying truth of "woke" lies in its call for recognizing and addressing systemic injustices to create a more inclusive and equitable society.

While it's understandable to feel frustrated when someone consistently plays the devil's advocate and seems unsupportive, attributing their behavior solely to jealousy and sabotage might not capture the full picture.

There are a variety of reasons why individuals might frequently adopt a contrarian position or appear unsupportive.

These reasons can range from a desire to engage in critical thinking to risk aversion, past experiences, personality traits, seeking attention or influence, and genuine concerns about the feasibility or ethics of an endeavor.

Jealousy and sabotage can indeed be motivating factors for some individuals, but it's important to consider other potential explanations before jumping to conclusions. Jealousy might lead someone to oppose ideas or projects out of a desire to prevent others from succeeding when they themselves feel insecure or inadequate. Sabotage, which involves deliberate actions to undermine someone else's efforts, is a more extreme form of opposition that usually stems from malicious intent.

However, it's crucial to approach situations with an open mind and consider the possibility that the person's intentions might not be negative. Sometimes, what appears as unsupportive behavior could be a misguided attempt to help by pointing out potential issues or challenges that they believe haven't been adequately considered.

If you're dealing with someone who always seems to be a devil's advocate and never supports any endeavors, it might be helpful to engage them in a constructive dialogue.

Try to understand their perspective and concerns, and clarify the reasons behind their skepticism. This approach can help you determine whether their behavior is rooted in jealousy, sabotage, or other motivations.

It can also open up opportunities for more effective communication and collaboration, potentially transforming their skepticism into constructive feedback that strengthens the endeavor.

It Should Be A Law

That if you are an Elected Government Official:

If you hear the Lord talk to you
If you hear God give you instructions
If you think God told you that you are the new Moses.

If you think you are having "actual" conversations with the Lord, God, or Jesus Christ.

It should be required that you be held in a psych ward for a 72-hour involuntary hold or until you're medicated and that prescribed medication is at the right level for your diagnosis of schizophrenia or Alzheimer's.

At that point, it would be up to your Mental Health Professional if you can be released unsupervised.

Schizophrenia: a severe mental condition of a type involving a breakdown in the relation between thought, emotion, and behavior, leading to <u>faulty</u> perception, inappropriate actions and feelings, withdrawal from reality and personal relationships into fantasy and <u>delusion</u>, and a sense of mental <u>fragmentation</u>.

More than 70% of people with this illness get visual hallucinations, and 60%-90% hear voices. But some may also smell and taste things that aren't there.

<u>**Alzheimer's disease.**</u> **Other forms of <u>dementia</u>, especially <u>Lewy body dementia</u>,** cause changes in the <u>brain</u> that can bring on hallucinations, hear voices, and have two-way conversations with no one there; it may be more likely to happen when your disease is advanced.

Which System Do You Think Would Be Better For Our Working Class?

The choice between implementing a minimum wage and a maximum salary cap (The maximum wage top official can make without raising the wage for everyone) with a bonus system that ties bonuses to the percentage of an employee's salary can be influenced by various factors and considerations. Here are some points to consider for each scenario:

Minimum Wage:

Pros

I was unable to find Pros for the working class.

Cons:

Provides a guaranteed minimum income level for all workers, ensuring a basic standard of living.

It helps increase poverty and income inequality by keeping the wages of low-income workers below the poverty level

It was supposed to offer financial security and stability for workers and their families. However, it has only increased company profits while widening the income gap.

The government thought it would lead to increased consumer spending as low-wage workers should've had more disposable income.

Major Cons:

Minimum wages lower the value of the working class, which could lead to job losses as some businesses may struggle to increase profits so they can afford to reduce labor costs while increasing workload.

Corporate Greed will result in higher prices for goods and services as companies pass the blame on increased labor costs to consumers when asked for a raise in minimum wage. The increase in prices because of labor costs is a lie and is the excuse that companies use whether there is a minimum wage increase or not.

Minimum Wage does not directly address the issue of excessive profits, higher executive compensation, and income inequality within the working class within a company.

Maximum Salary Cap with Bonus System:

Pros:

The salary cap plan Limits income inequality by capping the ratio between the highest and lowest earners within a company.

Encourages fairer distribution of wealth by tying bonuses to a percentage of an employee's salary, and has to be paid to everyone, not just management.

Wage Caps Promote a sense of shared success and teamwork among employees.

Wage Caps Ensure that bonuses are distributed in a way that reflects the overall compensation structure of the company.

Cons

False: It may discourage top talent from joining or staying with a company if the salary cap restricts their earning potential.

Fact: Top Talent can make as much as they want. They have to remember when they give themselves a hundred percent raise, every employee in the company gets a hundred percent wage increase.

False: This could lead to complexities and challenges in calculating and administering bonuses based on a percentage of each employee's salary.

False: If The CEO gets A Five Million Bonus. That bonus equals 33.33% of their salary, and then everyone in the company receives a 33.33% of their salary bonus. After all, the Working Class has made the company and its products profitable.

True: It might not fully address broader societal issues of income inequality beyond the company level.

Also, Fact: Unfortunately, not every company is up and up. Many have unscrupulous business practices like paying lower wages under the table, maintaining two sets of books, and coming up with backdoor incentives to pay the rich while ignoring the working class.

The effectiveness of either approach would depend on the specific goals and values of the organization or society in question. Some may argue for combining strategies or other innovative solutions to achieve fair compensation and address income inequality while incentivizing performance and productivity.

How Do You Act Or React To Any Event Whether It Is A Good, Bad, Major Or Minor Incident?

I have people in my life that fits the explanation below. Do you?

A reactionary personality or reactionary emotion typically refers to a tendency for individuals to react with extreme behavior or responses to various stimuli, events, or situations.

This can manifest as intense emotional reactions, impulsive behavior, and a strong inclination to respond in an exaggerated, extreme, or disproportionate manner.

People with a reactionary personality may exhibit heightened emotional reactivity and may struggle to regulate their responses to external stimuli.

Individuals with a reactionary personality may demonstrate the following characteristics:

Emotional Intensity:

They may experience emotions more intensely than others, leading to heightened reactions to both positive and negative stimuli.

Impulsivity:

They may be more prone to impulsive behavior, acting on their emotions without considering the consequences of their actions.

Black-and-White Thinking:

They may tend to see situations in extremes, with a tendency to view things as either entirely positive or entirely negative, without much nuance or middle ground.

Defensiveness:

They may be quick to react defensively or confrontationally when faced with criticism or challenges, often perceiving these interactions as personal attacks.

Difficulty in Regulation:

They may struggle to regulate their emotional responses, leading to outbursts, conflicts, or erratic behavior.

It's important to note that while a reactionary personality may involve extreme reactions, it's not necessarily a clinical diagnosis.

However, individuals who consistently exhibit extreme reactions that significantly interfere with their daily functioning and relationships may benefit from seeking professional support, such as therapy or counseling, to develop healthier coping mechanisms and emotional regulation skills.

Understanding one's own emotional reactions and developing strategies for managing intense emotions can be beneficial in fostering healthier relationships, improving decision-making, and promoting overall well-being.

Picture this:

Have you ever been in a rush and suddenly feel the urge to poo so bad that you run towards the bathroom and sit on the toilet seat?

You wait and wait for what feels like an eternity, but nothing happens.

So, you get up and button up your jeans. Just as you think it's all over, and you're exiting the room, your body screams, "NOW!" and you quickly try to lower your trousers.

The adrenaline rush makes it hard to get your pants down, and as you're halfway through the process, you start to poo before you're entirely seated! Sounds crazy, right?

No? Never Happened To You!
Me Either I Was Just Asking.

Potatoes are a staple in many households and are used in a variety of dishes. However, not many people are aware of the dangers that lurk within them. The green color that sometimes appears on a potato's skin is not an indicator of freshness as it is commonly believed. Instead, it is a sign of a natural defense mechanism that occurs when the potato tuber is exposed to light.

When potato tubers are exposed to light, they turn green and increase glycoalkaloid production. This is a natural defense to help prevent the uncovered tuber from being eaten. The green color is from chlorophyll and is itself harmless. However, it indicates that increased levels of solanine and chaconine may be present. Solanine is a poisonous alkaloid that is found in potatoes, tomatoes, and eggplants. In potatoes, 30-80% of the solanine develops near the skin, and some potato varieties have higher levels of solanine than others.

Solanine poisoning can cause a range of gastrointestinal and neurological symptoms, such as nausea, diarrhea, vomiting, stomach cramps, burning of the throat, cardiac dysrhythmia, nightmares, headache, dizziness, itching, eczema, thyroid problems, and inflammation and pain in the joints. In more severe cases, hallucinations, loss of sensation, paralysis, fever, jaundice, dilated pupils, hypothermia, and even death have been reported.

Therefore, it is essential to avoid eating potatoes that have turned green or have sprouted. It is also a good practice to store potatoes in a cool, dark, and dry place to prevent them from being exposed to light or moisture, which could lead to the development of solanine.

WARNING FOR ALL SPOUSES FROM ME: A Tale of Love, Electricity, and Misplaced Testicles

Last weekend, I was on a mission to find the perfect "I love you" / "I'm sorry in advance" gift for my hubby. And boy, did I hit the jackpot—a 100,000-volt Taser, pocket-sized and cuter than a kitten with a bow tie. The ad promised a zap with no permanent damage, perfect for a quick tango with a mugger before waltzing to safety.

SO COOL, I thought. So, I brought this little zapper home, popped in two AAA batteries, and pressed the button—nada. Zip. Zilch. But then, I discovered the magic trick: press it to metal, and voila! Blue sparks like the Fourth of July on a diet.

Cue the microwave incident. There's now a mysterious burn mark on its face that I've attributed to "culinary experimentation."

Alone at home with my electrifying pal, I pondered. "It's only powered by two AAA batteries," I mused, as my cat Tut gave me the "I dare you" look. I needed to know this baby packed a punch, for the sake of my husband's future mugger engagements.

So, there I was, clad in my best summer loungewear, glasses perched like a professor about to make a poor life choice, Taser in hand.

The manual was clear:

1-second burst: surprise!
2-second burst: interpretive dance of pain.
3-second burst: assailant does the worm.
Anything more: congrats, you're now a battery vampire.

This tiny gizmo looked as harmless as a rubber duck, but I had to know its power.

I aimed for the thigh, pressed the button, and BAM! I was on a first-name basis with every deity known to humankind.

It felt like the Hulk used me for bicep curls, while my cat scaled the walls to escape the chaos of my involuntary breakdance.

Here's some free advice: self-Tasering is a no-go. You'll hold onto that thing like it's the last piece of chocolate on Earth, and it will turn you into a human popcorn kernel.

When I finally came to, the scene was straight out of a home invasion by poltergeists:

- My glasses were auditioning for "Survivor" atop the TV.
- The recliner looked like it tried to flee the scene.
- I was twitching like a techno remix.
- My face was numb, my lip had its own gravitational pull, and I was drooling like a teething baby.
- And yes, I had an accident in my shorts, but my numbness was in denial.

I saw a smoke silhouette above me that could've been my hair's soul leaving its body.

And my testicles? If found, please return (reward included).

P.S.: Hubby finds my electro-shenanigans hysterical, adores his new gadget, and now uses it as leverage in every argument. "Remember the Taser," he says, and I immediately concede.

Black History Month, celebrated in February in the United States and in October in the United Kingdom, is a time to recognize and honor the achievements, contributions, and history of African Americans and people of African descent. As with many cultural observances, discussions about cultural appropriation and cultural inclusion can be relevant in the context of Black History Month.

Cultural Appropriation:
Cultural appropriation of Black History Month can occur when individuals or organizations engage in superficial or tokenistic gestures that fail to address the systemic issues facing the Black community. This can include using Black history or culture as a marketing tool without a genuine commitment to addressing racial inequality, or engaging in performative actions that do not contribute to meaningful change. Additionally, appropriative practices may involve misrepresenting or commodifying Black culture in ways that perpetuate harmful stereotypes or fail to acknowledge the complex and diverse experiences of Black individuals and communities.

Cultural Inclusion:
Black History Month can also be celebrated in ways that promote cultural inclusion and understanding. This includes engaging in educational activities that highlight the accomplishments and struggles of Black individuals throughout history, promoting awareness of systemic racism and inequality, and supporting initiatives that work toward social justice and equality. Black History Month also provides an opportunity for people of all backgrounds to learn about and appreciate the rich cultural heritage and contributions of Black communities, fostering greater understanding and solidarity.

To ensure that Black History Month is celebrated in a culturally inclusive rather than appropriative way, it's important for individuals and organizations to approach the observance with respect, sincerity, and a commitment to meaningful engagement with Black history and culture. This involves promoting authentic representation, listening to and uplifting Black voices, and actively working to address racial disparities and promote inclusivity throughout the year. When approached with genuine respect and inclusivity, Black History Month can be an opportunity to foster greater cross-cultural appreciation and understanding of the experiences and contributions of Black individuals and communities.

Saint Patrick's Day, celebrated on March 17th, is a holiday that honors Saint Patrick, the patron saint of Ireland. It has evolved into a widely recognized celebration of Irish culture and heritage, but like many cultural holidays, it can also be a topic of discussion regarding cultural appropriation and cultural inclusion.

Cultural Appropriation:
Saint Patrick's Day celebrations have been criticized for sometimes perpetuating stereotypes of Irish people and culture. This can include caricatured portrayals of Irish people, the perpetuation of harmful stereotypes, and the commodification of Irish culture for commercial gain. Additionally, some people may use the holiday as an excuse to engage in behaviors that mock or misrepresent Irish traditions, which can be seen as disrespectful and appropriative.

Cultural Inclusion:
On the other hand, Saint Patrick's Day can also serve as a time to celebrate and appreciate Irish culture in a positive and inclusive manner. Many people of Irish descent and others use the holiday as an opportunity to showcase the richness of Irish heritage, including through music, dance, food, and other cultural expressions. In many communities, Saint Patrick's Day parades and events provide a platform for people to come together and celebrate Irish identity and history, fostering a sense of community and inclusivity.

To ensure that Saint Patrick's Day is a celebration of cultural inclusion rather than appropriation, it's important for individuals and communities to engage with Irish culture respectfully. This can involve learning about the history and significance of the holiday, supporting authentic representations of Irish traditions, and being mindful of the impact of one's actions on the Irish community. When approached with understanding and respect, Saint Patrick's Day can be an opportunity to promote cross-cultural appreciation and inclusivity.

What I think are the responsibilities of Registered Democrats

Engaging in constructive conversations and providing information to empower individuals to participate in the democratic process is a valuable and essential endeavor.

Here are some considerations to keep in mind as you work toward these goals:

Informed Conversations:

Engage in meaningful and informed conversations with individuals open to discussing political issues and policy matters. Encourage dialogue, active listening, and the exchange of ideas. Providing accurate information and discussing the issues that matter to them can help inform their perspectives and decisions.

Voter Registration:

Support efforts to increase voter registration and participation, especially among those who are currently unregistered. Empower individuals to exercise their right to vote and participate in the democratic process.

Engaging Independents and Third-Party Voters:

Recognize the diversity of political perspectives and engage with independent and third-party voters respectfully and openly. Understanding their concerns and perspectives can help inform your outreach efforts.

Communicating Values:

Emphasize the values and policy priorities that matter to you and Democratic voters, such as empathy, understanding, caring, peace, love, equality, and gun control.

Articulating these values and their implications for policy can resonate with those who have similar priorities.

Building Community and Support:

Consider participating in community organizing efforts, joining or supporting local advocacy groups, and connecting with like-minded individuals to amplify your efforts and build a network of support.

Respectful Engagement:

Approach conversations with empathy, understanding, and a willingness to listen. Recognize that individuals may have diverse backgrounds and perspectives, and seek to engage with them respectfully and constructively.

Ultimately, by informing and empowering Democratic voters, encouraging voter participation, and engaging in meaningful conversations, you can contribute to the democratic process and help shape the political landscape that aligns with your values

Americans Are Americans Biggest Threat

YET AGAIN, ANOTHER MASS SHOOTING THIS TIME IN KANSAS CITY

SINCE WE CAN'T GET THE LEGISLATION TO ACT, I SAY WE TAKE IT THROUGH THE COURTS.

I would donate to a legal fund for this.

Although It May Be Tough. That Doesn't Mean It Is Impossible.

Suing to make semi-automatic firearms illegal in the United States would be an extremely challenging and complex endeavor. It's important to understand that this lawsuit would face significant legal, political, and practical hurdles. However, if you are determined to pursue this course of action, here are the general steps you might consider:

1. Legal Research: Conduct thorough research on federal, state, and local laws related to firearms, as well as relevant case law and legal precedents. Understand the legal avenues available for challenging or changing existing regulations.

2. Legal Basis: Identify a legal basis for your lawsuit. The case will involve in-depth research to make constitutional arguments, statutory interpretations, or claims related to public safety and welfare. You would need to work with legal experts who specialize in constitutional law and firearms regulation to build a solid legal argument.

3. Legal Representation: Retain experienced and knowledgeable attorneys specializing in constitutional law, firearms regulations, and civil rights litigation. Given the complexity of this issue, it would be essential to have legal representation with a deep understanding of the relevant legal principles and court procedures.

4. Plaintiffs and Standing: Identify individuals or organizations with standing to bring the lawsuit. Standing refers to the legal right to bring a lawsuit, and it typically requires a direct and concrete injury or harm. Plaintiffs must demonstrate how they are personally affected by the legality of semi-automatic firearms.

5. Filing the Lawsuit: Prepare and file a complaint in the appropriate court. The court could be a federal or state, depending on the legal and factual issues involved. The complaint should clearly outline the legal basis for the lawsuit, the relief sought, and the alleged harms or injuries.

6. Discovery and Evidence: Engage in the discovery process to gather evidence, including expert testimony, statistical data, and supporting

documentation that strengthens your legal arguments and supports your claims.

7. Litigation Process: Navigate the litigation process, which may involve motions, hearings, and a trial. Be prepared for legal challenges from opposing parties and rigorous scrutiny from the court.

8. Appeal Process: Be prepared for the possibility of appeals, as complex and high-stakes cases often involve multiple levels of judicial review.

It's important to emphasize that the steps outlined above are general and may vary significantly based on the specific circumstances of the case, the applicable laws, and the jurisdiction in which the lawsuit is filed.

Furthermore, pursuing a lawsuit to make a widely used type of firearm illegal would likely face significant opposition, legal challenges, and political obstacles. It's crucial to seek the advice of legal professionals and consider the broader implications and feasibility of such an endeavor.

To change or update the Second Amendment to the United States Constitution, a new amendment would need to be proposed and ratified. Here's a general overview of the process:

1. Proposal: There are two ways to propose a new amendment to the Constitution:
   a. By a two-thirds majority vote in both the House of Representatives and the Senate.
   b. By a national convention called by two-thirds of state legislatures.

2. Ratification: Once a proposed amendment is passed by either method, it must then be ratified by either:
   a. The legislatures of three-fourths of the states.
   b. Conventions in three-fourths of the states.

The process of amending the Constitution is intentionally difficult to ensure that changes are not made lightly. It's also important to note that the Second Amendment has been a highly contentious issue in the United States, and any attempt to change it would likely face significant political and legal challenges.

If there is a specific proposal for an amendment to update or change the Second Amendment, it would need to go through the formal process outlined in the Constitution. This typically involves support from a significant portion of both political parties and the states to succeed.

Okay, Republicans Want To Throw Out The Accusation That Democrats Are Communist

Democratic Party in The US consists mostly of Centrist.

Let's talk about Communist, Democratic, And Republican On The World Stage Regarding Politics.

Quick, what do Republicans and Communists have in common?

They demonize West European-style socialism.

When Republicans call Democrats "socialists," they want voters to hear "communists."

OK, it was the Union of Soviet Socialist Republics. But the defunct USSR was a communist dictatorship, not a Socialist country (and it became an authoritarian state under Trump's pal Putin).

The Democratic Party isn't a Democratic socialist party, either.

In terms of world politics, the Democratic party is centrist.

Globally, the GOP is way out on the far right-wing fringes.

Large democratic socialist, or social democratic, parties are common throughout Western Europe, including in NATO countries. So are labor parties, which embrace democratic socialism/social democracy.

The U.S. is the only industrial democracy without a viable democratic socialist, social democratic, or labor party.

Anyway, the Soviets hated all forms of democratic socialism. (So did Hitler and the Nazis.) If this hasn't explained why Democrats can't be communists, keep reading.

An English language paperback book published in Moscow in 1978 parroted the Communist Party line, dissing Democratic centrist, Democratic socialist, Socialist Democratic, and the Labor Party with the same ardor as today's GOP.

"'Democratic socialism,' whatever its guise, is nothing more than a reformist and bourgeois alternative to existing socialism [communism], which historically speaking is the only possible form of socialism," According to The Republican Party, GOP.

Also spewed by the Republican Party, "all Democrats have one characteristic in common — a scientific socialism [communism] and its basic ideas on the necessity for the radical, revolutionary transformation of capitalist society, the abolition of private ownership of the means of production, and the whole system of capitalist social relations."

Republicans Can't Understand that Democratic socialist, social democratic, and labor parties stand guilty as charged regarding parts of it.

Democratic Centrist want to reform only by the ballot box, not by the bullet.

They favor mixed public-private economies in which governments operate certain larger enterprises deemed vital to the whole country's well-being — such as health care, airlines, railroads, communications systems, and public utilities.

In addition, they support free trade unions and meaningful laws protecting workers, consumers, and the environment against the greedy excesses inherent in unregulated capitalism.

In short, Democrats, democratic socialists, social democratic, and labor parties have brought genuine democracy, security, and prosperity to millions worldwide.

Of course, Republican red-baiting goes way back. GOP reactionaries said Franklin D. Roosevelt was a socialist. "I am a Christian and a Democrat," the 32nd president responded. (Sounds like Biden and Harris.)

"Socialism is a scare word they have hurled at every advance the people have made in the last 20 years," recalled his successor, Harry S. Truman, a Democrat, Southern Baptist, and fierce anti-communist.

"Socialism is what GOP called public power. Socialism is what the GOP called Social Security. Socialism is what the GOP called farm price supports.

"Socialism is what GOP called bank deposit insurance (FDIC). Socialism is what the GOP called the growth of free and independent labor organizations. Socialism is what GOP gives the name to for almost anything that helps all the people."

The Republicans stepped up the "socialist" slamming against President Barack Obama.

Religious rightists get apoplectic at any linkage between their version of the Christian faith and socialism. Many of them are Republicans who act like "GOP" stands for "God's Own Party."

There once was a nationwide Christian Socialist movement that included adherents in Kentucky, many in Louisville. In 1911, a second annual Christian Socialist camp meeting in rural Graves County reportedly attracted 800 people.

"Democracy and socialism go hand in hand. Socialists have been among the harshest critics of authoritarian Communist states."

"The Republicans really didn't believe [Obama is] a socialist. They just know calling him one gives them an edge and puts the Democrats on the defensive."

They're bashing Biden and the rest of his party as socialists for the same cynical reason. But it could be that the GOP is screeching "socialist!" at Democrats so shrilly because they fear they're losing that edge.

There are some Democrat policies you might call socialist ideas: Social Security, which every Republic gladly accepts; Medicare, which Republicans gladly accept; subsidized housing, which qualifying Republicans gladly accept; food and children's help, which Republicans gladly accept when they are eligible. Since Republicans don't refuse but accept these services, does that also make them socialist?

It's important to understand that the terms "socialism," "Marxism," "communism," "Nazism," and "totalitarianism" have specific historical and ideological meanings, but these meanings can be distorted in political discourse. Each of these terms represents complex ideas and systems that have been interpreted and implemented in various ways throughout history. Here's a breakdown of each:

1. **Socialism**:
Socialism is an economic and political system where the means of production (like factories, resources, and land) are owned or regulated by the community as a whole or the state. The goal of socialism is to reduce class disparities and promote a more equitable distribution of wealth and power. Socialism encompasses a broad spectrum of theories and

practices, ranging from democratic socialism, where political democracy is combined with social ownership, to more authoritarian forms where the state has a central role in planning and control.

2. **Marxism**:

Marxism is a socio-economic theory and method of socioeconomic analysis that views class relations and social conflict using a materialist interpretation of historical development. It originates from the works of 19th-century German philosophers Karl Marx and Friedrich Engels. Marxism posits that capitalism, through its inherent exploitation and inequality, will inevitably lead to a proletarian revolution, after which a classless and stateless society (communism) will emerge.

3. **Communism**:

Communism, in its ideal form, is a classless, stateless society where all property is communally owned, and each person contributes and receives according to their ability and needs. Marxism is often seen as a theoretical foundation for communism, which has been the goal of various political movements, most notably in the 20th century. However, in practice, states that have claimed to be communist (like the Soviet Union or China under Mao) often diverged significantly from Marxist theory, resulting in authoritarian regimes with centralized control.

4. **Nazism**:

Nazism, or National Socialism, is a far-right, fascist ideology and movement founded and ruled by Adolf Hitler and the Nazi Party in Germany. Despite having «Socialism» in its name, Nazism is fundamentally opposed to Marxist socialism and communism. Nazis co-opted the term «socialism» to attract workers and to represent their (false) claim of supporting the common German (excluding those they deemed as «others,» such as Jews, whom they persecuted and murdered in the Holocaust). Nazism is characterized by extreme nationalism, racism, xenophobia, and the expansionist doctrine of Lebensraum. It is a totalitarian ideology, which means it seeks to control all aspects of public and private life.

5. **'Totalitarianism**:
Totalitarianism is a political system where the state recognizes no limits to its authority and strives to regulate every aspect of public and private life. This term is broad and can apply to various ideologies that seek total control, whether it›s far-right, like in Nazi Germany, or far-left, like in Stalin›s Soviet Union. Totalitarian regimes are often characterized by strong central rule, an extensive use of propaganda to maintain the personality cult of the leader, and the suppression of freedom.

In the American political context, sometimes terms like socialism and communism are used by some political figures and commentators as catch-all terms to criticize policies or politicians they view as too interventionist or redistributive. This usage can sometimes be more about political rhetoric than accurate ideological or economic analysis.

It's worth noting that political language is highly context-dependent and can be used in a variety of ways, not always strictly adhering to the original or academic definitions of these terms. Political labels can be misused to mischaracterize opponents or policies, which can lead to confusion about the true nature of these ideologies.

In American political discourse, "socialism" is sometimes used by members of the Republican Party, and indeed by some political commentators more broadly, as a pejorative term to describe policies that involve government intervention or expansion of social services. While this usage can be part of a legitimate debate about the role of government in society, it can also be a rhetorical strategy to frame such policies as inherently negative, suggesting a slippery slope toward an authoritarian or dysfunctional state.

This usage might oversimplify or misrepresent what socialism is, according to its academic or theoretical definitions. Socialism, as traditionally conceived, involves the collective ownership of the means of production, not merely government intervention or the provision of social safety nets. In the context of American politics, many policies labeled as "socialist" by critics are, in fact, examples of social democracy or welfare state policies, which are typical features of many capitalist societies.

The United States, like many other capitalist countries, operates with a mixed economy, which means it combines elements of free markets with social programs and government regulations. Some of these social programs have roots in or share characteristics with socialist ideals, such as providing for the common welfare and reducing economic inequality, but they operate within a fundamentally capitalist framework. Here are a few examples:

1. **Social Security**: A program designed to provide financial assistance to retirees, the disabled, and survivors of deceased workers. It is funded through payroll taxes and is a form of social insurance.

2. **Medicare**: A national health insurance program primarily for people aged 65 and older, but also available to some younger people with disabilities.

3. **Medicaid**: A program that assists with medical costs for some people with limited income and resources. It is jointly funded by the federal government and the states.

4. **Public Education**: Free access to K-12 education is a hallmark of the American system, and public funding for education can be seen as a socialist principle in that it is meant to benefit the entire community and is funded through taxation.

5. **Public Infrastructure**: Roads, bridges, public parks, and utilities are often provided by the government, which can be seen as a form of socialism in that the infrastructure is owned and maintained for public use and benefit.

Critics who label these programs as "socialist" often do so to suggest that they are steps towards a more comprehensive socialist system that could threaten individual freedoms or the free market economy. Proponents of these programs, on the other hand, argue that they are necessary components of a modern society that ensure a minimum standard of living, contribute to economic stability, and provide for the common good.

It is also worth noting that the use of the term "socialism" in American political dialogue can be historically and culturally loaded, reflecting Cold War era sentiments where socialism was directly equated with the ideologies of countries like the Soviet Union. This historical backdrop contributes to the emotional weight of the term and can sometimes overshadow objective discussion of policy.

In summary, the misuse of the term "socialism" in political rhetoric can serve to stigmatize certain policies or political opponents rather than foster a nuanced discussion about the actual content and merits of those policies. It's important for a healthy democracy to have accurate and honest discourse around economic systems and policies.

If you are Prejudiced, practice bigotry. If you're racist, you discriminate, show hatred towards others, practice intolerance, and believe in race-baiting. If you're pro-segregation, all for eugenics, see nothing wrong with separatism or slavery, you're Xenophobic, you're biased, Pro-Life, and practice intolerance.

People who practice what's listed above have no education when it comes to women, foreign-born people, black/African Americans, Asians, Indians, Chinese, Filipinos, Koreans, Japanese, Vietnamese, Other Asians, two or more races, Arabs, Islam and other Middle Easterners, Jewish 1, Native Hawaiians and other Pacific Islanders, yes Veterans are considered a minority, people with disabilities, people over 65, LGBTQ+, and any other nonwhite or lifestyle the MAGA Republican party does not approve of.

They have a narrow mind, believe in stereotypes, and have a lack of education on the part of the bigots.

What they don't know about the people listed above and the world around them has caused all this.

So remember, if you think negatively about any minority, it's because you're ignorant by choice, or you're ignorant because you're too stupid to be educated

All of the people that the words above are used to target may want to attempt to educate the uninformed.

If you're in a safe area and comfortable with yourself and your surroundings, give it a shot. You may change someone's mind.

The Liberals, Progressives, And Democrats are not immune to the above words. Many of us feel superior to the groups listed above.

Almost all Liberals, Progressives, And Democrats Feel All Of The List Above Toward The MAGA Republicans.

Hate does not stop Hate. We have taken the actions of a few and judged everyone based on that. We base everyone in MAGA on Donald Trump, Mike Johnson, Comer, J Jordan, Marjorie Taylor Greene, Lauren Boebart, and Matt Gaetz. I could go on, but these are an example.

We also take events caused by a few to judge them all, like Jan 6, 2021, the riots caused by the counter-protesters of a peaceful democracy protest.

Everyone needs to do their part so that we can learn to get along and we can live side by side peacefully.

I'm not trying to change a republicans mind

I'm not trying to change a nonvoter who is a constant bitcher but refuses to do something about the elections' minds.

I'm not trying to change the non-thinking or the easily influenced mind.

I am trying to keep Democratic voters informed.

I am trying to convince the unregistered to get registered and vote Blue.

I am trying to convince the independents to vote Blue.

I am trying to convince registered third-party voters to vote Blue.

I am trying to get those who have and believe in empathy, understanding, caring, peace, love, and acceptance of all individuals to vote blue.

I am trying to get people who agree with equality, gun control, and women's right to make their own choices to vote blue

There is no way that I want to change a Republican's mind. I only use my time talking to the people who can have a legitimate conversation, and a cult hasn't brainwashed them.

———————————

As responsible citizens, we all want to live in a safe and secure society. This requires us to have common-sense laws in place that protect us from harm and ensure the well-being of all individuals. Any person who opposes such laws may have an ulterior motive or may be attempting to conceal something.

It is essential to close the loopholes in existing laws that allow criminals to obtain firearms legally, without proper registration or licensing. This can be achieved through better legislation and stricter implementation of existing laws.

It is the responsibility of every adult who owns a firearm to ensure that it is used safely and responsibly. If a minor uses the weapon in a crime, the owner should be held legally accountable and charged with the same crime.

We must prioritize the safety of our children and take all necessary measures to protect them. Even if it means implementing stricter gun control measures, it is worth it if it saves even one child's life. Therefore, as responsible citizens, we should support common-sense gun control laws and work towards creating a safer society for everyone.

Married couples often fall into a pattern where they take each other for granted, and the most common problem in a dysfunctional or failing marriage is taking advantage of one's spouse.

Many couples often get so used to their partner being there for them and doing the little things that make them special that they stop noticing their efforts.

Sometimes, they even feel that their partner owes them something or doesn't mind constantly checking things off their to-do list simply because they are married.

Taking advantage of one's spouse is like taking advantage of anything else.

You don't realize how much you need something until it's gone. If your power goes out, you suddenly realize how grateful you are for electricity.

Similarly, if your water is turned off, you realize how much you use it during the day.

Unfortunately, when it comes to marriage, by the time people realize they've taken their partner for granted, it may be too late to save the relationship.

Sometimes, people take advantage of their spouse without even realizing it.

Some people naturally enjoy making others happy and are good providers, and that's great if you're married to one of them.

However, this inclination to satisfy others should not be taken for granted. Just because they love to do nice things for you, it doesn't mean you shouldn't return the favor by being grateful and thankful, even for the little things.

So, how can you avoid taking advantage of your spouse?

Here are a few questions to ask yourself:

How many times a day do you ask your spouse to do something for you?

Do you automatically assume that they will bring you a drink or turn on the coffee pot when they go to the kitchen?

Do you ask them to run to the store for you?

Do you expect them to say yes when you ask for favors?

Do you say thank you for the little and big things they do for you?

If you take advantage of your partner, you may forget to say thank you or please, which shows disrespect.

Do you answer the phone, respond to a text, or check Facebook while you're in the middle of a conversation with your spouse?

If you don't prioritize your spouse, it shows that you might be taking advantage of them.

When conversations get heated, do you tend to ignore the situation, not answer questions, or become indignant?

Do you tend to control conversations by getting louder or saying mean things?

If so, you may be taking advantage of your partner's inability to speak up and not providing them with the answers they need.

Do you get more than you give in the relationship?

If the relationship seems lopsided, meaning one person is always giving more in many areas, someone is likely being taken advantage of.

Do you ask your partner about their day, their life, their work, or their feelings?

If you only talk about yourself and don't care to listen to your partner's thoughts and feelings, you may be taking advantage of them.

Is your partner resentful?

If so, they may feel that they are being taken advantage of. If you're resentful, it may mean that your partner is taking advantage of you.

Do you offer to help?

If you see your spouse cleaning up or mowing the grass, do you offer to help or just sit idly by and allow them to handle it themselves?

Who gets their way most often in the relationship?

If one person tends to get their way more than the other, you can rest assured this person is being taken advantage of in the relationship.

Marriage is supposed to be forever, but very few people will be okay with being a doormat for the rest of their lives.

Being taken advantage of by someone you love is a heartbreaking experience that can damage a relationship beyond repair.

Chances are, you don't take advantage of your spouse (or they don't take advantage of you) on purpose, but rather because you've established a routine and are complacent with each other.

Therefore, take a few minutes to think of ten things you would miss about your spouse if they disappeared from your life tomorrow.

Of these ten things, how many do you expect on a day-to-day basis?

Take inventory of the ways your spouse goes out of their way to make you happy.

Are you thankful for them?

Do you return the favors easily?

Remember, marriage is about equality in a relationship, and each partner should respect and appreciate the other.

* 9 7 9 8 8 9 2 8 5 7 4 9 9 *